D1478556

AFFIRMING THE TOUCH OF GOD

A Psychological and Philosophical Exploration of Christian Discernment

---

Evan B. Howard

[signature]

University Press of America,® Inc.
Lanham • New York • Oxford

Library of Congress Cataloging-in-Publication Data

Howard, Evan B.
Affirming the touch of God: a psychological and philosophical
Exploration of Christian discernment / Evan B. Howard.
p.cm.
Includes bibliographical references and index.
1. Decision making—Religious aspects—Christianity. 2. Affect
(Psychology)—Religious aspects—Christianity. 3. Spiritual life—
Christianity. I. Title.
BV4509.5.H67 2000 248.2—dc21 00-029888 CIP

ISBN 0-7618-1689-5 (cloth: alk. ppr.)

Contents

List of Figures

Acknowledgements

While it is impossible to give adequate thanks to all those who contributed to the bringing of this book into existence, I would like to express special gratitude to a few of those who contributed most. I wish to acknowledge the support and care of professors Elizabeth Liebert, S.N.J.M. of San Francisco Theological Seminary, Donald Gelpi, S.J. and Alexander Garcia-Rivera of the Jesuit School of Theology at Berkeley, and Eleanor Rosch of the University of California, Berkeley. Their careful reading, stimulating dialogue, and helpful suggestions are greatly appreciated.

I would also like to thank the staff of the libraries of the Graduate Theological Union, Montrose Public Library, and the staff of the Graduate Theological Union Bookstore. They have made the task of research at a distance much easier. In addition, I would like to thank Helen Hudson and the staff at University Press of America for being so patient with all my publishing questions.

Finally, I extend my appreciation to those friends and family who have supported me throughout the process of research and writing. The friends of Spirituality Shoppe: An Evangelical Center for the Study of Christian Spirituality have made the time of research and writing possible and willingly paticipated as I shared this material in other forms. My two church families during this season, Vineyard Christian Fellowship of San Francisco and St. Paul's Episcopal in Montrose, Colorado, believed in my work. Many of the members volunteered to share discernment stories, for which I am very grateful. Above all I would like to thank my wife, Cheri and my two daughters, Terese and Claire for reading the text, for enduring family "discernment sessions," and for patiently listening to my many spontaneous discernment lectures.

Chapter 1

Introduction:
Background and Methodology

The Concept of Christian Discernment

On January twentieth, 1994, Randy Clark, pastor of St. Louis Vineyard Christian Fellowship, was invited by John and Carol Arnott of the Toronto Airport Vineyard Fellowship to help lead a series of healing and renewal meetings. Both Clark and the Arnotts had recently experienced powerful encounters with God after seasons of spiritual dryness. They hoped that these meetings might stimulate some of the same experience in the Arnotts' congregation. As it turned out, the meetings surpassed their expectations and they decided to extend the renewal indefinitely. They never expected that these meetings would kindle a flame that would burn to the present and spread throughout the globe. Christian leaders from virtually every Christian denomination have felt the fire of the "Toronto Blessing," as it is called, experiencing powerful encounters, and have returned to their home churches to spark similar phenomena elsewhere (Riss 1995). Hundreds of thousands have attended meetings in Toronto or elsewhere directly connected to this movement. Encounters experienced in the context of these meetings have stimulated fundamental religious conversions, major changes in marital relations, transformations of career direction, and other significant life-changes.

From the onset of the Toronto Blessing, a spectrum of rather
unique emotional/physiological phenomena played a major part in the
movement. It was this aspect of the movement in particular that drew
the attention of the press, and itself fostered exploration and participation in meetings. *National and International Religion Report* on July
11, 1994 stated that "Consistent reports describe a state similar to
drunkenness, including shaking with laughter, crying, slipping into a
trance, and falling to the floor. Repentance, warm feelings of love
and peace, the "return of the prodigals," and a number of salvations
also have been reported (*National and International Report* 1994, 1).
It is the preponderance of experiences of laughter that has given the
Toronto Blessing the label "the laughing revival." Some have even
reported experiences of "roaring" like a lion in these meetings (Arnott
1995, 172-76).

As might be expected, the Toronto Blessing became a source of
controversy. Some consider the Toronto Blessing to be a great work
of God, perhaps of apocalyptic proportions (Chevreau 1994; Arnott
1995; DeArteaga 1996). Others consider it a mixed blessing, containing both wonderful aspects but also dangerous and harmful aspects as
well (Beverley 1995; The Theological Commission of the Charismatic
renewal in the Catholic Church of Germany 1996). Some deny the
legitimacy of the movement as an authentic revival and are seriously
concerned with behaviors characteristic of the movement (Smith 1994;
Hanegraaf 1997). Finally, some are convinced that the Toronto
Blessing is, in fact, a delusion from evil or "seducing" spirits rather
than from God (Fruchtenbaum 1996).

In the midst of trends attached to such powerful feelings, the local
leader is called upon to give advice. "Is this movement *of God,* or
not of God?," a parishioner may ask. "Should I attend the meetings?"
"Should I pursue these experiences?" The answering of such questions is the stuff of Christian discernment.

A man I will call "Steve" was interested in a woman--but *how*
interested? All of his previous training in a particular Christian community taught Steve that dating and personal interest in sexual relationships were to be avoided. Steve was to pray, God would point
out his mate, and they would marry. That was that. Unfortunately,
however, the mate God "pointed out" by means of a significant
encounter was not similarly drawn to him, at least not in time. She
married someone else. That was years ago.

Over time, Steve began to doubt the belief system he had previously received. He began to learn that God was interested in Steve's own initiative in life. He began to ask himself for the first time, "what do *I* want to accomplish in life?" His career direction, his prayer life and his friendships all began to take new shape as Steve's own intentions were admitted and permitted. Eventually, Steve became aware that he wanted to get married. He began to develop relationships and one of these grew serious. He liked the woman. They had a great deal in common. She was attractive and was even interested in him. One day the subject of marriage came up.

But this relationship in the context of his new freedom stimulated new questions, questions both personal and spiritual. How was Steve to know that his interest in the woman was more than rational deliberation combined with the desire to get married and sexual interest? Were these enough to legitimize marrying a woman? Did *God* have any thoughts in this matter, and if so how could he know them? How could (or should) he separate God's will from his own in such a complex arena as romance? Steve's future depended on the answer to these questions. The answering of such questions is the stuff of discernment.

Deitrich Bonhoeffer grew up in the academic circles of early twentieth century Germany. He studied the theologies of the great thinkers of the time, ultimately serving as a student in America, a pastor in Spain, and a lecturer in systematic theology in Germany. From the first days of the Nazi accession to power in 1933, Bonhoeffer was involved in protests against the regime. He became a leading spokesman for the Confessing Church, the segment of the Christian community that stood against Nazi policy. For a time he retired to London for safety, but later returned to Germany. He was appointed to lead a seminary for this Confessing Church in 1935. Again in 1939, he considered taking refuge in the United States, but again returned, convinced that his authority to participate in the rebuilding of Germany depended on the integrity of his identification with his people through their trials. He became more active in the resistance movement and was arrested on April of 1943. His activity in the movement reached the point of involvement in a plot to assassinate Hitler. It was for this action that Bonhoeffer was executed (cf. Bonhoeffer 1963, 1971). At each step in Bonhoeffer's life a set of questions were addressed, "What was the authentically Christian act in this

circumstance?" "What would *God* desire in this point in time?" He
knew the answers may cost him his life, or may even threaten his very
eternal salvation. The answering of such questions is the stuff of discernment.

It has been said that in the field of business, a person is well
advised to risk very little; that in personal life and relationships it is
necessary to risk more; and that in the field of spirituality, we have no
choice but to risk everything. Discernment in spiritual matters, therefore, is of critical importance. In spiritual issues, one's earthly vocation and even eternal destiny is often ventured upon a judgment concerning the presence and activity of the divine. When not merely personal but corporate spiritual matters are addressed, and when the
presence of the divine or demonic is not merely discerned within the
believer or community of faith, but also in the world at large, the consequences of discernment become monumental indeed. One is well-
advised to judge carefully that which is, and is not, from God. Furthermore, the characteristic dangers of the spiritual life combine with
certain recent cultural trends to make the subject of discernment especially relevant in contemporary western culture. The plurality of religious beliefs and experiences currently available, the recent emphasis
upon individual agency in moral and personal choices, and the
unfamiliarity of the Post-Enlightenment West with spiritual matters all
serve to give discernment a special significance for this day and age
(Rakoczy 1980, 2-4).

Discernment is not only a significant topic today, it is also a popular topic. A casual search of the World Wide Web under the term *dis-
cern** renders over three thousand documents published on the Inter-
net mentioning the word. Web sites specifically identified with religious discernment include a Christian vocation project, a collection of
published reports of Quaker business meetings, a listing of Jesuit
retreats, an online Bible study, an archive of inspirational quotes, a
number of cult awareness groups, and a few groups not necessarily
connected with official religion. *Discernment Pro Arte*, a consultation
service accessible through the World Wide Web, advertizes a "discernment tool," an "Awareness Frequency Enabler, which will help
you chart the course of your spiritual journey from your earliest recol-
lections to present-day ventures." This tool is used to "begin the
process of selectively discerning what spiritual choices need to remain
a part of your journey, and which ones you may need to shed to
enable your Higher Self to be revealed" (Discernment Pro Arte 1997).

An awakening of interest in discernment is especially evident within the Christian tradition. Reflection within the Roman Catholic community, and particularly from within Roman Catholic religious and charismatic communities, has spawned an energetic reconsideration of the concept of Christian discernment (cf. Rakoczy 1980). But interest in discernment is also awakening within Protestant communities (Farrow 1989; Palmer 1988; Littell 1960; Clarke 1993; Chan 1998, 199-224; Thomas 1998, 127-36). Seminars and retreats cultivating Christian discernment are frequently available. The number of popular articles and books on discernment is increasing exponentially. Even within the academic community, significant contributions to an understanding of discernment are appearing regularly.

Reflective exploration of the topic of Christian discernment has unveiled a variety of issues which must be addressed in order to give it a coherent account. How should one define Christian discernment? How should one distinguish it from moral decision-making? What sources are to be used in the study of discernment and how are they to be interpreted? Should discernment be considered a gratuitous gift of God, available to a select few, or a virtue to be cultivated by all? Should one limit discernment within the exercise of ecclesial authority, or rather ought one to cultivate its development among the average lay person? What is the relationship between communal discernment and the government of a religious community? If one uses the phrase "discernment of spirits," to what should the term "spirits" refer? How should one properly prepare for Christian discernment? What is involved in the act of discernment? What identifiable procedures may be particularly appropriate for discernment in a given context? Ought "discernment" refer to the process or the product? By what criteria is the presence or activity of God discerned? What degree of certainty can an individual or group expect from their discernments (Orsy 1976; Dubay 1977; Lienhard 1980; Green 1984)?

Beneath these issues lie another collection of more properly theological questions. What approach to the nature of God and the nature of the human person grounds (or ought to ground) a theology of Christian discernment? What relationship exists between the grace/gifts of God and ordinary human capacities? What view(s) of the Church forms an adequate foundation for communal discernment? What ought to be understood by the "will of God," or the "call" of

God? Does God have two or three "wills"? How does (or how should) the Holy Spirit operate in the life of a believer? Ought we to expect the Holy Spirit to reveal specific guidance for non-moral decisions? Does the Spirit speak to the believer through identifiable affective impulses? Is the Spirit identifiably present in the world at large (Friesen 1980; Johnson 1990; Barry 1992; Lonesdale 1995)?

In addition to the questions above, a few issues related to philosophy and the human sciences raised in exploring the character of discernment can be mentioned. How do culture and community shape the discernment process? What similarities or differences can be identified between discernment practices of the world's religions? How do the dynamisms of the human person (developmental, psychodynamic, cognitive, interpersonal, etc.) influence the practice of discernment by a given individual or group? How do particular cognitive operations function to discover that which is or is not from God? How does one's sense of self or one's sense of meaning contribute to the framework from which discernment proceeds? What are the transcendental conditions of knowing involved in Christian discernment? In what does the "knowledge" of discernment consist? Does the act or history of Christian discernment provide sufficient warrant for belief in the objects of that discernment (Rahner 1964; Rulla 1978; Spohn 1983; Hughes 1990)?

Although some of the questions mentioned above will be addressed to a greater or lesser extent in the course of the present study, I will primarily focus on the issues related to the nature of the act of discernment. Cognitive-psychological and philosophical-theological questions will take priority. It is my conviction that a measure of insight can be offered to some of the other questions by cultivating precision on the cognitive and philosophical fronts. I will raise other questions in the present study only insofar as: (a) they bring clarity to an account of Christian discernment as proposed in the current chapter, or (b) they are necessary in order to explore the roles which affectivity plays in Christian discernment. The present chapter divides into three parts. First, I will introduce the problem of defining discernment and suggest a working definition which is able to comprehend the variety of horizons and referential objects associated with discernment. Second, I will provide a brief survey of the state of contemporary reflection on discernment, summarizing significant contributions to the field, and highlighting those insights and undeveloped areas of study which bear on the present study. Finally, I will specify the aims and methodology of the present study, identifying the precise issues that I intend to address and the resources and methods I intend on using to address them.

The Problem of Definition

A survey of the literature on Christian discernment immediately reveals the wide variety of horizons associated with the term. The term "discernment" is used to refer to: the identification of demonic or divine "spirits" and their influence upon individuals (Carter 1976), the selection of appropriate ascetical strategy in Christian growth toward sanctification (Carthusian 1995), the process of personal or corporate decision-making (Wolff 1993; Johnson 1996) the evaluation of cultural or religious trends (Rakoczy 1980), the evaluation of expressions within the gathered community of believers (Dautzenberg 1971), the selection of appropriate strategies for social or political action, (Antoncich 1975; Libanio 1977; McClain 1995), the means of making authentic ethical decisions (Gustafson 1974; Gula 1997), a faculty of spiritual perception (Hoke 1909), and the overall virtue of prudence or moderation (cf. Lienhard 1980). This diversity of reference does not usually present a problem for the casual practitioner of Christian discernment because the practitioner can make out the general meaning of discernment within the context of interest. But for the student of Christian discernment, this diversity of reference raises the difficult problem of definition.

The problem of defining discernment involves both historical and semantic complexities. It has its origins in the early history of the use of the term. Joseph Lienhard has traced the development of the history of "discernment of spirits" in the Patristic sources, demonstrating that there was a distinct development from the use of "discernment of spirits" to use of "discernment" (1980, cf. also Dingjan 1967). This development involved a shift in emphasized character from discernment as charismatic gift to discernment as virtue, and a shift in emphasized object from spiritual forces to psychological dynamics (Sweeney 1983). Thus, even at its earliest history, the term or sign "discernment" did not have a single, clear referential object.[1] The

[1]I am here using the terms "sign" and "object" as used in the Peircean semiotic system which speaks of a sign, its referential object, and the interpretant which links the two (cf. Hoopes 1991).

range of objects has expanded as reflection on discernment has developed (cf. Rakoczy 1980). Defining discernment is further complicated by the fact that in writings on discernment one finds a number of different terms used to refer to very similar phenomenological interpretants. For example, Therrien evaluates Paul's understanding of discernment not by analysis of διακρισις, but by evaluating Paul's use of δοκιμαζω. Outside the Roman Catholic tradition similar objects are referred to with a variety of terms. Thus, early Anabaptist communities speak of "judgment," Quaker communities talk of "making decisions," revivalist traditions speak of "testing," many Protestants speak of "finding" or "doing" God's will or of "guidance," and Protestant charismatics talk of "hearing God's voice," all generally referring to that which students of spirituality would call "discernment" (Sheeran 1983; Chacko 1996; Klug 1962; Billings 1987; Page 1954; Morgan 1978; Mumford 1971; White 1976; Willard 1993; Ryle 1993).

The variety of historical terms and meanings, combined with the variety of horizons associated with the term, gives rise to a variety of definitions of discernment expressed in contemporary literature on discernment. In spite of this variety, however, I would like to suggest that it is possible to comprehend the diversity of objects currently called "discernment" in a single phenomenological interpretant. To make this suggestion clear, it will be helpful to comment on definitions found in the literature. A few examples will suffice to supplement the historical illustrations already mentioned.

Discernment is the process by which one tries to stay attuned to the sense of self which God gives us. (Crampsey 1989, 28)

Discernment is awareness of inner states and the ability to so interpret these states that one's life can be gently guided by the Spirit of God. (Larkin 1981, 10)

Discernment, in the Christian tradition is "the process by which we examine in the light of faith and in the connaturality of love, the nature of the spiritual states we experience in ourselves and in others. The purpose of such examination is to decide, as far as possible, which of the movements we experience lead to the Lord, and to a more perfect service of him and our brothers, and which deflect us from this goal. (Malatesta 1970, 9)

It is the question of recognizing the action of God in concrete situations in the universe and in the community of God's people, and responding appropriately to it. (Upkong 1989, 416)

The working definition of discernment which will guide this study contains three elements. First, as religious experience, discernment describes the meeting of the divine and human. Secondly, the locus of the experience is interior psychological and religious experience expressed in affective language. Thirdly, the goal of discernment is decision and action, which in classical terms relates to knowledge of the "will of God" for the person or community. (Rakoczy 1980, 23)

First, one can distinguish between discernment as discovery attained and discernment as the process (or procedure) of that attainment. Ladislas Orsy makes this distinction in his *Probing the Spirit*, when he asserts that, "The correct theological meaning of discernment is in the perception or discovery of a movement of grace, although the term is often used to include the procedural technique that best disposes a person for such a discovery" (1976, 32). One can speak of "discernment" as (1) the moment of discovery/insight ("It was a tough process, but finally the Spirit enabled us to discern God's will in this situation"), (2) the process that led to this discovery ("It was a long and tough discernment, but the Spirit finally enabled us to affirm God's will in this situation"), (3) the procedure which embodies the process of discovery (either phenomenologically or prescriptively - "Discernment in tough situations must involve times of surrendering to God. Only then can one make a confident discovery."). Reference to discernment as both process and achievement can be seen in the above definitions in the use of the process terms like "process," "examine," "awareness," "stay attuned," on the one hand, and achievement terms like "recognize," and "decide" on the other.

Second, not only can one identify movement *toward* a point of achievement in the process of discernment. One can also recognize a motion *from* that point in the goals of discernment. This goal is frequently described as a "response," "decision," or "action."

Third, discernment is a noetic verbal noun. By this I mean that in discussion of discernment, the term nearly always has something to do with "knowing." Terms like "awareness," "interpret," "examine," "recognize," all give indication of the activity of discernment being cognitional. Whether the individual or community "mind" is operative, whether the focus is external or internal, discernment itself refers to a distinguishing which is a process/product of cognition - a kind of "knowing."

Fourth, when these noetic terms used to describe discernment are linked together in terms of their motion (awareness, perception, examination, interpretation, discovery, decision, response, action) one finds that discernment can be comprehended *in toto* as a process or act of knowing. Theologian/philosopher Bernard Lonergan has discussed knowledge in just such a manner (1958). In different settings or different communities one or another stage of this knowledge process is highlighted, but universally discernment refers to an act or process of "coming to know" that which is (or is not) from God. This act or process normally involves a series of logical stages.

Fifth, this discernment "has to do with" God. Discernment is a kind of *religious* knowledge. Whether in attending to the dynamics of affective inner states, in "testing" the validity of a prophetic utterance delivered in a charismatic gathering, or in evaluating cultural trends, the aim is to identify the presence, action, guidance, concerns, etc. of the *divine* therein. Thus Christian discernment differs from other kinds of knowledge which prescind from any involvement with the divine. In Christian discernment, God plays a central role, whether as perceived object, enabler of the process, determiner of the procedure, or revealer of the achieved product. Even when the aim described is not "finding God," but rather deciding a course of action or the like, a central "God discovery" pervades the determination of that course.

Sixth, this process of discernment involves the condition and conversion of the person or persons doing the discernment. Writers on discernment are careful to communicate that a discerning knowledge of God is more likely found by people with discerning hearts. This involves the entire faith and life of the discerner (Balthasar 1980; Morneau 1982).

Seventh, the specific dynamism of discernment as an act of knowledge involves a kind of sorting or *distinguishing* of that which is or is not from God. Even when one focuses on one's inner state, discerning attention aims at the identification of the presence of God therein. Whether the horizon in view is the inner life of the individual believer, the expressions of a community of faith, or the overall activity of "the concrete universe," discernment serves to distinguish elements of each horizon which are to be identified with the divine.[2] Indeed, it is this distinguishing aspect of Christian discernment which most clearly reflects the original meaning of discernment (from the Latin *dis*, "apart" and *cernere* "to sift or separate").

Finally, I would like to suggest the explicit inclusion of a characteristic of Christian discernment which, while not necessary to every instance of Christian discernment, is, nonetheless, central to most prototypes of Christian discernment and is an appropriate addition for the purposes of the present study. In sum, I shall approach discernment not only as an act of knowing, but also as an *affectively-rich* act of knowing. As I will demonstrate, contemporary reflection on Christian discernment supports this claim and the course of the study shall demonstrate the pervasiveness of affectivity in the act of knowing called Christian discernment.

Drawing the above comments together I am now prepared to express the single interpretant which can mediate the term "discernment" for the purposes of the present study. In doing so I am suggesting a working definition of discernment as generally described both in the breadth of Christian history and in the contemporary literature. I propose as a working definition for the present study the following:

> *Discernment is the affectively-rich process and act of coming to identify and know in a given situation, in the light of one's Christian faith tradition, that which is significantly related to God (or significantly not related to God).*

I have, in the above definition, left the aspect of response or action secondary. It is the decision, the choice, the identification, of the God-oriented action which to me is the central *discerning* aspect of

---

[2]Discernment also seeks to sort out, when appropriate, elements of the demonic and natural. In this study, however, I will emphasize the recognition and response to the divine since this aspect addresses the defining characteristics of Christian discernment most centrally.

the dynamism, even when the focus is upon concrete action. Having proposed this definition, it remains to explore the relevance of this definition in light of contemporary academic research in Christian discernment, and to describe more specifically how discernment as an act of knowledge will be explored in the present study. This will be accomplished in the two sections which follow.

Discernment As an Affectively-Rich Act of Knowing: Contemporary Reflections

It is my conviction that the phenomena known as discernment can be profitably studied when examined explicitly as an affectively-rich act of knowing. I derive this conviction not merely from a synthesis of terms and referential objects throughout Christian history, but also from an examination of recent research on discernment. Since 1960, the topic of discernment has received significant attention, especially in Roman Catholic circles, and not only in popular works, but in scholarly monographs as well. Discernment has been explored biblically, historically, theologically, and to a lesser extent philosophically and psychologically.

A number of significant contributions to the study of Christian discernment have appeared in recent decades. However, as mentioned above, these contributions (a) address discernment in the context of a wide range of horizons, and (b) are not always even self-consciously connected to the study of discernment as an independent topic of study. Many of these studies, without making the study of discernment as an act of knowledge an explicit aim, reveal, by means of numerous comments and the very structure of their presentations, that an understanding of discernment as an act of knowledge provides a helpful interpretant from which the diversity can be comprehended as a whole. Likewise, while not specifically focusing upon roles of affectivity in Christian discernment, these studies provide sufficient evidence of the significance of affective experience to warrant further exploration. In this review, therefore, I will attempt to bring a diversity of studies within a single focus and to draw attention to matters which may not be central to any single study but which are plainly noticed when seen in the context of the whole. I will indicate areas where insights from cognitive psychology and North American philosophy may make a significant contribution to the field. My aim, in this section, is not to present a thorough review of all recent litera-ture on discernment.[3] Rather I will comment on key publications as they bear on the topic at hand. I will follow the general order of the article in the *Dictionnaire de Spiritualite* (translated in Malatesta 1970), addressing biblical, historical, theological, philosophical, and pastoral/psychological research.

Biblical Studies

Jacques Guillet wrote the essay on Sacred Scripture for the article "Discernement des Esprits," published in the *Dictionnaire de Spiritualite* in 1957. Since this work a number of significant essays have been published which have advanced the Christian understanding of discernment in its biblical context. Unfortunately, however, with the exception of Dubay's *Authenticity* (1977), scholars in the biblical field have been content to examine discernment in terms of individual micro-specialties. The field of biblical studies has not yet consciously developed greatly as a theological discipline with regard to the study of Christian discernment as an independent topic. Individual studies in corporate decision-making, Old Testament or early Christian prophecy, spiritual guidance, demonology, and biblical pneumatol-ogy, and so on—many of which are not consciously associated with the study of discernment—make up the secondary source material from which a contemporary biblical theology of discernment must be pieced together.

Debate concerning the context and meaning of the Pauline διακρισις πνευματων ("discernment of spirits") was sparked by Ger-hard Dautzenberg's "Zum religionsgeschichtlichen Hintergrund der διακρισις πνευματων (1 Kor 12,10)." (1971; cf. also Dautzenburg 1975). His proposal was that the background of the phrase was a semantic one. He concludes that the gift referred to in 1 Cor 12:10 should not be understood as a "distinguishing of spirits," but rather as a charismatic interpretation of spiritual revelation (*Deutung von Geistesoffenbarungen*). Dautzenberg's proposal has received serious

[3]For a review of U.S. Roman Catholic literature between 1965 and 1978 see Rakoczy 1980. For a review of conservative Protestant literature concerning the notion of "God's will" from around 1910 to 1978 cf. Friesen 1978.

criticism, most notably from Jean Martucci and Wayne Grudem (Martucci 1978; Grudem 1978). Consensus currently appears to be inclined toward the traditional translation, although whether this "distinguishing of spirits" is to be understood as a general discernment of various influences in the believer (or congregation or culture) or as an evaluation of prophetic utterances remains an open discussion (cf. Dunn 1979; Grudem 1982; Schweitzer 1989; Fee 1994).

Outside of research on the term διακρισις, Pauline thought pertinent to the wider interpretant identified as discernment has been explored in a variety of independent studies. One important work in Pauline studies is the monograph by Gérard Therrien, *Le Discernement Dans Les Écrits Pauliniens* (1973). This work is a study of the term δοκιμαζω, as found especially in the Pauline literature. He associates the practice of δοκιμαζω in the Christian believer/community with a moral discernment or prudential judgment which has its foundations in a connatural knowledge (*connaisance cordiale*) of God effected by the Holy Spirit and in the context of the community of faith. James Dunn addresses predominantly Pauline literature in his essay, "Discernment of Spirits — A Neglected Gift" (1979). Dunn draws attention to the practice of the evaluation of prophetic utterance in the early Christian communities. He presents criteria related to the character of the prophet and the norm of earlier revelation as means by which prophecy was judged, describing the process as a dialectic of liberty, revelation, and authority. Drawing from the entire New Testament, Luke Timothy Johnson also addresses the practice of discernment in the early church in his *Scripture and Discernment* (1996). Unlike Dunn, however, Johnson's reference is communal decision-making, which he identifies as a *theological process*. It is an articulation of faith seeking understanding; it is the developing understanding of people's experience of God; it involves a long process accomplished by attention to the narratives of others and scriptural interpretation; it is completed in a sense of communal affirmation of God's work. Finally, James L. Jaquette's *Discerning What Counts: The Function of the* Adiaphora Topos *in Paul's Letters* (1995) contributes indirectly to an understanding of biblical discernment. As he states at the close of his work, "Paul calls believers to discover and do God's will. An important component of that task is discerning what things do not matter and, by implication, those things that count (Jaquette 1995, 225). Jaquette's aim in the study is to explore Pauline usage of a particular Graeco-Roman rhetorical pattern.

Biblical-theological contributions to an understanding of discernment phenomena are to be found in Thomas Dubay's *Authenticity: A Biblical Theology of Discernment* (1977), Garry Friesen's *Decision Making and the Will of God* (1980) and Dallas Willard's *In Search of Guidance* (1993). *Authenticity* is the first study to attempt a synthesis of biblical-theological material into a single work. Dubay draws upon exegetical research and Carmelite spirituality to address key questions in the study of discernment. He confronts the questions of how and when God speaks, the nature of "spirits" and the possibility of their distinction, the conditions for discernment, the criteria of discernment, the role of conversion in discernment, and verification. The final chapter applies the model developed in the test to the question of theological pluralism. His conviction, to which I shall draw attention in chapter four, is that "at the root of the whole matter is conversion, complete conversion" (Dubay 1977, 13). Friesen's biblical-theological essay has been influential in conservative Protestant circles. An adaptation of his doctoral dissertation (Friesen 1978), *Decision-Making and the Will of God* is a frontal attack on what Friesen calls the "traditional view" of guidance. He questions whether the Church is reflecting biblical tradition to speak of "God's will" in terms of a specific ideal life-plan which God has pre-ordained for every individual. Instead, he develops a case for what he calls "the way of wisdom," an approach to guidance and decision-making which emphasizes biblical revelation, moral integrity, personal agency, and reasoned decision. Willard, in his *In Search of Guidance* (1993), uses the issue of personal guidance to develop a theology of "conversational relationship with God." Starting from a theology of God's self-communication, he argues that God can be expected to provide guidance for the ongoing decisions of ordinary believers by means of an ongoing relationship. Willard's aim is to cultivate mature relationship with God as the context for personal choices.

The study of discernment in biblical studies has barely (if at all) reached the stage of conscious development as a topic of investigation. Contributions to an understanding of the biblical witness concerning discernment are, with few exceptions, found in separate specializations. In order to develop a more comprehensive biblical theology of discernment, a variety of sub-topics must be investigated within the various genre and corpi represented within the scriptures, each of which contributes to the investigation of a more general act of knowing, namely the process and act of coming to identify and know in a given situation (whether false prophets, corporate decisions, demonic spirits, the divinity of the man Jesus, etc.), in the light of one's Christian faith tradition, that which is significantly related to God (or significantly not related to God).

One interesting example of the "gaps" in biblical scholarship related to discernment is the lack of biblical research on affectivity. When one examines, for example, the theme of discernment of "spirits" within the background of the New Testament epistles, one discovers that within epistolary warnings concerning the work of the enemy, affective elements play a central part of the dynamics of the situation (lust: 1 Cor 7:5; unforgiveness: 2 Cor 2:10-11; anger: Eph 4:27; pride: 1 Tim 3:6-7; idleness, curiosity: 1 Tim 5:14-15; covetousness: 1 Tim 6:9-10). Much more emphasis needs to be given to developing the affective/psychological sensitivities of the biblical texts in light of the question of the nature of Christian discernment.

Historical Studies

The field of historical studies has given some of the finest contributions to the study of discernment in recent years. Indeed, it has been out of a recovery of historical traditions that much of the awakening of interest in discernment has arisen. The historical studies have set the stage for current research in discernment. Important questions and suggestive models have their origins in the recovery of particular historical representatives and through the interaction of these representatives with one another.

In addition to the general reviews found in the *Dictionnaire* article and in the article on discernment found in the German *Theologie and Philosophie* (Sweitek 1972), an understanding of Patristic and Medieval discernment has been advanced by a variety of studies published in recent decades (Levko 1997; Marty 1958; Canévet 1990; Raabe 1972; Halaska 1984; Ward 1989). Most significant of these are the articles by Joseph Lienhard, and the monographs by Fr. Dinjan and Christoph Benke. Joseph Lienhard, in a pair of articles (1980; 1993), focuses attention upon the use of the phrase "discernment of spirits" in the Patristic era. In his comprehensive accounting of the use of the phrase, Lienhard first covers the literature up to Athanasius' *Life of Antony*. He identifies a decline of the use of "discernment of spirits" after the *Life of Antony*, the phrase being replaced simply by "discernment" in the *Sayings of the Desert Fathers* and other Latin works. This shift in terminology reflects a shift in attention from evil spirits to human passions and with this shift discernment becomes less of a supernatural charism and more of a virtue necessary for ascetical life. Fr. Dinjan's study *Discretio* (1967) investigates monastic and patristic material insofar as they serve as sources for Thomas Aquinas' doctrine of prudence. His account begins with Cassian (with an appendix covering earlier material) and moves through Gregory, Isodore, Alcuin, Bernard, Anselm, Richard of St. Victor and others up to Aquinas himself. Dinjan's conclusion, that Aquinas' identification of *discretio* with the virtue of prudence is a natural development of the evolution of the term throughout the Patristic and early medieval period, serves to develop Lienhard's conclusions into the medieval period. The question of the relationship between natural and graced aspects of the discerning "coming to know" shall be addressed in chapter four of the present study. Christoph Benke examines the approach to discernment of Bernard of Clairvaux in his *Unterscheidung der Geister bei Bernhard von Clairvaux* (1991). Benke's study focuses upon Bernard's writings themselves rather than his predecessors. Situating Bernard's understanding of discernment within his theology and spirituality in general, Benke presents Bernard's approach to discernment as one which assumes spiritual conflict of good and evil spirits, spirits which can be recognized by the character of the interior movements they cause. The affective aspects of these movements are especially noted in Bernard, giving Bernard his distinctive contribution to the history of discernment, a contribution which is further developed in the work of Ignatius of Loyola.

The understanding of late Medieval and Reformation-period discernment has been advanced through a number of independent studies. Michael Proterra explored similarities between Luther and Ignatius (Proterra 1983), but most have focused attention upon the approach of a particular figure. John Gerson (Boland 1959), Heinrich von Friemar (Weismayer 1990), the author of the *Cloud of Unknowing* (Wolters 1980), Walter Hilton (1981 [1390?]), Catherine of Sienna (Schneiders 1982; Villegas 1997) and Anabaptist decisions (Littell 1960; cf. also Murphy 1990, 145-48) have all been explored. Historical research in Christian discernment has been dominated by research on and from within the Jesuit tradition. Studies in the approach of Ignatius himself and in the early followers of the Jesuit movement have perhaps outnumbered research on all other figures combined. This Jesuit dominance in discernment study has been so strong, in fact, that Richard Sweeney, concurring with others before him, asserted in 1983 that "very little has been written after Ignatius that appreciably alters or expands his presentation of the process of discerning spirits" (Sweeney 1983, 126). I will address the material on Ignatius in chapter two.

Sweeney's comment notwithstanding, a number of figures after Ignatius have also been examined with reference to their understanding of discernment. Spanish mystics (Culligan 1992; Larkin 1974; Giallanza 1978), Pietist leaders (Grossmann 1988), Puritan divines (Nuttall 1992, 34-47), Quaker fathers and mothers (Sheeran 1983), and Charismatic gatherings (Spohn 1973; Parker 1996) have all received particular attention concerning their approach to discernment. This research indicates that Ignatius may not have given the last word on discernment—indeed, among other representatives especially outside Roman Catholicism one finds unique contributions to an understanding and practice of discernment. I suspect that as investigation continues to explore discernment as understood and practiced by various figures the understanding of discernment will continue to broaden. I will contribute to this broadening in chapter two by exploring the approach to discernment found in the works of colonial American thinker Jonathan Edwards.

One tendency reflected in the popular historical surveys of discernment is to speak of a "discernment tradition" or a lineage of "discernment literature" which communicates a similar voice extending from the Patristic Fathers up to and through Ignatius. Susan Rakoczy exemplifies this tendency when she asserts that,

The essential teaching on discernment in the Christian tradition thus follows these lines. First, its biblical basis in the NT describes the Holy Spirit as the principle of active guidance in the life of the Christian, leading her to know the will of God. Secondly, the Patristic writers taught that various movements in the human heart can be caused by "spirits" of good or evil and that it is necessary to be attentive to one's psychological responses in order to determine both the source and direction of these movements. Thirdly, the tradition has been enriched by Ignatius of Loyola who synthesized a methodology from his own experience. Teresa of Avila and John of the Cross describe criteria for distinguishing the fruits of religious experience." (1980, 17)

My suspicion is that rather than thinking of a unified "discernment tradition" one should probably think in terms of an ongoing dialogue throughout history between various emphases concerning the means by which that which is significantly related to God is to be identified. Especially when one examines, not simply the use of the term "discernment" (διακρισις, *discretio, Unterscheidung*), but include the diverse horizons relevant to the wider interpretant captured in the use of "discernment," one finds that a wide variety of important and different contributions to an understanding of discernment appear, even within the same historical setting. The development of discernment wisdom through the history of the church arose in the context of mistakes, biases, conflicts, excesses, and discoveries. Much of the "discernment tradition" literature aims at correcting common erroneous approaches to discernment. Understanding of the presence and correction of bias in the act of coming to know will play a significant part of the analysis of discernment in the present study.

One aspect of discernment mentioned in some of the recent historical research is the cognitive/affective dimension of Christian discernment. Studies in Patristic figures, Bernard of Clairvaux, Ignatius of Loyola, Quaker spirituality, Protestant revivalists, and in the Pentecostal and charismatic renewals, have all given clear indication that one is on the right track in thinking of discernment as an *affectively-rich* act of knowledge. This dimension will receive special attention in the following chapters.

Theological Studies

The article on discernment in the *Dictionnaire de Spiritualite* does not survey theological or philosophical reflection on Christian discernment. After the final historical chapter (which is dominated by discussion of Ignatius and his followers), the article addresses discernment in the context of spiritual direction. In fact, there have been relatively few publications which have sought to explore the nature of discernment explicitly from within the discipline of Christian theology, although some of the biblical and historical studies reveal a theological sensitivity (Dubay 1977, Benke 1991, Toner 1982). Nevertheless, those works which have, by what is established, debated, and called for in them, emphasize the relevance of research which approaches discernment as an affectively-rich act of knowledge. Furthermore, these studies, approaching discernment in the context of a broad range of religious traditions and situational contexts, inform a philosophically and empirically sensitive account of Christian discernment with important themes to consider and helpful conceptual frameworks to use in exploration and interpretation. I will review a few key contributions, drawing attention to the points mentioned above.

The thesis *Vocation et Discernement*, published by Robert Gay in 1959, has established itself as an enduring contribution to an understanding of Christian discernment. The context of the work lies in debates concerning the procedures for affirming the priestly vocation in the Catholic community. The thesis aims to reaffirm that, "it is possible to verify the presence of interior grace," and in so doing to determine "the nature of this discernment, and its role in the discrimination of priestly vocations." (Gay 1959, 10[4]). After clarification of the nature of internal grace via the data of theology, he moves to clarify the nature of discernment. He summarizes his clarification of the doctrine of discernment of spirits as follows:

> The communication of the divine will by interior grace is an essential aspect of the economy of the New Law. Discernment of spirits is the doctrine which governs the verification of this work of the Spirit in the soul. It is a doctrine of orientation to God by way of knowledge. It acts to specify/clarify the object and the degree of certitude of this knowledge. (Gay 1959, 248)[5]

[4] " . . . que l'*on peut verifier la présence de la grâce interne*, et en tâchant de déterminer *la nature de ce discernement, et son rôle dans la discrimination des vocations sacerdotales*" (italics Gay's).

[5] "La communication du vouloir divin par la grâce interne est un aspect essentiel de l'economie de la Loi Nouvelle. Le discernement des esprits est la doctrine qui commande la vérification de cet agir de l'Esprit dans l'âme: c'est une doctrine d'orientation à Dieu par voie de connaissance. Il s'agit de préciser l'objet et le degré de certitude de cette connaissance."

Gay clearly understands discernment to be an act of knowledge. The chapters of the thesis are structured according to the "object, act, and author" of discernment. The author of discernment is the one(s) doing the discerning. The act of discernment refers to the process itself. The object of discernment refers to that which is being discerned. Gay further distinguishes between the "immediate," the "mediate," and the "next mediate" (*Objet médiat prochain*) objects of discernment (1959, 67-74). The immediate objects of discernment are the movements of the soul. He speaks specifically of attention to dynamics of "the intelligence" and "the will"; in his historical illustrations, however, he refers to affective terms like joy, sadness, consolation, and desolation. The mediate object of discernment, that which the discerner seeks to know beyond the movement itself, is the "principle" (*principe*) of the soul's movement. This principle is a recognized pattern of action within the soul which can be identified with the divine or some other influence (Gay 1959, 70-72). The next mediate object, then, is that which this identified pattern signifies, namely the activity or will of the Holy Spirit communicated to the discerner. I find this structuring of discernment very helpful, as it enables the identification of and reflection upon a variety of factors involved in Christian discernment explored as an act of knowing. I will develop Gay's categories throughout the following chapters.

Luigi M. Rulla contributes to an understanding of discernment of spirits in an article entitled, "The Discernment of Spirits and Christian Anthropology" (1978). In this article, Rulla weds aspects of depth psychology, philosophy, and theology into a unified perspective concerning discernment of spirits. He begins with the debate in Jesuit circles concerning the purpose toward which the *Spiritual Exercises* of Ignatius of Loyola were ultimately written: to foster elective choice or ongoing spiritual growth? His contention is that there is an intrinsic connection between these two, a connection which can be clarified through a more careful look at anthropological factors. In order to clarify these anthropological factors, Rulla distinguishes between a first and second dimension of the self, the first relating to a person's consciously held values, and the second to the totality of a person including conscious and unconscious inconsistencies between the ideal values and actual life. The presence of this second dimension in a person influences the possibility of a person responding accurately to values, and hence informs the dynamisms of discerning the work of God.

He relates this philosophically to Lonergan's four stages of cognitive process (Lonergan 1958). What Rulla calls "affective dispositions" are involved in the perception of value at the first three stages of Lonergan's epistemological schema (experience, understanding, judging). These affective dispositions "perceive and interpret" the content and attractiveness of the values which are presented to one in life (and in a discerning situation). What he calls "effective dispositions" are involved in the final stage (deciding/acting). At this stage there is a distinction between will (1) as mere capacity to make decisions, (2) as the act of deciding, and (3) as the state in which persuasion is no longer needed. Again, Rulla emphasizes the serious influence which unconscious factors (the second dimension) play in the apprehension of and response to values which are involved in Christian election (choosing a way of life which follows the values of God).

He then addresses the topic theologically by means of the exegesis of a few biblical passages. These passages emphasize the need for the renewal of the νοϋς, or the human mind. He suggests that the passages cited "offer a good foundation for the anthropological thesis that discernment is intrinsically connected with election and with the assimilation of the values of Christ. They also indicate that the mode of being of a person (also in the sense of the inconsistencies of the second dimension) influences the mode of acting as a Christian" (Rulla 1978, 559). He identifies the unconscious aspects of the second dimension neither as sin nor pathology but as an expression of concupiscence which is left for an interior struggle and which can continue to influence objective sanctity and apostolic effectiveness. He closes the article by offering some practical suggestions, especially concerning the need for spiritual directors to take the aspect of the second dimension seriously in their assistance to peoples' discernment. The nature of discernment as a process of knowing and the role of affective forces in shaping the nature and reliability of this knowing are important themes in Rulla's article. Furthermore, his emphasis upon anthropological factors, and more specifically his insistence that psychological factors affect epistemological considerations (how we come to know and discern), suggests the need for an integration of psychological and philosophical reflection on Christian discernment.

Susan Rakoczy offers a helpful contribution to a theological understanding of discernment in her review of American Catholic literature on discernment published from 1965-78 (1980). She reviews the substance of the literature as it addresses the questions of: (a) the prerequisites and functions of discernment, (b) the structures and processes of discernment, (c) discernment language: terms and functions (in particular the uses of the terms "spirits," "feelings," and "hearing and listening"), (d) discernment criteria, and (e) certitude. She takes a fairly broad contextual approach to the topic, addressing both personal and communal settings, discernments of "spirits," "elections," and social action discernments, and both religious and charismatic communities. I will highlight three aspects of her conclusions of this review here: indications in her work of an approach to discernment as an act of knowing, her call for increased specificity concerning the aspects of the discernment process, and her emphasis upon affectivity as a significant element in discernment.

Rakoczy never explicitly addresses discernment as an act of knowing. Yet comments throughout her work give indication that this is indeed assumed. For example, she defines discernment generically as "the experience of learning what God wants of one described as the "will of God" for that person" (Rakoczy 1980, 7). When discussing criteria of discernment she states that "discernment criteria operate on the principle that the spirits are known through their effects, both good and bad" (Rakoczy 1980, 167). Again, when discussing the certitude of discernment she asks, "If the criteria all point to the authenticity of the discernment experience, how should the knowledge of the will of God gained through discernment be evaluated?" (Rakoczy 1980, 186). Language like "learning," "known," and the "knowledge" of the will of God indicate that the aims of discernment are reached in the possession of some kind of knowledge or judgment which has a degree of certitude. Her reference to discernment as an "experience" emphasizes the aspect of discernment as a *process* of knowing.

One of the primary conclusions of Rakoczy's review is that there is a great need for clarity and specificity in future works on discernment. She calls for this repeatedly throughout her work. For example, in her chapter on the structures and processes of discernment she "highlights a central problem in the literature on discernment: the lack of clarity about discernment processes and the assumption that discernment needs little explanation" (Rakoczy 1980, 115). Later, when speaking of the use of language, she states, "The language used in the discernment literature does not appear to include an appropriation of the realm of interiority. This level of meaning would answer the question, 'What am I doing when I discern?' The literature does include descriptions of the process of discernment, but has not yet come to an appropriation of subjectivity which would provide a basis for a thorough analysis of the meaning of discernment" (Rakoczy 1980, 124). And again in her discussion of certitude Rakoczy complains that, "although the literature claims knowledge of the will of God and describes in terms relative to moral certitude, the emphasis in the literature is not on describing how this knowledge of God's will is to be understood in cognitional terms nor on the certitude of the knowledge as the most significant areas of authenticating discernment" (1980, 204; cf. also pp. 147,194,209-10). She emphasizes that literature on discernment tends to have a "confessional" rather than a "critical" character. I think this may be understood in part, because much of the thought on discernment has developed almost like a collection of wisdom traditions, and the authors (as well as the readers) are not interested in critical issues but rather in improving their practice of discernment in view of particular contextual horizons. Nonetheless, I concur with Rakoczy that a measure of critical reflection may help to clarify both thought and language as reflection on discernment develops further.

One aspect of the discernment process which Rakoczy makes special note of is that of affectivity. She summarizes her material on this matter by saying, "the language of discernment is rooted in the affective realm of human experience (Rakoczy 1980, 148). And again she claims, "The literature frequently speaks of affectivity as the locus of discernment" (Rakoczy 1980, 214). Her findings indicate that affectivity plays a significant role in the process of Christian discernment. For this reason she is especially concerned about lack of specificity with regards to this area. She speaks of the "lack of analysis of the emotional states described as 'fruits of the Spirit,'" which results in the inability to articulate the distinction between true and false peace (Rakoczy 1980, 182). Although she finds the Ignatian literature concerning the emotive states of consolation and desolation fairly clear, she states that on the whole,

> The area of affectivity raises the larger problem of the relation-ship of the psychological and spiritual dimensions of religious experience and the possibility of the conscious experience of grace. As with the discussion of "spirits," the literature evi-dences a lack of depth. Most of it is written to explain the meaning of these terms, not to attempt further interpretation of the relationship of psyche and spirit. (Rakoczy 1980, 141)

She calls for further work in this area, suggesting that, "acceptance of emotional states as demonstrating the direction of the will of God should be strengthened by further research and reflection on the dynamics of this type of experience" (Rakoczy 1980, 217). Rakoczy, like Gay, maintains that affective motions or states provide indications of the work of the Holy Spirit in a believer, and further, that one can identify these movements as from God or not from God. She pro-poses that this dynamic might be made clearer in light of critical reflection.

Brief mention should be made of the reflections of Maurizio Costa and the writings of William Barry. Both writers seek to unite reflec-tion upon theological themes, spiritual direction, and discernment. Costa, in his in his *Direzione spirituale e discernimento* (1993), identifies the notions of "doing the will of God," and of "spiritual dis-cernment" as foundational theoretical horizons of spiritual direction. A theology which takes seriously the revelation of the will of God must then address the means of arriving at the knowledge of that will. Thus, "it is not possible to ignore the doctrine and the practice of spiritual discernment" (Costa 1993, 31[6]). He distinguishes between two moments of discernment, a "passive" in which the motion of the divine is primary, and an "active" in which the human self is more involved. A critical element involved in the attention to these spiritual movements is the role of affectivity. He states that

> God does not speak with vowels and with consonants as in some kind of human language . . . . The consonants and

---

[6]"Non può ignorare la dottrina e la practica del discernimento spirituale."

vowels of the language of God to the human sound themselves
also through the sensible interior signs of consolation and
desolation. Spiritual discernment indeed acts a little like the
grammar and syntax of this language of God, and as such is the
key to interpreting its significance. (Costa 1993, 127[7])

Similar to Gay, Costa treats discernment under headings of the procedural techniques, the subject, the object, and the conditions for realizing the goal of discernment. As a set of procedural techniques, he
speaks of discernment as a "complex operation and as an interior
spiritual rhythm" (Costa 1993, 128). This interior rhythm is
identified with a process of knowing quite similar to the stages listed
by Lonergan above. Also like Gay, Costa distinguishes between the
various "objects" of discernment. He identifies the object which is
discerned (*che si* - associated with the will of God), the object by or
through which God's will is discerned (*sul quale o circa il quale* -
associated with spiritual experience), and the formal objects by means
of which spiritual discernment operates (*col quale* - associated with
the criteria of Christian discernment).

William Barry has sought to reflect on the theology and practice of
discernment in a variety of writings (Barry 1987b, 1987c, 1989a,
1989b, 1990, 1991, 1992, 1993; Barry and Connolly 1982). Barry's
starting point is the unity of the world as one single action, developing within the intention of God, yet at the same time dependent on
human action. His second step moves from divine to human existence, or more particularly, human *experience*. Barry asserts that all
human experience is encounter, interaction with the   subjective-
objective world. He identifies a variety of "dimensions of experience" within which humans live. Barry states:

There is a physical dimension because we are physical beings
in a physical universe. There is a biological dimension

---

[7]"Dio non parla con le vocali e le consonanti di una qualsiasi
lingua umana . . . Le consonanti e le vocali del linguaggio di Dio
all'uomo sono anche questi segni sinsibili interiori della consolazione
e della desolazione. Il discernimento spirituale si pone un po' come la
grammatica e la sintassi di questo linguaggio di Dio, è la chiave per
interpretarne il significato."

because we are biological beings in a biological universe. There are psychological and sociological dimensions because we approach any experience as a product of our psychological and sociological histories in the universe. We are not always aware of these dimensions of our universe, but they condition the experience nonetheless. (1992, 28)

To the above, Barry also includes a "religious dimension" supplied both by the believing person and the Mystery encountered. It is from this perspective that Barry begins to discuss the mediation of God to human experience—or the doctrine of revelation. God reveals the divine in and through a human experience that can be interpreted from the perspective of a variety of dimensions. Herein lies the significance. "Discernment is necessary," Barry writes, "not only because of the possible influence of evil spirits, but also because of the multidimensionality of human experience" (1992, 34).

Barry's next theological step is to clarify the nature of the human-divine relationship. This he accomplishes by a reflection on the nature of the divine Trinity--the community of Three-in-One, and by reflections on the biblical images revealing prayer as personal relationship. The portrait that appears is that of a God who desires ever-increasing intimacy and transparency and humans who vacillate between fear and freedom. Central to the modern human condition in the West is the underdevelopment of affectivity. The need is for people to learn to attend and to attune their affections to reality. This involves (1) a fundamental affective awareness of our acceptance by God, (2) a growing identification with God's own dream of love, and (3) a growing attunement with God's one action in the world. The final and most clear criterion emerging from this type of relationship as it develops positively becomes the sense either of harmony or a rasping of one's spirit. The central category of experience and the multi-dimensionality of that experience are themes which shall be developed in this study.

Other writers can be mentioned (e.g. Keane 1974; Sheets 1980; Parker 1996). Those discussed above are sufficient, however, to affirm the general direction of the current study as a study of discernment as an affectively-rich act of knowing. The review of this literature has also suggested some important theological themes relevant to reflection on Christian discernment. The doctrines of God's self-revelation, of the Trinity, and of the Holy Spirit are all doctrines which must inform reflection on Christian discernment. I will return to these doctrines in the exploration of the theological and philosophi cal thought of Donald Gelpi in chapter four. The theological review has also introduced valuable concepts and frameworks for exploring and interpreting Christian discernment. Notions of stages of knowing, of diverse objects of discernment, of multiple dimensions of human experience, of different "objects" in discernment, and of unconscious influences upon knowing are all ideas which shall inform the development of the present study in the following chapters.

Philosophical Studies

Only a handful of articles reflect upon Christian discernment with explicitly philosophical interest. These few articles, however, point even more directly to key issues that must be addressed in a study of discernment as an act of knowledge. For this reason, I will review these few articles in greater detail.

One of these articles, Karl Rahner's "The Logic of Concrete Individual Knowledge in Ignatius Loyola" (1964), has achieved something of a landmark status both in its novel interpretation of Ignatius and in its approach to discernment in general. I will reserve my comments on Rahner's interpretation of Ignatius for chapter two and will restrict myself to a few comments on his general approach to Christian discernment.

Rahner's "Logic of Concrete Knowledge" depends on, and really continues, an earlier work entitled, "On the Question of a Formal Existential Ethics" (Rahner 1963). In this earlier work he faces the problem of navigating ethical discourse between the Skylla and Charybdis of a nominalist situationalism on the one hand and an equally unacceptable "reigning conception" of Catholic moral theology, which he associates with the "application of universal moral norms to the concrete situation" (Rahner 1963, 220). His question in this essay is clearly a question of ethical philosophy. Rahner is not content to assume that mere rational application of norms to contexts determines ethical choice. Rather, he argues that "there must be some function of conscience which does not merely apply the universal norms to each of my particular situations but which moreover grasps also what has not yet been made absolutely clear by the situation and the universal norms, and which is precisely and as such what has to be done by me individually" (Rahner 1963, 229). In alluding to some "function of conscience" here, Rahner is explicitly identifying the conditions for the possibility of ethical discernment. He associates that function with a transcendental condition of individuality transformed by the Spirit into a "supernatural instinct and individual immediacy to the personal living God far beyond anything merely in the nature of a norm or law" (Rahner 1963, 230; cf. also Rahner's *Spirit in the World* (1968)).

Rahner raises a host of questions which "must be addressed" in order to consider this existential function of conscience. Key issues he raises are the need to "enter into a study of the peculiarities of a non-objective perception which is not merely a subsequent, reflected subsumption and articulation of an (adequately) given condition, but also a consititutive expression of the known thing itself," and to "treat of the fundamental option of the total basic decision about himself, in which the person, when he begins to reflect about himself, always finds himself already there." He refers to "certain phenomena of current depth-psychology" and the discussion of probabilism in ethical discourse. Needless to say these are questions which bear very closely upon a critical understanding of the nature of the process of Christian discernment as an act of knowing.

Near the close of this essay, Rahner suggests that perhaps this model of an existential ethics may shed light on "the whole teaching on Choice in the Spiritual Exercises of St. Ignatius" (1963, 231). In fact he suggests that perhaps, "our average theology and ethics has not yet caught up with the unconscious theology underlying the Exercises" (Rahner 1963, 232). Rahner returns to this issue in his "Logic of Concrete Knowledge." In this latter work the focus is not upon ethical discourse, but rather upon Ignatius' *Exercises* as an expression of a theology. He aims to re-ask a few theological questions of this classic work. He begins with the problem of election, the question, "In what way is this discovery of God's will for each human being meant and envisaged?" The relationship between this question and the earlier essay is obvious. Rahner suggests that for Ignatius, and for us today, an individual "discovery of God's will" is necessary because the norms of Church and circumstances are insufficient to give clear guidance. Furthermore, the theology of the

Exercises assumes a theology of the Holy Spirit which expects God to communicate God's will to the seeker. This communication is effected in some sense through interior movements. The (S)spirit active in the individual "has to be taken to be a reality different from the human being· and his own impulses and yet something that is operative as a psychological movement occurring in consciousness even though it takes its origin outside consciousness" (Rahner 1964, 100). Rahner's contention in this is that "the object of moral choice that Ignatius is concerned with in the Election is evidently, therefore, of a nature that makes it impossible for it to be apprehended in any other way than by a kind of cognition, a making known, which is in some sense directly due to God himself" (1964, 106). Here elective discernment is directly addressed as an act of knowledge. Rahner then identifies the same lack of precision mentioned by Rakoczy, asserting that "there is not yet clearly and explicitly enough a theology of the Exercises capable of bringing before the mind with sufficient precision the concrete ontological and gnoseological presuppositions regarding human living that are tacitly made and put into practice by Ignatius" (1964, 109).

Rahner identifies the key problem of individual election as being an epistemological one, "how this particular that cannot be inferred from general normative principles alone, can be known, especially when it is something imperative that is to be done, when it is the 'will of God'?" (1964, 115). He begins here with the problem of divine influences and their recognition. Rahner seeks to uncover the necessary conditions of the possibility of distinguishing that impulse which originates from the divine. The mere "goodness," or object-intention is insufficient to determine this, nor is an unidentifiable act of supernatural grace. Rahner argues that viewing these impulses as "miraculous," as "supernatural grace," as products of "secondary causes," as "gifts of the Holy Spirit," or as self-authenticating experiences, all leave the possibility of positive identification of that which is divinely originated incomprehensible. He believes the answer is to be found in locating the criteria of authenticity "intrinsic to the experience itself" (Rahner 1964, 128).

Rahner then searches in the *Exercises* for a principle of certainty from which to ground all other evaluation, what he calls a "supernatural logic." He identifies this foundational principle of his supernatural logic with the "consolation without prior cause," mentioned in

Ignatius' rules for the Second Week (Rahner 1964, 130). Ignatius claimed that this kind of consolation was indubitable with respect to its divine origin. The distinctive element of this consolation is the fact that it is absent of object, it is "utter receptivity to God, the inexpressible, non-conceptual experience of the love of the God who is raised transcendent above all that is individual, all that can be mentioned and distinguished, of God as God" (Rahner 1964, 135).

The question which flows from the identification of this contentless awareness of the divine, concerns how it can possess such "irreducible self-evidence analogous to that of the most general principles of logic and ontology" (Rahner 1964, 142). Rahner finds warrant for this kind of self-authentication in the identification of consolation without cause with the pre-reflective transcendental awareness of God described more thoroughly in his earlier works. Rahner argues that the human mind possesses a vague awareness and attunement to being itself. This orientation to being involves a necessary pre-reflective awareness of and participation in the life of God. This awareness can rise to a stage of reflectivity and as such becomes an "emergence into awareness." This awareness comes not as the product of conceptual thought or experience, but rather is the foundation upon which any experience can be grasped (cf. Rahner 1987, 1-81) It appears in the dynamism of the will. Rahner understands this as a gift of God. The authority of this awareness lies in its being an awareness of the term of all intellection and volition, an awareness of That to which the dynamism of human consciousness tends. As Rahner states,

> Where the whole of a person's being is poured into this pure movement of receptivity, we have the consolation which cannot deceive because it carries its own evidence with it, presupposes no other, does not stand in contrast to any other that might be preferred to it, and it is the foundation of all truth, certainty, and consolation. . . . And because it is the condition of the possibility of all cognition, it is without error, and is the ultimate certitude" (1964, 149).

Rahner argues that this awareness comes explicitly into conscious periodically and can be understood as a "perception" or a "sense."

Rahner reiterates that the emergence of awareness comes to the individual as a summons to the precise individual as existentially given, and not simply as a general vocation or norm. Having accounted for the emergence of this self-authenticating criterion of divinity, he must then determine how in practice this criterion, found in our experiences of consolation without cause, can serve as a determining criterion for the ongoing discovery of God's "individual will." This, Rahner suggests, is accomplished by means of frequent comparison. Thus he interprets Ignatius' approach to the "Second Mode of making an election" simply through the recognition of "a harmony or disharmony of the object of choice with this fundamental feeling he has about himself" (Rahner 1964, 166). And this, for Rahner, is Christian discernment.

Rahner has taken important steps toward a philosophical account of Christian discernment. In addressing election as a case of "concrete individual knowledge," Rahner recognizes the fundamental character of discernment - that of an act of knowing. In emphasizing the significance of consolation without cause, Rahner recognizes the important role which affectivity plays in Christian discernment. Rahner also identifies a key element of discernment process in the act of comparing. Categorization by means of comparing experiences to prototypes or exemplars is an element of discernment which shall be developed in chapter three. Furthermore, in raising the question of epistemology, the question of how the particular will of God can be known (and known to be known), I think Rahner has identified the critical question for philosophical reflection upon discernment as an act of knowledge. It is the question of the warrant(s) or grounds for the process and criteria of discernment itself. Upon what basis can the believer say that she has discerned (come to know or identify) the presence or guidance of God in a given situation? I think that Rahner's search for the "indubitable" criteria, for the foundations of a "supernatural logic" in Ignatius' Rules, however faulty, reflects this fundamental task. I shall return to reflection upon Rahner's solution to the question in chapter four.

Rahner himself acknowledges that "there is still much needed before theology can assimilate and bring forward for reflection this logic of the discovering of God's will" (1964, 169). It is the contention of the present study that a "logic" is present not only in moral choice or the elective discernment of "God's will," but also within all identification of that which is or is not significantly related to God. A primary aim of the study of discernment as an affectively-rich act of knowledge, therefore, is to explore the dynamics of just such a logic.

Rahner's work has stimulated much discussion among interpreters of Ignatius and students of discernment. Two essays have responded to Rahner's work from a philosophical perspective. The first of these is William Spohn's "The Reasoning Heart" (1983). Like Rahner, Spohn addresses discernment within a discussion of concrete moral choice. He identifies discernment with, "a graced ability to detect what is the appropriate response to the invitation of God." With reference to James Gustafson's use of the concept of "discernment" in ethical discourse (Gustafson 1974), Spohn proposes to identify and explore the use of symbol and affectivity in moral choice, operations which are both processes of discernment and neglected aspects of ethical theory. He calls these aspects the "reasoning heart." He argues that "a more adequate account of Christian discernment may be derived from American theologians, particularly Jonathan Edwards and H. Richard Niebuhr." He suggests, concerning these theologians, that, "they provide a richer analysis of the moral agent, extend discernment to a critical reading of the signs of the times, and also incorporate biblical material into the act of discernment more adequately than does Rahner" (Spohn 1983, 32). As with Rahner on Ignatius, I will reserve comments on interpretation of Edwards until chapter two.

Spohn begins his study with an exploration of the role of the symbol as a criteria. Spohn refers to Rahner's central criteria of the "fundamental sense of self" which is compared to prospective elective objects in discernment. While Rahner rests this sense of the self on the vague notion of radical freedom and transcendence, Spohn suggests that American theology emphasizes the symbolic history of a person as that which shapes and defines one's sense of the self. Drawing from the work of H. Richard Niebuhr, Spohn argues that the question of existential identity precedes moral choice, and that the question of identity is answered in image and metaphor. As images and metaphors or the self are re-considered in light of faith, the self is transformed and reawakened to new possibilities of being. This self comes to awareness through interpersonal life. "Discernment," Spohn asserts, "seeks to be responsible to social contexts by aid of the images with which they shape our self-understanding" (1983, 37). Thus by social identification and revisioning of symbols the discerner becomes aware of a "symbolic form" for how to respond to God.

Spohn argues that "the sense of self which guides discernment is more than a present awareness. It has been shaped over time through suffering and decision" (1983, 38). He emphasizes the centrality of story or narrative. Spohn draws from a number of theologians to emphasize the role which narrative plays in human life. As regards discernment, Spohn states that, "discernment operates by fitting the part into a whole which illuminates the significance of the part." He calls this an "aesthetic logic," and claims for this logic that "the self as an emerging character in time and society is a more adequate criterion for serious decisions than any religious experience which prescinds from the story of the individual or of the believing community" (Spohn 1983, 40). Spohn extends his analysis of discernment here not merely to the evaluation of personal life, but also of social trends:

> Discernment remains a personal search for the action of God in one's own history and in the events of the world. Although its conclusions are not morally generalizable as judgments of rationality are, the reasoning heart of the Christian finds normative guidance in the symbols and story of revelation. (1983, 45)

Spohn next moves to address "affective criteria for discernment." Spohn criticizes Rahner on his approach to affectivity stating that, "Rahner has no developed theory of human affectivity." He criticizes Rahner further in that Rahner "assigns the Gospels a minimal role in shaping the content of Christian ethics" (Spohn 1983, 46). Spohn proposes to develop precisely these points via the work of American philosopher-theologian Jonathan Edwards. Edwards contends that "true religion, in great part, consists in holy affections" (Spohn 1983, 47). As the Holy Spirit acts upon the heart of the believer a "specific set or constellation of affections" is produced in the Christian. This configuration of affective tendencies is, over time, shaped to the image of Christ, thus forming the foundations of an ethics of imitation which is centered in the reproduction of the dispositions which characterize the Redeemer.

Spohn identifies two specific roles which affections can play in elective discernment. "First," he says, "they set an affective matrix against which options are gauged to see if they are harmonious or not" (Spohn 1983, 50). Though Spohn does not mention it, this role parallels Rahner's "comparison," with the distinct difference that the transcendent experience of God is the ideal to which options are compared in Rahner's model, whereas for Spohn this ideal lies in the "qualities manifest in the Gospel story." Like Rahner, Spohn recognizes the function of categorization, of comparison with prototypical models as a means of identifying that which is can be associated with the divine. Second, affectivity can also function, especially in those whose affective operations have matured to conform to the divine pattern, to "intuitively suggest appropriate behavior" (Spohn 1983, 51). At times, believers can immediately recognize appropriate behavior, or as Rahner would call it, the "concrete existential ethical norm," simply by an affective grasp of the situation. Spohn identifies this function with the knowledge by "connaturality" common to Catholic moral theology (cf. for example, Maritain 1951). He sums up his analysis by linking moral decision-making and Christian discernment:

> Christian discernment brings to light rich elements in moral decision-making. Judgments of affectivity legitimately ground some moral decisions through the discriminating functions of memory and imagination. These judgments are evaluated not by formal logic but by aesthetic criteria: by the sense of self, the evaluation of events through biblical symbols, and the correlation between certain ways of acting and the configuration of Christian affections."

Throughout this discussion Spohn never doubts the central epistemological question of philosophical reflection on discernment. Spohn's debate with Rahner does not concern the importance of articulating the logic which underlies Christian discernment. Rather Spohn seeks to clarify the nature of this logic, a logic which he calls an "aesthetic logic." Needless to say, clarification of the role(s) of affectivity in human experience plays a significant part of this debate.

More recently Gerard J. Hughes has responded to both Rahner's and Spohn's approach to Christian discernment (Hughes 1990). Hughes is a Jesuit, and like the previous articles the perspective is that of moral philosophy. However Hughes proposes to address the subject not from Rahner's transcendental Thomism, nor from Spohn's North American context, but rather from the philosophy of Aristotle. He proposes to provide helpful insights into the philosophical structure of Ignatian discernment by comparing it with Aristotle's notion of φρονησις, translated as *prudentia* by the medieval scholastics. He argues that Aristotle, through Aquinas, may be more properly seen as the background of Ignatius' *Exercises*, and that therefore they should be read in light of Aristotelian philosophy.

Hughes begins by providing some general background into Aristotle's approach to practical wisdom. He differentiates between *intellectual* and *moral* virtues. The former correspond to valued skills or abilities. "Moral" virtues, on the other hand, are concerned with the quality of a person's emotional reactions to situations. He then notes the importance of practical wisdom for Aristotle, which is defined as, "the disposition to reach true and reasoned conclusions about actions concerning human goods" (Hughes 1990, 421). From this point Hughes moves to address three questions related to the interplay between Aristotle's *phronesis* and Ignatian discernment.

The first issue addresses the relationship between deliberation and affectivity. Hughes develops the affective side of Aristotle, noting that for Aristotle, "Moral training involves a schooling of the emotions" (1990, 422). Moral virtues, then, are an important foundation for practical wisdom. However, moral virtues, and the affective development which forms those virtues, are only a necessary *foundation*. Upon this foundation are laid the intellectual skills required to determine appropriate goods and decisions which promote these goods. He applies this basic framework of affectivity and intellect to interpretation of Ignatius, suggesting that, "what we find in Ignatius is not a Platonist distrust of emotions and feelings, nor a naïve trust in one's deepest feelings, but rather an Aristotelian view of the interactions between feelings and intellect, and an equally Aristotelian view that it is the mind which can discover the criterion for judging one's feelings" (Hughes 1990, 423-24). Hughes is reluctant to assert with Spohn that affectivity is a *criterion* for discerning judgments. Rather, "discernment and the moral virtues do indeed go hand in hand; but I suggest that it is a mistake to confuse them with one another, or to suggest that affective reactions are the criterion for sound decisions" (Hughes 1990, 426).

The second issue addresses the relationship between the universal and the particular. This is a central issue of Rahner's *existential ethic*. Hughes begins by asserting that one misinterprets Aquinas and Aristotle to read them as simply believing in an ethic reduced to the application of universal norms to concrete circumstances. First, Aristotle's scientific method focuses not on the formation of law, but rather on the production of insight which then is summarized in law. Furthermore, both Aristotle and Aquinas held that universal moral principles do not cover all possible situations. Indeed, for Aristotle, though familiarity with universal norms are necessary, "practical wisdom is almost a Wittgensteinian 'seeing as'" (Hughes 1990, 428). When faced with the situation of two people faced with the same decision and different moral obligations, Hughes rejects an uncheckable appeal to a "sense of self," whether based on religious experience (Rahner) or historical experience (Spohn). Rather, he asserts, "I think I am in line with Aristotle in saying that I would require to know which feature of that religious or affective history was the *relevant* one so far as this decision was concerned; and I would have to be able to integrate the answer into a coherent overall account of what it is to have such and such a vocation, or to be obliged to make this particular decision" (Hughes 1990, 429). Again he argues that Ignatius can be understood as holding to just such a view.

Hughes' final issue addresses the question of the choice of a way of life and discernment in this context. He notes that Ignatius' language in the statements about a choice of a way of life are very Aristotelian. He argues that Ignatian discernment is thoroughly deliberative and rational. Whereas Rahner sees the mode of election that focuses on distinguishing affective movements as primary, Hughes holds that the normal approach to discernment involves an interaction between rational analysis and affective attention. In conclusion, Hughes states that, "affective dispositions, whether they be patterns of emotional reaction or spiritual consolations, must themselves be assessed before they can be regarded as helpful or unhelpful, and this assessment involves the normal criteria of rational deliberation" (1990, 435).

Apart from issues dealing with Hughes' interpretation of Ignatius, which I will address in the following chapter, a few comments need to be made of his approach to discernment in general. First, although the emphasis in Hughes' account is upon elective action, Hughes agrees with Rahner and Spohn that the aim of discernment is a type of *knowledge*, in this case the practical wisdom which aims at the knowledge of particular options for action. Second, Hughes also offers suggestions concerning the roles which affectivity plays in the process.

His suggestions are different from Spohn or Rahner, but still he appears to claim that affectivity does indeed play a significant role in Christian elective decision. The need for clarification of the interaction of rational and affective elements in Christian discernment becomes ever clearer.

Hughes, Rahner and Spohn, are all clearly speaking within the context of *moral philosophy*. Rahner specifies in both articles that he is dealing with moral choice insofar as it regards not simply the universal norm, but rather, when there are multiple choices within the bounds of the universal norm, his interests concern what the existential or individual norm demands. Spohn seems to be offering a dialogue between the fields of moral discourse and reflection on discernment. He offers this as an alternative approach to an individual ethic, rooted more in story and affect rather than transcendent awareness. As such it would be best to suppose that Spohn addresses the same questions as Rahner. Hughes makes no such distinction of situational choice. Moral choice is based on various factors, and it is all part of practical wisdom. The significance of the philosophical emphasis on moral choice when discussing discernment is that many writers on discernment from within the field of Christian spirituality clearly distinguish Christian discernment from moral choice. Susan Rakoczy, summarizing the literature of U.S. Catholic writings on discernment from 1965-78 writes, "Moral choice concerns the decision to do good or evil; discernment, however, is oriented to the determination of one moral good among several goods" (1980, 58; cf. pp. 54ff.). While the term "discernment" is increasingly used to address ethical questions (Gustafson 1974; Dunstan 1975; McCarthy 1985; Poorman 1993; Gula 1997), many students of spirituality prefer to avoid associating discernment merely with ethical choice. Choosing a personal vocation or corporate apostolate is of a different order than a choice between right and wrong. For the purposes of the present study one may simply approach both these types of situation as acts of knowledge which involve the identification of that which is significantly related to God. Insofar as they approximate this definition, they are both to be regarded as discerning acts. However the criteria and approach to ethical choice may be distinguished from that of vocational choice, although I suspect that in the concrete, there will be some overlap of categories.

Having concluded the review of recent theological and philosophical contributions to an understanding of discernment, it may be appropriate to reflect on a few of the themes as a whole.

First, it appears appropriate to address discernment as an act of knowing. Theologians and philosophers alike appear to be moving toward addressing discernment in this manner. In the case of the present study, doing so enables one to unite the common interpretant linking together research on discernment from a wide variety of contextual horizons. Furthermore, I have shown in the literature a tendency to think of discernment as a *process* of knowing, frequently involving distinct stages.

Second, we have seen, especially in Rakoczy's thesis and in Rahner's work, that there is a need for greater specificity in writings on discernment. Discernment research needs greater theological, philosophical, and psychological sensitivity in its attempts to articulate what actually goes on in Christian discernment. There are a variety of terms and issues which demand greater specification in order for progress to be made in comprehending the nature of Christian discernment.

Third, our review has shown that affectivity is to be considered an important player in the discernment process. The importance of affectivity was mentioned time and time again in the literature. However, the exact nature of the role or roles which affectivity play(s) in Christian discernment was left ambiguous. Affectivity was mentioned as functioning as a sign or an effect by which the work of the Spirit can be identified (as with Gay and Costa). Affectivity was also mentioned as part of the prior shaping of the discerner either enabling (Hughes' "essential prerequisite," Spohn's "connaturality") or, when defective, hindering (as in Rulla) the discerning process. Affectivity was mentioned as being involved in the act of discernment itself, providing a norm or criteria at the point of categorical comparison (as in Rahner and Spohn), or providing intuitive suggestions for choice (again in Spohn). Affectivity itself can be seen as an *object* of evaluation, either as the immediate object of discerning attention (as in Gay), or as the object of rational evaluation (as in Hughes). Jonathan Edwards' own *Religious Affections* is a manual for evaluating of the character of affective movements in the church. For Hughes, affectivity forms the discerner and reason acts to guide the chooser. For Spohn, converting Gospel reflection serves to form the discerner and affective judgments serve to guide the chooser. While the importance of affectivity is recognized by nearly all, clarity is needed when it comes to the explicating the roles which affectivity plays in the processes of Christian discernment.

Another matter which deserves mention is the diversity of philosophical perspectives reflected in the few essays which address philosophical concerns. Karl Rahner recalls the thought of Aquinas, as do Gay, Hughes, and others (Sullivan 1980; Dussel 1979; Bellosa 1979). Rahner also reflects or reflects upon the thought of Suarez, Kant, and Heidegger. Spohn emphasizes the relevance of North American thought in particular that of Jonathan Edwards and H. Richard Neibuhr. Hughes returns to the work of Aristotle for a philosophical background for understanding discernment. Rulla bases his philosophical reflections on the thought of Bernard Lonergan. There is certainly no consensus on the matter of philosophical perspective toward discernment. In spite of this diversity, all of the authors, however, appear to be in agreement with the central philosophical *question* of Christian discernment, namely the question of what provides reason to believe that a claimed discernment has indeed achieved its aim, the identification of that which is (or is not) from God. Increased clarity concerning the integration of the rational and affective in the discernment process, increased clarity concerning how objects are compared in the discernment process, and increased clarity concerning the primary means of God's self-revelation all serve to bring light to the more central question of the means by which that which is from God can be confirmed or identified as such.

Finally, we have discovered that discernment has, as its distinctive feature, the character of sorting, sifting, comparing in order to *identify* that which is significantly related to God. Whether it is a process of "comparing" object or affective motion to a norm, or whether it is the synthesis of a part of experience into a whole in order to comprehend the nature of the part, or whether it is one set of cognitive operations (intellect) evaluating others (affectivity) to identify their appropriateness, at the core of Christian discernment is the act of categorizing experience.

Psychological Studies

As mentioned above, the article on discernment in the *Dictionnaire de Spiritualite* closes with a section on discernment in spiritual direction. I will reserve my review of current literature linking discernment and spiritual direction for chapter six. It is, however, relevant to the purposes of the present chapter to mention literature exploring Christian discernment from the field of psychology. A few recent psychological studies have offered contributions to an understanding of Christian discernment. These have served to advance the understanding of the dynamisms of the human-divine relationship in discernment and have helped to bring a measure of refinement to the understanding of key terms and structures. This review will also serve to indicate undeveloped areas of research, areas which will be developed in the current study.

In addition to the article by Luigi Rulla, mentioned above, a psychoanalytic perspective has been applied to Christian discernment in the work of W.W. Meissner. A Jesuit scholar, Meissner has applied his expertise in psychoanalytic psychology both to the *Spiritual Exercises* (1963; 1964a; 1964b) and to the life (1992) of Ignatius of Loyola, as well as to mystical experience in general (1984). Though Ignatius' life and works—and likewise Meissner's comments thereon—are laced throughout with the theme of discernment, Meissner's analysis of the nature of Christian discernment is most explicit in his commentary on Ignatius' Rules for the Discernment of Spirits (1964b, 178-88). In this commentary he seeks to recast Ignatius' Rules in terms of psychoanalytic ego-psychology. Meissner describes the conflict between good and evil "spirits," for example, in terms of intrapsychic mechanisms: activation of ego-systems conflicting with the pleasure principle and libidinal resistance to ego-control. He defines "consolation," a key term in Ignatian thought describing pleasurable affective motions toward God, in terms of ego-orientated responses (as differentiated from mere libidinal gratification). By providing enlightening commentary on numerous aspects of Ignatius' life and works, Meissner's work reminds the student of discernment (1) of the powerful conflict between unconscious forces and ego-control (the reality principle) underlying the dynamics of Christian discernment, and (2) of the interweaving of grace and nature (multidimensionality) within the spiritual life. In a recent thesis, Stephen Parker draws from Meissner and other ego-psychological works to identify charismatic discernment and decision-making as a "creative regression" (1996).

Insights into discernment from the Jungian perspective have been provided through a couple of contributions. Morton Kelsey, who has applied the perspective of Jung to a variety of aspects of Christian spirituality (e.g. 1972, 1973, 1976), gathered a few scattered lectures and articles together around the theme of discernment and published them in a single volume (1978). The chapters of this book deal with such diverse topics as the phenomena of "slaying in the Spirit," language, myth, and evil, and counseling practice. What ties them together is the realization that in each of these settings there is a need for the wise identification of that which is, and is not, from God. Both the nature of "spirits" and the psychology of the discerner who discerns the spirits are explored. Kelsey places the dynamics of Christian discernment in the psychological context of a "real spiritual world," full of archetypal conflict and mystery. Kelsey also emphasizes the complexity of the human person, bringing attention to the need for discernment. While not an analysis of the nature of discernment, Kelsey's work serves to illumine key issues that surround discernment research.

Richard Sweeney, in his doctoral thesis, applies Jungian insights directly to an analysis of Christian discernment (1983). Concerned that "efforts to appropriate today traditional approaches to the discernment of spirits are complicated by the fact that the language and conceptual structures of these approaches are derived from largely antiquated cosmologies and anthropologies" (1983, 1), Sweeney undertakes to recast three key issues of discernment research within the framework of Jungian psychology. First, he interprets the "spirits" which are discerned in terms of Jungian complexes, archetypes, and the unconscious integrating function, reframing an understanding of the works of these spirits and the responses to them. Second, Sweeney addresses the question of discernment as divine charism or natural virtue (in psychological terms - the acquisition and development of discernment). He does so by joining both sides together in a contemporary theology of nature and grace, by speaking of the growth of discernment in terms of the transformation of complexes that disorder affective experience and impede discernment, and by demonstrating the need for discernment to be developed in the context of one's psychological type or psychic function. Finally Sweeney suggests a four-stage process of discernment drawing from Jungian method: (1) submit to Impulses of the Unconscious, (2) Translate

Emotions into Images, (3) Strive to Understand the Images, and (4) Discover the Ethical Consequences.[8] Sweeney's work offers a second major psychological paradigm within which discernment can be explored and interpreted.

With the work of Elizabeth Liebert, an understanding of discernment receives insight from the field of developmental psychology. In her published volume on spiritual direction (Liebert 1992) and to a greater extent in her doctoral thesis (Liebert 1986), she seeks to apply insights from adult developmental theory to the understanding of Christian discernment. More specifically, she uses insights especially from Jane Loevinger and Robert Kegan to illumine structural-developmental aspects of Christian discernment, especially as presented in Ignatius' *Exercises*. Her chief contribution is to demonstrate that certain forms of discernment practice are meaningfully possible only for subjects who have reached certain milestones of ego-development. For example, the comparison and categorization of subtle inner motions involved in discernment as discussed in much spiritual direction literature, especially that informed by Ignatius' *Exercises*, requires the capacity for the recognition and evaluation of differentiated feelings, a capacity only possible when a person reaches the stage of development that Liebert calls "Conscientious" (1992, 106). By exploring the ways in which humans frame their reality and their sense of self throughout adult development, Liebert draws attention to an important and undermentioned aspect of discernment.

Having completed the review of psychological material, I will present a few comments by way of conclusion.

First, recent psychologically-oriented reflections on Christian discernment have opened up a range of interpretive categories to use in re-visioning Christian discernment in contemporary settings and in light of contemporary understandings of human experience. A responsible account of Christian discernment today must walk the tightrope of re-understanding old wisdom in new language and concepts without distorting the wisdom in the process. The research reviewed above has taken the first steps toward just such an account. I hope to continue this re-visioning in the chapters to follow.

[8]One should notice that there are important similarities between Sweeney's Jungian model and other models of "stages" within the process of knowing (cf. Lonergan 1958; Rulla 1978; Costa 1993). I will develop these similarities further in the following chapters.

Second, psychological studies of discernment have brought a necessary earthy refinement to many of the terms and concepts associated with Christian discernment. As a *human* act, Christian discernment necessarily involves all of the unconscious cathexes, archetypal associations, and developmental stages of ordinary humans. Spiritual terms such as "consolation" and "desolation" cannot be understood apart from the deep concerns of individuals and the structural framework within which these concerns become present to people. I will develop this refinement of terms and concepts of discernment in chapter five.

Third, one area of psychological research that remains unexplored with regard to the understanding of discernment is the field of experimental psychology--in particular the field of research in cognition and emotion. This field may offer increased empirical precision with regard to an understanding of discernment as an affectively-rich act of knowledge. I will explore this range of psychological material in the present study, especially in chapter three.

Aims and Methodology

I have established a working definition of discernment and, having reviewed a few significant contributions to an understanding of discernment, am now in a position to state more exactly the contribution the present study intends to make. I will first describe the methodology of the study generally as a study in Christian spirituality. I will situate the methodology of the study with relationship to the working definition of discernment. Then I will comment on the roles which the two cognate disciplines of experimental psychology and philosophical theology will play in the study. Having done this, I will outline the structure and limits of the study.

The aim of the study is to illumine an understanding of Christian discernment. Specifically I wish to demonstrate that the insights of experimental psychology, interpreted with the help of a philosophically-sensitive model of human experience, can provide helpful conceptual framework and empirical grounding for exploring and interpreting discernment as an affectively-rich act of knowing. My hope is that by exploring the functions of affectivity in Christian discernment through the eyes of experimental psychology, and by synthesizing the data of this human science within a framework capable of attending to important philosophical issues, I might contribute to the need for specificity in Christian reflection on discernment.

General Methodology

In view of the confusion created by multiple terms and horizons associated with Christian discernment, I have chosen to focus on an interpretant which can comprehend the similar form contained within the diversity of discernment situations. I have identified this interpretant with an *act of knowing*, defining discernment as the process and act of coming to identify and know in a given situation, in the light of one's Christian faith tradition, that which is significantly related to God. For this reason, the present study will not approach the study of discernment via analysis of terms. Nor will it focus on discernment within one tradition or contextual horizon (for example, discernment of spirits in the context of personal spiritual direction in Roman Catholic communities). Rather I will draw material from a variety of traditions and contextual horizons in an attempt to illumine the nature of Christian discernment. Hence the present study is essentially an interpretive analysis.

As an interpretive study in the field of Christian spirituality, this study follows the three step methodological framework set for the discipline of spirituality by Sandra Schneiders (1989, 1993, 1998 cf. also Downey 1997, 129). The works of representative figures from the history of spirituality will be used to *describe* discernment in the Christian tradition as an act of knowing. The phenomena of Christian discernment will then receive *critical analysis* via the cognate fields of experimental psychology and philosophical theology, fields suited to the exploration of discernment as an act of knowing. In its integrative conclusion, the study will offer *constructive interpretation* which contributes to an understanding of the process of Christian discernment as it is practiced today.

I am not, in this study, attempting to present a thoroughly descriptive analysis of Christian discernment, to describe how people actually discern that which is significantly related to God. Certainly, the historical, psychological, and philosophical material contributes to this understanding, and certainly an adequate understanding of this is valuable and worthy of formal research. However, that is not the final aim of the current study. I have taken no surveys and will be summarizing no formal interviews or seasons of participant observation of communal discernment processes. Nonetheless, the psychological material in particular will provide important insights concerning typical operations involved in Christian discernment as an affectively-rich act of knowing. My aim, however, goes beyond the real to the ideal. Discernment wisdom throughout history has aimed at *improving* the practice of Christian discernment, of bringing the practice of Christian discernment ever closer to the realization of the aim of discernment itself, namely the reliable identification of that which is significantly related to God. Thus one must, I feel, move beyond a *descriptive* account of Christian discernment toward a *normative* account, an account which indicates what ought to be done in order to insure the realization of the aim of Christian discernment with greater likelihood. The study will shift to the normative especially with the reflections in chapters four and five.

In exploring discernment as an *act* or *process*, the study will focus on the elements which structure discernment as an act or process: surrounding context, subject, object(s) and the process itself as understood in terms of preparation, apparent content, trajectory, completion, confirmation, and results/response. I shall demonstrate, for example, that the roles of affectivity in Christian discernment vary depending on which element of the process is in view. Writings on discernment emphasize these different elements in various measures. I will attempt to regard each of these elements as appropriate to the particular topic under consideration.

As an act of *knowing* my focus will ultimately turn, in chapters four and five, upon key epistemological questions. By what means is that which is significantly related to the divine recognized to be as such? How does affectivity mediate the "knowledge" of the divine, and in what does this knowledge consist? What grounds are there for the formation of the belief, in a given situation, that one has correctly identified that which is significantly related to God? In what does the warrant for such a belief consist? In order to clarify such questions it will be necessary to specify what is meant by the subject/author, the object, and the aim of discernment. I will also address the roles of specific "faculties" or cognitive operations as they bear upon the issue. Specifically, this study places its focus upon exploring the roles which affectivity and categorization play in discernment.

As an act of *religious* knowing I will focus my attention in this study upon discernment as it is described and practiced in one religious tradition (Christian). Primary and secondary works concerning the spirituality of discernment will be chosen from the Christian tradition. However, I have intentionally chosen representatives from two different major streams of Christianity (Roman Catholic and Protestant) in order to better comprehend the rich breadth of approach to Christian discernment.

The Cognate Disciplines

In order to explore what goes on in Christian discernment as an act of knowing I have chosen to utilize the findings of two separate "cognate fields" of study which focus upon the analysis of the human knowing process.

The first cognate field to be employed is the field of experimental psychology, and more specifically to approaches within this field referred to as "cognitive." During the past three decades, empirical understanding of human cognitive process has been significantly advanced through experimental psychology. Cognitive theories of affectivity are rapidly becoming dominant within social and personality psychological communities. Cognitive psychology has only just begun to consider religious phenomena, and has only recently been applied in any sense to issues of Christian spirituality (Watts and Williams 1988). This study will examine cognitive research related to affectivity and categorization in order to identify with greater precision both the evaluative sorting functions and the affective dimensions involved in the discernment process. Research in Christian discernment has implicitly understood discernment as an act of knowing, and even of sorting, distinguishing, and identifying its objects. It has yet to examine the cognitive processes of categorization by which human beings accomplish this identifying. Thus in this study I will examine empirical findings on human categorization in order to identify operations involved in establishing and maintaining taxonomic structures such as those differentiating "from God" and "not from God." Likewise, research in Christian discernment has emphasized the importance of affectivity but it has yet to examine the roles of affectivity in discernment in light of specific empirical research concerning the dynamics of emotional experience itself. Thus my review of research on affectivity will describe mechanisms such as concerns, coping processes, appraisals, and action tendencies, by which affective impulses convey and assess environment-person relationships, including the divine human relationship.

The second cognate field to be employed is that of philosophical theology. As an act of knowing, and especially as an act of knowing which has to do with *God*, philosophical and theological issues must be addressed. Greater interpretive precision will be provided to the present discussion of discernment through the use of the philosophical/theological perspective of Donald Gelpi. His corpus of works constitutes a thorough integration of North American philosophy and Christian theology with special sensitivity to the affective dimension. The theological/philosophical integration expressed in Gelpi's works is uniquely suited to the task of forming a conceptual framework adequate to interpret Christian discernment. This study will summarize Gelpi's relevant philosophical and theological categories (for example, his understanding of 'Experience,' 'general tendency,' and 'conversion') and will use these categories to provide an organizing principle which can unify disparate insights of cognitive psychology. In this manner, Gelpi's philosophical and theological categories form the beginning outlines of a conceptual framework within which the insights from cognitive psychology can be understood insofar as they bear on the understanding of Christian discernment as an affectively-rich act of knowing.

One must also address the question of how these two diverse fields might be properly coordinated. Gelpi himself has proposed a set of helpful guidelines for inter-disciplinary category coordination. His ideas were first presented in his *Inculturating North American Theology* (Gelpi 1988b) and have been incorporated in his integration of Christology and developmental psychology (Gelpi 1995). I concur with Gelpi that interdisciplinary coordination is best conducted as an integration of insights found within different categories. Categories from the humanities tend to interpret and contextualize categories from the sciences, philosophical logic validates the methods of scholarship and science by providing them with sound operational principles, theological categories verify, falsify, and transvalue certain kinds of philosophical and general categories, and categories from the sciences verify, falsify, and illumine categories from the humanities. By drawing specific attention to items of agreement, complementarity, convergence, or dialectical reversal between the current state of these two fields, insights from the field of cognitive psychology can be clarified and properly coordinated with the categories of philosophy, theology and Christian spirituality.

Structure of the Study

Chapter two will serve as the descriptive section of the study. Here I will employ two examples from the history of Christian spirituality: Ignatius of Loyola's *Spiritual Exercises* and Jonathan Edwards' *Distinguishing Marks* and *Religious Affections*. These works originate from two different continents (Europe, America) and two different branches of Christianity (Roman Catholic, Protestant). Yet each is a recognized classic on discernment and all specifically address the role of affectivity in this process. These works will be used to display aspects of discernment as an affectively-rich process of knowing: a process of recognizing, understanding, and evaluating within the context of a maturing Christian faith.

Chapter three turns to the field of experimental psychology to explore particular aspects of human affectivity and evaluation. Cognitive research on human categorization will be used to illumine the dynamics of human evaluation and the discrimination involved in Christian discernment. Then I will briefly survey research on affectivity, highlighting those findings relevant to the topic. I will then synthesize these findings, presenting an outline of the structure and function of affective operations within cognitive process and Christian experience in general. From the integration of research in affectivity and categorization we can begin (1) to understand how categorizing and affective operations condition and are conditioned within the process of Christian discernment and (2) how affectivity might function to assist or hinder the recognition and categorization of elements of experience as significantly related to God.

In chapter four, the study turns to theology and philosophy in the work of Donald Gelpi. The chapter will examine the important theological and philosophical issues necessary to construct a coherent account of Christian discernment as an affectively-rich act of knowing. After a review of Gelpi's primary philosophical categories, I will employ Gelpi's North American synthesis to address a few issues necessary to bring conceptual coherence to matters raised in previous chapters or to provide essential theological foundations. Then, the philosophical question of the warrant or grounds of religious knowledge will receive primary attention. I will retrace some of Gelpi's North American philosophical roots in order to establish a few logical steps necessary for an account of the reliability and limits of Christian discernment as an act of religious knowing. I will also draw attention to the relationship between epistemology and affectivity in Gelpi's philosophical theology, emphasizing the functions which affective operations play in bringing the believer to an adequate knowledge of God and God's activity. The thought of Gelpi concerning discernment will then be placed into dialogue with other philosophical reflections on the topic, illustrating where Gelpi's synthesis contributes specificity to an account of Christian discernment.

In chapter five, the study will utilize the insights gained from the two cognate fields to suggest an approach to Christian discernment which highlights the roles which affectivity plays in the process. I will draw the insights of the empirical and the philosophical material together to construct a model of human experience capable of interpreting the dynamics of Christian discernment. Using this model, I will offer a summary account of Christian discernment, commenting on a number of issues in discernment research in light of the integrative model constructed.

After the presentation of this approach, I will utilize this expanded understanding of the role of affectivity in discernment in chapter six to consider applications to two common discernment situations. First, I will suggest how a developed understanding of the role of affective operations in the discernment process can aid in the recognition and evaluation of the presence and activity of God (or other forces) in the context of personal spiritual direction and pastoral care. Second, I will also offer suggestions concerning the pastoral evaluation of affective trends and charismatic movements in the Church at large. These two situations are chosen for their similarity to the issues of Ignatius' and Edwards' works, and for their relevance for individuals and communities today. I will close with some general conclusions and suggestions for further research.

Chapter 2

Affectivity and Christian Discernment In the History of Spirituality: Two Examples

What does Christian discernment look like? This is the question of the present chapter. In the previous chapter I identified an interpretant which can comprehend the diverse phenomena identified by the Christian community as discernment. Discernment may be beneficially understood as an *affectively-rich act of knowing.* Having reviewed literature from a variety of disciplines, I showed the need for greater scientific and philosophical precision in studies on Christian discernment. The present study intends to contribute a measure of this precision via a critical analysis of Christian discernment in light of the insights of experimental psychology and those of the philosophical/theological framework of Donald Gelpi. Before one can move to critical analysis, however, It will be helpful to obtain, through historical description, an intuitive idea of the phenomena considered for evaluation. I will accomplish this by a presentation of discernment in the works of three representative works from Christian history: Ignatius of Loyola's *Spiritual Exercises* and Jonathan Edwards' *Distinguishing Marks of a Work of the Spirit of God* and the *Treatise on Religious Affections.*

I have chosen these works because each is a recognized classic on the subject of discernment. They originate, however, from different centuries, different branches of Christianity, and different continents.

They speak to widely different contexts and were written with different objects of discernment in mind. By exploring the similarities and differences of Christian discernment as presented in these documents I will be able to describe the process of Christian discernment as an act of knowing, illustrating the central aspect of the interpretant mentioned in chapter one. Furthermore, each of these works specifically addresses the role(s) that affective operations play in the discernment process, enabling this study to emphasize Christian discernment as an *affectively-rich* act of knowing.

The methodology used in this chapter is that of presenting a contextually "thick" description of discernment as it is found in these sample works (Schneiders 1994, 12; Geertz 1973). At this point my presentation bears similarity to McGinn's "historical-contextual" approach (McGinn 1993, 6), with the focus limited to factors necessary to give an adequate basic description of Christian discernment highlighting the factors emphasized in this study. While the study of Christian spirituality cannot be reduced to historical description (cf. Downey 1997,126-27), historical research is a necessary step in understanding Christian spiritual life. I will review the portrait of discernment as presented in each work, examining contextual factors and theological principles that shape each presentation of discernment. I will indicate structural aspects of each work that reveal the author's understanding of the process of Christian discernment. I will highlight the roles that affectivity plays in this discernment process, identifying the terms, concepts, and expectations that frame each work's approach to the roles of affectivity in Christian discernment. I will conclude by drawing insights from these two samples together, presenting a general description of Christian discernment as an affectively-rich act of knowing.

One other matter that should be mentioned at the onset of this "descriptive" chapter, is that in both Ignatius' *Spiritual Exercises* and Edwards' revival works the authors are presenting the readers with a portrait, not of actual discernment, but of ideal discernment. Consequently, although I recognize that the authors' personal experiences in discernment certainly shaped the formation of their writings, my primary aim in this chapter is not to recover the spiritual experience of each author, but is rather to grasp a sense of the ideal experience toward which each led his readers. Ignatius and Edwards were interested in showing what discernment looks like at its best. By exploring works of this type, I am involved not only in descriptive but also normative reflection.

The *Spiritual Exercises* of Ignatius of Loyola

The *Spiritual Exercises* of Ignatius of Loyola, founder of the Society of Jesus (the Jesuits), is the single most referenced work in recent discussion of Christian discernment. This small book contains the distilled essence of Ignatian spirituality, a spiritual vision that has empowered Jesuits for service to Christ and the Church for centuries. Begun in 1522, when Ignatius was thirty-one years of age, and repeatedly reworked and revised until it was finally published in 1548, the *Spiritual Exercises* served as a manual of spiritual direction for the Jesuit Order, and through this Order contributed significantly to the Catholic (or so-called "Counter") Reformation of the sixteenth century. The book is not a treatise on the spiritual life, nor simply a set of devotions to be used in times of private prayer. "Instead, it is a manual to guide exercises which are to be carried out by an excercitant, ordinarily with counsel from a director" (Ganss 1991, 50). It contains collections of instructions on how to pray and how to lead others into prayer, particular meditations and contemplations that people can use in prayer, and wisdom about the dynamics of the spiritual life for directors to understand what may be going on when people spend time in prayer. The book divides into four "Weeks," under the assumption that in the ideal use of this book an individual would set aside a full month for prayer following the format of the book and that in this ideal month-long-retreat, the exercitant would pass through four identifiable stages of spiritual experience. Meditations, rules and instructions are included in the text as appropriate to each stage or "Week." Ignatius' approach to Christian discernment is condensed in his "Rules for the Discernment of Spirits," (suited to the first and second "Weeks"). John O'Malley considers these rules "a critical introduction to the meaning of the whole book" (O'Malley 1993, 41). Nonetheless, for the sake of the present study, it seems best not to limit the exposition of discernment in Ignatius to a commentary on the "Rules for the Discernment of Spirits" but rather to explore how the phenomena of discernment, as defined by my interpretant, is portrayed and comprehended in the text of the *Exercises* as a whole.

The Context of the Exercises *in Ignatius' Life and Times*

The published *Exercises* being a product of twenty-six years of conscious development, the context of Ignatius' work in his life and times is not easy to determine. During these years Ignatius lived in four different countries (Spain, Israel, France, and Italy), attended different schools (at Barcelona, Alcalá, Salamanca, and Paris), and passed through major personal and career "stages" (mystic, pilgrim, student, charismatic leader, director/administrator of a religious order). During this period the Church and even the Holy Roman Empire itself suffered attack from many fronts (internal corruption, renaissance humanism, nationalism, Turkish encroachments, and the Protestant Reformation), all of which received some attention by Ignatius and the early Jesuits during the years of the writing of the *Exercises*. Although Ignatian scholarship continues to debate the various influences shaping the formation of the *Spiritual Exercises*, consensus is currently building around two points. First, more than likely, the *Exercises* was not a near-finished product when handed to his inquisitors at Salamanca in 1527 (*Autobiography*, 67[1]). Although "the essential parts of the *Exercises* were written in the context of the Manresa experience" (Meissner 1992, 423), important components of the work, along with revisions of the whole, probably were incorporated throughout the years of the development of the text, especially in light of Ignatius' Paris experience (Meissner 1992, 423; Dalmases 1985, 123; Bakker 1970; Endean 1989). Second, while national, academic, and ecclesiastical contexts certainly shaped the formation of the *Exercises*, the work should be regarded primarily as

---

[1]Following convention in Ignatian studies, references to key works of Ignatius will be made as follows: references to the Autobiography of Ignatius will be given as *Autobiography* followed by the standard paragraph number and the date indicated in square brackets (for example *Autobiography*, 67 [1527]). References to Ignatius' Spiritual Diary shall be given as *Diary* with the paragraph number (for example *Diary*, 13). References to the *Spiritual Exercises* shall simply indicate the standard paragraph number within square brackets (for example [318]). The text used for all of these works is that of Ganss 1991, and references to Ganss' commentary in this volume will be indicated as Ganss 1991.

the expression of the spiritual experience of Ignatius himself and those whom he served in ministry. John O'Malley summarizes this point succinctly, saying of the *Exercises*, "its origins lay not in a scholar's study, an academic disputation, an inquisitorial courtroom, or an ecclesiastical council. It was not a counterstatement to Luther, Erasmus, or the *alumbrados*. It originated in religious experience, first the author's and then others'" (O'Malley 1993, 42; cf. Meissner 1992, 87-108; Dalmases 1985, 66; Rahner 1953; 1968, 32-53).

Assuming these points, a few notes concerning contextual influences and personal experiences that shaped the formulation of Ignatius' understanding of Christian discernment as expressed in *The Exercises* may be made. Ignatian scholarship has established much of the context of Ignatius' thought and therefore only a brief summary is necessary here. First, the *Spiritual Exercises* is the product of Spanish chivalry. Not only modern scholarship but Ignatius himself makes reference to the influence of the ideal of the Spanish knight (Meissner 1993, 39, 43-65; Dalmases 1985, 43-48; *Autobiography*, 1 [1521-22]). The ideal of chivalry was not lost but transformed through Ignatius' conversion to Christ and is clearly present in the *Exercises* ([46, 91ff., 136ff.], cf. Rahner 1953 1-15). The impact of this ideal upon Ignatius' understanding of discernment will be seen first in his approach to the preparation for good discernment through the development of connaturality by means of meditation on the life and character of our "King," and second through the sense of pursuit of the "greater" (*magis*) which guides the discernment process, especially in the situation of an election of life.

Second, the *Spiritual Exercises* is a synthesis of a variety of sources. The genius of the *Exercises* may not have been the origination of new techniques of prayers but rather in that it combined elements from Ignatius' sources, in the light of his personal and ministerial experience, into a unique synthesis and practice of the Christian spiritual life, one which was well-adapted to the situation of his time. Ignatius drew from available mendicant histories, devotional techniques, and exhortations to sanctity to form this synthesis. Perhaps elements from other Patristic or medieval sources found their way into the formation of the *Exercises* (Bakker 1970; Benke 1991; Rahner 1953; Boyle 1983; Hughes 1990). Yet despite Ignatius' use and even dependency upon sources at times, the *Spiritual Exercises* was not simply a medieval compilation of meditations. Ignatius contributed original material to this work (e.g. the division into four "Weeks" and the Three Times for Making an Election), and synthesized and arranged the whole such that when used as a manual for shaping another's time with God through the ministry of a spiritual director, the *Spiritual Exercises* became a uniquely powerful tool for change.

Third, the *Spiritual Exercises* was not only a product of its sources, but also of its audience, the persons and contexts to which the book spoke. The most important audience to which the *Exercises* was addressed, and which shaped its formation was the individual. The precise formulation of the meditations, contemplations, annotations, and rules, grew not only from Ignatius' own personal experience, but also through his observations of the experience of other individuals. Ignatius' ministry of "conversation" with others, his giving of the *Exercises* to a wide variety of exercitants and his extensive correspondence gave Ignatius access to a significant informal "experimental group" from whom insights could be obtained for the refining and rewriting of the *Exercises*. With regards to the subject of discernment, this "working through" ideas in the context of his relationship with individuals is most plainly seen through his correspondence with Teresa Rejadell (Ignatius 1991d [1536], 332f.; Bakker 1970, 33-68; Endean 1989). A second context to which the *Exercises* was addressed was the need for reform in the Church. Ignatius answered this need, for himself and for those who received benefit from the *Exercises* by crafting a program of spiritual formation which (1) was tenacious enough to address the most serious of sins yet without falling into authoritarianism, (2) was flexible enough to address a wide variety of people, and (3) was simple enough to be "transferable" to the many directors who would follow Ignatius through the rapid expansion of the Jesuit movement. A final context to which the *Exercises* spoke was the configuration of religious movements that surrounded the early Jesuits. The rise of Erasmian humanism, the threat of the Moors, the excesses of the *alumbrados* and the progress of the Protestant Reformation movements were not unknown to Ignatius and his friends (Boyle 1983; Dalmases 1985, 95-105, 157; Caraman 1990, 62, 90). Indeed, Ignatius' band of followers had been brought before the Inquisitors' scrutiny more than once, accused of heresies associated with one or another of these movements. Certainly elements of his presentation of Christian discernment in the *Exercises* reflect a sensitivity to his ecclesial environ-

ment (e.g. the Rules for Thinking with The Church and Ignatius' obli-
que reference to the Holy Spirit; cf. Rahner 1953, 1968; Bakker
1970, 233-310). Nonetheless, while Ignatius took care to distinguish
his spirituality from that of contemporaries, it must be affirmed that
Ignatius' wrote the *Exercises* not as reactions or responses to those
contemporaries but rather simply as a manual for "helping souls."

Finally, I must mention something of the influence of Ignatius'
own experience upon the text of the *Exercises*, for, in spite of recent
scholarship correcting an earlier hagiographical inspiration theory, it
is still maintained that the primary force shaping the content of the
Exercises was Ignatius' own spiritual experience (Meissner 1993;
O'Malley 1993; Rahner, 1953; 1956; 1968). This is especially true
for Ignatius' understanding of discernment, which has been illustrated
elsewhere (Conroy 1993) and needs no detailed development here.
Ignatius himself shows the links between his spiritual experience and
his growing understanding of discernment in the *Autobiography*.
From his first encounter with discernment in his recuperation from a
leg injury (*Autobiography*, 6-8 [1521-22]), to his experience of
scruples (*Autobiography*, 22-25 [1522-23]), to his trip to Jerusalem
(*Autobiography*, 38-50 [1523]) and beyond, Ignatius details lessons he
learned from his experience concerning the practice of discernment.
We also possess Ignatius' record to both his personal reflections and
the corporate deliberations of his early followers concerning the issue
of voluntary poverty, excellent samples of Ignatian approach to the
"Times for the Making of an Election" (Ignatius *Diary*; 1991e [1544],
225-228).

Discernment in the Exercises

Though Ignatius of Loyola seldom uses the terms "discernment of
spirits" or "discern," the book is filled with wisdom about discernment. Hence I will not focus attention on Ignatius' use of the term.
Neither will I follow the common practice of presenting Ignatian discernment via an exposition of the "Rules for the Discernment of
Spirits" [313-336] or the instructions for "Making an Election" [168-
189]. Instead, in keeping with my interest in examining discernment
in light of a broad interpretant, I intend to explore the *Exercises* as a
whole document, exploring where and how, in this document,
Ignatius instructs his readers in the art of recognizing, appreciating,

and responding to that which comes from (or does not come from) God. I find this to be a very profitable approach to the *Exercises*. Indeed, to relegate discernment to the discernment of spirits or to the election may be to miss the primary thrust of discernment in the book. Ignatius, throughout the book, interweaves many types of discernment, each requiring different skills, different operations, different objects, and different results. By looking at discernment as defined above I will identify six distinct types of discernment in Ignatius' work. Ignatius' ideal exercitant is conducting discernments within discernments in the process of ordering one's life more closely to reflect the glory of God. In this manner I will approach the *Exercises* in its entirety as a tool by which believers are nurtured in their ability to recognize, appreciate, and respond to God as God is manifested to them. In doing so, I believe I am in harmony with those commentators who look not merely to the *Exercises*, but to the entire early Jesuit corpus to receive their understanding of Ignatian discernment (cf. Futrell 1970). I will present this exploration by way of a summary and notes concerning each segment of the *Exercises* in succession.

The interpretation of the *Exercises* is subject to a number of controversies. Some of the controverted issues significantly impact one's understanding of what discernment looks like. The limits of this study do not permit extended discussion of these points, yet some statement must be made in order to present a viable portrait of discernment as expressed in the *Exercises*. Therefore I will address the appropriate issues only as necessary to present a basic picture of Ignatian discernment as expressed in the text of the *Exercises*.

The book begins with a set of Annotations or introductory explanations designed "to gain some understanding of the spiritual exercises which follow, and to aid both the one who gives them and the one who receives them" [1]. They describe these spiritual exercises - such as examination of conscience, meditations, prayers, and such - analogically to physical exercises, as aids for the ridding oneself of all "disordered affections" and for the "seeking and finding God's will in the ordering of our life." A number of these Annotations deal with the manner in which exercitants should be led with regard to their experience of affective motions, giving instructions concerning their process through various situations [4,6-10]. These Annotations reveal that much of the discernment of the *Exercises* is understood to be a co-operative discernment, the retreat director assisting the exercitant to become aware, to notice, to recognize, to understand and to respond appropriately to the personal and spiritual dynamics that shape the experience of the *Exercises*. A number of the Annotations emphasize the adaptability of the *Exercises* to the life of individual exercitants [4,9,18,19].

The First Week

The *Spiritual Exercises* proper open with a title: "SPIRITUAL EXERCISES to overcome oneself and to order one's life without reaching a decision through some disordered affection"[21]. The language of this title re-introduces themes presented in the first annotation and provides the grounds for the first major controversy in Ignatian interpretation: the very aim and purpose of the *Exercises* itself. What was the intended result of the *Exercises*: personal sanctification ("overcoming oneself," ridding oneself of "disordered affections" cf. Meissner 1963, 352; 1964; Fleming 1983b; Toner 1982, 39) or the making of an election of life ("finding God's will," "ordering one's life," "reaching a decision" cf. Egan 1976, 111, 133; Rahner 1964)? Following Ganss (1991, 390), I would see the two ends as complementary. It is clear from the practice of Ignatius and his early followers that the *Exercises* were used in a variety of different contexts, some of which did not include an Election (O'Malley 1993, 127ff; Rahner 1968, 139-43). Furthermore, the Annotations themselves indicate that the *Exercises* are intended to be adapted for a wide variety of exercitants, some of whom will not progress "to matters pertaining to the Election or to other Exercises beyond the First Week" [18]. In this sentence, Ignatius reveals both the importance of the Election for those who proceed to this stage as well as the value of the *Exercises* for those who do not reach that stage. It thus seems best to view the purpose of the *Exercises* as dependent upon the particular exercitant taking them.

Understanding the flexibility toward which the *Exercises* was designed will help us comprehend the dynamic approach which Ignatius takes toward discernment in this book. On the one hand, discernment arises in the *Exercises* at the point which and to the degree which the exercitant is capable of comprehending and using the material. For those who are not prepared for the discernment involved in the Election, the director leads the exercitant into the discernment of self-examination and through the Meditations and Rules of the First Week. For others, the discernment of appreciation in the Contemplations on the life of Christ, the Rules for the Second Week, the Election, and even the discernment involved in the Contemplation to Attain Love may be appropriate. The procedure of the Election, for example, depends upon the lessons of discernment, while the most of the lessons of discernment do not depend upon the Election. The nature and character of discernment as understood and practiced by any exercitant will depend upon the potential of that individual. Yet, on the other hand, Ignatius assumes that God will be actively present in the life of every exercitant no matter how elementary [15]. Thus, while the particular exercises and the complexity of training in discernment may vary, the *Exercises* as a whole are a means of growth in discernment for every exercitant. The *Spiritual Exercises* are intended as a tool, in whatever measure possible, to aid all believers in recognizing, appreciating and responding to the presence and activity of God in the concrete experience of the individual. Because of this "flexible yet central" character of Ignatian discernment as presented in the *Exercises*, the basic portrait of ideal Ignatian discernment presented in this study is of necessity a developmental one, corresponding to "the best that each can accomplish" within the context of each Week of the *Exercises*.

    After the Title and a Presupposition, the *Exercises* are further introduced by means of a "Principle and Foundation" [23]. This introduction provides the theological perspective which grounds the structure and content of the *Exercises* as a text, and which must be present as much as possible in any exercitant who wishes to do the *Exercises*. It forms a concrete statement of the context within which Ignatius understands the act of discernment to exist. Central to this perspective are Ignatius' understanding of (1) the purpose of human existence, namely, "to praise, reverence and serve God our Lord," (2) the presence of "other things" at our disposal that may be used for this purpose (also called "creatures" - here Ignatius means objects, people, opportunities, experiences, cognitive faculties, and so on. cf. also [235ff.]), (3) the importance of an attitude of "indifference" with relationship to these things, and (4) the need to cultivate a desire and choice for "the thing which is more conducive to the end for which I am created" (cf. Ganss 1991, 393). The process of discernment, for

Ignatius, occurs within the context of a person (1) who is created to glorify the Lord and (2) who has access to a variety of "things" that may be used for that end. Yet, disordered affective attachment to any of these "things" (e.g. wealth, honor, pleasures, or experiences - as concretely experienced in the life of the exercitant) may also "hinder me" in the fulfillment of that end [23]. Thus there is the need (3) to attain a measure of indifference with regard to these things, "not to seek health rather than sickness, wealth rather than poverty, honor rather than dishonor" [23], and thus to discern: to recognize and understand/appreciate those things which come from God in order that this person might (4) "desire and elect" them in the concrete ordering of life.

The first of the actual exercises of the First Week relate to the examination of conscience [24-44]. The Daily Particular Examination of Conscience [24-31] assists the exercitant to review progress related to a particular sin at significant points throughout the day. The General Examination of Conscience [32-43] prepares the exercitant for confession [44] and reviews not one, but all sins which may have been committed throughout a period of time. The exercises in self-examination, the very first exercises in the book, introduce the exercitant to discernment at its most basic level by cultivating the skill of interior watchfulness. This is the first type of discernment introduced in the *Exercises*. The ability to notice interior movements (cf. Aschenbrenner 1983), most easily accomplished for the beginner through an awareness of the presence of sin, is a fundamental skill upon which all other discernment is built. Even the progressive focus upon thoughts, words, and deeds of sin foster a nuanced ability to recognize inner events. This training of awareness plays an important part in the First Week (cf. Meissner 1964a, 35,36; Meissner 1964b, 187). By regularly reviewing one's day for the presence of sinful inclinations in the manner of these exercises, the exercitant develops the ability to recognize, appreciate (in order to reject), and respond negatively to that which is obviously not from God and positively to divine graces.

The exercises of self-examination also introduce the exercitant to the theme of the First Week in general, that of sin. Having grounded oneself in the theology of God's glory, the First Week turns to a thorough review of one's sinfulness before God. The exercises of this Week lead the exercitant into a dis-engagement with values and patterns which tend away from God's glory. This dis-engagement is fostered through a series of meditations: on the sin of the angels, of the first humans, and of any human [46-54]; on the history of one's own sin [55-61]; and on hell [65-71]. The exercises aim not merely to bring a notional awareness of the presence of sin in one's life. Rather the exercitant "must arouse itself to a deeply felt affective response" (Meissner 1964a, 33). Each meditation is preceded by a prayer for "what I want," a very important element in the *Exercises* (Byrne 1989, 29-36). This suggested prayer for "what I want" [48,55,65] indicates the action of God expected in the life of the exercitant during the course of the meditations and is itself an important theme in Ignatian discernment (Barry 1989a, Byrne 1989). In the First Week these prayers petition God for "shame and confusion about myself," for "growing and intense sorrow and tears for my sins," for an "interior knowledge" and "abhorrence" of my sins, and an "intense sense of the pain suffered by the damned." The "First Week" exercises of dis-engagement help to free exercitants from "disordered affections" [21,140] and thus enable them to recognize, appreciate, and respond to the things of God in the concrete circumstances of their lives (Hughes 1975, 6-14).

These exercises are usually assigned to the exercitant by the director in the order designated by the *Exercises*. Part of this order is the inclusion of various "repetitions" of the meditations. For example the third exercise for the first Week is "a repetition of the first and second exercises" [62]. After the usual initial prayers exercitants are instructed to repeat the very same exercises they performed earlier. In these repetitions, Ignatius notes, "I should notice and dwell on those points where I felt greater consolation or desolation, or had a greater spiritual experience" [62]. The act of noticing in order to respond to identifiable elements of a meditative experience brings me to the second type of discernment, the discernment of spirits. In the instructions concerning the repetition of exercises, Ignatius simply instructs the exercitant to pay special attention to the presence of "consolation or desolation."

Later in the book Ignatius offers specific "Rules to aid us toward perceiving and then understanding, at least to some extent, the various motions which are caused in the soul: the good motions that they may be received, and the bad that they may be rejected" [313]. These rules are more commonly known as the Rules for the Discernment of

Spirits (Ganss 1991, 423, henceforth referred to as "the Rules"). The mastery of these Rules, "at least to some extent," is critical to the successful navigation of the *Exercises*. The Rules divide into those more suitable for the First Week [313-327] and those more suitable for the Second Week [328-336]. The Rules for the First Week summarize the habitual tendencies of good and evil spirits in response to various spiritual trajectories of people [314-15]. Then they provide definitions of consolation and desolation [316-17] and supply information for the director or exercitant concerning how to respond in times of desolation (Buckley 1973; Toner 1982, 47-212).

One aspect of the rules for the discernment of spirits of note is the assumption of conflict. Discernment appears in a context of conflict. This is fundamental to Ignatius' approach to discernment. The world of Ignatius is a world of opposing forces battling for supremacy. Ignatius saw this in terms of literal "spirits" (cf. Toner 1982, 260-270). This conflict occurs in the external world between Christ and Satan in their conflict for world domination [136-148]. It also appears in the Rules as an inner conflict, the forces drawing the individual believer toward or away from Christ.

The "good motion" caused in the soul by the good spirit is called spiritual consolation. The key elements which define Ignatian consolation are (1) it is spiritual and (2) it is pleasurable ("consoling"). Ignatius understands consolation to refer to the experience of the soul "inflamed with love of its Creator and Lord," to the shedding of tears related to the "service and praise" of Christ, and to an "increase" or intensification of one's experience of hope, faith, and charity ([316] cf. Murphy 1976). Some commentators have identified consolation simply with the spiritual term of the interior motion (Buckley 1973, 28-29). Yet the language of the *Exercises* and Ignatius' descriptions of consolation elsewhere indicate that spiritual consolations should be understood as pleasurable experiences that lead one to God (Toner 1982, 94-121; 283-290).

However, in the Rules for the First Week, desolation, not consolation, receives primary attention. Presumably, this emphasis on desolation derives from the fact that the exercitant is just beginning to notice, understand, and reject those aspects of life which are against Christ (a "putting off the old" dynamic) and is therefore more subject to open temptations to give up the Christian pursuit and return to the sins of the past. Ignatius describes desolation as "darkness of soul, turmoil within it, an impulsive motion toward low or earthly things, or disquiet from various agitations an temptations." By introducing confusion, discouragement, distraction, and temptation to the believer attempting to dis-engage from earthly values and patterns through the exercises of the First Week, the enemy seeks to destroy the believer's recognition, appreciation and response to the things of God before they have a chance to take root. A successful desolation has the effect, therefore, of preventing the reception of "what I want," in the First Week, the sorrow, grief, true interior knowledge of sin and so on. Thus the exercitant must recognize the presence of desolation when it appears in consciousness so as to defeat its intended goal through appropriate response.

The correct recognition of consolation and desolation, necessary both for determining elements of meditation for repetition and for battling the spirits involved in desolation, is guided by an analysis of the quality and trajectory of the experiences themselves (notice the value of the training in interior self-awareness provided by the self-examination exercises). Consolation draws one through "tears," through "peace," through "love" [316] In desolation "one is completely listless, tepid, and unhappy, and feels separated from our Creator and Lord" [317]. While consolation involves an increase in faith hope or love [316], the motions of desolation "move one toward lack of faith and leave one without hope and without love" [317]. Similarly, "the thoughts which arise from consolation are likewise contrary to those which spring from desolation" [317]. This approach to the recognition of consolation and desolation is further borne out in the prayers for "what I want" and the instructions for repetitions throughout the *Exercises*. Ignatius provides no instruction for recognizing consolation or desolation through comparison with a previous experience of "consolation without prior cause" or of one's primordial consciousness. Discernment of spirits is conducted as an affectively-sensitive and rational reflection upon the quality and trajectory of the motions experienced in consciousness.[2] The "extent" of the accuracy of discernment of spirits is governed by the maturity, practice, intelligence, and grace given to each exercitant at any moment.

[2]Ignatius presents the same emphasis on inner watchfulness toward the quality and trajectory of experiences in his "Notes Concerning Scruples" ([345-51] cf. Meissner 1964b 190).

The Second Week

Whereas the First Week focuses attention on developing skills of interior watchfulness, fostering awareness of sin, and cultivating the initial recognition of and response to the diverse spirits which prompt various motions during the experience of the *Exercises*, the Second Week adds a new dimension through attention to Christ. The Second Week is a season of re-engagement with the person, concerns, and values of Jesus (Meissner 1964a, 41). As Futrell says of the exercises of the Second Week, "Through these contemplations, the exercitant is gradually brought to experience the interior resonance with the feelings of Jesus Christ (*sentir*) which will enable him to discern the word of God to him in the Election and ever after" (Futrell 1970, 75). Ignatius structures the Second Week around three types of exercises. First, there are a number of meditative Contemplations on the earthly life of Christ. Nestled within these Contemplations are a few key Meditations and considerations, designed to intensify the exercitant's identification with Christ. The Second Week climaxes and closes with the instructions for Making an Election.

The meditation which opens the Second Week, sometimes called a "second foundation" (Ganss 1991, 400), compares "Christ our Lord" to an earthly king [91-100]. The exercitant, in this meditation, is to place in mind a human king "whom all Christian princes and all Christian persons reverence and obey" [92]. Ignatius instructs the exercitant to observe this king in his or her imagination and to consider "what good subjects ought to respond to a king so generous and kind" [94]. Then the meditation moves from the earthly king to the heavenly, who is "much more worthy of consideration" [95]. The aim of the meditation is the response of wholehearted devoted sacrifice in the desire to "distinguish themselves in total service to their eternal king" [97]. The exercises of self-examination, which began the First Week, introduced the skill of interior watchfulness. This interior watchfulness was both a preliminary skill for developed discernment and a type of discernment in itself. In a similar manner, the meditation on the heavenly king introduces a new discernment skill: that of aesthetic and empathetic appreciation. In this meditation "that which comes from God" is Christ himself - his person and his characteristic values, standards and feelings (Sobrino 1978, 396-424). By focusing attention on the Christian model of perfection, the exercitant, having dis-engaged from the life and values of sin, is now re-engaged with the supreme values of the Christian faith.

The appreciative dynamic is intensified through the contemplations on the life of Jesus Christ. In these contemplations, the exercitant takes a segment from the Gospel narratives as the object of contemplation. The exercitant pictures the scene in his or her imagination, watching, listening, feeling, "entering into" the events of the passage. In these contemplations, "what I desire" is "an interior knowledge of our Lord, who became human for me, that I may love him more intensely and follow him more closely" [104]. Thus the aim of the contemplations is to cultivate a felt-recognition, appreciation and response to Jesus through repeated reflection upon the Christian Gospels. This is the third type of discernment presented in the *Exercises*. This third type of discernment, the discernment of appreciation for Christ, along with an attitude of desire for generous response to Christ's call, provides the context of Second Week discernment.

As the exercitant proceeds to the key meditations on the Two Standards [136-148] and the Three Classes of Persons ([149-157] cf. Rahner 1953, xii), introduced by the Introduction to the Consideration on States of Life [135], the direction of the *Exercises* shifts slightly. The appreciative gaze upon Christ now begins to finds its term in personal sacrificial abandonment in concrete service to Christ. The meditation on the Two Standards recalls the conflict between Christ and Satan, each calling their forces to conquer the world. The exercitant reflects upon the character and strategies of each in turn, praying to receive "insight into the deceits of the evil leader, . . ; and further, for insight into the genuine life which the supreme and truthful commander sets forth, and grace to imitate him" [139]. In the meditation on the Three Classes of Persons, the exercitant considers three persons who attempt to rid themselves of an attachment to some "thing," cultivating the inclination to abandon all for Christ and praying for "the grace to choose that which is more to the glory of his Divine Majesty" [152]. The dis-engagement of the First Week and the re-engagement to Christ through the contemplations of the Second Week has its effect in the exercitant in a "progressive deepening of the realization and commitment to the basic principle of indifference which was proposed in the foundation in the first week" (Meissner 1964a, 45). Disordered affections are released in the wake of grief for sin and the desire to follow and serve the heavenly king. Patterns of thinking and responding that would distort the perception of the Lord's presence and activity are set aside through an identification with the person, values and concerns of Christ. Glorious opportunities that lie ahead for the particular life of the exercitant in service of Christ have been inspired through the meditations and contemplations. By the latter part of the Second Week the exercitant is now prepared to recognize, appreciate and follow his or her own call to serve God our Lord.

During the Second Week, as with the First, Ignatius assumes that the exercitant will be experiencing "various motions which are caused in the soul" [313] in the course of the retreat. Thus he offers a second set of Rules for the Discernment of Spirits [328-336]. Because the exercitants are better able to perceive the subtleties of the forces opposed to Christ, and because the attacks themselves are more subtle for those in the Second Week, Ignatius offers here a "more probing discernment of spirits" [328]. Whereas in his Rules for the First Week, Ignatius identified consolation with the work of the good spirit and focused his attention upon the recognition and response to desolation, here he brings greater nuance to the presentation. He mentions that consolation can be caused by either the good or evil spirit for contrary purposes. In this manner evil can be introduced to the believer under the appearance of good. As in the Rules for the First Week, attending to the quality and trajectory of one's experience enables the recognition of the diverse spirits. It is characteristic of the evil angel to go along with the devout soul and then entice the soul away little by little [332]. By examining the "beginning, middle, and end" one can notice the tendencies which are introduced by various spirits at different points in life [333]. The good angel touches the devout soul "gently, lightly, sweetly. The evil spirit touches it sharply, with noise and disturbance" [335]. Again, one should attend to these motions in one's experience because the inclinations to various choices of life or to the exercitant's options for serving Christ will be affected by the presence of these consolations and desolations. The elective aim of the Second Week, the free choice of a way of life that brings God the greatest possible glory through the life of the exercitant, may be thwarted by a temptation under the appearance of good.

Ignatius names one type of consolation the origin of which can be identified confidently. He refers to it as the "consolation without a preceding cause" [330]. The correct interpretation of this consolation is a much controverted point in Ignatian scholarship. Some see it as the emerging into consciousness of one's primordial awareness of transcendental Mystery and a key to Christian discernment (Rahner 1964, 131ff; Egan 1976). Others (Toner 1982) disagree, pointing to the lack of centrality of this form of consolation in Ignatius' work and to the relative infrequent expectation of this in Ignatius. While scholarship has not reached consensus on the precise meaning of consolation without previous cause, I think it is fair to say that Toner's point is well taken. As I have already pointed out, Ignatius directs the exercitant not to some universally experienced consolation without cause to guide the reader to the recognition and comprehension of consolation. Rather he directs the exercitant to an awareness of the quality and trajectory of the motions in experience. Informed watchfulness to the precise configuration of consciousness, rather than a comparison of a given experience to one's "supernaturally elevated transcendence," is Ignatius' "first principle" of discernment. Ignatius mentions consolation without cause here in the Rules for the Second Week, not to provide a foundation for interpreting all the other rules but rather to indicate, in a section that will deal with various nuances of consolation some of which are formed by the good and others by the evil spirit, one type of consolation the source of which can be confidently determined.

One must remember that while Ignatius' Rules for the Discernment of Spirits possesses an identifiable structure as a unit (cf. Buckley 1973), they are still an outline, not intended on being comprehensive. In particular, Philip Endean, in an analysis of Ignatius' famous letter to Teresa Rejadell notes that "we need to supplement Ignatius' rules for discernment with material on the role of the good spirit in the process of conversion" (1989, 42). Later in this study, I will suggest that the work of Jonathan Edwards provides just such a supplement. The important matter to keep in mind with regard to Ignatius' Rules is the context of the exercitant, experiencing various motions and inclinations while meditating on the Gospels or other exercises. It is through the informed awareness and appropriate response to these motions that the exercitant becomes more and more able to "order one's life" in accord with the greater glory of God.

This ordering of life reaches a climax in the Second Week with the Making of an Election [169-189]. After a challenging exercise on humility ([165-168] cf. Meissner 1964a, 49-50), the exercitant is then led to consider specific means by which he or she might best serve God. Major choices of a state of life (vows of religious life, marriage) receive primary attention but Ignatius intends the *Exercises* to be accessible to any who might find themselves already having made this prior choice and are simply making a "changeable election" [171, 172-174] or have a need to "Amend and Reform One's Life and State" [189].

Ignatius' instructions here are structured around "Three Times for Making a Sound and Good Election" [175]. Rather than presenting the exercitant with a "how to" find God's will and guidance, Ignatius, always conscious of the presence of grace in Christian discernment presents his approach to election in terms of "times," existential spiritual conditions in the presence of which it is more appropriate to make a decision concerning one's choice of life. The First Time follows a profound movement of God in one's life, when "the Lord moves and attracts the will in such a way that a devout person, without doubting or being able to doubt, carries out what was proposed" [175]. While on the surface this experience may appear like Ignatius' description of the consolation without previous cause, the First Time election and consolation without previous cause experiences should not be identified, nor should one consider a consolation without previous cause necessary for the First Time election (contra Egan 1976, 141). In the First Time election it is the *will*, not the affections, which are raised. Toner (1991, 109) identifies the key elements of this experience: in this experience the will is (1) moved and drawn (2) without the power of doubting (3) to what is proposed, presumably the content being some element of elective reflection. In the First Time the exercitant is simply inclined beyond his or her own power to doubt to a certain choice of life.

The Second Time is present "when sufficient clarity and knowledge are received from the experience of consolations and desolations, and from experience in the discernment of various spirits" [176]. Ignatius says no more about this occasion. His sentence certainly draws attention to the importance of the discernment of spirits, not only for the purposes of selecting elements of meditations for repetition and for defeating the strategies of the enemy intended to hinder growth toward indifference, but also for the evaluation of options of states of life. Yet the sentence also leaves the reader somewhat uncertain about the exact nature of the process or event(s) which lie(s) behind the Second Time election. Scholars who follow the approach of Karl Rahner in interpreting the *Exercises* understand this Time to involve a comparison of the object of election with one's "fundamental desire for God" (Rahner 1964, 158; cf. Futrell 1970, 79f; Egan 1976). This approach to the interpretation of the *Exercises* has been evaluated correctly, I think, by Avery Dulles, who when speaking of Rahner's essay writes, "Having first reduced the *Spiritual Exercises* to the election, he then proceeds to reduce the election to the 'second time,' and the second-time election to the rules of discernment for the Second Week. Finally he shows that these rules themselves can be reduced to the 'first principle' of pure consolation, which is self-validating" (Dulles 1965, 149-50).

Ignatius himself, as I have shown, does not present consolation without previous cause as the "first principle" of discernment, either the discernment of spirits or the discernment involved in making a good election. Not only would such an approach assume that the experience of consolation without previous cause occurs much more frequently than Ignatius indicates by his works (Toner 1982, 306-312), but it would also distort Ignatius' understanding of the exercitant's process in discernment of spirits. If clarity is to come through the examination of consolations and desolations and the discernment of spirits, it will come through an attention to the quality and trajectory of the experiences that surround the movement toward election. Thus, a young man seeking wisdom concerning whether or not to join the Jesuit order meditates on the passages of the Gospel, cultivating connaturality with the ideals of the heavenly king. He may find himself, in the course of these meditations, receiving (repeatedly!) the consolation desired. He may find that he is drawn to serve and imitate Christ and rushes of sacrificial abandonment rise in his heart. During these times of consolation, the Second Time approach to the discernment of spirits is conducted as this young man asks, "To what do I feel drawn as I am in the midst of this consolation: to join, or not?" "When I am spiritually at my best, shown by both the quality and trajectory of my experience, what option am I most inclined to choose?" Conversely, when in desolation one asks the same question. By exploring the inclinations of the will during various spiritual/affective experiences, it is possible, over time, for this exercitant to come to a "sufficient clarity" concerning the choice that flows from his best and therefore would more than likely be the best choice of a state of life. This approach to the interpretation of the Second Time Election is developed much further in Toner (1991, 130-160; for Ignatius' own elective process cf. Dalmases 1985, 263 and Munitiz 1988).

Ignatius' mention of conditions that can be described as "without doubt" (in the First Time) and "sufficient clarity" (in the Second Time) indicate that the election itself is viewed by Ignatius as a kind of discernment. It is a process of recognizing and understanding, in order to respond to, that which comes from God. The election, then is the fourth specific type of discernment. The discernment of self-examination addressed patterns that were not of God, the discernment of spirits identified motions of various sorts and the discernment of appreciation recognized the values and heart of God through the person of Christ as revealed in the scriptures. Elective discernment evaluates inclinations of the will in light of the movements of God upon the soul, whether indubitably, with sufficient clarity, or through the ordinary processes of rational evaluation (The Third Time).

"The Third Time," Ignatius writes,

"is one of tranquility. I consider first the end for which I was born, namely to praise God our Lord and save my soul; then, desiring this, as the means I elect a life or state of life within the bounds of the Church, in order to be helped in the service of my Lord and the salvation of my soul.

By a time of tranquility I mean one when the soul is not being moved one way and the other by various spirits and uses its natural faculties in freedom and peace.

If an election is not made in the first or second time, two methods are given below for making it in the third time" [177-178].

These methods involve (1) the cultivation of indifference, (2) the prayer for God to move the exercitant's will that his glory would be accomplished "by reasoning well and faithfully" and by choosing in conformity with his will [180], (3) the application of sound reason (pros and cons) and imagination (what would you advise a friend in your situation?) to the election, and (4) the offering of the choice made in this manner to God for confirmation. As opposed to the First or the Second Time, this third time involves coming to a decision through "the preponderating motion of reason" [182]. Yet the Third Time, as the other Times for making an election, should be viewed as grace-assisted processes by which exercitants come to recognize, appreciate and respond to that which comes from God (Meissner 1964a, 52). The discernment of election, in all of its "Times," involves and synthesizes the use of other types of discernment already learned earlier in the *Exercises*.

A couple of further points should be made concerning the election for the purpose of presenting a basic portrait of discernment as expressed in the *Exercises*. First, one must understand that Ignatius does not assume that the *content* of a given election will necessarily come through a time of consolation or obvious divine influence. Ignatius very carefully guards the freedom of the individual to explore, evaluate, and choose. Rather, as one abandons "disordered affections" and cultivates connaturality through the exercises, then reason, desire, and choice are brought into a place where human freedom and divine will become one. While Ignatius does not here deny the possibility of divine revelations (cf. Ignatius 1959 [1549], 196-211), here in the election it is more a matter of God's inclination of the will to ends already considered, rather than His giving instructions to the mind. Thus elective discernment is more a recognition of the movement of the will than an identification of information arising in the mind.

A second matter is the question of the priority of these "Times" for making an election and their interrelationship. This issue continues to be a matter of debate among Ignatian scholars, with some emphasizing the priority of the Second Time (Rahner 1964; Egan 1976) and others emphasizing the priority of the Third Time (Hughes 1990). Egan (1976, 150), following Bakker (1970, 281ff) notes that there has been a trend in Ignatian interpretation and possibly in Ignatius' own practice from interest in the First to the Second to the Third Time. Correlated to the question of priority is the issue of interrelationship. Should these three Times be viewed as parts of one activity, mutually dependent upon each other, or as three separate and autonomous approaches to the election? Once again, Jules Toner has addressed these questions in some detail (1991, 233-254). I have followed his approach in this study by presenting the Times as three autonomous potential existential conditions within which an election may be made. The recognition of autonomy does not prevent the use of methods connected to another Time (grace permitting) to supplement or confirm the election chosen at any particular Time. Indeed this is the recommended approach. Nonetheless, Ignatius presents these Times as separate situations, each of which are sufficient to make an elective decision. If there is any indication of "priority" among the three Times, I see the First and Second as having some slight advantage only insofar as Ignatius turns to the Third time, "if an election is not made in the first or second time" [178].

I have shown that the Second Week builds upon and develops elements of discernment begun in the First. Drawing upon the skills of interior awareness, the first lessons in discernment of spirits and the dis-engagement of the exercitant from "disordered affections," the exercises of the Second Week introduce a more nuanced discernment of spirits and a cultivation of the discernment of appreciation through the meditations and contemplations on Christ the heavenly king. The Week climaxes with the elective discernment of a state of life, a process which requires a synthesis of all that has been learned thus far.

The Third Week

The Third Week of the *Spiritual Exercises* is a period of confirmation and solidification (Meissner 1964a, 55-56). Outside of a set of "Rules to Order Oneself Henceforth in the Taking of Food" [210-217], there are no special meditations in the Third Week. This section of the *Exercises* is entirely composed of contemplations upon the passion of Jesus [190-209]. The transition between the Second and Third Weeks is much subtler than that between the First and Second. Additional points in the contemplations give the contemplations a more intimate dimension. "What I desire" in this Week is described as "heartfelt sorrow and confusion," "sorrow with Christ in sorrow; a broken spirit with Christ so broken; tears; and interior suffering because of the great suffering which Christ endured for me." The emphasis here is less on the imitation of Christ and more toward ""staying with" or "being with" him in his passion and death. To be able to enter into his sorrow and to enter beyond the observation of exterior pain to the inner suffering of Jesus expresses the grace asked for in this Week" (Fleming 1983, 16), as the Third and Fourth Weeks contextualize the paschal mystery.

One element of Ignatius' instructions for the Third Week that bears upon the subject of discernment is a note he gives concerning the colloquies or petitionary prayers that close the times of meditation. Ignatius develops a point he made earlier [54] concerning the varied content of these prayers, perhaps because the exercitant is now more adept at discernment; with greater comprehension the exercitant can now take greater freedoms in prayer. Ignatius writes,

> In the colloquies we ought to converse and beg according to the subject matter. That is, in accordance with whether I find myself tempted or consoled, desire to possess one virtue or another, or to dispose myself in one way or another, or to experience sorrow or joy over the matter I am contemplating. And finally I ought to ask for what I more earnestly desire in regard to some particular matters [199].

Ignatius here sets the exercitant free to recognize and respond to movements of affect and will that may arise through the retreat. In this passage one can see that, for Ignatius, discernment plays a part not only in the choice of meditations for repetition but also in the selection of matters for petitionary prayer at the end of an exercise.

The Fourth Week

W.W. Meissner writes in his "Psychological Notes on the *Spiritual Exercises*" of the Fourth Week, "Even more than was the case in the third week, psychology begins to overextend itself in trying to analyze what transpires in this fourth week" (Meissner 1964a, 56). With the Fourth Week one moves toward higher and higher levels of mystical experience. "What I desire" here is "to be glad and rejoice intensely because of the great glory and joy of Christ our Lord" [221]. Only one contemplation is given, that of the Lord's appearance to Mary, although in the Notes which follow Ignatius refers to other mysteries of the Resurrection and Ascension that may be used during this Week [226]. The aim in this Week is to enter into the joy of the Lord through identification with his victorious risen life.

The climax of the Fourth Week, and indeed of the *Spiritual Exercises*, is the "Contemplation to Attain Love" placed at the end of the Fourth Week [230-237]. The exercise takes the exercitant back over much of the material covered in the *Exercises*. God's wondrous gifts and activity through creation, redemption, and the particular gifts which the Lord gives each believer are brought to mind. It cultivates a response of grateful, self-giving abandonment to love and serve the Lord. "What I desire" in this exercise is "interior knowledge of all the great good I have received, in order that, stirred to profound gratitude, I may become able to love and serve his Divine Majesty in all things" [234].

With this key phrase, "in all things," Ignatius pushes discernment to its limits. "This contemplation is not simply of sin and its forgiveness," Michael Buckley writes, "nor of the mysteries of Christ: it is the contemplation of everything" (Buckley 1975, 97). The approach to discernment throughout the *Exercises* has been to instruct the exercitant, to the extent possible, in the recognition, appreciation and response to that which is (or is not) from God. Whether in the inner motions of the exercitant's affective experience, the patterns or choices of life, or in the person of Christ as revealed in scripture, Ignatius has trained the exercitant to possess an informed sensitivity to the things of God, wherever they may be found. And in the Contemplation to Attain Love he specifies exactly where Christ is to be found—in all things. The loving discernment of Christ in all things is thus the fifth and most comprehensive type of discernment. This type of discernment makes use of all that has come before, both in the contemplations on scripture and the consideration of life, and brings them together into a comprehensive unity which in itself is a discernment operating on a different level. The only appropriate response is loving service to all people, in all times, in all things.

One more set of Rules, located as an appendix at the end of the *Exercises* must be mentioned. This is Ignatius' "Rules for Thinking, Judging, and Feeling with the Church" [352-370]. It was probably written later in the development of the text and, of all sections of the *Exercises*, this set of Rules bears the marks of a "response" to the ecclesiastical climate of the sixteenth century. It is structured as a list of recommendations ("we should _____," "we ought to _____") divided into eighteen separate "Rules." The rules list a variety of ecclesiastical doctrines and practices to "praise," many of which had come under much criticism in his time. His list includes confession, reception of the Sacrament, frequent Mass, religious vows, relics, pilgrimages, fasts, penances and the veneration of images [354-360]. He states that one should praise the precepts of the Church, the recommendations of our superiors, and positive and scholastic theology [362-364]. He gives advice concerning the discussion of such doctrinal "hot potatoes" as predestination and the relationship between faith and works [366-370]. The original title for this set of Rules is uncertain as several formulations are extant. George Ganss, addressing this variation, finds evidence of a dual purpose for these rules: "The very differences of formulation indicate the founder's hope that his exercitant would think both *with* the Church, by obediential acceptance of her pronouncements, and rightly *in* the Church, by speaking and acting habitually in a manner likely to increase his own and the Church's spiritual vitality" (Ganss 1973, 73). Ganss also indicates the intended audience of this set of rules: "these rules were meant for a serious retreatant nearing the end of the thirty-day Exercises, who is now far advanced in the love of Christ and eager to help in spreading his Kingdom; who also, perhaps, will soon be working among heretics or weak and disgruntled Catholics" (1973, 77).

The bearing of this set of rules upon Ignatius' understanding of discernment is indicated through his oft quoted thirteenth rule:

> To keep ourselves right in all things, we ought to hold fast to this principle: What I see as white, I will believe to be black if the hierarchical Church thus determines it. For we believe that between Christ our Lord, the Bridegroom, and the Church, his Spouse, there is the one same Spirit who governs and guides us for the salvation of our souls. For it is by the same Spirit and Lord of ours who gave the ten commandments that our holy Mother Church is guided and governed [365].

One may see, in this statement, a hint of Ignatius' chivalrous loyalty. Yet one can also see an important theological assumption guiding his approach. God will not work contrary to His own purposes. God's guidance through the Church will not contradict the guidance given through the discernment of spirits or a Third Time election. Indeed, even if one were to claim a First Time elective experience which controverted the recommendations of the Church, Ignatius' would be skeptical about the experience. Ignatius here is reminding his exercitants of another type of recognition, appreciation, and response to that which comes from God. The Church originates from and is led by the same Spirit who "governs and guides us." An informed respect for the Church as "of God" will serve to shape the attitudes and decisions of the exercitant and of those he or she may encounter. This, the sixth type of discernment, flows not from embittered polemics, but rather from loving loyalty.

Summary and Implications:
Ignatian Discernment as an Afffectively-Rich Act of Knowing

We have seen, in this review of Ignatius' *Spiritual Exercises*, a profound synthesis of teaching concerning Christian discernment. This teaching concerning discernment is not limited to his "Rules for the Discernment of Spirits" nor to the Election (cf. Peters 1979, 30-32) but encompasses the entire program of the *Exercises*, seen as a developing whole. Some exercitants who take the *Exercises* will only progress through some of the First Week. They will not make an election; they may not even have the Rules of Discernment for the First Week explained. Yet these exercitants will still learn discernment. Through the exercise of self-examination and the first method of prayer they will learn the skill of interior watchfulness and acquire experience in noticing and appreciating (in order to reject) that which is not from God. Others may progress further. They may become acquainted with the environment of spiritual conflict and learn the Rules for the Discernment of Spirits. They may find themselves able to recognize consolations and desolations and thereby are capable of defeating the enemy's strategies or of selecting meditations for repetition. Still others may progress to the Second Week. Having disengaged from disordered affections, they may learn the skill of Gospel appreciation, contemplating the life of the earthly king. They may learn the more nuanced Rules of Discernment for the Second Week, distinguishing true consolation from the consolation which appears good at the start but little by little proves to be a trap of the enemy. Some may progress to the making of an Election, discerning the movements of the will in order to determine that state of life which would give God the greatest possible glory.

Finally there may be some who proceed through the whole course of the *Exercises*. These will learn the discernment of Attaining Love, learning to recognize, appreciate, and respond to the presence and activity of God in all things. They will learn the discernment of Thinking with the Church, recognizing, in the recommendations and leadership of the hierarchical Church, a deposit from God. Through all these stages the exercitant acquires new methods of discernment but in reality it is simply the maturing of the one discernment of a believer learning to recognize, appreciate and order his or her life around the presence and activity of the living God. It is a matter of growing in an affectively-rich process of knowing.

Although he never reflected upon discernment in an academic manner, the *Spiritual Exercises* indicate that Ignatius implicitly understood discernment as an act of knowing. Harvey Egan writes, "The Exercises have to do with an experiential knowledge of God's Gift, an existential knowledge arising from the Holy Spirit's touches and the touches of the enemy of our human nature, a special knowledge born from struggle, a special enlightenment from above" (Egan 1976, 124). This implicit epistemological approach can be detected in not only in the Rules, but also in Ignatius' composition of the contemplations and meditations. Part of the power of the *Exercises* lies in its intuitive grasp of the link of imagination and affect to cultivate experience and motivate action (cf. DeNicolas 1986). In this linkage lies a grasp of fundamental aspects of human experience. The meditations and contemplations, designed with this link of imagination and affect, frequently call for "knowledge" as that which is desired [63, 91, 104, 113, 139, 233].

The full title of the Rules for the Discernment of Spirits also indicates this epistemological approach. The full title reads, "Rules to aid us toward perceiving and then to understanding, at least to some extent, the various motions which are caused in the soul: the good motions that they may be received and the bad that they may be rejected" [313]. Discernment is proximately achieved in the recognition/identification (perceiving) and the appreciative grasp (understanding) of the phenomena at hand. An informed differentiation of consolation from desolation in the experience of an exercitant, for example, achieves "to some extent" the aims of Christian discernment. So also would the appreciative recognition of Jesus' humility in his passion. Discernment is finally incarnated in praxis: a response appropriate to the understanding perception of the phenomena of life. Discernment is not knowledge simply for knowledge sake, but rather knowledge *to be embodied* in action.

Hugo Rahner, in his study of the background of Ignatian discernment of spirits, traces the usage of the metaphor "shrewd money changers" through the history of discussion about discernment (1956, 475-483; 1968, 171-180). Although this metaphor is used variously throughout the Patristic and Medieval periods, its chief use was as a symbol for the wise differentiation of the genuine from the counterfeit. Rahner's survey of church history closes with the early commentary on the *Exercises* by Fr. González Dávila, who identifies Ignatius with the best teaching of the Church Fathers. Dávila refers to John Cassian's use of this image and states,

"By this he [Cassian] meant those whose office it is to be able to distinguish good money from false. So we, too, should not allow ourselves to be taken in as regards the value, weight and stamp of money: this means that we must investigate the origin, course and outcome of the inward movement, so that one may recognize which author it is to be ascribed to. And we believe it was to this end that our Father [Ignatius] left behind in his writings the many Rules for this matter. (cited in Rahner 1968, 179)

It is this "distinguishing," this differentiation, this categorization of that which is from God as opposed to that which is not from God, the genuine from the counterfeit, which is the distinguishing feature of discernment as an act of knowledge. Of all kinds of knowledge that can be obtained in the Christian life, *discernment* focuses on the identification of that which is (or is not) from God, a categorization of human experience. I shall return to this in the following chapter.

Finally I must say something about Ignatian discernment considered as an *affectively-rich* act of knowing. It is impossible here to give a comprehensive treatment of Ignatius' presentation of affect in the *Exercises*. It is ironic that in spite of Ignatius' universally acknowledged depth on affective matters, so little is published concerning his approach to affectivity. The subject deserves much more detailed attention than has been given it in the literature. All that can be accomplished here is to present a few suggestive conclusions concerning Ignatius' understanding of the roles of affective operations in Christian discernment.

One must appreciate that Ignatius refers to affective operations with a very broad range of terms and expressions. Frequently he simply speaks of "affections" generally, referring to felt patterns, states or tendencies [3, 50, 60, 150, 234, 338, 342, 363]. As these are oriented toward or away from God they are labeled "ordered" or "disordered" affections [1, 21, 150, 153, 157, 164, 172, 174, 179, 342, and esp. 169]. In keeping with the common Aristotelian/Thomist framework of psychology, Ignatius refers to the "sensitive" human nature, indicating tendencies and feelings that are more physiologically based, often identified with the illicit "pleasures of the senses" [35, 87, 97, 182, 314]. When emphasis is upon any cognitive operation perceived as arising from within, Ignatius uses the term "motion" [6, 15, 175, 177, 180, 182, 184, 186-87, 227, 313, 316-17]. G. Ganss states that "motion" is a "technical term, taken from scholasticism, to designate the interior experiences, such as thoughts, impulses, inclinations, moods, consolations, desolations, and the like" (Ganss 1991, 388; cf. also Peters 1979, 28). Very often Ignatius refers to affective operations by giving concrete examples of the types of experiences he intends. References to tears, sorrow, joy, brokenness of heart or being inflamed with love are common [4, 55, 48, 60, 65, 78, 96, 104, 113, 157, 193, 195, 203, 206, 213, 221, 229, 233, 252, 315-17, 322, 329, 338, 347, 370]. Key affective terms with relationship to discernment that I have already discussed are "consolation" and "desolation." These terms designate particular affective motions which are spiritually oriented and have distinct pleasurable or unpleasurable characteristics [6, 62, 118, 176, 199, 213, 252, 316-36; see also Ignatius' use of the term "relish" 2, 227, 252] (cf. Murphy 1976). Ignatius also speaks frequently of "inclinations." At times he uses the term in a discussion of affective operations. Other times he gives more direct reference to the "will" or choice [3, 15, 16, 135, 155, 157, 175, 180, 197, 199, 316-17]. A special affective/volitional state for Ignatius is that of "indifference" [23, 165-68, 189]. "The key term in the Ignatian vocabulary of discernment," writes John Futrell, "is *sentir* [interior knowledge]." He identifies *sentir* as "above all a kind of felt knowledge", an affective, intuitive knowledge possessed through the reaction of human feelings to exterior and interior experience" (Futrell 1970, 56. cf. [44, 63, 104, 322]). The wide range of vocabulary for affective experiences and operations used by Ignatius can be accounted for in part by the ambiguity of the material he is trying to describe. As I shall demonstrate in the following chapter, emotions are notoriously diffi-

cult to define. Ignatius covers all the angles, identifying affectivity
by means of action tendencies, feeling states, moods, appraisals, and
more. In this sense, Ignatius' wide affective vocabulary is not only
indicative of the subject at hand, but also of his genius in addressing
the subject (cf. Letemendia and Croft 1968).

Ignatius understands discernment to be an integrative process.
While I will highlight the roles of affectivity in this study, I do not
wish to minimize the important place Ignatius gives other elements of
human experience. Ignatius' self-conscious inclusion of all elements
of human experience into the *Exercises* is one of the strengths of his
kataphatic mysticism. His systematic use of imagination in meditation, though not unique in the literature of the time, was certainly a
highly developed expression (cf. DeNicolas 1986). Ignatius also frequently places cognitive and affective terms together, desiring that the
retreatant would "know and grieve" for sins [44], "feel an interior
knowledge" of my sins, "perceive the disorder" in my actions and
"have a knowledge of the world in order to detest it" [63], "note . . .
where some insight, consolation or desolation was experienced"
[118], praise both positive theologians who "stir up our affections"
and scholastic theologians who "define and explain for our times the
matters necessary for salvation" [363, cf. also 104, 213, 252, 329].
He systematically applies the use of the "faculties" [45], "operations"
[46] or "powers" [51] to the pursuit of God. Periodically he speaks
of these faculties in the traditional divisions of his time: memory
(including imagination), understanding, and will [50-52, 234, 246].
Elsewhere he links intellect, affect and will [104]. His third *Annotation* illustrates his approach to affectivity in relationship to intellect
and will. He states,

> In all the following Spiritual Exercises we use the acts of the
> intellect in reasoning and of the will in eliciting acts of the
> affections. In regard to the affective acts which spring from
> the will we should note that when we are conversing with God
> our Lord or his saints vocally or mentally, greater reverence is
> demanded of us than when we are using the intellect to
> understand. [3]

Even his use of *sentir* ("interior" or "felt" knowledge) reveals
Ignatius' intentional integration of intellect and affect. He makes this

integration most explicit in his application of the three powers of the soul to the meditations [50-52, 65-71], in his application of the five senses to the matters of contemplation ([121-126]; cf. Rahner 1968, 181-213), and in his suggestions for the three methods of praying [238-260].

Using Robert Gay's categories of discernment analysis, one can say that affectivity functions first of all in Ignatian discernment as a factor which is shaped by the *context* of discernment.[3] The context of Ignatius' times cultivated openness to affective sensitivity and expression. The reforms of Cisneros, the development of groups of *alumbrados* and the more general atmosphere of romantic chivalry all contributed toward the openness to direct religious experience which is expressed in Ignatian discernment (Letemendia and Croft 1968, 27-28; Meissner 1992, 3-29). Ignatius was not unaware of the affective trends of his time, and while he did not engage in polemics to distinguish his own position vis-à-vis his contemporaries, the *Exercises* show themselves as a pioneering expression within the general trends of the period. Ignatius also drew attention to the impact of the cosmic context of spiritual forces upon the affective atmosphere of discernment. Indeed, for Ignatius, this was the more important context. The individual exercitant dwells within a much larger universe inhabited by "angels" [329] "spirits" [315-16] and divine mediators ([199] cf.Egan 1976, 112-115). Thoughts arise in the exercitant internally from the self and externally from the good spirit or from the evil spirit [32]. As spirits cause thoughts to arise the affective atmosphere of the exercitant is altered. Thus, for example, in the case of an exercitant who is "progressing from good to better . . . it is characteristic of the evil spirit to cause gnawing anxiety, to sadden, and to set up obstacles" [315]. The configuration of affective motions in an individual exercitant is, in part, a function of the precise strategies being played out by these forces. The contexts of the exercitant, both cultural and cosmic, thus serve to shape the affective experience of the exercitant's own search for that which is from God.

With the individual exercitant, the one doing the discerning, I move to the *subject* of discernment. Affectivity exists in the subject

---

[3]Whereas Gay spoke of the author, object(s), and act of discernment, I will speak of subject, *context*, object(s), and act of discernment.

of Ignatian discernment as patterns of personal life that hinder or help the exercitant to recognize, understand, and respond to that which is from God. With the very first exercises of self-examination, and then even more as the First Week progresses, Ignatius emphasizes affectivity as a force hindering spiritual growth. On the one hand, Ignatius' catalog of sins falls into the traditional order of thought, word, and deed. Affectivity is not mentioned specifically as the content of sin in the meditations of the First Week [33-42; cf. 45-72]. Yet Ignatius' repeated mention of the difficulty of "disordered affections" ([e.g. 1, 21, 169, 172, 179, 342]; note also his mention of disordered "inclinations" [157], disordered "excess" [217] and "attachments" [153-57, 342]) indicates that one ought to take a broad approach to Ignatius' understanding of "thoughts." Hence the First Week functions as a season of dis-engagement with the affective patterns that support sinful thoughts, words and deeds and which disenable the freedom which is necessary for authentic Christian action (Rulla 1978; Meissner 1963, 1968; L. Hughes 1975, 39). In this sense affectivity functions much the same as the "passions" of Greek philosophy.

As one moves to the Second and Third Weeks, however, one finds that affectivity can not only serve as a hindrance, but also as a help to discernment. When feelings, tendencies, inclinations and patterns of attraction or avoidance are ordered and oriented toward the Creator and Lord (not merely a change of intellectual belief, but a comprehensive transformation of belief-system) through the development of appreciation (not merely an intellectual regard for the truth of Christ, but a delight in and desire to share and imitate the thoughts, feelings, words, and deeds of Christ) one finds the cultivation of an affective pattern designed to assist the discernment process by intuitively responding to that which is from God. This is the fostering of the connaturality of faith. The process is intensified in the Third Week through the development of compassionate appreciation, and in the Fourth Week through the development of affective patterns which can "sense" Christ in all things. I briefly mentioned above Ignatius' value for the state of "indifference." It is hard to call indifference an affect or emotion, though certainly it is not the absence of emotion (cf. Toner 1991, 79-86). Indifference really involves the dominance in the exercitant of the desire for the glory of God, which supersedes all other preferences. Through disordered affections, and through the cultivation of appreciation and indifference, affectivity functions in Ignatian discernment as a pattern of personal life which can hinder or help the exercitant's ability to recognize, understand, and respond to that which is from God. In this aspect affectivity functions as a conditioning factor with regards to the *subject* of discernment.

Affectivity also functions in Ignatian discernment as a sign of God's presence or activity, an indication of where "that which is from God" may be found. As mentioned in the previous chapter, Robert Gay refers to affective motions as the *immediate object* of discernment (1959, 68-70). I have already described this function above (cf. also Toner 1982, 1991). First, human thoughts and feelings have multiple causes (Sauer and Horn 1994, 109). By examining the quality and trajectory of affective motions in an informed manner one can recognize certain predictable patterns of the affective experience (Gay's *objet médiat*) which in turn gives reason to sort out what spirits may be acting upon one and what thoughts arising are from oneself. This, finally, guides one to the presence, activity or will of the Holy Spirit (Gay's *objet médiat prochain*). Whether the exercitant is recognizing consolation for the sake of meditative repetition, or identifying desolation (or a false consolation) for the sake of defeating the enemy's strategies, or discerning inclinations of the will in conditions of consolation or desolation for the purpose of making an election, affective motions must be examined as an *object*, an indication of "that which is from God."

Finally, affectivity functions in Ignatian discernment, as presented in the *Exercises*, as a component of the *act* of discernment itself. Discernment is not simply the reasoned reflection upon affective experience. Rather, the reflection itself is, in part, an affective process. The knowledge of the divine, for which the exercitant searches, is a felt-knowledge, a knowledge of the heart (Rahner 1968, 147). Affective operations function to mediate a "mystical perception" (Alston 1991, 9-67) through "spiritual senses" (Rahner 1968, 164) which appraise the presence of spiritual reality for the exercitant. Again, affective operations are not necessarily the primary component in discernment. As mentioned, the First Time of making an election arises when the will is so moved by the Spirit that there can be no doubt but that a certain option is from God. There need be no significant contribution of affective operations in this discernment. So also with the Third Time (cf. Toner 1991, 107-129, 161-189). Nevertheless, affective operations are quite often involved in the discernment process. Here one is involved in what Dunne calls "different kinds of knowing" (Dunne 1974, 23). The Second Time of making an election depends upon "sufficient clarity" arising from affective dynamics. The consolation without prior cause is an affective experience which carries within the experience its own self-authenticating grasp of the divine. Futrell writes of the confirmation of Ignatian elective discernment, "Ordinarily, however, in both individual and communal discernment confirmation is experienced interiorly as profound peace, contentment, satisfaction, recognition in tranquility that the way has been found to respond to the word of God here and now" (Futrell 1970, 63). It is both as object and as component of an act that one must think of affectivity as a "criterion" of discernment (cf. Buckley 1973, 35-36). The recognition and understanding of that which comes from God is not simply achieved through intellectual reflection. The act of discernment itself is an act involving affective operations and is confirmed in affectivity.

Jonathan Edwards' *Distinguishing Marks* and *Religious Affections*

Jonathan Edwards (1703-58), American Puritan divine and "father of American evangelicalism," though not unknown in the field of Christian spirituality (Handy 1986; Dupré and Wiseman 1988, 369-91; Magill and McGreal 1988, 359-366,372-78; cf. also Clebsch 1973, 11-56), is due for increased attention by students of Christian discernment. Pastor of the congregational church in Northampton, Massachusetts and primary leader of the Great Awakening in America, Edwards was not treated in the volumes on Christianity in *World Spirituality* (Dupré and Saliers 1989), nor in historical surveys of Christian discernment (Malatesta 1970, Sweitek 1972, Wulf 1965; cf. also Rakoczy 1980, 6-17; Sweeney 1983, 43-160; yet cf. Spohn 1983 and Colacurcio 1972). Though scholarship in Christian spirituality has largely neglected Jonathan Edwards, scholarship in American history and philosophy has experienced a revival of interest his works. The research developing from this interest has transformed the image of Edwards from an eccentric Calvinist theologian to a highly creative thinker. Historian Perry Miller, who first stimulated the interest in Edwards, writes of him, "The truth is, Edwards was infinitely more than a theologian. He was one of America's five or six major artists, who happened to work with ideas instead of with poems or novels" (Miller 1981, xxxi). Edwards is now frequently regarded as one of America's premiere philosophical thinkers (Lee 1988, 1-3; Smith 1981-82, 28; Daniel 1994, 1).

Although there appears to be consensus that Edwards was a brilliant thinker, writing original works of philosophy, science, theology, ethics and spirituality, there is certainly no consensus on how he is to be imaged. As Ian Murray, a recent biographer writes, "to say that writers on Edwards are divided is an understatement" (Murray 1987, xxiii). The broad range of Edwards' sources and the disheveled state of his manuscripts, combined with the complex originality of Edwards' own writing, have made comprehensive understanding of his works impossible and adequate interpretation difficult. Needless to say, he has received different fundamental interpretations in the hands of his interpreters, each of which identifies a new "key" with which Edwards' thought can be opened.[1]

Although Jonathan Edwards spent most of his life as a parish pastor, he produced a wide range of writings. In addition to both a private "Diary," and a "Personal Narrative," we possess a large collection of sermons and published treatises on matters theological, spiritual and ethical. He kept notes and outlines on Scripture and on scientific and philosophical topics, which were never published in his lifetime but are available now. He also kept folders of notes on a variety of other topics. These latter are known as the "Miscellanies," some of which have recently been published. A complete picture of Edwards' thought can only be obtained from a careful and simultaneous examination of his sermons, treatises, correspondence and personal reflections with careful attention to the dating of the documents, the circumstances of his life, and the full range of sources upon which he drew. The present study cannot even begin to develop such a portrait. I will rather, in this section, attempt to explore Edwards' approach to Christian discernment as portrayed in two pub-

---

[1] For a review of the literature up to 1981 see Donald Weber's Introduction to Miller 1981. A sample of diverse contemporary interpretations can be found in Murray 1987, Lee 1988, Gerstner 1991, and Daniel 1994.

lished treatises that address the subject of discernment directly: his *The Distinguishing Marks of a Work of the Spirit of God* (1972a [1741] abbreviated DM) and *A Treatise Concerning Religious Affections* (1959 [1746] abbreviated RA). Whereas the state of Ignatian research permitted less background and textual detail in the present study, the underdeveloped state of research on Edwards' approach to discernment and the misunderstandings of Edwards perpetuated by some who apply his works to discernment (which I will address in the final chapter) demand greater explanation concerning the background, structure and texts of Edwards' works.

Distinguishing Marks began as a Yale College Commencement address, which was presented in 1741 in the heat of the Great Awakening. It was released in print the same year, making it one of the first published treatments of the revival. The treatise is divided into three parts. The first part enumerates nine "negative signs" by which detractors of the revival incorrectly sought to discount the event as a work of God. The second part identifies five "positive evidences" or "distinguishing marks" by which a work of God can be correctly identified. The final part of the treatise applies these signs to the events of the Great Awakening, concluding that it is truly to be regarded as a work of God, and making suggestions for contemporary application. *Religious Affections* began as a series of sermons preached in 1742 and early 1743, while he was writing another revival treatise: *Some Thoughts Concerning the Present Revival of Religion* (1972c [1743] abbreviated ST). Unpublished manuscripts indicate that *Religious Affections* received significant revision before going to press in 1746. Indeed the progress of the revival itself underwent a fair amount of transformation during this period. "To use Edwards' own illustration," Murray writes, "when he spoke in 1742, it was 'springtime' and he viewed 'the multitude of blossoms'. In 1746 the view was no longer like that of the month of May; it was October, and the actual 'fruit' resulting from the blossoms which had all appeared 'fair and beautiful' told another story" (Murray 1987, 251). The structure of *Religious Affections* is similar to *Distinguishing Marks*. After Part One, which provides the necessary definition of religious affections and defends their value in Christian religion, Edwards presents a set of "negative signs" "Shewing what are no certain signs that religious affections are truly gracious or that they are not." (RA, 125). Part Three then shows "what are distinguishing signs of truly gracious and holy affections" (RA, 191). Edwards makes application throughout this work rather than being placed in a separate section at the end. Many of the points made in Sections Two and Three are expansions of material included in *Distinguishing Marks*. Because of the similarities of structure and content in these two works, *Religious Affections* is often treated as a development (and a matured expression) of the earlier treatise and consequently scholars consider *Distinguishing Marks* minimally, if at all. As I will suggest below, however, Edwards himself states two distinct purposes for the two works, and in doing so identifies two separate objects of discernment: the revival movement "in general" and affective patterns that people experience in the context of a movement. In order to present a clearer picture of discernment as understood by Edwards, therefore, I will summarize discernment as presented in each of these works separately.

The Context of Distinguishing Marks *and* Religious Affections *in Edwards' Life and Times*

In contrast to the difficulty of identifying the contextual influences surrounding the composition of Ignatius' *Spiritual Exercises*, it is relatively easy to identify the factors surrounding Edwards' two works. They were both written and published within a period of six years. During this time Edwards lived in one location (Northhampton) and was occupied solely in the pastorate there. Edwards clearly states his purpose for each work and cites his sources when he refers to them. Indirect sources are harder to identify, but recent research has helped to clarify even these difficulties.

First, Edwards wrote in the context of a booming pioneer America. During Edwards' lifetime New England experienced remarkable expansion. Although the Puritan "experiment" had been abandoned, the New World still held hope for a new future for many. Edwards reflects this hope in *Some Thoughts* when he suggests that perhaps the current revival may be the first fruits of the Millennium (ST 323-24; 353-58). The rapid expansion of New England also brought with it new tensions to congregational life, tensions which would ultimately influence the removal of Edwards from his post in 1750, and would shape the content of *Religious Affections* (Murray 1987, 16, 313-29; cf. RA 412-41;).

Second, Edwards' original contributions in these two documents are informed by a wide range of sources. Jonathan Edwards, even in pioneer America had access to, and studied, literature from a variety of fields and perspectives. Although there appears to be consensus that Perry Miller's assessment of Edwards' dependence upon Locke and Newton was overstated, it is clear that Edwards utilized Newton and Locke, especially, as important interlocutors in the development of his thought (Miller 1981, 44-99; Anderson 1980, 52-236; Smith 1992b, 14-28). Though Edwards does not explicitly refer to the thought of Locke or Newton in *Distinguishing Marks* or *Religious Affections*, I shall show that Edwards' adaptation of British empiricism is implicitly present in his presentation of the "new spiritual sense" or the "sense of the heart." Edwards also received help in the development of this and other doctrines from some of the sixteenth century "Cambridge Platonists" (Anderson 1980, 53-68). Another implicit influence upon the structure of Edwards' thought is his training in logic (Anderson 1980, 13; Daniel 1994). Edwards indirectly refers to one particular logical fallacy concerning the assessment of the revival in *Some Thoughts* (ST, 316; cf Goen 1972, 67). More important is the Ramist approach to "agreement" and "disagreement" which shapes Edwards' doctrine of "consent" to divine excellency (Anderson 1980, 89-90; Daniel 1994, 67,179).

Edwards' explicitly referenced sources in *Distinguishing Marks* and *Religious Affections* reflect the specifically theological and spiritual purpose of these works. Most important of these sources are the Christian scriptures themselves. The importance of Scripture for Edwards can be seen, in that during the period of the writing of the "Diary," "Personal Narrative," and "Resolutions," the works which most intimately treat of his experiences during the most philosophical season of his life, "he alludes to no other book than Scripture" (Simonson 1982, 23). For example, his "Diary" entry for August 28, 1723 reads, "When I want books to read; yea when I have not very good books, not to spend time in reading them, but in reading the Scriptures, in perusing Resolutions, Reflections, &c. in writing on types of Scripture . . ." ("Diary" I.xxxi). His massive "Notes on the Scriptures" and "Blank Bible" are considered some of his most important writings (Murray 1987, 138-39). There is no work more referenced in Edwards' works than the Bible. Both of the works under consideration here had beginnings as orations directly structured at least in part, by a text of scripture. Indeed, Edwards consciously states in *Distinguishing Marks* that, in developing rules for judging phenomena, "we are to take the Scriptures as our guide in such cases" (DM 227).

After the Scriptures, the writings of the Puritan divines received primary reference in Edwards' revival works. This is especially the case with *Religious Affections*. Edwards' use of individual Puritan sources in *Religious Affections* has been examined in detail elsewhere and need not be recounted here (cf. Smith, 1959, 52-73). Nevertheless, a few points should be made for the sake of the topic at hand, for Edwards' understanding of Christian discernment was a development of Puritan thought and practice steeped in discernment concerns (cf. Hambrick-Stowe 1989, 338-353).

Puritan thought was a conscious development of the thought of John Calvin in the area of affectivity. John Calvin himself approached the human psyche with the same twofold primary division of faculties (intellect and will) that Edwards presents in a much more developed form in *Religious Affections* (Calvin 1964 [1536?], I.xv.6-8; II.ii.2-12; cf. RA, 96). While Calvin did not wholly ignore the role of affectivity in Christian spirituality (cf. Calvin 1964 [1536?], I.ii.1; I.vii.5; III.ii.7,36; III.viii.8-11), it was left to the English Puritans to develop this area of his thought. As Smith writes of Calvin, "His interest accordingly was directed more to discerning and stating the true marks of the church—discipline, sacraments, and the preaching of the Word—than to discovering the distinguishing marks of solitary piety. This is not to say that Edwards and other Calvinists were not concerned for the church; the fact remains, nevertheless, that conversion, sincerity, and humiliation—the marks of the inner life—were uppermost in their minds. For Calvin, theology was not yet that psychology of the Spirit it was to become for his later followers" (Smith 1959, 65. For a representative of early Puritan development see Bayly 1714 [1613?], 3,34-35). The question of how the sovereign God, through the work of the Holy Spirit, operated upon the human individual was a primary issue in Puritan dialogue (cf. Nuttall 1947). It is a chief theme in Edwards' revival works (cf. Steele 1994, 52ff.; Cherry 1990, 6; Delattre 1968, 121).

One important distinction related to the question of the role of the Holy Spirit made by Puritan divines was the differentiation between "common" and "saving" influences of the Holy Spirit. The former designates all those movements by which the Holy Spirit invites, convicts, touches, and woos a person prior to initial conversion. The latter refers to the transforming work which the Spirit accomplishes at regeneration and thereafter. Jonathan Edwards quotes at length from the classic work of John Owen on the Holy Spirit concerning this distinction. Owen's chapter, "The Work of the Spirit Preparatory Unto Regeneration," clarifies this distinction with regards to the potential effects of the Spirit's work on a person's mind, affections, and reformation of life in general (Owen 1965 [1674], 238-41; cf. RA, 250-51). Edwards follows Owen's main line of thought (as that of his grandfather Stoddard. cf. Murray 1987, 255) on this issue in his own writings. As I shall demonstrate, this distinction will play an important role in identifying the unique purposes of *Distinguishing Marks* and *Religious Affections*.

The distinction between "common" and "saving" influences brings us to the much-discussed issue of identifiable preparatory works of the Spirit. Puritans often recounted the path to salvation in particular steps. These steps attempted to identify distinct works of the Holy Spirit grounded in Puritan theology, but also observable in the affections of persons moving through stages of conversion (comparable to Ignatius' "Weeks"?). A number of schemata were developed in Puritan circles to clarify these steps (Cherry 1990, 62-63; Wilson-Kastner 1978, 15-20; Laurence 1979, 269-71), however a primary point of agreement among nearly all was that saving conversion was expected to be preceded by sensible experiences of conviction, or terror, or humiliation (again comparable to Ignatius' "First Week" experiences? cf. DM 266). Edwards struggled with the order and precise identification of these stages in experience. As I will show below, Edwards, in *Religious Affections*, finally placed his emphasis on the encouragement that we "try ourselves by the *nature* of the fruits of the Spirit" rather than "by the Spirit's *method* of producing them" (RA, 162).

Questions like the above lead directly to the inquiries concerning the role(s) of the individual in the salvation process and, consequently, to the question of how individuals might obtain confidence or assurance of saving grace. I shall show below that this question is at the heart of Edwards' arguments in *Religious Affections*. In Puritan circles, reflection on these issues led to the development of lists of "signs" of true faith (of what is and is not from God). Lists of indicators by which one would examine ones heart and life in a search for evidence of "true faith" were common in Puritan circles. For example, in Richard Sibbes' "The Bruised Reed and Smoking Flax," a treatise from which Edwards quotes (RA, 433), one finds a number of such lists. One of them provides a set of "rules" and "signs" to "try whether we be such as Christ will not quench." Sibbes' "signs" include enlightenment from the Holy Spirit, a corresponding impact upon the affections (here the language of Sibbes' description is very similar to Edwards'), a new direction of life, a new sense of discernment of the work of the Spirit, a willingness to deal with weaknesses when they are discovered, and an orientation towards God (Sibbes 1973 [1635], 59-62; cf. 87-88 and Lovelace 1989, 303-04). Edwards developed his own list of "signs" as early as his 1734 sermon "A Divine and Supernatural Light" (Edwards 1834 [henceforth abbreviated *Works*] 2.12-17; cf. Smith 1981-82, 32). He develops the technique much further in his revival treatises.

Third, Edwards' presentation in these two documents is shaped by the ecclesial and social contexts which surrounded him. Though not as volatile as Ignatius' setting, the ecclesiastical and social setting of colonial New England provided sufficient tension to encourage the best from this brilliant thinker. A creeping "Arminianism" cultivated a relaxation of the foundational doctrine of salvation by faith and formed an important part of the background to the Great Awakening itself (Cherry 1990, 160-61; Goen 1972; 4-18; cf also ST, 502-04; RA 173 and Edwards' *Faithful Narrative of the Surprizing Work of God* (1972b [1737], abbreviated FN, 148). The adoption of the "Half-Way Covenant" regarding the requirements for communion also stands as an important contextual factor, especially in the Northampton church Edwards pastored. The Half-Way Covenant was a measure which enabled the children of persons, baptized in infancy though not professing Christians, to present their own children for baptism and to maintain connection with the church, provided they were upright citizens who would accept the discipline of the church (Goen 1972, 13; Cherry 1990, 203-15). Solomon Stoddard, Edwards' highly influential predecessor at Northampton (and his grandfather), took the further step of eliminating the relationship between profession of inward faith and association with the church. Stoddard simply received all who assented to the articles of faith, along with their descendants, assuming these were moral citizens.

Edwards' concerns with this practice and the personal issues surrounding the dispute at Northampton (detailed in Murray 1987, 271-
76, 311-350) resulted in the loss of his post. In 1949 Edwards published his own position in a treatise on this issue (cf. Edwards 1994).
Three years prior, he foreshadowed these views in an earlier treatise—
Religious Affections (RA, 412-418). The revival had brought the
issue to a head, as many people came to profess faith who had hitherto
already been received into communion and membership. Thus the
question of evidences of saving faith, and the discernment thereof,
became central issues to the Northampton congregation. Edwards'
local controversy, however, was merely a small example of a much
bigger question: how is one to discern true saving faith?

The primary ecclesial context within which *Distinguishing Marks*
and *Religious Affections* were written was the Great Awakening itself.
The details of this complex historical event cannot be rehearsed here
and a brief summary must be sufficient (cf. Gaustad 1957; Rutman
1970; Murray, 1987 155-267; Smith 1992b, 29-56; Cherry 1990,
164-76). Early sparks of this revival in America were felt in New
Jersey around 1726 under the preaching of T.J. Frelinghuysen. These
sparks caught flame in the Scotch-Irish Presbyterian churches in New
Brunswick where Gilbert Tennant was serving. Edwards himself
experienced premonitions of a greater movement of God in
Northampton under the tenure of his grandfather Solomon Stoddard.
But in 1734, Edwards writes, "a great and earnest concern about the
great things of religion and the eternal world became universal in all
parts of the town, and among persons of all degrees and all ages; the
noise among the dry bones waxed louder and louder" (FN, 149). The
interest in and conversion to "things of religion" spread to the surrounding towns, and for over two years New England saw revival as
it never had before. Edwards' published his influential account of
this work (*Faithful Narrative*) in New England in 1737. Regional
awakenings were appearing throughout the colonies. These regional
awakenings were tied together and given a new burst of strength after
1740 by the powerful preaching of the English revivalist, George
Whitfield. Edwards writes of this period that "souls did as it were
come by flocks to Jesus Christ." Stories of faintings, weepings, leaping for joy and more spread like wildfire from New England to the
European continent. By the time *Distinguishing Marks* was published
in 1741, resistance to the phenomena of the Awakening was beginning

to be felt. *Distinguishing Marks* anticipated this resistance and was written with this critical audience in mind. Open criticism of the movement appeared in print the very next year. Edwards addressed these criticisms in his treatise *Some Thoughts concerning the present Revival* (1742). In this treatise Edwards also addressed difficulties with the revival from another direction—the excesses and errors of those who promoted the revival. Advocating of lay preaching in churches, spontaneous and inappropriate outbursts of emotion, over-attention to physical manifestations associated with converting experiences, denunciation of clergy unsupportive of the revival and like phenomena harmed the reputation of the movement and prevented others from receiving of this work of God. Edwards' chief critic, Charles Chauncey, published a point by point attack upon Edwards in 1743 in his *Seasonable Thoughts on the State of Religion in New England* (Chauncy 1743). By the time Edwards published *Religious Affections* (1746) the flames of the revival in New England had died down and Edwards' immediate concern turned from Chauncey and the critics of the revival, toward the supporters of the movement themselves. The Awakening during this period inspired unprecedented missionary activity, the founding of colleges and the development of an evangelical consensus throughout the colonies which would galvanize the diverse peoples of the colonial US such that they could confront England in a Revolutionary War. Needless to say, the question of how to come to a confident knowledge of what is or is not from God in the midst of such an event was the central question of the Awakening. Edwards' addresses *Distinguishing Marks* and *Religious Affections* directly to this question.

Finally, Edwards' writings were shaped by his own experiences and observations. As with Ignatius, his own experiences of God offered to him a paradigm of the divine-human relationship (and Christian discernment) consistent with yet unique within his ecclesial environment, a paradigm which would be developed over the years and find some of its best expression in the treatises explored in this study. As with Ignatius, Edwards records these insights in his own "Personal Narrative." He writes of his boyhood in the context of a time of awakening in his father's congregation: "I was then very much affected for many months, and concerned about the things of religion, and my soul's salvation; and was abundant in religious duties. I used to pray five times a day in secret, and to spend much time in religious conversation with other boys; and used to meet with them to pray together." Edwards notes, however, that his interest in religion wore off, and he "returned like a dog to his vomit and went on in the ways of sin." Edwards concludes, "And I am ready to think, many are deceived with such affections, and such a kind of delight as I then had in religion, and mistake it for grace" (Edwards 1998, 791).

He had especial difficulties with the doctrine of God's sovereignty and it was enlightenment concerning this issue that brought Edwards fully to Christ. I quote at length from his "Personal Narrative," describing an event that took place most probably in May or June of 1721 (Murray 1987, 35):

> The first instance, that I remember, of that sort of inward, sweet delight in God and in divine things, that I have lived much in ever since, was on reading those words, 1 Tim.i.17. *Now unto the King eternal, immortal, invisible, the only wise God, be honor and glory forever and ever. Amen.* As I read the words, there came into my soul, and was as it were diffused through it, a sense of the glory of the Divine Being; a new sense. quite different from anything I ever experienced before. Never any words of Scripture seemed to me as these words did. I thought with myself, how excellent a Being that was, and how happy I should be if I might enjoy that God and be rapt up to him in heaven; and be as it were swallowed up in him for ever! I kept saying, and as it were singing, over these words of Scripture to myself; and went to pray to God that I might enjoy him; and prayed in a manner quite different from what I used to, with a new sort of affection. But it never came to my thought, that there was anything spiritual, or of a saving nature, in this.
>
> From about that time I began to have a new kind of apprehensions and ideas of Christ, and the work of redemption, and the glorious way of salvation by him. An inward, sweet sense of these things, at times, came into my heart; and my soul was led away in pleasant views and contemplations of them. And my mind was greatly engaged to spend time in reading and meditating on Christ, on the beauty and excellency

of his person, and the lovely way of salvation by free grace in
him. (Edwards 1998, 792-93)

Although the "Personal Narrative" was written years after the event,
indications from the earliest extant entries in his "Diary" confirm the
general thrust of Edwards' conversion. On December 22, 1722 he
writes, "This day, revived by God's Holy Spirit; affected with the
sense of the excellency of holiness; felt more exercise of love to
Christ, than usual. Have, also, felt sensible repentance for sin,
because it was committed against so merciful and good a God"
(Edwards 1998, 759 "Diary").
    Much of what Edwards says in the above self-reflections
anticipates his thought on discernment expressed in his works on
revival. The evaluation of the character and trajectory of the affections of his youth as deceptive and easy to mistake for [saving] grace,
especially when considered in light of the nature of the later more
inward experiences, reveals a sensitivity to diverse affections that
characterizes his approach to discernment in the revival works. The
repeated use of words like "beauty," "excellency," "glory" and
"lovely" indicate the aesthetic element of Edwards' approach to the
knowledge of God, an element which forms an essential part of his
presentation of Christian discernment. The narratives are full of
affective language ("delight," "enjoy," "pleasant," "affected,"
"exercise of love"), the importance of which the entire first section of
Religious Affections defends. The object of these affections was the
character of God and his salvation more than the benefits to be gained
from God. Indeed, Edwards' enlightenment was even more narrowly
an illumination concerning the sovereign character of God,
accompanied with a renewed appreciation for the doctrine of salvation
by faith and grace alone. He speaks of a "new sense" of "new ideas"
and of the "sweetness" which he perceives in divine things. The "new
sense" or new perception of spiritual reality is the epistemological
foundation stone upon which Edwards' approach to discernment is
built. Finally, in a little aside, Edwards notes that "it never came to
my thought that there was anything spiritual or of a saving nature in
this." Edwards is struggling, even here, with the difficulty of recognizing particular motions of the Spirit (especially those required by
the Puritan fathers to be accounted for in order to gain assurance of
salvation). It was only later that Edwards was able to recognize the
saving influence of the Spirit in that event.

If Ignatius used his own spiritual direction relationships to provide insight and information from which the thought of the *Exercises* was refined, Edwards had similar opportunity during the Awakening. And he took advantage of it. In addition to the well known account of the experiences of his own wife Sarah (ST 331-42; cf. Goen 1972, 68, Edwards *Works* 1834, 1.xlv-xlvi, lxiii-lxx), his *Faithful Narrative* reads like a journalist's account of the event, detailing locations, manifestations, and consequences. Edwards writes in *Distinguishing Marks* of the "many instances I have been acquainted with" (DM, 236-37). He finds himself fortunate that God had placed him in the Northampton church where he could become "acquainted with" those that were revived and "wrought upon" during the seasons of renewal under Stoddard's leadership (DM, 268). He thus "knows by experience" of what he speaks concerning the dynamics of the human response to the Spirit (DM 285). It is this knowledge by "experience" which guided his approach to the order of the Spirit's work in salvation (RA, 160-63), and it is his observations which provide insight to matters of discerning between true and false affections (RA 319, 370). He presents his motive for the use of these observations in *Distinguishing Marks*:

And as I am one that, by the providence of God, have for some months past, been much amongst those that have been the subjects of that work that has of late been carried on in the land; and particularly, have been abundantly in the way of seeing and observing those extraordinary things that many persons have been much stumbled at; such as persons crying out aloud, shrieking, being put into great agonies of body, and deprived of their bodily strength and the like; and that in many different towns; and have been particularly conversant with great numbers of such . . .; many of them being persons that I have long known, and have been intimately acquainted with them in soul concerns, before and since: so I look upon myself called on this occasion to give my testimony, that so far as the nature and tendency of such a work is capable of falling under the observation of a bystander, to whom those that have been the subjects of it have endeavored to open their hearts, or can be come at by diligent and particular inquiry, this work has all those marks that have been spoken of [of a work of God]; and

particularly in many of those that have been the subjects of
such extraordinary operations, all those marks have appeared
in a very great degree. (DM 263-64)

Discernment and Affectivity in Distinguishing Marks

Distinguishing Marks is a brief treatise, amounting to sixty-two
pages of text in the Yale University Press edition. It was published in
1741, four years after the release of Edwards' *Faithful Narrative*.
Faithful Narrative was the most influential book in the early stages of
the Great Awakening, going though three editions and twenty print-
ings between 1737 and 1739. A "general revival," as opposed to
smaller local awakenings, was unheard of at the time and people read
Edwards' account of the revival with both disbelief and excitement.
Faithful Narrative stimulated awakening on both sides of the Atlantic.
By the time *Distinguishing Marks* was published, interest in the
revival was quite high. Critics of the event were surprisingly silent
up until this time, but Edwards' knew that this would not last. He
took the first word in defending the revival with *Distinguishing
Marks*. This word was a lesson in discernment.

Edwards' text for this work was 1 John 4:1, "Beloved, believe not
every spirit, but try the spirits whether they are of God; because many
false prophets are gone out into the world." Edwards highlights both
the duty of trying the spirits and the presence of counterfeits. Then
he states his purpose: "My design therefore at this time is to shew
what are the true, certain, and distinguishing evidences of a work of
the Spirit of God, by which we may proceed safely in judging of any
operation we find in ourselves, or see in others" (DM, 227). By "any
operation" Edwards is referring to the experiences and phenomena
related to the revival. He mentions the judging of operations "in ourselves" and "in others," yet it becomes clear as the treatise develops
that his primary interest is the evaluation of the Awakening as a
whole. This is clear (1) from his use of language in the list of "negative signs" ("'Tis no sign that a work is not the work of the Spirit of
God, that . . ." DM, 228, 234, 235, 236, 238, 241, 243, 244, 246),
(2) from his explicit evaluation of "the work in general" (e.g. DM,
243, 244, 254; cf. ST, 314), and from the applications presented in

the third part of the treatise, the first of which states plainly that "that extraordinary influence that has lately appeared on the minds of the people abroad in this land, causing them an uncommon concern and engagedness of mind about the things of religion, is undoubtedly, in the general, from the Spirit of God" (DM, 260). Edwards' aim in this treatise, then, is to model an appropriate procedure for Christian discernment and then to apply that model to the Awakening "in general."

As mentioned earlier, *Distinguishing Marks* is divided into three parts. The first part clarifies appropriate discernment procedures by identifying a list of *negative signs*: "what are not signs that we are to judge of a work by, whether it be the work of the Spirit of God or no; and especially, what are no evidences that a work that is wrought amongst a people, is not the work of the Spirit of God" (DM, 228). In order to come to identify and know that which is from God, one must approach the phenomena concerned with an appropriate set of criteria. Edwards was convinced that wrong evaluations of the revival were being made due to improper criteria being used, criteria which didn't isolate the specifically divine elements in a revival movement. In the first part of this treatise Edwards identifies nine of these inappropriate criteria and argues in each case why judgments based on these criteria are necessarily inconclusive.

Edwards states, for example, that the unique and highly expressive character of the Great Awakening cannot be used to determine the lack of divine origin. Nor even can the fact that in the midst of the Awakening bad is found to be mixed with the good. On the contrary, Edwards argues that "extraordinary" and "high" affections might be expected in a general work of God. Drawing examples from Scripture and history, Edwards demonstrates, for example, "that a true sense of the glorious excellency of the Lord Jesus Christ, and of his wonderful dying love, and the exercise of a truly spiritual love and joy, should be such as very much to overcome bodily strength" (DM, 232). Edwards argues concerning the presence of bad mixed with the good, "A thousand imprudences won't prove a work not to be the work of the Spirit of God; yea if there be not only imprudences, but many things prevailing that are irregular, and really contrary to the rules of God's holy Word. That it should be thus may be well accounted for from the exceeding weakness of human nature, together with the remaining darkness and corruption of those that are yet the subjects of the saving influences of God's Spirit, and have a real zeal for God" (DM, 241). The power and beauty of God's character and works, and the frailty of the human person, make the use of such criteria as the above highly suspect for an adequate discernment of the situation.

In *Distinguishing Marks*, every negative sign ("what are not signs that we are to judge of a work by, whether it be the work of the Spirit of God or no") is developed solely for the sake of demonstrating that these signs cannot be used to determine that the revival is *not* a work of God. The critics of the event are at the forefront of Edwards' mind in this treatise. In reading through Edwards' arguments, one can hear the voices of his opponents behind the text: "But this is not what we are used to" (cf. DM, 229); "This is just the same enthusiasm Luther and Calvin condemned" (cf. DM, 234); "All these bodily effects are not in the Bible" (cf. DM, 232-33); "Their imaginations are deceived by what they think they experience" (cf. DM, 237); "They are being persuaded by the example of others, rather than by reason or Scripture" (cf. DM, 238f., 240); "How can something full of errors be of God?" (cf. DM, 244-46); "They are just being manipulated by the preaching" (cf. DM, 246); "They are being deceived by Satan masquerading as an angel of light" (cf. DM, 259); "God is a God of order, not confusion; hence this disorderly movement must not be from God" (cf. DM, 267). And in every case Edwards has a reply: Novelty does not necessitate lack of divine origin, but rather it may indicate the powerful presence of God (DM, 229-30); bodily effects and strong impressions doesn't make a movement enthusiastic, for many in scripture experienced these things and we must examine the root rather than mere "motions of the blood and animal spirits" (DM, 234); just because every bodily exercise isn't described in the Scripture proves nothing, for the Scripture provides no rule to determine acceptable or unacceptable bodily effects (DM, 232-33); wild imaginative experiences can be accounted for by the fact that humans think with the use of the imagination and that elevated experiences will naturally impact the imagination - in fact "God has really made use of this faculty to truly divine purposes" (DM, 236), and so on.

Having destroyed the critics' criteria of judgment in the first part, Edwards proceeds, in the second, to construct an alternative criteriological model for discerning group phenomena, to "shew positively what are the sure, distinguishing, Scripture evidences and marks of a work of the Spirit of God, by which we may proceed in judging of any operation we find in ourselves, or see among a people, without danger of being misled" (DM, 249). He takes his structure for this section from the passage of scripture which introduces the treatise, confining his discussion to five signs found in 1 John 4.

The first criteria of a work of God Edwards identifies is that it *"raises their esteem"* of Jesus and of the truth of the Gospel concerning him (cf. 1 John 4:2-3). Edwards states, "if the spirit that is at work among a people is plainly observed to work after that manner, as to convince them of Christ, and lead them to Christ; more to confirm their minds in the belief of the story of Christ, . . . and to incline their affections more to him; it is sure sign that it is the true and right Spirit" (DM, 250). The second indication is when the spirit *"operates against the interest of Satan's kingdom"* (cf. 1 John 4:4-5). When the spirit at work in a people leads them to lay aside attachment to things of the world, and inspires them to overcome the lusts of the world, "to lessen men's esteem of the pleasures, profits and honors of the world, . . . the spirit that operates after such a manner, must needs be the Spirit of God" (DM, 251). The third criteria states that "that spirit that operates in such a manner, as to *cause in men a greater regard to the Holy Scriptures,* and establishes them more in their truth and divinity, is certainly the Spirit of God" (DM, 253; cf. 1 John 4:6). The fourth criteria is built from the epistle's distinction between the "spirit of truth" and the "spirit of error" (1 John 4:6). Thus, Edwards states, "if by observing the manner of the operation of a spirit that is at work among a people, we see that it *operates as a spirit of truth,* leading persons to truth, convincing them of those things that are true, we may safely determine that 'tis a right and true spirit" (DM, 254). The final criteria is that of *love* (1 John 4:7,12-13). Concerning this criteria Edwards states, "Therefore when the spirit that is at work amongst a people tends this way, and brings many of them to high and exalting thoughts of the divine Being, and his glorious perfections, . . . and works in them an admiring delightful sense of the excellency of Jesus Christ; . . . winning and drawing the heart with those motives and incitements to love. . . . And also quells contentions among men, and gives a spirit of peace and goodwill, excites to acts of outward kindness . . . . I say when a spirit operates after this manner among a people, there is the highest kind of evidence of the influence of a true and divine spirit" (DM, 256).

A couple of points should be made concerning Edwards' understanding of Christian discernment reflected in his presentation of the above criteria. The first concerns the process of discernment. Edwards understands "trying the spirits," or the act of discernment, to be a process of "observing the manner of the operation of a spirit that is at work among a people." Discernment involves careful observation of something. Edwards calls this something an "operation." One can legitimately understand this word to be comparable to Ignatius' use of "motions," only applied here to corporate as well as individual experience. Motions or operations arise from and point to the activity of diverse "spirits." Thus behavior patterns or affective tendencies in persons and groups ("a people") can arise as consequences of the activity of a "spirit" within the circumstances. To use Gay's categories, the "operations" function as the immediate object leading one to recognize the activity of diverse spirits (the next mediate object). However, Edwards' approach to discernment looks not merely to the operations, the affective and behavioral experiences as such, but rather he draws attention to the *manner* of the operation (Gay's mediate object - the "principle" of the motions). In every instance mentioned above, Edwards associates the discernment process with the identification of the manner of these operations. It may be best to think of this "manner" as a *tendency* ("when the spirit . . . tends this way") or concrete orientation. The notions of "habit," "tendency," "disposition" and "manner" are not insignificant concepts for Edwards. Indeed, as Sang H. Lee asserts, "Edwards' contention is that habits and tendencies belong to the order of being" (Lee 1973, 33). By carefully observing affective and behavioral phenomena with an eye toward the tendencies in their quality and direction, and by comparing these with normative tendencies derived from scripture, one can "proceed safely in judging" that which is (or is not) from God. What do you see? Is the dominant affective/behavioral pattern among great numbers of people in a movement one of love, being drawn toward and inspired by God, and reaching out in kindness to others? Then you are likely to be looking at a move of God. Thus careful, biblically-informed attention to "what's going on" forms the core of Edwards' approach to the process of discernment in *Distinguishing Marks*.

Mention of "spirits" brings me to the subject of Edwards' demonology. Without going into detail, it needs to be noted that, like

Ignatius, Edwards believed in the real influence of Satan and evil "spirits" in the course of human life. Like Ignatius, Edwards understands the Christian life to be lived within a conflict of kingdoms. In *Distinguishing Marks* Edwards' references to evil forces (more often "Satan," or "the Devil") for the most part to address three types of concerns. First, Edwards argues that one need not assume that Satan is the cause of particular phenomena, for other factors may better account for the phenomena at hand. Such is the case with the presence of ecstasy in the revival: this can be explained both by the work of God and the weak frames of a human person (DM, 237). Second, Edwards emphasizes the power of his "positive signs" by arguing that they are not likely to be counterfeited by the Devil. Satan would not lead great numbers of people to exalt Christ (DM, 250); the Devil would not go about raising up scripture (DM, 253); love and humility are contrary to the Devil (DM, 258); "it is not supposed that Satan would go about to convince men of sin" (DM, 251; cf. 252). Third, he mentions that even if the Devil may be involved in some events of the Awakening, this does not disprove the nature of the movement "in general." Even if Satan masquerades as an "angel of light" (2 Corinthians 11:13-14) this does not constitute an adequate objection to the sufficiency of the marks of the Spirit of God. Rather it simply indicates the necessity of careful discerning observation, to distinguish the difference between a mere shew of light and the real fire from God (DM, 259-60). Edwards does mention, by way of aside, a rule for discerning the work of the enemy, namely that "Satan will keep men secure as long as he can; but when he can do that no longer, he often endeavors to drive them to extremes, and so to dishonor God and wound religion that way" (DM, 269). He warns the promoters of the revival to be especially careful against misconduct in their behavior in the context of the revival, for "the great Enemy of this work will especially try his utmost with us; and he will especially triumph if he can prevail against any of us, in anything to blind and mislead us" (DM, 277). For Edwards, as for Ignatius, one improves discernment as strategies of the enemy are understood in advance. But for Edwards, the emphasis is upon the biblically certain evidences, the "distinguishing marks," of the work of the Holy Spirit. Based on these, one can judge safely.

In the third and final section of *Distinguishing Marks*, Edwards applies the criteria advanced in section two to the Awakening. He first asserts the general conclusion that, "unless the Apostle John was out in his rules, [they] are sufficient to determine it to be in general, the work of God" (DM, 261). He recounts what is "notorious" or evident to all concerning the event: regard for the scriptures, improvement of the means of grace, increased sense of the dreadfulness of sin and of the value of Christ and his death - and these not merely in a few people but "in all parts of the land." There has been little feigning manifestations, and the fright associated with many experiences appears to be a real terror of the consequences of eternal death. He notes, however the need for competent spiritual guides who can help people to interpret their experiences (DM, 269; cf. ST, 320). He notes that, "the work of God that has been carried on there this year, has been much purer than that which was wrought there six years before. It has appeared more purely spiritual; freer from natural and corrupt mixtures, and anything savoring of enthusiastic wildness and extravagance" (DM, 270). Secondly, he warns against any opposing this work and to encourage all to promote it. The time of waiting and watching has ended. He predicts that "the stumbling blocks that now attend this work will in some respects be increased, and not diminished. Particularly, we probably shall see more instances of apostasy and gross iniquity among professors" (DM, 274). Now is the time for aggressive support of this work. Finally he moves to "apply myself to those that are friends of this work, and have been partakers of it, and are zealous to promote it" (DM, 276). He urges them to avoid errors or misconduct. He especially emphasizes (a) the dangers of spiritual pride, and of (b) too much heed to impulses and strong impressions, (c) the importance of not despising human learning, (d) the harm of censuring other professing Christians, and of (e) managing controversy with opposers with too much zeal. He closes by encouraging a measure of prudence in behavior. Each of these corrections draws the promoters back to a focus on the "positive" rather than the "negative" signs for their own sense of religious self-identity. I will suggest that this is the primary focus of *Religious Affections*.

For Edwards, as presented in *Distinguishing Marks*, discernment is a process of coming to know, to find an empirically confident and biblically grounded understanding of what is and is not from God, in this case an affective-behavioral trend in the churches of his time and place. The means by which one gains knowledge concerning this event is, for Edwards, through well-informed observation of the affective-behavioral phenomena. By observing the "manner" of the event, the tendencies which the quality and the trajectory of the phenomena exhibit, and by comparing this to normative descriptions of the "manner" of the Christian faith as presented in the scriptures, similarities or differences begin to show themselves and a safe judgment can be formed concerning the event.

Finally, I will offer a word concerning the role(s) of affectivity in Edwards' approach to discernment as presented in *Distinguishing Marks* (I will briefly compare Ignatius and Edwards on this point below). Edwards does not develop his theology of the affections in this treatise. He broaches the topic in *Some Thoughts* and develops it fully in *Religious Affections*. He refers to affections periodically in *Distinguishing Marks* (DM, 229, 239, 248, 250) and in all cases he refers to affections much as we would use the term "emotions" today. Yet without developing a theology of the affections, Edwards makes it clear throughout this work that affections are a large part of "what is going on" to be discerned. People are being caught up in affective experiences. Terrors, delights, tears, leaping for joy, feeling "swallowed up" in God, unbearable grief for sin: all of these are the symptoms of this work of God. The affections themselves, and the behavior of the people experiencing them, become the objects of discernment. It is really the group affective-behavioral trend which is the primary matter of discernment in *Distinguishing Marks*. While Edwards does not develop the roles of affectivity with regards to the subject or the process of discernment here, affectivity clearly plays a role in this treatise as the object of discernment. I will show how the focus changes as I turn to Edwards' *Religious Affections*.

Intervening between the release of *Distinguishing Marks* and *Religious Affections* was the publication of Edwards' *Some Thoughts Concerning the present Revival of Religion in New England, And the Way in Which it ought to be acknowledged and promoted* (1742; on ST cf. Goen, 1972, 65-78; Murray 1987, 233-248). In the first part of this book, Edwards reaffirms his approach to discernment presented in *Distinguishing Marks*. He begins the first part by presenting the errors of judgment made by those "who have had ill thoughts" of the revival. Rather than making scripture the rule by which to judge of the operations, they have judged the work *a priori*, from its origins, its instruments, its methods. Edwards states, "such a work is not to be judged of a priori, but a posteriori: we are to observe the effect wrought; and if, upon examination of that, it be found to be agreeable to the Word of God, we are bound without more ado to rest in it as God's work" (ST, 293). Rather than judge by observation of the effects of the revival in comparison with biblical criteria, the critics of the event have based their judgment on false criteria: philosophical assumptions about the human person, uncertain signs (like effects on the body), accidental similarities to enthusiasts or their own experience (ST, 296-314).

With the mention of the use of philosophy to judge the work, Edwards introduces an issue which will become central for *Religious Affections*, namely the nature of "affections." Edwards hears his opponents saying, "There is but little sober, solid religion in this work, it is little else but flash and noise. Religion nowadays all runs out into transports and high flights of the passions and affections" (ST, 296). The philosophical assumption which underlies this criticism, Edwards notes, is that the affections are a distinct faculty from the will, associated with the animal nature and therefore are accidental or even harmful to the cause of religion. Edwards attacks this scholastic faculty psychology, this "myth of the passions" (cf. Solomon 1983) as error. He states, "But it is false philosophy . . . and false divinity to suppose that religious affections don't appertain to the substance and essence of Christianity: on the contrary, it seems to me that the very life and soul of all true religion consists in them" (ST, 297). This sentence anticipates the entire first part of *Religious Affections*.

Finally, in the fourth and largest part of *Some Thoughts*, Edwards turns to address a number of "things to be corrected or avoided." He repeats and emphasizes the rule for discerning the work of the enemy presented in *Distinguishing Marks*, that "it has been a common device of the Devil to overset a revival of religion, when he finds he can keep men quiet and secure no longer, then to drive 'em to excesses and extravagances" (ST, 410). Edwards states that "the errors that attend a great revival of religion usually arise from these three things: 1. Undiscerned spiritual pride. 2. Wrong principles. 3. Ignorance of Satan's advantages and devices" (ST, 414). Two of these, the first and third, give rise to mention of discernment. The first cause of errors is undiscerned spiritual pride. Edwards spends a full fifteen pages addressing this issue, and his treatments here and in *Religious*

Affections are some of the best writings on humility in Christian spiritual literature. Edwards' special concern here is that "spiritual pride in its own nature is so secret, that it is not so well discerned by immediate intuition on the thing itself, as by the effects and fruits of it" (ST, 418). He then proceeds to describe "the manner" of spiritual pride: it disposes to speak of others' sins, it is apt to suspect others. "Some that have spiritual pride mixed with high discoveries and great transports of joy, that *dispose* 'em in an earnest *manner* to talk to others, . . . sharply reproving them." (ST, 418; italics mine). He develops his understanding of the works of the enemy in his discussion of the third point. Here in the fourth part of *Some Thoughts*, Edwards turns from evaluation of the whole to discernment of the parts. He assumes that the revival in general is a work of God. That has been established in the first part of the book. Yet lack of discernment concerning the *parts,* the "imprudences and irregularities," causes damage to the reputation and progress of the revival in general. The process is similar in both instances, yet now the object of discernment is not the affective/behavioral trend facing the church as a whole, but the affective motions operating within the experience of a single individual. The discernment of affective motions of the individual within the midst of a work of God becomes the chief topic of *Religious Affections.*

Discernment in Religious Affections

The Setting

A Treatise Concerning Religious Affections was originally a series of sermons begun in 1742. Murray writes, "It was in part, Edwards' knowledge of the existence of opposition which led him during 1742 to give close attention both to a defense of the Awakening and to the kind of Christian experience which it had revived. The result was that even amidst so many engagements he wrote a book of 378 pages entitled, *Some Thoughts Concerning the Present Revival of Religion in New England*, in 1742, and began to lay the foundations of a second, yet larger work, *A Treatise Concerning Religious Affections* in a series of sermons which he commenced that same year" (Murray 1987, 204). In *Some Thoughts* he addressed the defense of the Awakening. In *Religious Affections* Edwards addresses Christian experience.

Shortly after the publication of *Some Thoughts*, serious opposition to the revival arose in New England. A Convention of ministers met in May of 1743 and published a list of errors and disorders which they denounced, refraining from "any positive assertion on the existence of a true revival" (Murray 1987, 208). In September of 1743, Charles Chauncy, pastor of First Church in Boston and Edwards' most significant opponent, published his *Seasonable Thoughts on the State of Religion in New England*, stating that in the main, the revival was simply the proliferation of enthusiasm. Chauncy begins the Introduction to the book with an extended quotation from Thomas Shepard's *Parable of the Ten Virgins*, exhorting ministers to due caution with regards to professions of faith and religious affections. Persons may come extolling their conversion, yet their boasts may not in the end reveal the true heart. Chauncy agrees wholeheartedly with Shepard's call for caution, stating that in these days,

> "There has certainly been too much *Haste*, as well as *Positiveness*, in declaring these and those, in this and the other Place, to have *passed from Death to Life*; A Judgment has been too commonly formed of Men's *spiritual* condition, more from their *Affections*, than the *permanent Temper* of their Minds discovered in the habitual *Conduct* of their Lives; not duly considering, how precarious that Religion must be, which has its *Rise* from the *Passions*, and not any *thorow* (sic) *Change* in the *Understanding* and *Will*." (Chauncy 1743, 3; italic Chauncy's)

By late 1743 Jonathan Edwards himself was quite concerned of the imprudences and irregularities of the revival. Edwards writes on May 12, 1743 in a letter to a correspondent in Scotland that, "we have run from one extreme to another, with regard to talking of experiences; that whereas formerly there was too great a reservedness in this matter, of late many have gone to an unbounded openness. . . . Among other ill consequences of such a practice, this is one, that religion runs all into that channel. . . so that other parts of religion have been really injured thereby: as when we see a tree excessively full of leaves, we find so much less fruit" (Edwards 1998, 107). John Davenport, the living symbol of the enthusiastic element of the Great Awakening, gathered on March of 1743 with a group of followers in New London, Connecticut to form a new church led by the direct inspiration of the Holy Spirit given to Davenport. Having condemned numerous ministers as unconverted, they burned a number of articles, some of them books of the Puritan fathers. Between 1743 and 1746, when *Religious Affections* was published, Chauncy's concerns, in light of the obvious visible excesses, had won the day and interest in and involvement in "the things of religion" waned.

The Aim

While Edwards never refers to Chauncy or Davenport by name, nor to any of the specific events or people involved in the Awakening, one can see from the preface of *Religious Affections* that the course and concerns of this, and perhaps all, revivals were foremost on his mind when he wrote the book. Edwards echoes Chauncy's own question in the very first sentences when he states that "there is no question whatsoever, that is of greater importance to mankind, and that it more concerns every individual person to be well resolved in, than this, what are the distinguishing qualifications of those that are in favor with God, and entitled to his eternal rewards? Or, which comes to the same thing, What is the nature of true religion?" (RA, 84). He confesses his sense of mystery at the work of revival "so much good, and so much bad, should be mixed together in the church of God." Yet this is not new, for all works of God have exhibited this mixture. He concludes, "'Tis by the mixture of counterfeit religion with true, not discerned and distinguished, that the devil has had his greatest advantage against the cause and kingdom of Christ, all along, hitherto" (RA, 86). He notes how the enemies of God have repeatedly appeared after religion has been revived and "gives them a fatal stab unseen" through the entry of evil under the appearance of good. "And so it is likely ever to be in the church," Edwards states, "whenever religion revives remarkably, till one has learned well to distinguish between true and false religion, between saving affections and experiences, and those manifold fair shows, and glistering appearances, by which they are counterfeited" (RA, 88). He reiterates the dangers of undiscerned affections, mentioning the enemy's strategy of driving people to extremes. Then he reasserts his main point of the preface:

Therefore, it greatly concerns us to use our utmost endeavors clearly to discern, and have it well settled and established, wherein true religion does consist. Till this be done, it may be expected that great revivings of religion, will be but of short continuance: till this be done, there is little good to be expected, of all our warm debates, in conversation and from the press, not knowing clearly and distinctly what we ought to contend for (RA, 89).

Immediately following this paragraph he presents the aim for which he writes *Religious Affections*. He states that his design in this book is different from that of *Distinguishing Marks*, "which was to show the distinguishing marks of a work of God, including both his common and saving operations." His purpose here is unique, and he is clear about this purpose, stating that

> what I aim at now, is to show the nature and signs of the gracious operations of God's Spirit, by which they are to be distinguished from all things whatsoever that the minds of men are the subjects of, which are not of a saving nature (RA, 89).

Three things need to be noted by way of clarifying Edwards' aim in *Religious Affections*.

First, Edwards' concern is not the present but future revivals. Edwards has noticed a pattern, and he has seen it manifested in his lifetime. The Spirit initiates a mighty work of God, and in the early course of that work many people are drawn to the things of religion. But when least suspected, the Devil introduces spiritual pride, false principles concerning the promotion of a revival, and like errors. People are led to extremes in opinion concerning the value of this work in general, leading to the development of factions, discontent and disorder. Finally interest in revival and hope in God are both damaged. This pattern can be identified both in scripture and history. In Edwards' mind, the Great Awakening is over. He has his eyes set on the next move of the Spirit (remember he saw a number of separate waves in Northampton). "Until," Edwards repeats, "the church learns to distinguish between the divine and that which is not revivals are doomed to be of short continuance." Edwards' aim, in *Religious Affections* is not to provide evaluation of the Great Awakening, rather it is to provide the principles for ensuring that the next Awakening can have long lasting (and wider-spreading) impact upon the communities affected.

Second, Edwards does not make an effort in *Religious Affections*, to evaluate, or to provide principles for the evaluation of, the divine origin of this or any supposed "work of God." He explicitly mentions that he accomplished this evaluation in his earlier writings. Rather than the discerning of "a work of God," his interest in this book is "to show the nature and signs of the gracious operations of God's Spirit," phenomena that "the minds of men are subjects of." No longer is he talking, as in his earlier revival works, about "the work in general." In *Religious Affections* the foci of the book, and the objects of discernment, are the various motions which people experience *in the context* of a work of God.

Finally, Edwards does not aim this work toward establishing principles for distinguishing between the work of the Spirit and other operations. He is not merely interested in discerning between "true" and "false" affections in a general sense. Again, Edwards makes himself explicit on this point. While in *Distinguishing Marks*, Edwards treated of the distinction between all work of the Spirit ("both his common and saving operations") and the work of other spirits, in this work Edwards explicitly limits his attention to the "gracious" or "saving" influences of the Spirit. In order to make this critical distinction clear one must recall the Puritan teaching concerning "the works of the Spirit preparatory to regeneration" mentioned above. Puritan practice commonly identified those works of invitation, conviction and such which do not actually effect a transformation of the person in fundamental orientation to Christ as separate from those works of the Spirit which do effect that change, either in initial or ongoing conversion (regeneration/justification and sanctification). To confuse these separate works of the Spirit was dangerous. Thus in *Distinguishing Marks* Edwards notes that, "beside the vain shews which may be from the Devil, there are common influences of the Spirit, which are often mistaken for saving grace: but these are out of the question [of the revival being a work of the Spirit], because though they are not saving, yet they are the work of the true Spirit" (DM, 260). This matter which was "out of the question" in *Distinguishing Marks* is the main point in *Religious Affections*. Just as Chauncy's concern in his *Seasonable Thoughts* was for the hastiness in judging of the "spiritual condition" of professors, whether "they have passed from death to life," so the most important question for Edwards, in *Religious Affections* is the identification of "the distinguishing qualifications of those that are in favor with God, and entitled to his eternal rewards." Edwards' aim in *Religious Affections* was to establish those principles by which people can confidently identify the "saving" influences of the Holy Spirit. For, as Edwards repeatedly points out in this book, by mistaking the common influences for saving influences, by failing to rightly to discern the signs and presence of the "gracious" or "saving" affections, people are led to base their assurance of faith and religious self-image upon the fact and circumstances of God's invitation to transformation, rather than upon God's transformative work itself. This point must be kept in mind as the reader of *Religious Affections* surveys the negative and positive signs of religious affections.

The First Part

Religious Affections divides into three parts. The first, "Concerning the Nature of the *Affections* and their Importance in *Religion*," develops what was only broached in *Some Thoughts* concerning the psychology of the affections and their significance for religion. The second part, "Shewing what are *no certain Signs* that *religious Affections* are *gracious*, or that they are *not*" develops and adapts the "negative signs" listed in *Distinguishing Marks* for the particular aims of this book. The third part, "Shewing what *are distinguishing Signs* of truly gracious and *holy Affections*," enumerates a new set of "positive signs," reviewing human experience from beginning to end, designed to isolate those influences which can only be accomplished through a saving work of the Spirit. Rather than reserve the chief application for a separate section as in his earlier works, here he applies the themes of his parts to situations throughout the work.

After a brief scriptural introduction to the book, he defines his key term, the "affections." He states plainly, "Affections are no other, than the more vigorous and sensible exercises of the inclination and will of the soul" (RA, 96). He immediately, and without reference to the scholastic faculty psychology that his approach will seek to replace, identifies the psychological framework within which this definition can be understood. He identifies two distinct faculties in the human "soul." The *understanding* relates to the world by perception, speculation, discerning, viewing, and judging. The second faculty he labels the *inclination*. The inclination relates to its surroundings not "merely" through perception and the like (neutrally) but is in some manner "inclined." Involved in inclination are such elements as like and dislike, attraction and aversion, approval and rejection. As the inclination impacts human action Edwards calls it the *will*. However, insofar as human inclination does not impact concrete human action, but rather simply expresses an inclination of the mind, Edwards refers to this aspect of human life as the *heart*. He notes that the inclinations of the heart can be experienced in different degrees, from a slight attraction to an overwhelming lust. Edwards states that when "the motion of the blood and animal spirits begins to be sensibly altered; whence oftentimes arises some bodily sensation, especially about the heart and vitals, ... And it is to be noted, that they are these more vigorous and sensible exercises of this faculty, that are called the *affections*" (RA, 97; italics Edwards'). Edwards separates *affections* from *passions* for with the passions, the inclinations "are more sudden, and whose effects on the animal spirit are more violent, and the mind more overpowered, and less in its own command" (RA, 98). John Smith rightly notes that "this distinction [between affections and passions] is of great importance, because most of Edwards opponents thought he was defending religious passions at the expense of intellect and they did not understand that by an affection he meant the response of the self to an *idea*, an apprehension of the nature of a thing" (Smith 1992b, 33). Unlike the later psychologist William James (cf. James 1961 [1902]), Edwards did not identify affectivity with the physiological activity, for "it is not the body, but the mind only, that is the proper seat of the affections" (RA, 98). Physiological states only signal and manifest the presence of affectivity, a state of mind, to or through the person affected. Edwards understands affections generally to have a polar character (love-hatred, desire-fear, joy-grief, etc.), but he acknowledges the existence of affections which are "mixed," which involve elements of both attractive and aversive poles (pity, zeal). By such distinctions Edwards seeks to identify affections, and in doing so he develops a construct of affectivity unique to his time (cf. Smith 1992b, 17).

Edwards links the will and affections close together, and it is not always clear how to separate them in this book (cf. Smith 1959, 14). At times Edwards highlights the physiological manifestations by which affections are known to be present in an individual (RA, 98). Yet as an inclination *to* something, especially to a divinely excellent

Something, affection is often portrayed as an "apprehensive-intentional response to value" (cf. Tyrrell 1987; cf. RA 225,253). Edwards distinguishes an affection both from the activity of the bodily spirits and from apprehensions which may give rise to affections in a discussion of enlightenment (RA, 269). Yet again, Edwards' understanding of the role of affections in the "sense of the heart" in the converted individual (which I will treat below), appear to imply that the affections do not mediate merely the *value* of their object but also carry something of the *nature* of their object to the one affected (cf. RA, 272). Edwards certainly understands affections as the "motive springs of action" (RA, 100; cf. Lewis 1994). Smith suggests that, "if we stick to the idea that an affection is a "warm" and "fervid" inclination involving judgment, we shall not go wrong" (Smith 1959, 14). As I will show in chapter three, Edwards, like Ignatius, is reflecting something of the multi-dimensional character of human affectivity.

After defining the nature of affections, Edwards proceeds, in the first part of his book, to defend the value and significance of affections in the Christian religion. This section of the book is a splendid biblical defense of Christian experience (known to the Puritans and Methodists as "experimental religion"; cf. Steele 1994). In contrast to Chauncy's understanding of religion as "precarious" when founded on the affections (understood as "passions"), Edwards argues that "true religion, in great part, consists in the affections" (RA, 99). Edwards defends this thesis by a number of arguments. He concludes that "although to true religion there must be something else besides affection; yet true religion consists so much in the affections, that there can be no true religion without them" (RA, 120). Edwards urges his readers to make use of such means as "have much of a tendency to move the affections" and cries "what great cause we have to be ashamed and confounded before God, that we are no more affected with the great things of religion" (RA, 122). It is clear that Edwards' prayer for "what he desires" is rich in affectivity. The application of this to the question is presented in his application:

> There are false affections and there are true. A man's having much affection don't prove that he has any true religion: but if he has no affection, it proves he has no true religion. The right way, is not to reject all affections, nor to approve all; but

to distinguish between affections, approving some, and rejecting others; separating the wheat and the chaff, the gold and the dross, the precious and the vile" (RA, 121).

Edwards provides the principles by which this distinguishing is done in the sections which follow.

The Second Part

Edwards indicates his purposes in the title of the second part of his book, "Shewing what are no certain signs, that religious affections are truly gracious or that they are not." Like the first part of *Distinguishing Marks*, Edwards clarifies the discernment process by identifying inappropriate criteria which are used to evaluate the object of discernment. However, in contrast to *Distinguishing Marks*, which treated inappropriate criteria used by the critics of the Awakening to reject the divine source of the event, in *Religious Affections* the inappropriate criteria are those by which "zealous promoters" of Awakenings evaluate themselves to be under the influence of saving affections. Edwards lists twelve.

That Edwards is applying similar methodology (clarification and application of criteria) to different objects in these two treatises can be demonstrated by an examination of his enumeration of the criterion of effects on the body. In *Distinguishing Marks*, Edwards lists this criterion as follows: "A work is not to be judged of by any effects on the bodies of men; such as tears, tremblings, groans, loud outcries, agonies of body, or the failing of bodily strength" (DM, 230). In *Religious Affections* Edwards asserts, "'Tis no sign that affections have the nature of true religion, or that they have not, that they have great effects on the body" (RA, 131). In *Distinguishing Marks* the *work* is in view; in *Religious Affections* it is the *affections*. Yet in both cases, Edwards applies the same basic principles of discernment. In *Distinguishing Marks*, Edwards devotes the entire argument to proving that it is possible, if not probable, that these effects on people's bodies can be excited by a work of the Spirit of God, even though natural elements may be present. In *Religious Affections*, Edwards devotes equal space to demonstrating both that these affections *can* be manifestations of saving influences of the Spirit (contra the critics) and that it is wrong to assume that these affections *must* be manifestations of saving influences of the Spirit (contra the enthusiasts). Indeed, as Edwards develops part two, he places greater emphasis on dissembling the confidence that promoters have that their affections are "certain signs" that they are transformed by God.

Whereas in *Distinguishing Marks*, Edwards operated by a principle of inclusion, in *Religious Affections* he operates by exclusion. In *Distinguishing Marks*, Edwards mentions the possibility of natural elements, corruption, even Satanic deception, to argue that these factors do not preclude an awakening being a genuine work of God. All can be included. In *Religious Affections*, however, Edwards mentions the counterfeits of Satan (RA, 141, 144, 147, 158, 166, 183), the constitution of human nature (RA, 136, 142, 148, 156), and the corruption of people (RA, 145, 157) for the sake of indicating the variety of influences which may be primarily influencing the presence of a given religious affection. Just because the "work in general" may indeed be a work of God's Spirit in spite of the presence of all these non-divine factors, this does not mean that a given affection experienced in the context of that work must therefore be a result of the influence of the Holy Spirit. For though the work in general may be from God, individual experiences must be evaluated on a case by case basis, and by more certain criteria.

Edwards applies the same principle to the distinction between "common" and "saving" influences. As mentioned above, Edwards makes it clear that whereas in *Distinguishing Marks* he developed principles for identifying the work of the Spirit "in general," both common and saving influences (appropriate to the evaluation of a work of God upon a wide range of peoples and places), in *Religious Affections* he focuses attention upon those influences of the Spirit which are of a "saving nature." Consequently, just as he excludes affections resulting from natural elements, elements related to human corruption and spiritual deception, so also he excludes those resulting from a "common" work of the Holy Spirit. For example, when speaking of the experience of impressions being received during heightened affectivity, Edwards states, "And besides, it is to be considered, that persons may have those impressions on their minds, which may not be of their own producing, nor from an evil spirit, but from the Spirit of God, and yet not be from any saving, but a common influence of the Spirit of God" (RA, 142). Likewise when speaking of the appearance of texts of scripture to the mind, he states that they may "not be from Satan, nor yet properly from the corruptions of their own hearts, but from some influence of the Spirit of God with the Word, and yet have nothing of the nature of true and saving religion in them" (RA, 145). Similarly when he speaks of the order of affective experiences he wonders, "how far God's own spirit may go in those operations and convictions which in themselves are not spiritual and saving, and yet the person that is the subject of them, never be converted, but fall short of salvation at last" (RA, 159-60). So also when he addresses the last sign (RA, 183). He reiterates this point in the third part of *Religious Affections* (RA, 308-09). Edwards' concern here is that people are basing their sense of salvation upon accidental elements of God's work of invitation (whether or not they have truly responded to that invitation), and thus are assuming things about their spiritual state without proper indication from the more "distinguishing and certain" signs of the saving influence of the Spirit.

While each sign cannot be treated individually in the present study (cf. Smith 1992b, McDermott 1995), I may use, as an example of Edwards' approach to discernment in the second part of this book, the issue of the "order" of affections. As mentioned above, it was common in Puritan circles to think of the work of the Spirit with an individual as proceeding through a number of separate stages, each of which can be identified by the presence of particular experiences in the recipient. Thus, it was expected that people would experience a stage of "conviction" or "legal humiliation," in which they would feel a sense of their own sinfulness and the rightful judgment of God upon them, or similar affections. Only after this, and after "closing with Christ," would they experience the acceptance of God on the basis of Christ's work on the cross, the glories of their salvation. Thus, in much Puritan tradition, the discernment of "saving experience" was tied to the sequence of affections experienced. No sorrows, no salvation.

As noted in passing above, Edwards, struggled with this assumption. He states, in the first extant entry in his "Diary" [December 18, 1722],

The reason why I in the last question my interest in God's love and favour, is,—1. Because I cannot speak so fully to my experience of that preparatory work, of which the divines speak:—

2. I do not remember that I experienced regeneration, exactly
in those steps, in which divines say it is generally wrought.
(Edwards 1998, 759)

Months later, he repeats this concern, and attaches to it a resolution:

The chief thing, that now makes me in any measure to question
my good estate, is my not having experienced conversion in
those particular steps, wherein the people of New England, and
anciently the dissenters of Old England, used to experience it.
Wherefore, now resolved, never to leave searching, till I have
satisfyingly found out the very bottom and foundation, the real
reason, why they used to be converted in those steps. (Edwards
1998, 779 [August 12, 1723])

Edwards' own turn to Christ grew not from first a sense of terrors and
then of the joys of salvation. Rather it came for him from a realization of the blessed beauty of God's sovereign holiness. David
Laurence has drawn attention to a few "Miscellanies," written by
Edwards somewhat after this time, in which Edwards inquires of the
presence of faith in the experience of humiliation (Laurence 1979,
272).

In *Religious Affections*, Edwards appears ambiguous on this point.
For this reason, Edwards' interpreters are not agreed in their portrait
of Edwards concerning his approach to the preparationist scheme of
conversion (cf. Cherry 1990, 62-70; Smith 1992b, 6; Wilson-Kastner
1978, 15-20; Laurence 1979; Lovelace 1989, 304-305). On the one
hand, Edwards explicitly distinguishes between "legal" and "evangelical" humiliation (RA, 311-315), and here in the second part of the
book he asserts and defends from scripture and history that a development from law to gospel is "God's ordinary manner" of operation
(152-155). He uses this point to defend the thesis that the order *may*
be evidence of these affections being from saving influences of the
Spirit. But, on the other hand, he argues that the order of experiences
does not *necessitate* confirmation of a saving experience of the Spirit.
The terrors or joys may be a consequence of the person's "constitution
and temper" (RA, 156-57); their own corruption may lead them to
experiences which closely resemble those assumed to be in connection
with salvation (RA, 157-58); or Satan can counterfeit the external

appearance and order of experiences (both common and saving), though he cannot "*exactly* imitate divine operations in their nature" (RA, 159). Indeed the Holy Spirit, apart from saving grace, may have a tremendous influence on a person (RA, 159-60). Finally, he points to "experience" or observation. He appeals to the ministers of the land. They have seen those who account for their conversion with all the right stages, yet "don't prove well." He says, "The manner of the Spirit's proceeding in them that are born of the Spirit, is very often exceeding mysterious and unsearchable: we, as it were, hear the sound of it, the effect of it is discernible; but no man can tell whence it came, or whither it went" (RA, 161). He points to the manifest variation in the works of the Spirit, as seen in the awakening. Edwards' conclusion on this point is worthy of being considered a "saying of the Fathers" on Christian discernment:

> What we have principally to do with, in our inquiries into our own state, or directions we give others, is the nature of the effect that God has brought to pass in the soul. As to the steps which the Spirit of God took to bring that effect to pass, we may leave them to him. We are often in Scripture expressly directed to try ourselves by the *nature* of the fruits of the Spirit; but nowhere by the Spirit's *method* of producing them (RA, 162).

Thus while God ordinarily progresses people through successive stages of "law" to "grace," the categories used to identify this development easily become overly rigid. Indeed, the Spirit may choose to work sovereignly in a manner one has not expected. Good discernment requires a respect for the sovereignty of the Spirit's work and the frailty of our own categories.

The Third Part

Having eliminated, in part two, those criteria for discernment of religious affections which are "not certain," Edwards turns to identify those criteria which "are distinguishing signs of truly gracious and holy affections." Edwards aims not merely to identify those indications of the work of the Spirit in general, but rather to point to those characteristics which distinguish the gracious or saving influence of the Spirit in the experience of particular affections. For this reason, the lists of "positive signs" between *Distinguishing Marks* and *Religious Affections* are similar yet different. While the raising of scripture or the exaltation of Jesus may be a sign of the work of the Spirit of God in general, it does not necessarily follow that just because scripture is exalted or that there is an increase of interest in Christ in a given experience, one has experienced a saving transformation. As noted, even the appearance of love can be counterfeited. Edwards' task in *Religious Affections* is to distill the essence of authentic Christian conversion and to display this essence in such a way that by careful observation of one's affective tendencies, in comparison with this essence so displayed, one can come to a fair judgment concerning his or her spiritual state. Edwards marshalled all of his philosophical, theological, and psychological brilliance for this task, and in so doing, he presents one of the finest treatments on Christian conversion written.

Edwards proceeds in the third part of the book by presenting twelve signs of gracious affections. They are as follows:

1. they arise from influences that are spiritual, supernatural, and divine
2. the first objective ground is the excellent and amiable nature of divine things as they are in themselves
3. they are founded on the loveliness of the moral excellency of divine things
4. they arise from the mind's being enlightened
5. they are attended with a reasonable and spiritual conviction of the truth of the things of religion
6. they are attended with evangelical humiliation
7. they are attended with a change of nature
8. they tend to and are attended with the lamblike, dovelike temper and spirit of Jesus Christ
9. they are attended and followed with a Christian tenderness of spirit
10. they possess beautiful symmetry and proportion
11. the higher the affections are raised, the more spiritual appetite and longing of soul after spiritual attainments are increased
12. they have their exercise and fruit in Christian practice.

John Smith notes that Edwards, "pays attention to three 'directions' in connection with signs; in some cases the direction is the affection itself, in others the emphasis is on the ground of the affection or what calls it forth, and in still others, Edwards is concerned with the consequences or what issues from an affection" (Smith 1992b, 37). I am convinced that this same division structures the twelve signs which Edwards presents in the third part of *Religious Affections*, such that the entire part forms a structure for Puritan self-examination which covers the beginning, middle, and end of affective motions. Edwards introduces the first four signs by language which speaks of the affections "rising from" or having their "foundation" in the sign mentioned (RA, 197, 240, 241, 253, 254, 257, 267). The fifth through seventh signs are introduced by speaking of the affections being "attended with" certain characteristics (RA, 291, 311, 340, 395). The eighth and ninth signs supplement and enlarge the seventh. They speak of the affections as "tending to and attended with," as "begetting" or "promoting," as being "under the government of," or as "attended and followed with" (RA, 344, 345, 346, 347). The affections of the tenth sign both "are" and "extend" symmetry and proportion (RA, 365, 370). And finally, the eleventh and twelfth signs indicate consequences which flow from the affections, either as tendencies which follow changes in the affections ("the higher, the more" RA, 376), or as the "exercise and fruit" of the affections (RA, 383). I believe that this structure in itself is part of Edwards' approach to discernment. His own diary reveals how deeply the practice of self-examination by a review of "resolutions" or signs was ingrained in his experience of God (cf. Edwards 1998, 752-59 along with 759-89). *Religious Affections* forms the framework of such a self-examination both for aspirants for profession of faith, and for the ministers who assist others in the knowledge of their experiences, especially in the context of a work of God.

As in *Distinguishing Marks*, the reader of *Religious Affections* will discover the views and practices of his audience and context by a careful review of Edwards' applications scattered throughout the book. Edwards' concern is to expose the traps and snares into which many people have fallen by failure of discernment, causing damage to themselves and to the revival of religion in general. He lists a number of these "forms of enthusiasm" in his discussion of the fourth sign:

"all imaginary sights of God and Christ and heaven, all supposed witnessing of the Spirit, and testimonies of the love of God by immediate suggestion; and all impressions of future

events, and immediate revelations of any secret facts whatsoever; all enthusiastical impressions and applications of words
of Scripture, as though they were words now immediately
spoken by God to a particular person, . . ." (RA, 286).

Edwards concedes, following his treatment in *Distinguishing Marks*
and *Some Thoughts* that such experiences may attend saving
influences of the Spirit (e.g. RA, 290-91). However, to make these
the *foundation* of one's sense of salvation or religious self-image, or
to make them into a normative "practice" or a criteria of a Christian
community elite, is going beyond their purpose and crosses over into
false discernment procedure. Edwards would ask the reader to look
and see what the affections *arise from*. Do they arise from the
regenerating, sanctifying work of the Spirit? Then, attended or
unattended with "impressions," it is likely to be gracious. Do the
affections arise from the mere presence of or association with the illu-
minations themselves? Then probably these affections are not saving.
What are these affections *attended with?* Do you see them attended
with humility or the dovelike spirit of Christ or do you see them
attended with an excitement and pride over the possession of the experiences themselves? What fruit is produced from the affections? Do
the experiences of God lead the person to acts of charity, service, and
love, or do they lead the person into self-righteous self-service? A
review of questions like these will indicate the divine character of the
religious affections experienced. Once again, as in *Distinguishing
Marks*, Edwards indicates that by careful observation of the "manner"
of the affective motions in comparison with biblically-consistent
criteria, one comes to a safe judgment concerning the objects of discernment.

The mention of a "safe judgment" brings me to the question of
certainty. How certain did Edwards think the judgments based on his
criteria were? Edwards addresses this point in the introduction to his
third part of *Religious Affections*. He states, "that I am far from
undertaking to give such signs of gracious affections, as shall be sufficient to enable any certainly to distinguish true affection from false
affection in others; or to determine positively which of their neigh-
bors are true professors, and which are hypocrites" (RA, 193; and
with this he condemns the practice of censuring so damaging to the
revival). Furthermore he warns the readers that "no signs are to be

expected, that shall be sufficient to enable those saints certainly to discern their own state, who are very low in grace, or are such as have much departed from God" (RA, 193; so also for the "hypocrite" with false confidence). Edwards does not intend *Religious Affections* for neophytes or backsliders but rather for mature believers or the ministers who assist them. While Edwards at times appears to expect an overlarge transformation in initial conversion, he does acknowledge the developmental aspects of conversion (cf. RA, 283, 306-07, 356; cf. DM, 236), and he is aware that discernment is dependent upon the maturity of the discerner. Assurance of one's own state, is ultimately (and especially for those mentioned) a matter of practice, not self-examination. Edwards, realizing the limits of his own treatise, asserts that

'Tis not God's design that men should obtain assurance in any other way, than by mortifying corruption, and increasing in grace, and obtaining the lively exercises of it. And although self-examination be a duty of great use and importance, and by no means to be neglected; yet it is not the principle means, by which the saints do get satisfaction of their good estate. Assurance is not to be obtained so much by self-examination, as by action (RA, 195).

He defends this thesis at length in his discussion of the twelfth sign. Illusory absolute certainty or false confidence based upon wrong criteria are precisely what Edwards argues against in *Religious Affections*. This book is offered to mature believers and those who help others to provide a framework which can help lead to "moral certainty," a sufficiently reasonable confidence to act upon the judgment. Indeed, if one considers the large percentage of space given to the final sign, *Religious Affections* can not only be seen as a framework of self-examination, but also as a call to action.

Edwards spends more time in *Religious Affections* than in his other revival works describing the strategies of the enemy. Whereas in *Distinguishing Marks*, Edwards referred to the quote about the Devil masquerading as an angel of light in order to argue that the presence of the enemy's's work is insufficient evidence to conclude that a work can't be a work of God, here he uses the same passage to warn his readers of the enemy's ploys under the appearance of good (RA, 287-

88). Indeed, as mentioned above, it is concern with the ground gained over revivals by the enemy under the appearance of good that stimulates the writing of *Religious Affections*. Edwards is especially conscious of the ploys of the enemy with regard to people's experiences of imaginative "impressions." Just as Ignatius witnessed the great good that could be stimulated through the use of human imagination, so Edwards witnessed the great damage that can be done by undo confidence in undiscerned imaginative images (RA, 288-91). By means of impressions, texts of scripture and such, the tendency of the enemy is to draw people "little by little" away from the purity of their first response to God, much as Ignatius spoke of the critical dynamics in the moment after an experience of a consolation without previous cause (cf. RA, 309-10).

In spite of Edwards' heightened awareness of the enemy in *Religious Affections*, his overwhelming focus remains upon the dynamics of the Spirit of God. It is a book on discerning "gracious affections" and the distinguishing signs of the Spirit of God remain primary in *Religious Affections*. One brief sample of his insight on such matters must suffice. Edwards, reminiscent of Ignatius' first rule for the discernment of spirits, states,

> For so hath God contrived and constituted things, in his dispensations towards his own people, that when their love decays, and the exercises of it fail, or become weak, fear should arise; for then they need it to restrain them from sin, and to excite 'em to care for the good of their souls, and so to stir them up to watchfulness and diligence in religion: but God hath so ordered that when love rises, and is in vigorous exercise, then fear should vanish, and be driven away; for then they need it not, having a higher and more excellent principle in exercise, to restrain 'em from sin, and stir 'em up to their duty (RA, 179).

It is impossible here to present an exegesis or a summary of each of Edwards' twelve positive signs of gracious affections (cf. Smith 1992b, 38-55; McDermott 1995). However, because a grasp of Edwards' notion of "spiritual understanding," or the perception of excellency by means of the sense of the heart, is critical to a proper understanding of Edwards' approach to discernment as presented in

Religious Affections, I will give a sense of Edwards' approach by means of a presentation of Edwards' fourth positive sign. Edwards' fourth sign states that "gracious affections do arise from the mind's being enlightened, rightly and spiritually to understand or apprehend divine things" (RA, 266). He presents his conclusion concerning the nature of this "spiritual understanding" a few pages later: "that it consists in a sense of the heart, of the supreme beauty and sweetness of the holiness or moral perfection of divine things, together with all that discerning and knowledge of things of religion, that depends upon, and flows from such a sense" (RA, 272). My comments on this sign will follow the structure of this passage, as well as that of the first two parts of the dissertation by Robert Colacurcio on this topic (cf. Colacurcio, 1972, 1-147).

First, spiritual understanding, for Edwards consists in a "sense of the heart." Here, he briefly distinguishes this sense of the heart from a mere "notional understanding" which does not involve inclination. However, to gain a more adequate grasp of Edwards' notion of the sense of the heart I must turn to one of his Miscellanies, number 782. Perry Miller, who first published this Miscellany, dates the piece at about 1745, the year before *Religious Affections* was published (Miller 1948, 124). The starting point for Edwards' reflections in this Miscellany is a dialogue with John Locke's treatment of the relationship between words and ideas (Locke 1961 [1722], III.i.1; III.ii.6). Human thought can proceed with actual ideas of things in the mind, or it can proceed by substituting words for these ideas, allowing signification to simplify the thought process. As Colacurcio summarizes, "An actual idea makes sense out of the manifold of experience without abstracting from or impoverishing its sensible components" (Colacurcio 1972, 91). Edwards labels the thought by signs "cogitation" or "indirect apprehension." He calls thought which involves an actual idea of the thing "ideal apprehension." Ideal apprehension can pertain to the faculty of understanding or that of the will or heart (foreshadowing the division of faculties he presents in *Religious Affections*). Common language refers to an ideal apprehension that has reference to the heart as "having a sense of it." All that understanding which either (a) involves mere cogitation or (b) involves ideal knowledge, yet without involvement of the will or heart, Edwards labels "speculation." He calls that ideal apprehension which involves the heart "the sense of the heart" (Edwards 1948

[1745], 136). This sense of the heart or "sensible knowledge" is oriented to polar realities (good-bad), perceiving and responding to an "inward tasting or feeling, of sweetness or pleasure, bitterness or pain."

Now this sense of the heart or sensible knowledge can come in one of two ways, either purely naturally or with some "immediate influence of the Spirit." Furthermore sensible knowledge can also be divided with regards to its object: either natural or spiritual good. Because a sense of spiritual good and evil do not possess "any agreeableness, or disagreeableness to human nature as such" (Edwards 1948 [1745], 141; on agreeableness and disagreeableness and consent cf. Miller 1981, 241; Delattre 1968, 42, 211; Smith 1992b, 108; Anderson 1980, 89-90), Edwards reflects, "therefore men merely with the exercise of those faculties, and their own natural strength, can do nothing towards getting such a sense of divine things, but it must be wholly and entirely a work of the Spirit of God, not merely assisting and coworking with natural principles, but as infusing something above nature" (1948 [1745], 141). Upon this basis he distinguishes between common or preparatory influences of the Spirit and saving influences. He concludes, "The special work of the Spirit, or that which is peculiar to the Saints [that which is "saving"], consists in giving the sensible knowledge of the things of religion with respect to their spiritual good or evil; which indeed does all originally consist in a sense of the spiritual excellency, beauty, or sweetness, of divine things, which is not by assisting natural principles, but by infusing something supernatural" (Edwards 1948 [1745], 142). In this sentence, One not only sees the foundations of the quote from the fourth sign, but one also sees the roots of the first through the fourth and seventh signs. Immediately following this sentence Edwards indicates how conviction of the truth of the things of religion (sign five) and true saving faith (the theme of religious affections) flow from this spiritual understanding (1948 [1745], 142-43).

Second, the object of this sense of the heart is "the supreme beauty and sweetness of the holiness or moral perfection of divine things." "Beauty" or "excellency" in the thought of Edwards has been the topic of a great deal of discussion in the past few decades (cf. Delattre 1968; Holbrook 1973; Lee 1988, 146-169; Daniel 1994, 177-196). To quote Delattre (1968, 2), "for Edwards beauty is the key to the structure and dynamics of the moral and religious life." Edwards treats the character of excellence in his first entry in the set of reflections titled, "The Mind." Starting from the proposition of his contemporaries that excellency or beauty (he uses these words inter changeably here and elsewhere) involves symmetry or proportion, Edwards identifies this proportion as equality of relation, and thus concludes that, "all beauty consists in similarness, or identity of relation" (Edwards 1980 [1723?], 334). The more complex and yet harmonious the relations, the greater the beauty. The "relation" between elements involves a certain orientation, called by Edwards "consent" or "dissent" (also labeled "agreement" or "disagreement"). Thus Edwards writes,

> Excellency consists in the similarness of one being to another—not merely equality and proportion, but any kind of similarness. . . . This is an universal definition of excellency: The consent of being to being, or being's consent to entity. The more the consent is, and the more extensive, the greater is the excellency. (1980 [1723?], 336)

Consent exists proper to the "being" in relation. With human and divine beings that consent is a "consent of spirits to one another" and is fulfilled in love. From this understanding of consent one can see how Edwards understands the sovereign God to be the objective foundation of beauty and the object of the sense of the heart. "Now God is the prime and original being," Edwards writes, "the first and the last, and the pattern of all, and has the sum of all perfection. We may therefore doubtless conclude that all that is the perfection of spirits may be resolved into that which is God's perfection, which is love" (Edwards 1980 [1723?], 363). Edwards states in *Religious Affections*, "This infinite excellency of the divine nature, as it is in itself, is the true ground of all that is good in God in any respect" (RA, 243). The goodness God *possesses* toward humankind derives from the goodness which God *is* (cf. Delattre 1968, 82).

Third, since spiritual understanding involves ideal apprehensions that pertain to the heart which responds to value, and since God, as pure excellency, is the highest value, it follows that the heart serves as the proper vehicle of human-divine relationship. Thus the affections become central. As the excellency perceived is greater, the heart is greater affected. Thus, spiritual understanding or "true religion" lies greatly in the affections. It involves the development of interest, passion, and feeling (cf. Cooey 1989).

Yet, as Delattre notes, "the attractive power of the apparent good is in part, then, a function not only of the apprehension of the beauty in that good but also of the manner of view of that beauty, whether "sensible" and grounded in personal experience or "notional" and acquired at second-hand" (Delattre 1968, 92). One can speak of the beauty of God either with an actual idea of this beauty in the mind, or one can speak of it reflecting words heard or read, having no "sense" of what is spoken. The frame of mind with which one approaches reality affects the ability to recognize the excellency therein. And when dealing with divine beauty, the human frame is so weak and corrupt it has no ability to orient itself such that it can grasp the divine excellence as it is in itself. This kind of re-orientation requires "a work of the Spirit of God, not merely assisting and coworking with natural principles, but as infusing something above nature" (Edwards 1948 [1745], 141). The Holy Spirit, who *is* the substantial love and beauty of the Godhead (cf. Delattre 1968, 152-156), communicates this sense of God's excellence to the believer through regeneration. The perception of excellency is a gift given to the believer at conversion (Colacurcio 1972, 106-118).

Finally, spiritual understanding manifests itself in "all that discerning and knowledge of things of religion, that depends upon, and flows from such a sense" (RA, 272). Gerald McDermott writes, "it is not just the beauty of God himself that the saint knows and sees. Once we have caught a glimpse of the beauty of the Godhead, everything else in life—all the world and all of existence—takes on a new color. Everywhere we look there is beauty" (McDermott 1995, 129). Edwards develops this at length in *Religious Affections*. "By this sense of the moral beauty of divine things," he writes, "is understood the sufficiency of Christ as mediator. . . By this is seen the excellency of the Word of God . . . by this is seen the true foundation of our duty . . ." (RA, 273-74). The truth and character of "the things of religion" are truly perceived when viewed in the light of this spiritual understanding, which has as its object the beauty of God; thus "there arises from this sense of spiritual beauty, all true experimental knowledge of religion" (RA, 275).

The consequence of this for discernment is that whereas Ignatius emphasized the development of a connaturality to Christ formed through the discernments of self-examination and appreciation in ongoing conversion, Edwards draws attention to the need for the presence of an intuitive dimension of discernment which derives from an *infused connaturality* given to the believer at initial conversion. This connaturality involves understanding and inclination, head and heart. In the regenerated believer, the inner work of the Spirit functions to give a taste, a sense, a permanent template of divine excellency, which develops by degrees and which can serve as an inner criterion against which the phenomena of discernment can be compared. Edwards gives an excellent example of this in a note on prophetic inspiration in his notes on "The Mind":

> The evidence of immediate inspiration that the prophets had when they were immediately inspired by the Spirit of God with any truth is an absolute sort of certainty; and the knowledge is in a sense intuitive, much in the same manner as faith and spiritual knowledge of the truth of religion. Such bright ideas are raised, and such a clear view of a perfect agreement with the excellencies of the divine nature, that it's known to be communication from him. (1980 [1723?], 346)

For Jonathan Edwards, discernment not only involves the careful observation of phenomena in light of biblically-grounded criteria, but it also involves the exercise of an intuitive dimension. "Much in the same manner" as the prophets of old, there is, within the converted and maturing believer, an immediate and "felt" grasp of the things of religion, rooted in a connaturality instilled and developed by the regenerating and sanctifying Spirit of God. However imperfectly exercised in the context of revival movements, Edwards maintained that it was this transformation of understanding, and not mere experiences of illumination, that is the true foundation of gracious affections and Christian discernment.

Summary and Implications

Edwards was concerned about discernment. He states that, "it is a subject on which my mind has been peculiarly intent, ever since I first entered on the study of divinity" (RA, 84). In *Distinguishing Marks* and *Religious Affections* Edwards presents his approach to discernment.   The process of discernment is basically the same in both works.   He corrects false criteria used to evaluate phenomena.   He presents biblically-grounded criteria which are used as guides for careful observation.   In *Religious Affections*, Edwards develops the intuitive aspect of discernment, by which the converted believer perceives divine excellency, and in so doing, perceives the "things of religion" anew.   By careful observation in light of appropriate and biblically-grounded criteria, attentive to the intuitive sense of the divine given through the Spirit, the believer can be make a fair judgment concerning the phenomena which confronts oneself or others.   In this sense Edwards, like Ignatius, intuitively approaches discernment as a process of "coming to know," an act of knowing.

While I have revealed that the process of discernment presented in each of these treatises is essentially the same, I have also demonstrated that the object of discernment in each work was different.   In *Distinguishing Marks*, the object in view was the work of God "in general."   The phenomenon evaluated was the awakening in process—whether it be a legitimate "work of God" (and worthy of promotion) or not.   In *Religious Affections* the object was not the work of God in general, but rather the affective operations experienced in the context of a work of God.   It was the parts, rather than the whole, that were evaluated in *Religious Affections*.   Likewise, while it was the critics who were the opposition in *Distinguishing Marks*, in *Religious Affections* it was the "enthusiasts" who received the strongest attack.   In the first treatise it was an affective trend which served as the object of discernment; in the second it was the affections themselves as experienced by the individual.

Because of the similarity of process envisioned by Edwards, yet the difference of object, I indicated that the criteria of discernment in these two treatises were similar, yet distinct.   The positive signs presented in *Distinguishing Marks* were those that were sufficient to determine a work of God in general.   Exaltation of Jesus, increased respect for the scriptures, increase of love and decrease of sin: all of these indicate where the Spirit of God is at work in a people over a wide space and time.   Yet in *Religious Affections* the target is much more specific.   Edwards pursues the distinction not merely between that which is from God and that which is not from God, but more specifically between that which is a *particular type* of work of God— namely a "gracious" or "saving" work—and all else.   Only those signs which point to the transformative (not merely invitatory) work of the Spirit were allowed for consideration in *Religious Affections*. For this reason, Edwards' positive signs in *Religious Affections* provide an outline of a theology of Christian conversion.

Finally, I must summarize Edwards' understanding of the role(s) of affectivity in Christian discernment. As noted already, affections served in each treatise as the object of discernment; however, they served in different ways. In *Distinguishing Marks*, Edwards addressed the general affective trend that was impacting numbers of people in New England, and established principles by which such an affective trend could be fairly evaluated. In *Religious Affections*, he addressed the affections themselves, as experienced by individuals in the context of a revival. For Edwards' situation the affectivity which shaped the *context* of discernment also became the *object* of discernment. Edwards' works present a uniquely brilliant and balanced articulation of reflection on the roles of affectivity in the light of his contemporaries (cf. Proudfoot 1989, 167). Edwards was aware of the impact of spiritual forces upon the affective experiences of individuals. Divine and evil spirit could both be involved in the exciting of affections in a given person. While Edwards presents insightful comments on the strategies of the enemy, however, his primary focus was upon the signs and work of the Holy Spirit.

In these two treatises, Edwards is less interested in the formation of the discerner, than in articulating appropriate criteria for discernment, in proposing "rules for the discernment of the Spirit." He speaks little of the affective preparation of the believer for discernment. Edwards' thoughts on the role(s) of affectivity in the *subject* of discernment are, for the most part, limited to his comments on the transformation of the discerner through the enlightenment of conversion, what might be called infused connaturality through regenerative transformation. As the Holy Spirit infuses the believer with a spiritual understanding, the "sense of the heart" for divine excellency, and as that understanding or sense is increased and purified through the sanctifying work of the Spirit, there arises an increased intuitive resonance with the things of religion. In this manner the discernment of that which is from God becomes gradually more and more natural.

Finally, affectivity functions within Edwards' understanding of affectivity as a part of the act of discernment itself. Contrary to Chauncy's scholastic psychology, Edwards' approach to affectivity gives it an important role in apprehending value and something of the nature of things. Especially in *Religious Affections*, where the objects of the discernment are individual affections, affectivity functions as essential components of the positive signs for a thorough examination of the beginning, middle, and end of one's course of affective experience. In both treatises it is attention to the "manner" of affectivity which is key to the evaluation. For Edwards, affectivity is involved in the process of discernment insofar as it is active in the review of positive signs. Observing the quality and trajectory of affective experience through its beginning, middle, and end, requires the engagement of affectivity itself, as well as an "affective memory." Though Edwards does not develop this aspect of the role of affectivity in the discernment process, his approach cannot be understood without it. Edwards also understands affectivity to be involved in the act of discernment in a more intuitive fashion simply by enabling one to "sense" that which is from God more easily by virtue of the active presence of the Spirit bringing to the believer an enlightened grasp of divine excellency.

Conclusions: Discernment as an Affectively-Rich Act of Knowing

Having reviewed the approach to discernment in Ignatius of Loyola and Jonathan Edwards, I am now in a position to summarize the picture of discernment that appears from looking at their works. What does discernment look like? This is the question of the present chapter. I have been examining the possibility of understanding Christian discernment as an affectively-rich act of knowing, and have presented the works of two representatives from the history of spirituality in order to give a more intuitive portrait of Christian discernment as defined in chapter one. In these conclusions, I will address the notion of discernment as an act of coming to know. Then I will discuss the notion of discernment as affectively-rich.

Coming to Know

Ignatius of Loyola and Jonathan Edwards discuss a similar topic in two very different contexts. Ignatius wrote from the context of Roman Catholicism at the onset of the Reformation. Edwards wrote from the context of American Puritanism at the onset of Protestant liberalism. Ignatius wrote a carefully structured manual for spiritual directors. Edwards wrote a carefully argued treatise for ministers and mature believers. Insofar as they offered books for "helpers of souls" they were similar offerings. Each identified different objects of discernment in their works. I showed that Ignatius applied discernment to six different areas of life, thus identifying six different "types" of discernment: the discernment of sinful patterns through self-examination, the identification of the influence of different forces through the discernment of spirits, the orientation of the mind and heart to Christ through the discernment of appreciation, the making of a choice of life through the discernment of election, the recognition of the presence of God in all things through the discerning contemplation to attain love, and the affirmation of the presence of God in the Church through the discerning rules for thinking with the Church. Edwards aimed *Distinguishing Marks* and *Religious Affections* at two separate concerns, thus identifying two separate objects for discernment: the revival movement "in general," and the particular affections which are experienced in the context of a work of God. Yet in the midst of these different contexts and aimed at these different objects, the question is the same: how is one to come to know that which is significantly related to God? Whether the issue was the distinction between influences of good or bad spirits, or the identification of a choice of life that flows from the influence of God, each work, each type of discernment attempted to demonstrate a way to "come to know," that which is "from God." It is their presentation of the identification or categorization of the presence or activity of the divine which makes these works of discernment.

Both Ignatius and Edwards approached discernment with an assumption that discernment was enacted in the context of conflict. Both Ignatius and Edwards made reference to the evil forces that create the need for discernment in many situations. Both understood the ways the enemy works "little by little" to draw people away from the truth. Both understood that the Spirit of God tends to operate towards those moving from "bad to worse" (or to use Edwards' language, "when the exercises of love fail") with force, while that same Spirit tends to woo those who are moving from "good to better" ("when love rises") with sweetness. Both understood that the enemy will deceive people by influencing them "under the appearance of good," although Edwards did not restrict this rule to the more mature believers (Ignatius places this Rule in those for the Second Week). Rather Edwards saw how this type of strategy is frequently used by the enemy even to prevent people from receiving the first fruits of saving grace. Ignatius offered some insight concerning the ways of the good spirit but focused his attention, in the first set of "Rules" in particular, on the works of the evil spirit. As noted above, Phillip Endean suggests that it would be appropriate to supplement Ignatius' rules with "material on the roles of the good spirit in the process of conversion" (Endean 1976, 51). Edwards, making some mention of the work of the enemy but centering attention upon the nature of the works of the Spirit of God, provides just such a supplement.

Neither Ignatius nor Edwards sought to give a merely descriptive account of Christian discernment. Though well acquainted with the practices of those around them, their interest in discernment was not *describing* current practice, but rather in *improving* current practice. Both were well aware of common errors of discernment caused by natural categorization biases and heuristics. Edwards in particular goes into great detail in his works to demonstrate the fallacious nature of such criteria, even though he recognizes the natural tendency to look to the salience of particular features (noise, bodily effects, and the like) or commonly known prototypes (example being used) as indicators of the divine. Instead both Edwards and Ignatius present a normative approach to discernment, a format of self-controlled actions which, when properly followed, should result in a more reliable grasp of that which is or is not from God. I will turn attention to this normative ideal, which if not fully obtainable (neither Ignatius nor Edwards held to absolute certainty of knowledge) could at least be approximated through self-controlled acts, as well as to the epistemological underpinnings for such an ideal, in the philosophical portion of this study.

It seems reasonable to understand discernment, as presented in these works, as a process or act of knowing in the context of a converted and converting faith. Discernment, for Ignatius, was a process of coming to recognize, understand/appreciate, and respond. This same basic structure was present, with more or less emphasis, in each of the various types of discernment discussed in the *Exercises*. Edwards does not address the structure of the discerning process other than to indicate by the order of his "positive signs" in *Religious*

Affections, a movement from beginning, through middle, to end in the process of self-examination. Edwards' emphasis is less on the *process* of discernment, as the *criteria* which insure a "safe judgment" from the process. For Edwards, as for Ignatius, discernment at its best is accomplished through the careful observation of the tendencies of thought, feeling, behavior of oneself or others in light of (1) biblically-grounded criteria, and (2) the enlightenment of the Holy Spirit, resulting in a judgment. In both figures one can see epistemologically significant language being used to describe discernment. Furthermore, this discerning act of knowing occurs within the context of a converted and converting believer. In Ignatius, the emphasis on the context of conversion is stressed both in the important role that the Foundation plays at the inception of the *Exercises* and in the emphasis upon the healing of "disordered affections" found throughout the *Exercises*. In Edwards, it is stressed in his developed theology of the works of the Spirit, preparatory works, saving works, and sanctifying works.

Affectively-Rich

Ignatius and Edwards struggled with language to describe the nature of affectivity. Ignatius uses a variety of terms to refer to affective experience. He uses, but stretches, the scholastic psychological framework he inherited. Interpreters frequently dispute the precise referent of such terms as "consolation," "without prior cause," "inclination" and "will." Likewise, Edwards develops a philosophical psychology unique to his time in order to express his understanding of affective experience. Yet, their attempts at describing the nature of affective experience touch upon many aspects which have been mentioned by contemporary scientific studies on "the emotions." In the following chapter I will show how contemporary research in affectivity supplies both a language and a measure of scientific precision to an understanding of the roles which affectivity plays in the process of Christian discernment.

Nonetheless, both Ignatius and Edwards affirmed the valuable role which affectivity plays in human experience. While these two men came from different contexts and probably understood the nature of affections slightly differently, rather than relegating affective experience to a unhealthy vestige of the animal nature, both Ignatius and

Edwards regarded affectivity as a special means of the communication of the Spirit of God to the human soul. Repeatedly in the *Exercises*, Ignatius urged the excercitant to pray for what she or he desires. Indeed the success of the *Exercises* depends upon the reception of "what I desire." The "what" of that desire are affections: to be moved with tears for my sin, to be inspired to imitate Christ, to feel sorrow for Christ's death, to rejoice exceedingly. Ignatius expected and assumed the excercitant will experience consolations in the course of the *Exercises*, times when the exercitant will be drawn to Christ through specific pleasurable experiences. For these reasons He encourages the exercitant to alter posture, light, surroundings, meditations—anything that will cultivate the experience of the consolation desired [89]. For Ignatius affective "motions" mediate and indicate the activity of the Spirit of God. Edwards also considered affectivity an important element in the faith. For Edwards, "true religion, in great part, consists in the affections" He defended this from every possible angle in the first part of *Religious Affections*. The religion of scripture is affective; the religion of the saints is affective; the religion of heaven is affective; religion ought to be affective. The supreme excellency of the divine nature is perceived through affectivity. The love of Christianity is lived through affective experience. Thus, like Ignatius, Edwards encouraged the use of such means, "as have much of a tendency to move the affections" (RA, 121).

Ignatius and Edwards understood the affective context of discernment to be that of a converted and converting believer. Thus, affectivity plays a role in shaping the *subject* of discernment. This is assumed for Ignatius in the procedure of giving the *Exercises*. Exercitants begin with the Foundation; they are given no more than they are able to handle; they learn the lessons in discernment cumulatively. As watchfulness improves, the exercitants develop affective sensitivity and disordered affections are purified. Then the affective context of the excercitants change, and they can grasp discernment more deeply. Edwards emphasizes less the purifying disordered affections through spiritual formation, but rather the correction of enthusiastic or dead affections through spiritual information. Edwards' treatises were presented to expose the snares and traps by which the enemy had gained ground over the revival, either in the rejection of affectivity or in the misconduct surrounding its promotion. Disordered approaches to affectivity itself were at the core of these errors, and Edwards wrote *Distinguishing Marks* and especially *Religious Affections* in order to correct them. Both Ignatius and Edwards understood that quality discernment was contingent upon the development of a certain connaturality or sympathetic identity of consciousness. Furthermore, both understood this connaturality to be mediated through a affectively-rich sight of the divine excellency. Ignatius cultivated this connaturality in his excercitants through the fostering of appreciation in Gospel contemplation. By setting the eyes of his excercitants upon the person of Christ, they are attracted to and re-engaged with the values, feelings, and concerns of the divine. Edwards emphasized the connaturality which comes through the initial transforming work of the Holy Spirit. Apart from the enlightenment of the Spirit, persons have no possibility of tasting the sweetness of divine excellency. Then as the Spirit continues to sanctify the believer, this sense of the heart is increased and the sight of divine beauty increases, bringing light not only to one's sight of God, but to all life.

Affectivity also functioned as part of the conscious and unconscious *context* of both Ignatius and Edwards. Ignatius was aware of the background of the *alumbrados*, of the Roman hierarchy, and therefore of the approaches to the use of affectivity his excercitants might bring to the *Excercises*. It was for this reason that he crafted the "Rules for the Discernment of Spirits" so carefully. Likewise Edwards was intensely conscious of the contagious aspects of revival, which both promoted and hindered the processing of affect in Christian discernment. It was with these complexities in mind that Edwards clarified discernment by discriminating between "no certain" and "distinguishing" signs of the work of the Spirit in the affective experience of groups and individuals.

Affectivity also functioned in both Ignatius' and Edwards' works as an *object* of discernment, as discussed above. In Ignatius, affectivity operates as the internal immediate object, the principle of which becomes the sign or indicator (mediate object) of the (S)spirit's movement. Consolations and desolations are important objects of discerning evaluation, though they are not the sole objects (movements of the will, behavior patterns, church teachings and such are all appropriate objects of discernment as well). For Edwards the affective trends of a group or the particular affections of an individual become an immediate object of discernment, the "manner" or tendencies of which serve as the mediate objects indicating the source of a given affective object.

Thus, for both Ignatius and Edwards, affectivity functions also as an important element in the *act* of discernment itself. Affectivity functions as a means of perception itself. According to Ignatius, it is by attending to the quality and trajectory of affective operations that their nature and source are discovered. The affections themselves reveal something of the universe around. I emphasized this point in the work of Edwards by drawing attention to his concern for the regard to the "manner" of affective operations. Tendencies, qualities, patterns *within* affective experience reveal something of the nature of spiritual reality. Thus careful observation, attentive to affective experience and informed by biblically-grounded criteria, can lead the discerner to a reasonable judgment of that which is from God. This judgment, however, is not merely of a matter of reason, but a felt intuitive judgment. Both Ignatius and Edwards struggle with language to communicate this aspect of discernment. I shall indicate in chapters four and five how the epistemological significance of "tendencies" in affectivity can be more clearly articulated by means of the framework of American philosophical theology.

I have painted an intuitive portrait, through the work of two figures in the history of Christian spirituality, of Christian discernment understood as an affectively-rich act of knowing. In Chapter Three I shall explore, through the field of experimental psychology, the nature of human categorization, which distinguishes this from that, as well as the nature of human affectivity. In doing so I will attempt to bring a measure of empirical precision to an understanding of Christian discernment.

Chapter 3

Categorization and Affectivity

I have been exploring the idea of Christian discernment as an affectively-rich act of knowing. By doing so I hope to illumine aspects of Christian discernment undeveloped in research to date. As a descriptive introduction to Christian discernment, chapter two presented an overview of Christian discernment in the works of two representatives from the history of Christian spirituality, Ignatius of Loyola and Jonathan Edwards. I demonstrated there that although discernment aimed at a wide variety of "objects" (experiences, decisions, corporate trends, patterns of behavior— even "all things"), the essential process of discernment remained the same. This process consisted of a recognition and understanding in order to respond—a process of knowing. I noted that this process often involved the comparison of some "object" with appropriate criteria. By observing the quality and tendencies of phenomena in light of norms gained through education, conversion, or appreciation, the maturing believer would be best able to differentiate that which is or is not from God. Furthermore I have illustrated the significance of affectivity for this process. Affectivity is involved in discernment at the level of the subject, the context, the object(s), and the very act itself. Discernment is suffused with emotion.

One thing I have not accomplished thus far is the clarification of the central *operations* of discernment. I call "operations" those patterns of mental-physiological activity involved in evaluating, adapting, and responding, to something *as* something, both those that perform a very specific function (such as image-retrieval, concept recognition, event appraisal, or hormonal activation), as well as those that combine particular operations to form larger functions (such as perception, choice, desire, and disgust). My aim in the present chapter is to contribute a measure of specificity to an understanding of the activities involved in Christian discernment, by exploring them as operations in light of the insights of experimental psychology.

Thus we will now move from the descriptive to the "critical" portion of this study. If indeed, Christian discernment can be beneficially explored as an affectively-rich act of knowing, then one ought to be able to provide some illumination to the act of discernment by examining more carefully what takes place in human knowing and human affectivity. Hence I have chosen, in this chapter, to explore empirical research in human categorization and affectivity. Christian discernment aims at a particular kind of knowing: the discrimination of that which is significantly related to God. As such discernment finds its realization in the confident application of a category ("from God" or "not from God") to an instance (an experience, event, decision, etc.). Experimental psychological research in human categorization has recently uncovered a number of significant insights that can help provide a measure of the specificity desired in an intellectually coherent theory of Christian discernment. Similarly, research in affectivity has mushroomed in the past three decades, providing empirically-rooted insights that can help clarify some of the confusion about affectivity in classical discussions of discernment. In this chapter then, I will explore insights from these two fields of study in order to illumine a theory of Christian discernment.

I should give, at the onset of this chapter, a sense of what I expect experimental science to contribute to a theory of Christian spirituality. Donald Gelpi has outlined something of my intentions in his own multidisciplinary integration of insights from developmental psychology to the field of Christology (Gelpi, 1994-95 1:130-32; cf. also Gelpi 1988b, 168-69). He identifies three "positive tasks" that empirical investigations can provide philosophical/theological theories. First, they can validate or strengthen a hypothesis or theory when that theory can coherently and successfully interpret empirical findings. I might add that empirical research can also serve to prevent the validation of a hypothesis when the hypothesis fails to adequately interpret the findings. Second, empirical research can amplify a theory when it supplies more detailed information about particular realms of experience than can be provided from theological/philosophical reflection alone. Finally, scientific research can provide illumination of the particular topic of study. In a similar vein, cognitive psychologist Eleanor Rosch articulates that which she intends her own empirical research to provide to a theory of human cognitive process. She writes, "What the facts . . . contribute to processing notions is a constraint—process models should not be inconsistent with the known facts about prototypes" (Rosch 1978, 40). My assumptions about the integration of empirical and theoretical information parallel those of Gelpi and Rosch. I expect that empirical findings will place a certain constraint upon discernment theory such that one would not espouse interpretations of either actual or ideal Christian discernment that were clearly inconsistent with the clear results of experimental research. I also hope to see the empirical material provide much more detail concerning "what goes on" in the categorizing and affective elements of Christian discernment, detail less available to theological studies. Unfortunately, space allows only for suggestions of how this detail might amplify an understanding of Christian discernment. Nonetheless, I expect that this exploration of Christian discernment in light of experimental psychology will illumine the understanding of Christian discernment by enabling one to see aspects of the discernment process that were not as clear previously.

I have not attempted original empirical investigations in this study. Although empirical research in religious experience is a growing field, developing in both quantity and quality of output (cf. *Journal for the Scientific Study of Religion*, Hood 1995, Hood et al. 1996), the present study is not a direct contribution to that field. I hope that my work will contribute sufficient theoretical groundwork to enable future research to begin the difficult task of defining "discernment" within the parameters of such fields. If this can be accomplished, perhaps future empirical studies can explore more concretely just how Christians today actually "discern" the presence and guidance of God. This chapter is also not simply an "application" of scientific models to religious. I am not interested in simply showing what discernment looks like "in the eyes of," or "from the perspective of" a particular cognitive psychological model. That approach has been utilized to

142   *Affirming the Touch of God*

provide helpful illumination of discernment theory through psychoanalytic and Jungian models as reviewed in chapter one. Rather, in order to maintain a focus upon *empirically grounded specificity* as an aim, I have chosen to stress convergent experimental findings rather than psychological models.

I will summarize empirical findings concerning human categorization and affectivity that will act as constraints upon and amplifications of a theory of Christian discernment, a theory which will be developed in the following chapters. Hence, while I will apply the insights of experimental psychology to Christian discernment throughout the chapter and especially in the summaries, I will reserve a more comprehensive integration and application of the material for the final two chapters. Needless to say, I cannot review all relevant literature in a study of this kind. Nor can I provide detailed descriptions of experimental conditions of individual studies. I have chosen to summarize the work of key scholars and review key themes in hopes that a dialectical investigation of a few key figures might most conveniently yield the discovery of points of convergence, complementarity and agreement that will prove fruitful for the development of a theory of Christian discernment.

The material used here was selected for a variety of reasons. First, I drew largely from literature within the field of "cognitive studies," or "cognitive approaches" to experimental psychology. This branch of psychology proved most appropriate both for exploring discernment as an "act of knowing," and for keeping a focus on measurable experimentation as a primary method of analysis. "Cognitive psychology" grew out of behavioral research in the past few decades. It has retained the emphasis upon experimental method, but shifts in theoretical frameworks and topics of interest toward the exploration of human mental process (cf. Neisser 1967). Most of the research in emotions arises not from the field of "cognitive psychology" per se, but rather represents a dominant approach to affective research in the fields of personality and social psychology. Cognitive approaches to religion are beginning to appear in anthropology (Malley 1996; Boyer 1995), in philosophy (Proudfoot 1985) and in studies of the psychology of religion in general (Hood et al. 1996; McCallister 1995; Watts and Williams 1988). This study represents the first attempt to review the literature with regards to a theory of Christian discernment.

Second, as mentioned above, I have centered my attention on key figures and themes in the development of research in categorization and affectivity. In the section on categorization I will use a roughly historical review of the field (following the structure of Rosch 1994 and Medin 1989), paying special attention to research related to "prototypes" and "basic categories," to exploration of scripts/schemata, and to more recent inquiries concerning categories as "theories." In the section on affectivity I will summarize and synthesize the research of four major figures in emotions research (following the lead of Cornelius 1996).

Finally, I selected material relevant for the illumination of Christian spirituality. For this reason, I will supplement the summary of work with other material relevant to the subject.

Categorizing Meaningful Information: Discernment as an "Act of Knowing"

A theory of Christian discernment should provide an account of "from God" and "not from God" as legitimate categories to which may be attached a variety of experiences, events, or objects. Insofar as the discernment involves an organization of experience *with reference to God*, it becomes the subject of theological and philosophical investigation. However, insofar as discernment involves *an organization of experience* with reference to God, it is appropriately illumined by exploration of the properties of the human organization of experience, classified in psychological literature as the study of "concepts and categories." Christian discernment does not simply address how believers come to awareness of the presence or guidance of God in their experience. Numerous studies in mysticism have addressed this issue through the centuries. Discernment takes the question of the knowledge of God one step further by pursuing the question of how one comes to awareness of the presence or guidance of God *as* the presence or guidance of God. When a Christian discerns a particular calling in life as "from God," she or he moves beyond the mere experience of the calling of God to the identification and categorization of that experience *as* the calling of God. Thus discernment moves from *quid sit* to *an sit*, from perception and inquiry to understanding and judgment (cf. Lonergan 1967 [1949]; Lonergan 1958). This aspect of discernment makes it especially appropriate for investigation as an act of conceptual knowing or categorization. What operations are involved in the retrieval of the category "from God" and its application to individual experiences or situations? From where do the categories related to Christian life and discernment come? By what processes are the categories of the Christian faith—categories essential to the determination of that which is or is not significantly related to God—established, perpetuated, revised, and used? These questions reveal the relevance of the analysis of human categorization for the understanding of Christian discernment, especially as an act of knowing.

Needless to say, in approaching discernment as an act of knowing through research in categorization, I am only examining one aspect of a much larger universe. Human knowing involves much more than the conceptual categorization of experience. Nonetheless, clear understanding of the processes underlying human categorization is valuable for developing an understanding of human knowing and Christian discernment. Standard texts in cognitive psychology place discussion of categorization in chapters on knowledge acquisition (Matlin 1994; J. Anderson 1995). Recent discussion of epistemology has acknowledged the critical relationship between cognitive psychological "categorization" and philosophical "justification of belief" (Goldman 1986; less directly Plantinga 1993). By exploring the dynamics of human categorization, I am addressing a central element of the human knowing process.

Some might argue that in the investigation of such elements as "concepts" and "categories" I am approaching the question of knowledge of God and Christian discernment from an entirely inappropriate direction. Knowledge of God, and the sense that a given phenomenon is actually "from God," is a matter of experience, intuition, or feeling rather than of conceptual frameworks. However, I hope to show through the course of the next two chapters (1) that conceptualization of religious experience involves not merely semantic cognition, but a variety of operations, and (2) that well-formed conceptual judgments of categorization need not distort or diminish experience of God, but rather can facilitate increasing clarity of that experience.

Categorizing Categorization: Defining the Field

Psychological research in "concepts and categories" studies how humans organize their experience. Human beings constantly are confronted with a "world." Myriad sensations, feelings, thoughts, and inclinations all demand some kind of attention constantly. Humans interact with this flood of "input" in part, by grouping instances into categories or concepts. A concept for "cat," for example, may group numerous sensory experiences (sight, feel, smell, sound), mental ideas (mental image of physical shape, generalizations of well-known cat behavior patterns, memories of things people do with cats) and personal inclinations (perhaps related to allergies or a personal devotion to cats), into a single category. This grouping distinguishes all "cats" from all that is "not cats." The psychology of human categorization investigates just what this process involves.

The field is divided slightly differently by scholars in cognitive psychology, with key terms defined in slightly different ways (Glass and Holyoak 1986; Matlin 1994; J. Anderson 1995). Douglas Medin defines a *concept* as "an idea that includes all that is characteristically associated with it." He defines a *category* as "a partitioning or class to which some assertion or set of assertions might apply" (1989, 1469). Rosch defines categorization as "the process by which distinguishable objects or events are treated equivalently" (1994, 513). The differences in division and definition correspond, for the most part, with the questions that are being asked and the model of mental process that underlies the presentation of results.

A number of interrelated questions surround the study of human categorization, questions not dissimilar to the questions that have long hounded philosophers inquiring of the nature of "universals" (Woozley 1967). Roger Brown, in a review of categorization research listed the major themes of the field as follows:

> (1) Is a cognitive category a well-defined set with diagnostic characteristics or is it a fuzzy set with no absolutely diagnostic characteristics? (2) Is membership within the set a binary absolute or is it a matter of degree? Is there any sort of internal structure? (3) Are all categories of an entity of equal importance or is there some level in the vertical dimension of a taxonomy that is more basic than any other? (4) Are categories, named or otherwise, culturally and individually relative or are they universals? (1979, 192)

Rosch identifies a number of questions in a later review of the field for the *Encyclopedia of Human Behavior* (1994, 513): "Why do we have the particular categories we do and not others; how are the categories acquired, stored, and used in the mind; and what is the relationship between categories in the mind and objects, cultural forms, and contingencies in the world?" Later in the same article two other key questions are mentioned: How does the development of categorization progress from childhood to adult life? What is the relationship between the acquisition and use of language and human concepts and categories? With questions like these in mind one can see that it is important, when we speak of a concept or category, to distinguish between (a) the meaning of a word, (b) a representation of apparent reality in the mind, (c) the activation of a process of mental organization, (d) the structure of reality itself. Each of these horizons becomes primary in different research settings.

Medin (1989) and Rosch (1994), summarize the history of categorization research into four basic periods. Through the course of each of these four periods of categorization research different questions were emphasized and different fundamental perspectives concerning human categorization were suggested and defended. Each fundamental perspective formed the framework for the research of the next period. Along the way, a variety of secondary-level insights regarding the operations of human categorization were discovered. I will review the questions, perspectives, and insights of each period, drawing attention to those findings relevant to the categorization process of Christian discernment. I will then summarize the review of this research, providing a set of principles that appear to grasp the most certain findings of the research. I will suggest, by means of this synthesis, a working notion of the nature of and operations involved in human categorization. Finally, I will demonstrate ways in which an empirically-grounded understanding of human categorization constrains or amplifies an understanding of the categorization process known as Christian discernment.

Early "Classical" Research

The first period of categorization research can be labeled the "classical" or "definitional" period, ranging from the 1950's until the early 1970's. The behaviorist analogue to cognitive research in categories was the notion of "stimulus generalization." Stimulus generalization was the process by which an organism, conditioned to respond to a particular stimulus (for example, reacting to a mild electrical shock when a musical note was played), would give the same response to a similar stimulus (for example the sound of a musical note an octave above the previous one). Unfortunately the significance of stimulus generalization research for a theory of categorization went unrecognized until many years later.

In 1956 Jerome Bruner, Jacqueline Goodnow and George Austin wrote *A Study of Thinking*. This book documented a significant program of research into what they called "cognition." Their experiments tested the process by which subjects learned logical rules related to various patterns displayed to the subjects. They discovered, "that people tend to use systematic strategies in their effort to discover some unknown concept. These strategies were difficult to describe in terms of elemental stimulus-response associations" (Bourne, Dominowski, and Loftus 1979). Their research helped to overthrow the dominant stimulus-response (S-R) associationist approach to human learning in favor of a viewpoint that emphasized the role of the learner as a strategist in the learning process (S-O-R). Thus a true "cognitive" psychology was born. Bruner and his associates initiated a series of early "hypothesis-testing" theories, examining how people learn concepts by sampling and adjusting hypotheses. Bourne and his associates summarize their understanding of a concept as follows:

> A concept is an abstraction in the sense that it refers to no particular object, process, state of affairs, or event but rather to a collection of such concrete entities. Concepts have two fundamental components, a set of defining features and a relationship among them. Concepts are learned through experience with real entities. When a person learns a concept, he learns both the defining features and their relationship. (Bourne, Dominowski, and Loftus 1979, 194)

This understanding of concept as a logically related set of "defining features," or of "necessary and sufficient conditions," forms the fundamental perspective of the first period of research and comes into question during the second stage of research. Approach to categories as "hypotheses" will appear in the fourth stage of categorization history.

Both the possibility of human categorization involving a set of defining features or necessary and sufficient conditions and the possibility of human categorization involving a kind of hypotheses-testing operation must be addressed in the development of descriptive and normative accounts of Christian discernment. Are the criteria of Christian discernment such that they indicate conditions which when obtained determine conclusively the presence or guidance of God? Does discerning categorization posit hypotheses concerning God's presence or guidance, only to refine and revise these hypotheses in the course of a discerning process? I will address these questions in the summary and applications at the close of this section.

Prototypes and Basic Categories

The second stage of category research (roughly the 1970's; cf. Gleitman, Armstrong and Gleitman 1983; Medin 1989; Rosch 1994), was characterized by the development of research concerning (1) *prototypes*, roughly described as "best examples" or representatives surrounding which human concepts and categories are constructed, and (2) *basic categories*, or the fundamental level of categorization around which concepts and categories are organized. As research concerning prototypes and basic categories was significantly pioneered and developed during this period through the work of Eleanor Rosch and her associates (cf. Heider 1972; Rosch 1973; Rosch and Mervis 1975; Rosch et al. 1976; Rosch 1977; 1978), I will utilize Rosch's essays as a way of summarizing the developments of this period.

Rosch's research began with investigation of the relationship of language and thought in color categorization. Research by Rosch's predecessor, Roger Brown, had suggested that language (color names) affected the coding of color categories in memory. Rosch identifies the question that confronted her in a later review, "Might there be, I wondered, aspects of cognition, even for colors, that linguistic codes did not affect?" (1988, 376). Research on this question was carried out in the context of the Dani people of New Guinea, a group who had only two basic color names. Through a variety of memory tests given to both Dani and American subjects, Rosch first demonstrated, contrary to Brown's work, that, for basic color terms, categories were formed first around salient points in the color space rather than around color names. She called these salient points in color space *prototypes*. The research also identified a universal aspect of color cognition: people across diverse cultures categorized color in memory similarly even when their names for colors differed significantly. Finally, the work illustrated, contrary to the classical "necessary and sufficient conditions" approach to conceptual category membership, at least one category in which membership was conceived not by a "bounded structure" determined by the presence of a set of defining features that provide necessary and sufficient conditions for category membership, but rather by a *graded structure* in which category membership is based upon degrees of similarity to the prototype.

The question then broadened from color categories to concepts in general. Perhaps the idea of salience or "focal point" could apply to categories other than just color. Experiments with geometric shapes indicated that prototypes could be identified for *square, triangle,* and *circle* as well. People of diverse cultures appeared to organize their mental categories around their similarity to "best examples" of a geometric concept. An initial experiment using semantic categories suggested that the idea of prototypicality might have a broader range of influence. An extensive research program confirmed that indeed a host of natural categories are organized around forms or models called prototypes.

This, in turn led to research concerning why some items are regarded as more typical of a category than others. Rosch and her associates, following the lead of Ludwig Wittgenstein's notion of "family resemblance," hypothesized that the members of a category considered most typical were those having the most attributes in common with other members of the same category and least attributes in common with other categories (Rosch and Mervis 1975). Wittgenstein (1953) had drawn attention to the habit of identifying a given human family by means of a variety of features (for example, long nose, red hair, square chin, and so on) no one or set of which provide necessary and sufficient conditions for membership in the family but which together provide a sense of "family resemblance" through their accumulated number and degree of similarity. Wittgenstein suggested that this manner of relating features to families may be characteristic of human conceptualization in general. Rosch and her associates tested this hypothesis with a series of experiments. Their interest in the first set of experiments was upon the "correlational structure" of the world. The world is categorized or structured, they suggest, because it possesses attributes that appear co-related to others. Thus, creatures with feathers are more likely to have wings than creatures with fur. Rosch and her associates (Rosch et al. 1976) explored taxonomies of natural categories (such as "clothing," "furniture," and "fruit"). By exploring lists of attributes given or recognized, motor movements related to objects, similarity of basic shape, and identifiability from average shape, they were able to establish the existence of at least three separate levels of taxonomical categorization: a superordinate level (e.g. "furniture"), a basic level (e.g. "chair"), and a subordinate level (e.g. "rocking chair"). Furthermore, their research in the first set of experiments demonstrated that the *basic* level identifies objects that possess the greatest number of co-occurring attributes.

In the second set of experiments, the research shifted from taxonomical interests to psychological processing interests. If there are "basic object categories" in the world, possessing a high degree of co-occurring attributes, these basic categories ought to play an important role in the conceptual organization of the human mind. They ought to be the most inclusive categories represented by a mental image. Basic level objects ought to serve as a reference point for evaluations of category membership. They should be the first divisions of the world learned as young children. Basic level terms should be the most used terms to refer to objects. Each of these hypotheses was tested and confirmed. Rosch and her associates concluded,

> The categorizations that humans make of the concrete world are not arbitrary, but rather are highly determined. They are determined, in the first place, because the perceived world is not an unstructured total set of equiprobable co-occurring attributes. Unlike the artificial stimulus arrays typically used in concept identification research, the material objects of the world possess high correlational structure. Categories are determined, in the second place, because, in so far as categorization occurs to reduce the infinite differences between stimuli to behaviorally and cognitively useful proportions, the basic category cuts in the world would be those which yield the most information for the least cognitive load. (Rosch et al. 1976, 428)

In the same article, Rosch and her associates relate the findings of the "basic objects" research to earlier work on prototypes. They observe that prototypes of categories appear follow the same principles as basic level objects. "Categories form to maximize the information-rich clusters of attributes in the environment and, thus, the cue validity of the attributes of categories. Prototypes of categories appear to form in such a manner as to maximize the clusters and cue validity within categories" (Rosch et al. 1976, 433).

Rosch summarized and developed these findings in two separate articles (1977; 1978). From these articles, and in light of her earlier work, it appears that four empirical conclusions can be made about human categorization with a high degree of probability.

First, humans frequently organize concepts or categories by attention to *prototypes.* Just what a prototype *is*, however, is not altogether clear. Although she repeatedly asserts the significance of prototypicality for psychological models of mental representation, she explicitly denies any necessary connection between the notion of a prototype and any particular theory of mental representation. One is incorrect to assume that a prototype is a mental "average" or "idealization" of a given category. Likewise, it is incorrect to assume that a prototype is an actual object of some "best case" (or the memory of that object) of a given category. What seems to be central, whatever the model of processing, is that human conceptual thought appears frequently to organize around readily identifiable "representatives" of a given concept or category.

Second, membership for many categories does not depend upon the identification of well-defined features and rules (necessary and sufficient conditions), but rather upon "degrees" of similarity to a prototype. Thus what one calls a "plant," a "chair," or "genuine spiritual experience" may be determined not by the presence of features and rules which definitively identify that concept (for example, plant - growth by photosynthesis, chair - four legs, genuine spiritual experience - absence of "enthusiasm"), but rather by collections of features none of which are determinative but all of which are weighed in terms of their relative similarity to a model or representative case. Thus category membership, at least for some categories, is based upon a *graded structure* rather than a bounded structure, analogue, rather than digital. As noted above, the assumption of defining features and logically discrete rules of membership was central to the "classical" approach to concepts during the first period of research. Rosch's work has been viewed as an overthrow of this earlier notion of a concept. Yet Rosch herself is careful to acknowledge that "undoubtedly, some categories and some kinds of processing of categories do involve digital codes" (1977, 20; cf. 1983). One should look at the results of the empirical research of this second period as expanding the notion of concept to include a very important and hitherto neglected aspect.

Third, human categorical organization appears to be structured around a *basic level* which maximizes the similarities between properties of the category. Rosch repeatedly relates this element to assumptions concerning the nature of the environment. She states, "that basic objects are categories at the level of abstraction that maximizes cue validity and maximizes category resemblance is another way of saying that basic objects are the categories that best mirror the correlational structure of the environment" (Rosch 1978, 31). One can reasonably conclude at least that in ordinary human life, the environment is encountered at a "basic level," in which objects, events, and persons, all share co-related attributes significant for human interaction.

Finally, Rosch's work has demonstrated that at least for some concepts, humans possess a *universally* applied measure of categorization. The research on color demonstrated that humans from very diverse cultures organize color concepts around salient examples more than by color name. Evidence indicated that physiological reasons may contribute to color categorization. But what of other examples of prototypicality? Are there universal properties of categorization in general (physiological, mental, social), or does human categorization develop merely by the transmission of the individual cultures within in which humans develop? Rosch readily acknowledges that the content of categories should be expected do differ among people and cultures. What *is* universal, she argues, is the principle of categorization itself.

Through the work of others, the notions of prototypicality, graded structure, basic categories, and universal conceptual processes were confirmed, developed, and extended far beyond the categorization of natural objects. Roger Brown, as early as 1965, addressed the problem of prejudice or "stereotypes" as a categorization issue (Brown 1965). Amos Tversky and Daniel Kahneman pioneered research in decision-making in the 1970's. Their identification of a variety of "heuristics" and "biases" revealed that orientation toward salient instances and representatives judgments significantly influenced the way humans make judgments and mis-judgments (cf. Tversky and Kahneman 1974; Kahneman and Tversky 1981; Dawes 1988). Psychological situations, event taxonomies and environmental scenes were all evaluated according to Rosch's methods (Cantor, Mischel and Schwartz 1982; Tversky and Heneway 1983; Rifkin 1985). More recently, notions of prototypes, exemplars, and the like have played heavily in the investigation of interpersonal understanding and misunderstanding (e.g. Smith and Kihlstrom 1987; Zarate and Smith 1990; Smith and Zarate 1990; John, Hampson and Goldberg 1991; Linville and Fischer 1993). Categorization within these various domains has been shown to behave similarly to the categorization of natural objects researched by Rosch. Studies of event schemata and emotion prototypes will be discussed below. The range of domains confirming this approach gives reason for the present study to consider the involvement of prototypicality, graded structure, basic categories and universality in the categorization process known as Christian discernment.

One other relevant aspect of basic category research was the notion of "expertise." Rosch and her associates had noted in their own research on basic level categories that "different amounts of knowledge about objects can change the classification scheme" (Rosch et al. 1976, 430). They recount the presence of an airplane mechanic in their experimentation subject pool. While most subjects related to *airplane* as a basic level object, this man organized his own thought as if types of airplanes were basic categories. The lists of motor movements, similarities, and groupings of attributes and such were more detailed for this mechanic than for others. Tanaka and Taylor (1991) have investigated the impact of expertise upon categorization more fully, demonstrating the diversity of conceptual structure as a function of expertise. As I will show below, I think it is reasonable to think of discernment wisdom as examples of expertise in the spiritual life.

A Note on Schemata

A kindred concept to that of prototype is the notion of "schemata." The term "schema" itself derives from Immanuel Kant's *Critique of Pure Reason*. Kant developed the notion that a person's experiences are remembered as collections defined by common elements. The common elements serve to permit categorical access to and synthesis of large amounts of material without constant reference to instances of a category. Humans maintain schemata for objects (giving a sense, for example, of "rooms in a house"), for events (suggesting expectations for a "first date"), and even for spiritual life (creating a sense of ritual to personal and corporate worship). Cognitive research has developed this notion. Thus "a schema represents 'generic' information that includes not only events from one's life, but also general knowledge about procedures, sequences of events, and social situations" (Matlin 1994, 235). Like prototype research, the notion of schemata has been used to investigate a variety of domains (Thorndyke 1984). Rosch recounts that the notion of schema assisted her development of the idea of a prototype (Rosch 1977; 1987). Both "prototype" and "schema" refer to a representation of something (objects, events, plots, etc.) indicating typicality with reference to a category. The similarity between the two notions can be seen by a review of the properties of schemata. Thorndyke (1984, 173) lists the following:

1. A schema represents a prototypical *abstraction* of the concept it represents encoding the constituent properties that define a typical instance of its referent.
2. Schemata are hierarchically organized in memory [taxonomically].
3. The properties that characterize a schema are represented as variables that can be filled, or *instantiated*, whenever the schema is used to organize the incoming information.
4. The use of general schemata to organize new incoming data permits reasoning [predictions] from incomplete information.
5. Schemata are formed by *induction* from numerous previous experiences with various exemplars of the generic concept, presumably through a process of successive refinement.

Anderson (1995) presents the idea of schema as an organizing mechanism which locates information concerning particular features in predetermined "slots." For example the concept *house* might contain slots for its parts, materials, function, shape, size, and reference to its superordinate category.

A great deal of research has been invested in the exploration of schemata related to ordinary events, often referred to as "scripts." Experimental studies have demonstrated that people store well-structured sequences of events in memory, such as the notion of what to do in a restaurant. Experimental evidence indicates that people encode new events with reference to general scripts which reveal what to expect in a given event. There is also evidence that event scripts are processed differently than concepts of objects. With objects, the schema indicates attributes and subjects are able to list them rapidly. With scripts, it appears that subjects "proceed" mentally through the elements of an event script. Anthony Rifkin has established a "basic level" for event scripts following the lines of Rosch's research (Rifkin 1985). Schemata or scripts appear to shape the organization of memory storage in that they affect selection of material remembered, and recovery of material from memory, in that they organize background knowledge which signals particular interpretations of stimuli, and in that they inform the selection of short-term and long term memory (cf. Matlin 1995).

The notion of schema, like that of prototype, suggests that human categorization has a tendency to organize material around a central idea. This tendency aids in the synthesis of the mass of individuality humans face each moment. But it can also serve to distort the understanding of that which confronts one. Schematic and script-oriented operations are not obligatory, but they may at least be common if not "typical" of human categorization. The tendency to organize around a central idea and to form somewhat normative patterns used to categorize events, objects, people will have an impact upon the operations involved in Christian discernment. Key "objects" of faith, religious events and spiritual experiences are often evaluated and identified within the context of prototypes, schemata, and scripts. I shall explore these below.

Modeling and Critique

From the mid 1970's through the mid 1980's research in categorization assessed the findings of the previous decade. This assessment took two primary forms. First, the findings regarding prototypes, graded structure and such served as the stimulus for the development of a number of "models," or conceptual reconstructions of human categorization.   Second, prototype and basic category research received critiques regarding various aspects of its formulation.   This reassessment of the perspective of the previous period helped pave the way for the insights of the fourth period.   Thus while the findings of this second period are less significant for the construction of a theory of Christian discernment, it is helpful to understand the refinement of the perspective of prototype and basic category research and the important questions raised during this third period so that an adequate synthesis of the field of categorization study can be made.   Only then can an adequate account of Christian discernment as categorization-knowing be presented.

Interest in model building centered attention upon the nature of the "prototype" used for comparison in the formation or application of a category, with the models falling into two main groups.   The first group, called "prototype" or "abstraction" models, suggested that the mind formed an image or representation of a concept that was used in memory when a concept was used.   This mental representation was formed as an idealized image: a "mean," "average," or "composite" of instances of the concept actually experienced (cf. Posner and Keele 1968; J. Anderson 1995).   The second group, called "exemplar" or "instance" models, denied that the mind created a mental abstraction that served as the prototype for a concept; the mind rather utilized particularly relevant actual instances or "exemplars" of the concept (Medin and Schaffer 1978).   Others suggested that perhaps both mental syntheses and remembered examples played a role in the categorization process (cf. Glass and Holyoak 1984).   Empirical findings appeared not to favor one approach or the other.   Nearly all information-processing models of categorization joined in rejecting the earlier "classical" model, as recently discovered mental operations (comparison to an abstraction or comparison by use of exemplars), rather than the identification of defining features and rules, were seen to explain the origin and maintenance of concepts in the mind. Likewise, concepts were not seen as propositional sets, bounded by clear and distinct limits but rather as hazy collections of family resemblances.

During this same period research in prototypes, graded structure and such came under significant critique, both theoretically and experimentally.   First, prototype research appeared to examine (and account for) only simple nouns or "natural concepts," and not to account for complex concepts or grammatical terms (Osherson and Smith 1981). Second, conceiving of category membership through graded structure resulted in a number of logical contradictions and truth-value confusions, especially when joined to recently explored "fuzzy set" theories (Osherson and Smith 1981). Third, empirical research after Rosch demonstrated that graded structure of "typicality" could be found for a host of concepts, even such well-defined concepts as "odd number" or "female." When interviewed, subjects would claim that membership in such categories was an "all-or-none" affair. Nevertheless, when rankings of "typicality" for the particular concept were requested, the same subjects provided clear indication of "prototypical thinking" for the same concepts (e.g. 2 ranked higher than 106 on the prototypicality scale for the category "even number"). Some (e.g. Gleitman, Armstrong and Gleitman 1983) argued, therefore, for a more careful distinction between questions related to *membership in* a category and questions related to *exemplariness of* a category. This led to the critique that prototype categorization theories are unable to account for the specification of features that are relevant for the delineation of a concept.

Fourth, subject assessment of prototypicality was found to be unstable, varying in criteria and method between individual and cultural contexts (Barsalou 1987; cf. Medin 1989). Fifth, the notion of comparison by *similarity* to a prototype came into question. This critique argues that stating that concepts are formed or utilized by noticing the similarity between a prototype or exemplar and a concrete instance does not necessarily indicate which, of a near-infinite pool of possible features or attributes, are relevant for a given category. Empirical research indicates that categorization is constrained by factors that limit which features are assessed. Furthermore, prototypicality has been demonstrated for goal-related categories (e.g. "things to take on a camping trip"), where the category is derived not from similarity to a prototype or exemplar but rather comparison to an ideal (Medin 1989). Thus probabilistic theories based upon similarity-comparison to a prototype (either abstraction or exemplar) are insufficient to account for the formation of human concepts or categories (Medin and Wattenmaker 1987; cf. also Gluck and Corter 1992 on cue validity). Finally, the "structural" aspect of category formation and use has been questioned. Gluck and Corter (1992) wonder whether the reason for basic categories is related to the cor relational structure of the environment. The simple assertion of basic categories and their mirroring the environment is insufficient to account for both the significance and flexibility of human categorization demonstrated in the empirical literature. They suggest that *utility* rather than *structure* might be a more appropriate way to account for category development and use.

The work of the third period of research resulted less in the development of a third fundamental perspective concerning human categorization. Rather this period served to reassess of the findings of the previous decade in light of new data and new models. Thus empirical discoveries served to expand expectations concerning the range of prototypicality use, while at the same time restricting any claims for comprehensiveness by prototype operations. Narrowly defined models of prototypes and exemplars struggled for images with which to grasp the operations of the mind in categorization. Logicians debated the function of graded structure categories in language and thought. Finally, trends in research suggested that perhaps some features of the second period of study may have to be adjusted or abandoned.

Theory Theory

In recent years the trends in categorization research have begun to shift once again, causing human concepts and categories to be evaluated less from the viewpoint of the perceptive grasp of the environment and more as from the viewpoint of the frameworks which shape the nature of perception itself. A few factors contributed significantly to this shift. First, the critiques of similarity, structure and feature identification forced categorization research to account not simply for the comparison of a case to some ideal but also for the selection of, framework within, and context in which the attributes or features of the case and ideal are considered relevant or worthy of notice. Second, models of human information-processing were changing, and older models of linear processing were giving way to models of global activation. This led to a decreased emphasis on invariant representations as the content of categories and toward an increased emphasis on ad hoc concepts contained in "working memory" (Barsalou 1987) or "category utility" (Gluck and Corter 1992). Third, research in developmental psychology and linguistics supported some kind of theory

theory. Objects tend to be named first; discovery and delineation of causal properties of the category appear later. Children tend to develop from a process of classification by means of characteristic attributes to a process that establishes defining features by means of a kind of "theory" refinement. Fourth, trends in philosophy of science were increasingly emphasizing the theory-laden character of observations. As I will show, theory theory emphasizes hitherto neglected aspects of human categorization and puts human categorization into the larger contexts of inquiry and world-view, aspects of categorization vital to an understanding of the categorization processes of Christian discernment.

One of the chief proponents of "theory theory" in cognitive psychology is Douglas Medin. I will draw material from two of his articles (Medin and Wattenmaker 1987; Medin 1989) to summarize some of the main points of theory theory. Medin contends that similarity "gets at the shadow rather than at the substance of concepts" (1989, 1474). Prototype/exemplar theories only account for the collection and comparison of data. They do not indicate what gives the data *meaning*. Medin and Wattenmaker propose that analyses of relational properties within concepts may offer more hope for interpretation than the previous foci on attributes. Research suggests that people not only notice feature correlations, but that they also deduce *reasons* for these correlations based on knowledge about how the world works. This is what Medin calls "knowledge-based" categorization (1989). Research also indicates that some aspects of categorization common to the summing of evidence or adding similar features (such as linear separability cf. Wattenmaker, Dewey, Murphy, and Medin 1986) are subject to control by prior theory. Thus attributes are not simply "added" to produce a summary prototype which serves as the model for a concept. Rather some interproperty coding, or "theory-building" holds the features involved in a meaningful whole.[1] Medin claims that approaching concepts as theories also facilitates reconciliation of the critiques of prototype models regarding context dependence and ubiquitous typicality,

---

[1]This aspect of categorization can be discussed with relationship to discernment under the heading of "criteriology," in which not only the listing, but the selection and ordering of criteria for various discernment situations are determined.

insofar as theories (or underlying dimensions) determine typicality structure in different contexts. Finally, Medin and Wattenmaker propose that the flexibility of concept use suggests a "theory-driven" approach to concepts (1987). Their conclusion: "concepts should be viewed as embedded in theories" (Medin and Wattenmaker 1987, 41).

Having given reason that some type of a theory or knowledge-based approach might serve the interpretation of human categorization, Medin and Wattenmaker offer guidelines for determining constraints on theories. Their first constraint is parsimony or *simplicity*. They conclude that simplicity is inadequate in itself as a constraint on theories. They suggest that a process oriented (rather than product-oriented) rule induction theory may help to explain the development of theories. The experimental methods (use of pictures of trains with logically distinct differences) and results bear a striking similarity to the research of the 1950's and 60's. Borrowing from Kant and Wittgenstein, they suggest that the attention to salience in conceptual thought is helpfully considered "seeing the object as." Borrowing from perception research, Medin and Wattenmaker suggest that the constraints in conceptual thought may preserve some of the constraints afforded by phylogenetic history and present relationship with the environment. In this view adaptive specialization orients humans to particular features of the environment and enables the application of adaptive specialization (somewhat metaphorically) to other domains of life. Thus theory construction may embody many of the same constraints as used for learning memory and perception. They show possible linkages with this notion to previous research, emphasizing the need for a way of explaining sensitivity to correlated attributes without conscious computations. Their general point is that "there may be interesting linkages among structural constraints in the environment, nonconscious and relatively inflexible perceptual and memorial mechanisms, and more flexible theories" (Medin and Wattenmaker 1987, 57). I find little difference between this and Rosch's emphasis on the "correlational structure of the environment."

Medin is not suggesting that one abandon similarity as an approach to conceptualization. Rather he considers it *insufficient* to explain human concepts and categorization. His desire is to link similarity with knowledge-based categorization. A type of approach to similarity that can accomplish this includes the following principles

- Similarity needs to include attributes, relations, and higher order relations.
- Properties in general are not independent, but rather are linked by a variety of interproperty relations
- Properties exist at multiple levels of abstraction
- Concepts are more than lists (Medin 1989, 1476)

He posits, based on empirical observation, the existence of an "essentialist heuristic" whereby people intuitively act as if things (objects, events, etc.) have essences or underlying natures that make them the things that they are. Thus *men* and *women* are seen to have genetic determination, although the concept *man* may normally retrieve a set of physical or visual characteristics. This heuristic, they suggest, "may be one way of reconciling classification in terms of perceptual similarity or surface properties with the deeper substance of knowledge-rich, theory based classification" (Medin 1989, 1479). Similarity may point to, but not constitute, category structure.

It is possible to claim not that concepts *are* theories, but rather that they are *embedded in* theories. Needless to say, in the articles reviewed, Medin spends more time explaining the formation of theories than describing the nature of concepts or categories. It appears that Medin, assuming that concepts are embedded in theories, wants to explore the structure of theories to glean those insights concerning concepts which can be found. At the present these insights are only suggestive. Rosch, in a recent review article on categorization (1994), communicates awareness of the speculative state of theory theory. She notes that theory theory has been silent on many of the questions one might think it would address: "What is meant by a theory? . . . How does the theory view itself account for similarity? Likewise for the problem of attributes—given a theory, how are we to derive or predict attributes from it?" (Rosch 1994, 522). Her hope is that the current trends will serve to place categorization research in the larger context of "forms of life."

Eleanor Rosch's later material (1987; 1988; 1992; 1996; 1997; Varela, Thompson and Rosch 1991) issues a significant challenge to categorization research as a whole. Drawing from as diverse influences as Ludwig Wittgenstein, Maurice Merleau-Ponty, and Chogyam Trungpa, Rosch questions whether cognitive studies has the theoretical and methodological equipment to offer adequate explanations of categorization. In her paper on "Wittgenstein and Categorization Research," she takes categorization researchers to task on their narrow use of Wittgensteinian ideas like prototype and family resemblance. Rather than taking seriously Wittgenstein's challenge to the "object of reference" approach to human language (cf. Wittgenstein 1953), cognitive scientists have reified concepts or category structures such that they are expected to fulfill the roles of classical thought of categories, namely that they serve as "objects of reference that give meaning to words and make true knowledge possible" (Rosch 1987, 159). She, following the later Wittgenstein, suggests that one look at concepts not as representations of objects, or as "things," but rather as forms of life, part of the activities, language-games, meanings in use and conventions of human existence.

In *Embodied Mind* (Varela, Thompson and Rosch 1991), Rosch, along with Evan Thompson and Francisco Varela, challenge the theoretical and methodological framework of cognitive science. This work draws heavily from Maurice Merleau-Ponty's idea of the mutuality of conditioning of subject and object in the embodiment of the human situation (Merleau-Ponty 1963) as well as from a wide range of sources from the Buddhist "mindfulness" traditions. A chief aim of the book is the offer of a "third" approach to cognitive science as an alternative to the cognitivist and connectionist predecessors. Their alternative is labeled "enactive," emphasizing (1) that perception consists in perceptually guided action, and (2) that cognitive structures emerge from the recurrent sensorimotor patterns that enable action to be perceptually guided. The point here is that humans actively determine their world while repeated interactions with the environment determine the human. They call upon Rosch's work in basic categories, upon the pioneering work in kinesthetic image schemas (frameworks of understanding and conceptualization governed by one's relationship to the human body) of Mark Johnson (1987), and upon George Lakoff's (1987) work in linguistics, to suggest that concepts may be more helpfully viewed as embodied action rather than mere representation.

The mindfulness traditions take center space in Rosch's most recent articles (1996; 1997). In "Transformation of the Wolf Man" (1997), Rosch likens the perspective of cognitive science to the kinds of knowing of a beginning meditator, a kind of knowing which reveals an isolated information-processor and an equally isolated "world-out-there." As attention is trained, however, self, body, emotions, action, and others are experienced in a much different fashion. Finally, a truly novel mode of knowing may be reached wherein subject and object distinctions fade away and the knowledge itself is "not graspable, describable, conceptualizable, formulatable, or modelable; it is a nonconceptual knowing" (Rosch 1997, 20). With this background she offers suggestions for the building of a new psychology from the point of view of the meditative mode of knowing. Rosch gives a similar challenge to the dualism of cognitive science in her "The Environment of Minds: Towards a Noetic and Hedonic Ecology" (1996). She begins with a (surprising for a pioneering cognitive scientist) defense of behaviorist thinking. Then by exploration of research in a wide range of fields she concludes that "the ecological environment of goal directed, acting minds is not a neutral world describable by physics but a noetic and hedonic environment consisting of affordances, normative reference points, counterfactual possible worlds, and a continual emotively toned process of comparison" (Rosch 1996, 19).

As mentioned above, Rosch's later work expresses a significant challenge to categorization research. She presses one to think of categorization, indeed all cognition, less as subjective representations of a "world-out-there," and more as moments of lived experienced arising from one's actions, one's body, and one's environment. This later work focuses on the theoretical re-visioning of cognitive studies, and as such moves from the aim of "experimental constraint" chosen for the present chapter into topics reserved for the chapter on philosophical/theological matters.

The fourth period of research in categorization emphasized the roles of theories or general conceptual structures and operations upon human categorization. Models of "prototype" or "exemplar" comparison simply proved insufficient to explain the data, which demonstrated that humans categorize and develop concepts not by simple comparison, but by comparison *in the context of meaning* (cf. also J. Anderson 1995). Selection of attributes for comparison, inter-property relationships of features, assignments of levels of attributes, all give reason to see human categorization as a multi-leveled process involving not merely "bottom-up" constraints in terms of the perceptual/conceptual impact of the environment upon the human organism, but also "top-down" constraints in terms of the impact of the world-view and inherited cognitive processes placed upon the person prior to (and active during) a conceptual event. And perhaps, one must re-vision even the fundamental frameworks of cognitive psychology in order to provide adequate explanation for the data of human categorization. The findings of the fourth period, as the summary and application will show, suggest how the operations of Christian discernment function within the life and exploration of a lived Christian faith.

Summary

Research in human concepts and categories has wound its way through diverse terrain over the past few decades. A number of models, methods, and issues have characterized categorization study in experimental psychology. In spite of this diversity, I think it is fair to say that the empirical study has provided a number of "constraints" for which a theory of human categorization (and Christian discernment) must give account. As well, I think the research provides material for the amplification of a theory of Christian discernment.

It is important to remember, as mentioned above, that just as categorization operations are not the only operations involved in human knowing, they are also not the only operations involved in dis-cernment. Indeed, it is even difficult to examine categorization itself without including exploration of other operations connected with it, as was demonstrated by the contextual interests of the fourth period. Exploration of categorization took me into questions of perception, inference, judgment, theory formation, language development and decision making (for the relationship of categorization with these and other operations cf. Gopnik 1997; Glass and Holyoak 1984; Paivio 1971; Kosslyn 1980). There is, therefore, reason to respect the portrait of categorization in *Embodied Mind* as dependent upon "a tangled hierarchy of perceptual and cognitive processes." Untangling these mental processes is further complicated by the fact that the field of cognitive psychology has developed as a collection of micro-specialities, making integration of research cumbersome. I have chosen a "safe" approach to the field, summarizing the most plausible results of empirical studies which may illumine a theory of Christian discernment.

When I speak of human categorization, therefore, I am speaking of the system of operations used to "divide up" the human's world. Categorization is the process whereby humans acquire, maintain, and revise the concepts and categories by which they relate to elements in human experience, and by which elements in human experience are responded to *as* instances of these categories. A few comments can be made about this process by way of summary.

First, one must be clear about what one means by such terms as "concept," "category," "category formation," and "categorization." One must distinguish between (1) cultural category-system development and transmission (both socially and phylogenetically), (2) personal category-system formation - the incorporation/assimilation of culture, physiology, personal experience, and such into a *personal* category-system (on category-system cf. Rosch 1994), (3) the delineation of category membership criteria (inclusion/exclusion of attributes, naming of prototypes, rule induction, and the like), (4) category "storage" - the operations by which information about concepts or categories is remembered (short-term, long-term, working memory, etc.), and (5) category "retrieval" - the use of category-related information in particular concept-attribution instances (for example the recognition/identification of objects, events, experiences *as* instances of a particular concept). As mentioned above, one must distinguish and relate word-meaning and thought-pattern, taxonomical structure of things and habit of the mind, bottom-up and top-down constraints. Even an adequate summary of the research is impossible without being sensitive to the fact that key terms will mean different things when used in different contexts.

Second, the very fact that one can posit such an activity or "thing" as *concept* or *categorization* entails the recognition that the perceived world possesses some kind of identifiable regularity. This recognition is assumed in much of the research reviewed above. It is present in Bourne's approach to the identification of rules in his classical research on category learning. It is implied in Rosch's emphasis upon the correlational structure of the environment (1976), and in her later discussion of "affordances" (1997). It is present in Mark Johnson's insistence that what makes an image-schematic gestalt identifiable is its "repeatable pattern" (Johnson 1987). It is evident in Gluck and Corter's identification of "regularities in the environment" which are captured by categories (1992). Anderson mentions that schema are "ways of encoding regularities" (1995). Finally, Varela, Thompson and Rosch assert, "because this relative, conventional, codependently originated world is lawful, science is possible—just as possible as daily life" (Varela, Thompson and Rosch 1991, 228). Some of this regularity (as in color perception) appears to be universal. I think that the regularity underlying human categorization also implies that human concept and language, while acting as fallible and context-dependent forms of life, nevertheless possess correlationality with the perceived environment—indeed, following C. S. Peirce and Donald Gelpi, I will argue in chapter four that it is this correlationality between human concept and regularities that forms an important foundation for the reliability of any theory of human categorization and of Christian discernment. Whether this identifiable regularity originates from physical embodiment, cultural heritage, phylogenetic inheritance or divine design (or perhaps all of the above?), recognition of real affordance gives concept and language a semiotic function without imprisoning them in classical representational theories.

    Third, it appears that humans do learn some concepts by hypothesis testing or rule induction. Especially when the concept in view is perceived to be well-defined, people appear to use "sample and replace" (Bourne, Dominowski and Loftus 1979) or "theory development" (Medin 1989) approaches to conceptual learning. Medin's suggestion that humans often operate under an "essentialist hypothesis" in their conceptual processing is worth attention apart from any metaphysical issue attached. Thus, even though the nature of a concept presented in the first stage of categorization research may prove insufficient, the main point of the classical category learning research can be affirmed for some cases.

    Fourth, I think it is safe to say that prototypical sorting and representativeness judgment are significant, though not "necessary and sufficient" elements of conceptual processing. Judgments of prototypicality, or judgments according to a "best example," have been demonstrated for the widest possible range of concepts and categories. Basic level categories, those categories which serve to organize the most common and fundamental approach to a given segment of experience, have also been identified for a wide range of domains. The use of graded structure, that is the development and use of categories according degrees of similarity rather than strict defining features, is also found in a variety of categories. Schemata and scripts form expectations and grids which structure a variety of domains. Thus, it appears that one can affirm the basic principles of the second period of research. Nonetheless, a review of the research as a whole suggests that concepts and categories not be *reduced* to the principles listed here. A given category-stimulus may retrieve non-prototypical data under certain conditions, for example, when a recent encounter with a decidedly *atypical* exemplar of a category is triggered at the mention of a category name. Abstract concepts like grammatical prepositions, mathematical sets, or logical distinctions may be encoded by semantic properties rather than judgments of perceptual similarity. Human categorization appears to be a "rich" process (Medin 1989), dependent upon a "tangled hierarchy" (Varela, Thompson, and Rosch 1991) of operations. While important insights, the findings of the second stage are insufficient in themselves to explain human categorization.

Fifth, for the reasons mentioned above, it would appear that the models of the third period of research largely fail to do the job. Strict prototype or exemplar models of information-processing for the most part have been unable to account for attribute selection, attribute leveling, strategic learning and other factors of human conceptual processes. Furthermore, while pointing to the need for wider theorizing, the critiques of prototype research often revealed their own misunderstandings of early prototype research and thus expected more of notions like "prototype" and "family resemblance" than they were intended to carry (Rosch 1983; 1987).

Sixth, I think the chief value of the "critique" research of the third period has been to point the way to a broader approach to human categorization explored in the fourth period. Conceptual process must take account for such elements as (1) the information forming the background of human concepts, (2) the kinesthetic image schemas developed from human embodiment, (3) the central paradigms governing development of concept, (4) the context of categories, and a number of other factors constraining conceptual process and human categorization prior to its inception. While the research of the fourth period has failed to identify just what a theory *is*, it has succeeded in demonstrating that concepts and categories are at least embedded in larger cognitive processes.

Seventh, while one can present a general outline of the categorization/conceptualization process, one is still left wanting for a precise definition of just what a concept *is*. Whether a concept is an abstraction rooted in definable features and rules (Bourne), or an idea that includes all that is characteristically associated with it (Medin), or a representation (early Rosch), or an action (later Rosch), is not clearly proven in the empirical research. What one must gain from the research are the helpful insights concerning the conceptual operations themselves.

Eighth, categorization and human conceptual process appears to serve a variety of functions. It helps to "divide up" human experience into reasonable units. It also serves to facilitate memory and the retrieval of experience. This facilitation can at times can be very beneficial, enabling one to "fill in" data from an incomplete encounter. It can also prove detrimental, fostering misjudgments, biases, and inaccurate stereotypes. Conceptual processes also predispose one's response to that which confronts, by means of by priming responses associated with the schema/category in general. Categories, therefore, appear both to represent the perceived world to humans and serve in themselves as "enactions" of that world. They embody one's interaction or adaptation with that which confronts, whether an internal environment or an external one. In all these ways, it seems fair to say that categorization *mediates* human experience. As mediation, categorization serves semiotic, adaptive, and enactive functions.

Ninth, the correction of human conceptual process appears to be possible. Attention can be trained; one can become aware of stereotypes, biases, and misjudgments. Through careful self-controlled awareness and adjustment of the patterns of categorization process itself, one can have the potential of adjusting patterns of human categorization according to various norms. Habits of inaccurate categorical judgment due to overreliance upon a single salient example, for instance, can be noticed and changed as an improved criteriology refines the arrangement of family-resemblance configurations signalling the presence of a given category. Indeed, categorical expertise can be developed. In this way research in human categorization informs not only a descriptive account of human conceptual thought, but also provides important groundwork for normative approaches to human categorization, explored in the field of logic.

Finally, this process is thoroughly infused with emotion. Categorization research seldom addresses this point, and so in making this point I deviate from my emphasis on consensual empirical grounding. I merely point out a significant lacuna in the research. Research periodically acknowledges that concept formation notices what is "relevant," without bothering to explore just what this may mean. Barsalou speaks of "context-relevant information" (1987) provided through conceptual thinking to service goal-related action. Rosch conceives of categorization as involving a "continual emotively toned process of comparison" (1996). However, the relationships between conceptual process and emotional process have been for the most part neglected in the field of categorization research. I will develop this in the section to follow.

Perhaps these insights concerning the nature and operations involved in human categorization process can be best synthesized by an imaginary picture of a developing conceptual experience. I will begin with a subject, calling her Jane. Jane appears as a person already "given." Her phylogenetic and ontogenetic history have predisposed her to notice certain things and not to notice others. Her cultural and social background, and the forms of language she is familiar with also constrain what and how Jane can notice. Jane is an adult, and so has developed a large store of concepts and categories already. But today she is confronted with something she has never experienced before. This "something" can be an object, an event, an experience, a feeling, a thought - anything. I will call it a *wal*. Needless to say, her embodiment permitted this novel experience of *wal*, but upon the moment of the experience, Jane is involved in a subtle choice. She can either ignore the novelty of this event and subsume this "something" into another familiar category which may bear some resemblance to *wal*, or she can classify this *wal* as novel and say to herself, "I have never experienced anything like this before." If she chooses the former, she will simply include perhaps a bad or distant case of this other familiar category, which will remain so categorized until sufficient experience (perhaps enough salient examples) demands otherwise. If she chooses the latter, she will have created a new concept, that of *wal* (yet usually unnamed at this stage). When she thinks of *wal*, the concept itself may highlight a few significant or salient features provided by environment cues, probably highlighting attributes that made it unique. Her concept is, at this-stage, chiefly determined by this recent experience with one exemplar. But perhaps she begins to find herself confronted by a few more "somethings" which bear great similarity to *wal*. At this point her concept of *wal* expands. She begins now not simply to compare *wal* with all other experience, but also to compare different instances of *wal*. Perhaps certain features begin to show themselves as character-istic of *wal* experiences. Perhaps a shape, a feeling, a pattern of some sort, or a central exemplar begins to serve as a "prototype," a means by which other experiences begin to be heuristically judged as *wal* or *not wal*. Theoretical thinking is beginning to form a clearer perceived understanding about *wal*, and initial hypotheses are formed.[2] Fur-thermore, interaction with other people shape her concept of *wal*. Perhaps they have names for experiences that appear similar to Jane's. At this point the public dimension of concepts begins to play a role as concepts are shared between people. Their observations shape her understanding of *wal*.

In time, *wal* begins to find a place in Jane's taxonomical understanding of her perceived world as the concept begins to have place as a category. By now she probably has attached a name to the concept. However, recall of the concept *wal* will vary slightly for Jane at any given situation. Goal-orientation associated with *wal*, recent experience with particular exemplars of *wal*, state of develop-ment of *wal* concept all will adjust as Jane represents and enacts *wal* in experience. Different features or similarity-comparisons will be highlighted in various situations. Furthermore, the kind of concept that *wal* is (e.g. concrete or abstract) will shape her conceptual process related to *wal*. As Jane encounters sufficient experience with *wal*, her essentialist heuristic may be triggered. Deductive com-parison with other experience and rule inductive operations are set in motion. Her repeated contact with *wal* may suggest a feature or fea-tures that appear to consistently identify *wal*. Perhaps her functional relationships cause her to interact with *wal* in very specific ways at certain times (identifying a particular *wal*-related language-game, for instance). Perhaps Jane is gaining some measure of expertise in *wals* by now. Thus Jane finds it very beneficial to refine her concept of *wal* to include a set of defining features, identification of "necessary and sufficient" conditions for the existence of *wal*. Once again, com-munication with other people may confirm or disconfirm her

---

[2]These are usually formed unconsciously through the development of responses to the repeated interaction with novel phenomena.

hypothesis concerning these conditions. Of course, recall of the concept may still be associated with abstracted prototypes, particular exemplars, or attributes that are more connected with other factors, and she may still have ideas of more or less typical *wals*, but when asked "what makes a *wal* a *wal*?" she will respond by the giving necessary and sufficient condition(s). Jane's confidence in her understanding reaches a high point at this stage, and she begins to share her wise expertise with others, helping them to recognize the salient features of *wal* and to distinguish them from *not wal*. Finally, this developed concept of *wal*, in turn, both enables and inhibits what Jane can and can't notice. It is in some fashion similar to this intuitive description that I summarize the integration of operations of feature selection and inhibition, attention, memory storage, memory retrieval, comparison, logical inference, synthesis, theory incorporation, concept representation, categorical judgment, enaction; body, environment, social history, language, emotion and spirit involved in the form of knowledge-action known as human categorization. A chart illustrating this process is presented in Figure 1.

Categorization and Discernment

Having explored something of the nature of and operations involved in human categorization in experimental psychology, I am now prepared to describe with greater psychological specificity what a theory of Christian discernment as an act of knowing/categorizing must account for. A few points can be made here.

First, one must acknowledge that Christian discernment does not appear in a vacuum. The Christian discerner comes to the act of discernment as a "given." I use the term *given* not in the sense that a person is to be considered a static entity, but rather to indicate that the nature and character of a person at any present moment are provided or donated (given) by one's heritage in time and space. In addition to personal-developmental and cultural factors (Rizzuto 1979; Berger 1967), cognitive-structural factors act to shape the religious framework the believer brings to any religious event (Boyer 1995). This is the transmission of religious "tradition" (on religious tradition as "scripts" (cf. McCallister, 1995, 343). The range of experiences capable of being noticed *as* religious, the image of God and God's activity (much more than a mere intellectual concept - cf. Rizzuto

FIGURE 1:
HUMAN CATEGORIZATION PROCESS

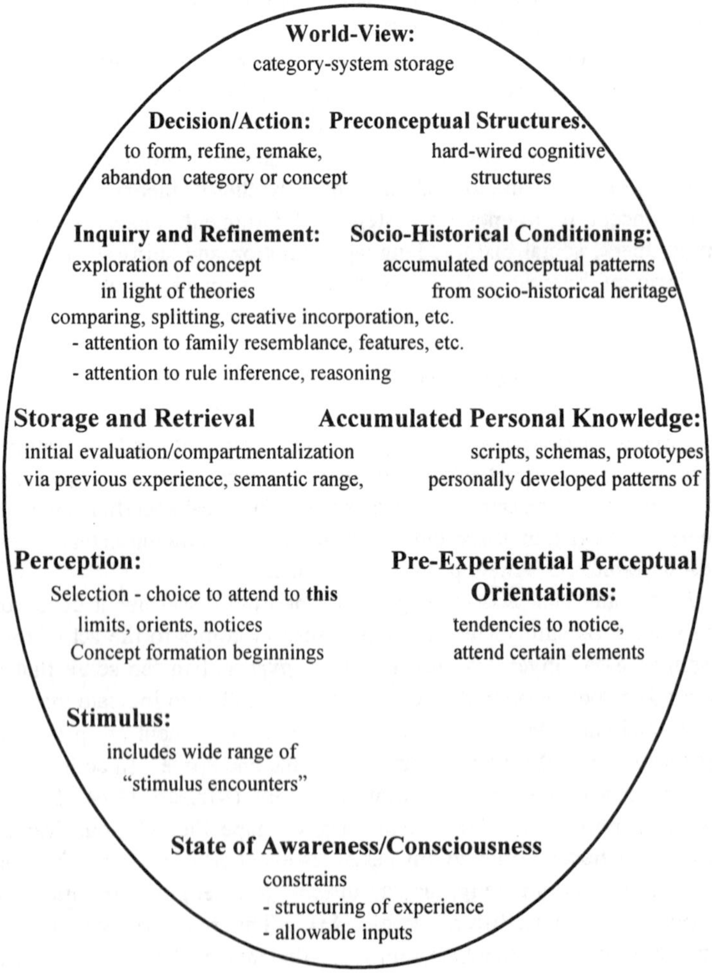

World-View:
category-system storage

Decision/Action: **Preconceptual Structures:**
to form, refine, remake,   hard-wired cognitive
abandon category or concept   structures

Inquiry and Refinement: **Socio-Historical Conditioning:**
exploration of concept   accumulated conceptual patterns
in light of theories   from socio-historical heritage
comparing, splitting, creative incorporation, etc.
- attention to family resemblance, features, etc.
- attention to rule inference, reasoning

Storage and Retrieval   **Accumulated Personal Knowledge:**
initial evaluation/compartmentalization   scripts, schemas, prototypes
via previous experience, semantic range,   personally developed patterns of

Perception: **Pre-Experiential Perceptual**
Selection - choice to attend to **this**   **Orientations:**
limits, orients, notices   tendencies to notice,
Concept formation beginnings   attend certain elements

Stimulus:
includes wide range of
"stimulus encounters"

State of Awareness/Consciousness
constrains
- structuring of experience
- allowable inputs

1979), habitual goal-related activities or interests which bear on matters of religion, and more, are shaped to some extent by what has gone before. Thus the individual discerner does not enter discernment "neutral," but already somewhat religiously configured. Thus the act of identifying what is from God always begins from what is given in the individual.

Second, discernment addresses real tendencies, regularities afforded in the perceived environment. Patterns (e.g. consolation) are recognized, habits (e.g. love) are identified and numinous experiences are categorized into somewhat recognizable and communicable taxonomies. However fallible in practice, Christian discernment aims at the adequate correlation between concept (concept formation and concept retrieval/attribution) and the regularities of the perceived environment (in this case the presence or guidance of God). It is within the context of such spiritual affordances that exemplars and salient features are coded in mind and society by prototype or by more abstract means. Without trying to solve the debate regarding the social construction or universality of mystical experience (on this cf. Katz 1978; Proudfoot 1985; Forman 1990; Alston 1991; Yandell 1993), it appears at least fair to state that religious literature, and the wisdom of Christian discernment in particular, points directly to mutually identifiable regularities in the perceived world, regularities which appear to have religious significance.

Third, discernment should be seen as a special type of categorization. Rather than discriminating between numbers of objects, events, experiences that naturally occur in separate domains of life, much of Christian discernment identifies one binary concept (*God* or *not God*) in many, perhaps unlimited, domains of life. Categorization literature has focused upon conceptual operations insofar as they relate primarily to objects, events, rules, and procedures, and has neglected the categorization of adjectival concepts (outside of research on color). I think that Christian discernment may function like a subtle adjectival concept, identifying one particular element or tendency (divinity) within other realms of experience. This type of approach naturally blends into the study of aesthetic categorization, which, as I have indicated with Ignatius and Edwards and shall develop below, plays an important part in Christian discernment. Aesthetic categorization involves a very simple labeling that requires an increasingly thorough knowledge of the related category-system. It is within this empirical framework that one can begin to see the impact of Edwards' spiritual understanding or Ignatius' discernment of appreciation upon specific discernment situations.

Fourth, a theory of Christian discernment must respect categorization as a *process*. While *God* may be revealed in an overwhelming manner at times (e.g. Ignatius' First Time election), usually confident determination of category membership in complex categories requires completion of various stages of evaluation, ensuring that biases have been circumvented and that all appropriate information has been integrated. As I shall suggest, key shifts in these stages are often signalled by changes in affectivity. The process of the attribution of category membership (noticing God) by means of simple salient features under ordinary circumstances will differ from the careful discernment of God's guidance in a matter of critical importance. In either case, however, the categorization of God's presence or guidance is, as categorization, a process involving a variety of separate operations.

Fifth, discernment will be different for different people. The contexts (charismatic worship, personal spiritual direction, social transformation, etc.), the associated goal-related activities (personal decisions, corporate evaluations, responding to impulses in prayer, etc.), the history with "God" in particular domains (novice to the faith, mature believer) all will affect how *God* and *not God* can be or are best perceived. In some contexts noting a few salient features of *God* are all that is needed or appropriate (e.g. pointing to the "harbor lights" of scripture, circumstances, and Spirit - cf. Mumford 1971). In other circumstances the need for subtle recognition of the dynamics involved is much greater (e.g. an Ignatian thirty day retreat; cf. Toner 1982; 1991). At times what may look like God may prove only to be an "angel of light" (Diadochus 1979 [450(?)]; Jonathan Edwards *Religious Affections*; for this theme in Buddhism cf. Tson-kha-pa 1978). The capacity for, contexts of, and experience with religious categorization differs between people. Approaches to Christian discernment must take this diversity into consideration.

Sixth, one must recall distinctions between category features, category exemplariness, and category membership with relation to Christian discernment. Recall of *God* may encode a variety of category features of the concept *God*: recent experiences, abstract concepts, particular feelings, or something entirely different, depending on the occasion.   Furthermore, there may be prototypical or exemplary events, experiences, ideas with which some can point to *God* with confidence.   Yet, as mentioned above, particularly salient experiences which one readily associates with God may not always be the most reliable criteria for category membership.   Discernment deals particularly with category membership.   For example, Boyer (1995) notes that Medin's "essentialist heuristic" appears to apply in tribal religious social stratification.   Cultures may point to a variety of surface features when asked what makes an individual a shaman, but their assumption is that there is some underlying "essence" (possession of the spirit) that is *the* defining feature.   This same essentialist assumption may also lie beneath Gay's (1957) distinction, mentioned in previous chapters, between the "immediate," "mediate," and "next meditate" objects of discernment, in which some features become signs of an underlying critical feature.   A theory of Christian discernment must reflect carefully on category membership issues, and distinguish them from category exemplariness and feature identification with respect to the various domains in view.

Seventh, in this context then, the development of connaturality as mentioned in the previous chapters becomes, for discernment as categorization, the increase of experience and facilitation of "noticing" important features.   Cue validity, feature similarity, rule-inductive patterns and such remain unnoticed until sufficient exposure to exemplars enables distinction.   As a discerner gains increasing expertise in the overall "material" of the Christian faith, familiarity with a wider and richer range of related attributes is acquired and distinctions are made possible which are not available to those with less exposure to the domains and material involved in discernment.

Eighth, Christian discernment is conducted within the developing "category-systems" (Rosch 1983, 42; 1994; Glass and Holyoak 1984, 157) of Christianity itself.   Categories are embedded in theories, and the selection of relevant attributes for comparison in application of a category, interproperty relations holding features together in a meaningful whole, and the leveling of features indicating importance of different features are ordered in the context of theory and theory-developing communities (Medin 1989).   As experiences, events, and such are evaluated over the centuries, taxonomies of concepts and partonomies of scripts (J. Anderson 1995) are developed around relevant domains and goal-related fields of interest.   New and important concepts related to these domains (e.g. "consolation" and "desolation") are established, and means of recognizing these are developed (e.g. self-examination exercises). Since concepts are not merely a private but also a public phenomena, communication can serve to refine these concepts (it can also serve to harden stereotypes and biases - cf. Lonergan 1958). In terms of categorization research, I think it is helpful to regard the historical "discernment tradition" as the insights and arguments of Christian spiritual expertise pointing out relevant salient features to notice (and pointing away from inappropriate features). Edwards' emphasis on the distinction between "no certain signs" and "more certain signs" certainly reflects this kind of category-system. At times the tradition may become sufficiently developed on particular matters to move toward a more "classical" understanding of the category in that the understanding of that category is understood in terms of "defining features" which when present provide (nearly) "necessary and sufficient conditions" of the category itself.

Ninth, as individual believers discern particular objects, they call upon this tradition, these category-systems, to facilitate the recognition of God in individual phenomena. Informed discerning individuals sort out the regularities and tendencies of the mix of stuff that confronts them in light of schema and prototypes given by expertise. This helps them avoid judgment biases caused by cognitive-structural heuristics, environmental factors and affective concerns, and to focus on key features and processes. For the informed discerning believer, this will involve a fair degree of attention training, as some natural patterns of categorization may need to be corrected for the sake of accurate assessment of category membership. At times the tradition itself must be refined. A theory of Christian discernment must account for this ongoing use and correction of personal and corporate category-systems in the act of discernment.

Tenth, as was made clear in the review of the empirical literature, a theory of Christian discernment will also acknowledge the important role that prototypes, similarity comparison, and graded structure will play in category recognition. Salient features will be identified and events, objects, experiences will frequently be compared to these salient features (e.g. looking for peace as confirmation in an elective situation) in order to determine the presence or guidance of God. Some experts in the tradition refer not merely to prototypes and particular exemplars, but also to a *range* of exemplars that give an intuitive sense of the concept (e.g. Ignatius' description of consolation). Yet the attention to similarity is also embedded in an implicit theory of spirituality that is more than simply inherited tradition but also a felt sense of the whole, which gives direction to the selection, organization and expression of the similarities under concern (e.g. certain features of "peace" are more explicitly noticed as significant in Christian discernment than in other domains).

Finally, discernment, in all its diverse forms, is merely one element of an adaptive, semiotic, enactive mediation of experience. It is both an act of knowledge and a knowledge-in-action. It both represents and forms its environment. It is not neutral and static, but rather dynamic and alive. It is suffused with emotion. To that point that I now turn.

Affectivity: Discernment as an "Affectively-Rich" Act of Knowing"

I am examining discernment not merely as an act of knowing, but as an "affectively-rich" act of knowledge. I have already noted the centrality of the affective dimension of life. Thus Robert Roberts writes,

> Whatever else Christianity may be, it is a set of emotions. It is love of God and neighbor, grief about one's own waywardness, joy in the merciful salvation of our God, gratitude, hope, and peace (Roberts 1982, 1).

In a similar manner, Donald Saliers states, "because our existence is known most deeply and intimately through our emotions and passions, the place of encounter with God is in their midst" (Saliers 1991, 99). William McNamara emphasizes this point, issuing believers the challenge that,

> No puny passions will do, but the total thrust of our erotic being toward the Absolutely Loving God, and therefore toward full participation in the Christlike life on earth. . . . This is the earthly destiny of every person: to be so alive, so completely

awakened, that he moves in and out of concrete human exigencies at a passionate pitch of loving awareness (McNamara 1977, 124).

These writers merely echo the words of Jonathan Edwards that "true religion, in great part, consists in holy affections."

This significant role of affectivity in Christian life creates special problems for the categorizing act of knowledge known as discernment. It is disconcerting to have something as mysterious as emotions play a significant role in the process intending to bring clarity to the most important area of human existence (relationship with God). Sometimes confusion regarding affectivity is the very problem to be discerned, as one tries to determine whether a particular emotional experience ought to be considered "from God." Sometimes emotions influence Godward predispositions, either hindering or helping one's capacity to notice God's presence or guidance. Affectivity also assists (or complicates) the knowledge-acquisition function of discernment. The inclusion of affectivity in the midst of discernment adds a measure of "messiness" into a process that one otherwise might consider rather neat. For this reason some are tempted to distrust and minimize their role in discernment (e.g. Friesen 1980).

Clarification of the roles of affectivity in discernment is further complicated in that a variety of conflicting notions concerning emotions are in circulation. Some, following many classical and medieval thinkers, hold a suspicion of emotions as ranking low on a hierarchical scale of human "faculties." Others, following psychological trends after Freud, emphasize the danger of emotional repression, and encourage unrestrained expression of emotions. Writers on Christian discernment span a wide range of times, places, and approaches to affectivity. I have noted this in Ignatius and Edwards already. I also mentioned in chapter one that others have called specifically for "further research and reflection on the dynamics of this type of experience" (Rakoczy 1980, 217). Hence the section which follows will attempt to provide greater empirical grounding to an understanding of affectivity in order to clarify affective experience in the context of Christian discernment.

Rather than review the history of experimental psychology with relationship to affectivity, I have chosen to summarize the approach of four chief figures in the field of emotions research. Research related to affectivity has for the most part focused on the exploration of human emotions (such as anger, sorrow, and the like) and for this reason implications for the broader concept of affectivity (by which term I refer to a variety of evaluative responses including emotions, moods, desires and other operations) will be reserved for my synthesis at the close of the review of emotions research. The history of emotions research has not developed as neatly as research in categorization. Rather than passing through distinct shifts of focus, emotions research has developed with somewhat parallel competing models. Major representatives have risen to represent these models over the years. Recently, all have been forced to acknowledge something of the insights of the other approaches. The result is that emotions research is, I think (along with Cornelius 1996), developing some measure of consensus. The present section will point toward this measure of consensus. I will represent emotions research by developing the thought of four different figures, each of which emphasizes a different aspect of affectivity: (1) the Dutch scholar Nico Frijda, whose work on the adaptive dimension, especially in the form of "action tendencies" is well-respected in the field, (2) the American Richard Lazarus, who helped pioneer the "cognitive" approach to emotions, (3) Keith Oatley, the British/Canadian scholar who has developed a "communicative" approach to emotions, and (4) Lazarus' student James Averill, who has led the way into development of a "social constructionist" approach to emotions. I will present the figures separately, pointing out the unique contributions of each. Because of the massive range of psychological and physiological data involved in forming a theory of emotions, I will approach each figure by summarizing their own summaries of findings. I will then add a few notes from other relevant research. Following this I will pull the research together into a kind of synthesis of insights concerning affectivity and apply this synthesis to the understanding of affective experience that is directly connected with the Christian faith and finally, more specifically, to Christian discernment. Because of the diversity of approaches, a firm definition of "emotion" must develop cumulatively, being finally developed in the synthetic presentation of affectivity given at the close of the review.

Nico Frijda: The Adaptive Dimension

The topic of human emotion has become a popular one in recent decades, both in popular literature (cf. Goleman 1995) and in scholarly circles (for review cf. Cornelius 1996). Psychologist Nico Frijda has been one of the chief participants in academic research in emotions for over three decades. Frijda's main work is his review and synthesis of emotion research, *The Emotions* (Frijda 1986; cf. Averill 1988, 81; Oatley 1992, xii). I will develop Frijda's contribution especially as presented in this work, but will supplement with some of his later thought.

Frijda takes his starting point with a broad definition of *emotional phenomena*. Emotional phenomena involve (1) non-instrumental behavior (such as stroking a child or smiling while nursing), (2) physiological changes, and (3) evaluative subject-related experiences, as evoked by events and their significance. An emotion itself is the occurrence of these or their inner determinant. His notion of emotional *behavior* has its origins in Charles Darwin's principles of serviceable associated habits, antithesis, and direct action (cf. Darwin 1998 [1872]). Frijda's Darwinian emphasis, however, is not upon the development of specific emotion expressions through phylogenetic history. Rather he is interested in understanding the current functions that emotions serve by way of adapting the human to the challenges of the environment. He states,

> The fact that expressive movement can be interpreted as behavior with functional significance in the subject's interaction with his environment is of central importance for clarifying the relation between expression and emotion; or for clarifying what is meant by an *emotion* for that matter (Frijda 1986, 12 italics Frijda's).

Frijda replaces Darwin's three principles of emotional expression with four of his own. The first is the principle of "relational activity." By this Frijda notes that emotion behaviors seek to change relationship with the environment. Quite often this change is not accomplished by changing the environment, but rather by an alteration in the sensory and locomotor readiness of the individual (e.g. tenseness). At times, however, emotion behaviors move toward influencing the behavior of someone else. Frijda calls this second principle "interactive effectiveness." Frowning at a child to correct poor behavior is an example of this. The third principle of emotional behavior is the principle of "activation." Activation involves the presence of attention, readiness, or striving for something. A final principle involved in emotional expression is "inhibition." Some expression can be understood best as the inhibition of behavior, as when one quietly grits one's teeth in rage. Modes of activation (apathy to excitement), inhibition (controlled to unrestrained) and relational motion (approach to withdraw) all combine to modify states of readiness to act in a given situation. This brings Frijda to his chief point, *action readiness*. "Emotions," says Frijda, are "modes of relational action readiness, either in the form of tendencies to establish, maintain or disrupt a relationship with the environment or in the form of relational readiness as such" (1986, 71). For Frijda, action tendency is the primary feature of emotions as emotions. It is action tendency that distinguishes emotions from intentional behavior.

Frijda is exceptionally thorough in his discussion of the *physiological* aspects of emotional response. He reviews the background of emphasis in physiology in terms of the well known James-Lange theory (cf. Lange and James 1967 [1922]), and the debates about specific physiological responses to particular emotions which followed, concluding that "the importance assigned to cognitive and behavioral aspects depends upon the answer to the question of physiological specificity" (Frijda 1986, 126). He reviews evidence for autonomic responses (heart rate, blood pressure, respiration, etc.), hormonal changes, electrocortical changes (α and β rhythms) and muscle tension. While the findings are sufficient to show that physiological response is certainly an important element in action readiness, Frijda concludes that it does not define emotion.

The third major element of emotional phenomena is *experience*. Emotional experience involves three elements: situational meaning structure, awareness of arousal, and awareness of action readiness mode. It is the combination of these three elements that gives the "experience" of emotion. Frijda regards situational meaning as the output of an appraisal function, which evaluates a situation in light of personal concerns. The structure of situational meaning is constructed from a variety of specific operations or components. "Core" components evaluate objectivity, relevance, difficulty, urgency, positive or negative valence and other key features of a situation that may give it emotional significance. Other operations called "context" components attend to the presence or absence of the matter in view, the possibility for change in the situation, the object or event orientation, and other factors which affect which emotion would be expressed in a given emotional episode. "Object" components, such as ego-role and value relevance also give shape to the particular emotion evoked in a given situation. Value relevance is especially significant in light of the present study, because it codes a valence upon a graded scale from possessed concern to supra-personal value. Frijda examines awareness of arousal through research regarding autonomic awareness, concluding that it contributes to the intensity and quality of an emotion "although it is probably not the cue for distinguishing the different emotions" (1986, 230).

Frijda deals with the third element of emotional experience, awareness of action and action tendency, through a review of self-attribution theory and the evidence from propioceptive cues (such as facial movement). He stresses the importance of this element for emotional experience. He states, "Felt action readiness modes contain the information needed to account for the distinction between the major emotions like anger, fear, and joy and for many distinctions within those concepts. Action readiness modes contain all the information needed for the subject to distinguish one major emotion experience from another" (Frijda 1986, 238). Along with the sensed hedonic quality of emotion, these factors combine to make emotional experience. Thus emotion as experience is defined as:

> awareness of some mode of action readiness of a passive and action-control-demanding nature, involving readiness to change or maintain relationships with the environment (or intentional objects generally); which action readiness is experienced as motivated or caused by situation appraised as relevant, urgent, and meaningful with respect to ways of dealing with it; which situations are felt to affect the subject, and to affect him bodily" (Frijda 1986, 257).

Having presented an outline of the primary elements of emotions (non-instrumental behaviors, physiological changes, felt experiences), Frijda moves, in *The Emotions*, to address emotions as *elicited* behavior. Why do stimuli elicit emotional phenomena and how are emotions stimulated? The elicitation of emotion involves two separate entities, "the stimulus event and a concern that exists prior to the stimulus event and that the subject carries with him when the event confronts him" (Frijda, 1986, 278). A *concern* is a disposition to prefer the occurrence of a given state of affairs. Concerns develop through the life-history of the subject. They are tied up in relationships, goals, and valued objects. They are often rooted in primary needs, desires or aversions. Some concerns are related to the general functioning of the subject as an organism. Some concerns are related to supra-personal values. Frijda understands *stimuli* as that which confronts the human subject. Stimuli are elements of experience that are relevant to particular concerns. It is not, however, simply the stimuli itself that triggers emotion; rather "constellations" or "stimuli-as-signals of given modes of promise of concern satisfaction, or of threat thereto" serve this function (Frijda 1986, 470). When a stimuli signals some kind of match or mismatch with regard to a concern, an emotion is evoked (as, for example, when concern for personal safety is signalled by being confronted by a mountain lion during a hike, and fear is elicited). The concern must be present for an emotion to be evoked (a young child without knowledge or concern about mountain lions does not experience the same fear, to his or her danger). The stimuli may be real or imagined (research demonstrates that to some extent fear may be elicited among subjects simply by vividly imagining the mountain lion situation). General activation heightens emotional experience (the fear will be stronger if you are running when you meet the mountain lion).

Emotion is elicited by stimuli through an evaluative *process*. *Appraisal* mechanisms, as mentioned above (and will be described in more detail below), operate to turn stimulus events into a situational meaning structure. The meaning structure of the appraised event actually serves to elicit the emotion. An initial comparison of stimulus event appraises the event in light of the core components mentioned above (urgency, difficulty, etc.) and issues a primary sense of relevance. A more diagnostic operation compares the event to the set of context components, giving direction to the type of emotion elicited. Further evaluation weighs seriousness and other components to assess the degree and type of emotion. These operations together produce a summary picture of the situation meaning structure (for example the assessment of urgency, seriousness, largely helpless condition, etc. combine to form the situation meaning structure of the mountain lion situation). *Regulation* plays a part in the entire process. Inhibitory mechanisms can respond to the external stimuli themselves (we can deny the presence of the mountain lion), the process (we can imagine that the lion will be nice to us), or proposed actions (we may want to run, but choose to walk slowly and carefully away). Appraisal and regulatory inhibition operate both consciously and unconsciously. The output of this stage of the process is a *proposed action*. This, in turn, triggers *action readiness* modes (on the relationship between emotion, appraisal, and action readiness cf. Frijda, Kuipers, and Schure 1989). What particular emotions are experienced depends upon the range of action programs, the behavior systems, and the activation or deactivation mechanisms available. The match of situation-meaning, action proposed, and program available indicates which action-tendency and emotion appears. Action readiness then elicits physiological changes, emotional responses and emotional experience. Overt responses flow from these.

The sense of the varying intensity of emotions is well-known. Frijda and Joep Sonnemans explored the factors affecting the intensity of emotions in 1994 (Sonnemans and Frijda 1994). The question this study asked was "*what* is it in emotions that varies to give this sense?" They administered a questionnaire exploring the sense of intensity in subjects' emotional experience. Factor analysis of the questionnaire yielded six primary factors including duration of the emotion, perceived bodily changes, strength of action tendency and belief changes and influence upon long-term behavior. The findings indicated that emotional intensity is multidimensional. In spite of probable individual differences in the weighting of each factor, it appears, therefore, that a variety of factors can be coded to give a sense of the intensity of an emotional experience.

In an article for the American Psychologist, Frijda addresses the theme of regularity, mentioned in the discussion of categorization,[1] by addressing emotions as "lawful phenomena" (1988). His aim in this article is to discuss what he considers to be "empirical regularities" concerning the way emotions operate. Frijda presents a num-

---

[1] I will discuss terms like "habit," "manner," "pattern," "law," and "regularity," under Gelpi's understanding of "tendency" in chapter 4.

ber of specific laws relating to the elicitation, persistence and regulation of emotion. A few, listed below, are especially relevant to Christian discernment:

The Law of Apparent Reality - *Emotions are elicited by events appraised as real, and their intensity corresponds to the degree which this is the case*

The Law of Change - *Emotions are elicited not so much by the presence of favorable or unfavorable conditions, but by actual or expected changes in favorable or unfavorable conditions.*

The Law of Comparative Feeling - *The intensity of emotion depends on the relationship between an event and some frame of reference against which the event is evaluated.*

The Law of Conservation of Emotional Momentum - *Emotional events retain their power to elicit emotions indefinitely, unless counteracted by repetitive exposures that permit extinction or habituation, to the extent that these are possible.*

The Law of Closure - *Emotions tend to be closed to judgments of relativity of impact and to the requirements of goals other than their own.*

The Law of Care for Consequence - *Every emotional impulse elicits a secondary impulse that tends to modify it in view of possible consequences.* (Frijda 1988 352-55; italics Frijda's).

By emphasizing the role of action tendencies as a central component of emotional experience, Nico Frijda reminds one that affectivity is *adaptive*. Human emotions involve tendencies to respond, to adapt, to interact with the environment confronting us with personal significance. By emphasizing the various elements which combine to constitute emotion, he also emphasizes that affectivity is a *process*. Emotions are not simply "reactions," or libidinal "energy release." Emotions involve an interrelated network of cognitive, physiological, and uniquely affective operations, mutually influencing one another over time. It is this process as a whole that structures human "emotion."

Richard Lazarus: The Cognitive Dimension

Frijda writes, "Richard Lazarus is one of the grand old men of current emotion theory. I think that one may say that, together with

Magda Arnold and Stanley Schachter, he created the cognitive approach to emotion" (Frijda 1994, 473). Lazarus' work began in post-World War II research concerning stress. He identified important differences between physiological and psychological stress, the latter being tied up with "personal meaning." He also distinguished between three kinds of stress: harm, threat, and challenge. Lazarus' research in stress proved to be a key step toward a fully cognitive approach to emotions, for in the difference between harm, threat, and challenge, Lazarus identified the central element of emotional appraisal. Threat appraises a situation as being imminently noxious. Challenge appraises a situation as being potentially noxious, but that the negative potential can be avoided with sufficient effort. Research in stress appraisal led to research in the related concept of "coping" with stress, the thoughts and actions humans take to manage specific demands appraised as noxious in some form. The research of Lazarus and his associates led to the development of precise tools for measurement of stress and coping, and to the formulation of a set of "laws" of coping behavior (Lazarus 1993, 9).

The study of stress served as a subset of emotion research, and Lazarus began to formulate his research into a larger, more comprehensive approach to emotions in general. This approach is fully developed in his *Emotion and Adaptation* (Lazarus 1991a). I will follow this book to summarize Lazarus' main themes. He calls his approach a "cognitive-motivational-relational" theory of emotion (cf. also Lazarus 1991b). The theory is "cognitive" because it emphasizes the importance of appraisal and cognitive factors in the formation of emotion. Lazarus writes, "The most important *content* in the emotion process consists of *knowledge* (that is about how things work in general and in the specific adaptational encounter) and *appraisals* of the significance of the person-environment relationship for personal well-being" (1991a, 127; italics Lazarus'). It is "motivational" in that, for Lazarus, emotions are responses to the state of affairs with relationship to goal commitments. A sense of personal investment lies behind the matters appraised and "felt" in emotion, and this investment motivates thoroughly. The theory is "relational," because the appraisal is always about relationships, changes in the "person-environment relationship." Emotions are not simply a matter of the person; nor are they simply a matter of "what is out there." Rather, emotions address the intersection of the two. In a statement that reflects Frijda's work, Lazarus writes,

> In effect, universal statements about environmental or personality-centered provokers of emotion are, theoretically incomplete. They do not specify the *conditions* that are harmful or beneficial for any given *type of person*, or conversely, the *types of persons* for whom *particular environments* are especially harmful or beneficial, and they do not help us understand the varieties of emotional patterns that result. The bottom line is that the quality and intensity of an emotion are products of actual, anticipated, or imagined adaptational encounters with an environment, which are appraised by the individual as having either positive or negative significance for well-being. (1991a, 92; italics Lazarus').

One of Lazarus' chief contributions is his clarification of the nature of emotional *appraisal*. Using repeated experiments measuring slightly different factors Lazarus has developed a theory of emotional appraisal that is quite nuanced. He distinguishes between situational and generalized appraisal, the former directed at specific situations, the latter referring to patterns of evaluation on a broader level. Both must be addressed in order to account for the emotion process. He also distinguishes between knowledge, which informs the subject of the world in general and appraisal, which evaluates the significance of events (cf. Lazarus and Smith 1988). Lazarus approaches the role of appraisal from two separate complementary perspectives. From what he calls the *molecular* perspective (looking at appraisal from the view of the particulars involved), Lazarus distinguishes separate appraisal operations which evaluate situations to bring the sense of harm or benefit characteristic of emotion. *Primary* appraisal addresses motivational relevance (the degree to which an encounter touches goals or concerns), motivational congruence (consistency or inconsistency with goals), and type of ego-involvement (self and social esteem, moral values, ego-ideals, meanings and ideas, other persons and their well being, life goals). Type of ego-involvement includes those value-laden goals that Frijda addressed under "value relevance." *Secondary* appraisal assesses accountability (blame or credit), coping potential, and future expectancy (whether things are likely to change for the better or worse). With a few minor differences, the output from primary and secondary appraisal roughly parallels Frijda's situational meaning structure. Lazarus, however, orders his appraisal components in such a way that the development of emotion follows the appraisal process. He writes,

> Notice that the appraisal components are ordered in such a way that they proceed from very broad decisions - for example, whether or not there will be an emotion (goal relevance), whether the emotion will be positive or negative (goal congruence or incongruence) - gradually narrowing down to a precise discrimination between one emotion or another. As the options are narrowed, it becomes possible to say that only one emotion is possible in this context (Lazarus 1991a, 151).

From the *molar* perspective (looking at the whole), the particulars of appraisal coalesce into general themes related to the person-environment relationship. Lazarus calls these "core relational themes." He identifies each emotion with a particular core relational theme, much as Frijda identified each emotion with a particular "action tendency." For example, Lazarus' core-relational theme for "fright" is "facing an immediate, concrete, and overwhelming physical danger." His conviction is that "this approach treats the emotions as relational categories, each of which not only describes a different kind of psychophysiological reaction, but also defines a different person-environment relationship implying a particular kind of harm or benefit" (Lazarus 1991a, 290).

Whereas Frijda speaks of "regulation," Lazarus draws from his background in stress research to speak of "coping." He divides coping into two kinds. Problem-focused coping attempts to change the person-environment realities behind negative emotions. Emotion-focused coping attempts to change what is attended or how it is appraised. Rather than understanding coping simply as efforts to control the emotion or the situation Lazarus proposes that coping "also directly follows an initial appraisal of harm, threat, or challenge and can modify the subsequent appraisal, thereby changing or even short circuiting the emotional reaction" (Lazarus 1991a, 113). Lazarus' description of coping processes, while very informative, is limited to emotions related to stress, making application to positive emotions (and religious emotions) limited.

In spite of Lazarus' insistence upon the primacy of cognition in emotion (for the debate on this point cf. Zajonc 1980; 1984; Lazarus 1984; Leventhal and Scherer 1987), he is careful to preserve an approach to appraisal that "does not imply rationality, deliberateness, or consciousness of the cognitive processes involved in emotion" (Lazarus 1991a, 152). The key to this clarification lies in a grasp of the achievement of meaning. Lazarus draws from various fields to suggest that meaning, perception and processing of personal-relevant information need not be reflective or deliberate. Quite often it is unconscious and automatic (at times, to our detriment). Whether conscious or unconscious, however, Lazarus and his associates have demonstrated that people also can and do engage in *reappraisals* which adjust evaluation and emotion. He relates his findings concerning unconscious appraisal to depth psychology in *Emotion and Adaptation* in a brilliant comparison, suggesting that what depth psychologists aim for in their approach to the unconscious, is a depth psychology of goal, intention, or concern.

Whereas Frijda emphasizes emotion as a *process*, Lazarus uses the word *system* to describe the dynamics of emotional experience. The cognitive-motivational-emotive system consists of a network of variables and outcomes. *Antecedent* variables include personality/motivation variables, which relate to values and commitments, beliefs, existential sense of control, and environmental/situation variables, which relate to demands, constraints, resources, ambiguity or immanence of harm. *Mediating process variables* are the stages of appraisal itself: primary, secondary, reappraisals, and coping strategies. Short term *outcomes* include physiological changes and subjective feelings. Long term outcomes include somatic health/illness, morale/well-being, and social functioning. Later sections of *Emotion and Adaptation* deal with individual emotions, emotional development, social influence and practical applications.

Using different language and different methods Lazarus supports much of what was presented in the discussion of Nico Frijda. In addition, Richard Lazarus gives a much more nuanced recognition of the importance of cognitive functions in emotions. Appraisal and coping processes rely on cognitive operations in order to form and shape emotional experience. Emotions, whether consciously or unconsciously, *know* something. It is often the emotions that give humans the clearest sense of awareness of a certain state of affairs. Emotions evaluate, through knowledge, appraisal, reappraisal, and coping mechanisms, the significance of the person-environment relationship.

Keith Oatley: The Communicative Dimension

The third representative of emotions research is Keith Oatley. Whereas other scholars in emotions hail from personality or social psychology, Oatley's research spans the fields of brain/mind studies and cognitive science, making him more strictly a "cognitive" psychologist. Oatley developed primary elements of his approach to emotions in partnership with P. N. Johnson-Laird (Oatley and Johnson-Laird 1987). He developed his thought more fully in his well-respected monograph, *Best Laid Schemes: The Psychology of Emotions* (1992; cf. Frijda 1987, 51; Averill 1994, 73). This book and the 1987 article will serve to provide an outline of Oatley's insights. *Best Laid Schemes* is a unique book in emotions research in that it draws material from a variety of fields to develop his points. Not only cognitive science and emotions research, but also Aristotelian philosophy and world literature are heavily employed to provide the reader with a more intuitive sense of the material handled. For the purposes of the present paper I will focus attention upon summarizing empirical material and pointing out Oatley's unique insights.

Oatley and Johnson-Laird consider their approach to emotions a "conflictive-cognitive" theory. As *conflictive*, they consider their work to be a development of the ideas of John Dewey, who in attempting to reconcile differences between Darwin's and William James' theories of emotions, developed the ideas that emotions arise at points of goal conflict (cf. Dewey 1894; 1895. on conflict theories of emotions cf. Mandler 1984). As *cognitive* they refer to "psychological explanations in terms of the representation and transformation of knowledge which may or may not be conscious" (Oatley and Johnson-Laird 1987, 30).

Drawing from artificial intelligence and cognitive science, their approach emphasizes the role of goals or *plans* in the origin of emotional experience. Oatley describes the nature of a plan in his summary of the actions of a character in Tolstoy's *Anna Karinina*:

One formulation would be that by operating with his mental models (involving, perhaps, times, routes, places) he assembles a series of subgoals, and hence the actions he will perform, to achieve the overall goal. After assembling the plan in the simulation space of his mend, he can act, directing himself, as it were, by reading off the actions in sequence. This idea of the planning hierarchy captures a principle of what we mean by acting intentionally (Oatley, 1992, 27).

Although plans can be structured in a very simple manner, as in the quote above or in many computer programs, everyday life involves a more complicated approach to plans. Human actions are often influenced by multiple goals simultaneously. Human knowledge and resources related to the formation and performance of plans are limited. Human actions often involve the coordination and influence of a number of agents whose plans are more mysterious than one's own. These complications necessarily create occasions where conflicts appear. Oatley calls these moments "junctures." Emotions arise in the context of these junctures.

Oatley and Johnson-Laird tie their conflictive-cognitive approach to a "modular" theory of human information-processing (increasingly popular in cognitive circles). This theory suggests that cognitive process develops from a networked set of *modules*, each functioning to perform a discrete operation or achieve a specific goal. In a modular system, there are problems of coordination, as "one part often does not know what the other part is doing." Thus a modular system requires a certain amount of monitoring and "inner communication" in order to maintain proper functioning of the system as a whole. This, in turn leads to the central postulate of the Oatley/Johnson-Laird theory of emotions:

Each goal and plan has a monitoring mechanism that evaluates events relevant to it. When a substantial change of probability occurs of achieving an important goal or subgoal, the monitoring mechanism broadcasts to the whole cognitive system a signal that can set it into readiness to respond to this change. Humans experience these signals and the states of readiness they induce as emotions (Oatley 1992, 50).

The similarity to Frijda's "action tendencies" or "states of action readiness" is obvious. However, Oatley specifies the idea through an information-processing model. In doing so, the focus shifts slightly from the adaptive response of the subject to changes in the *environment* ("out there" situations) to the adaptive response of the subject to changes in *mental state*. Thus Oatley and Johnson-Laird emphasize correspondence or mis-correspondence within the appraisal process itself (my language) as the central causal factor in emotion elicitation.

As suggested by the words "broadcast" and "signal" in the above postulate, Oatley's approach to emotion is a *communicative* approach. It begins with the "inner communication" of the human mind. Oatley distinguishes between two kinds of mental communication to indicate how emotions function in this regard. *Semantic messages* are referential. They have syntactic structure, specific hierarchically organized destinations and require interpretation. *Control messages*, however, function by a diffuse spreading operation which signals a simple change in the modules within range of the message "spread." Oatley and Johnson-Laird's hypothesis is that "there are control signals that correspond to basic emotions. Each occurs when a particular kind of juncture is recognized" (Oatley 1992, 54).

Oatley and Johnson-Laird, following the lead of Ekman and others, postulate a small number of universally occurring basic emotion modes. Their approach to these (five) emotions is very similar to Rosch's understanding of prototypicality with regard to salience in color. He draws upon a variety of empirical data to argue that happiness, sadness, anxiety (or fear) anger, and disgust should be regarded as basic (on the "basic emotions" debate cf. Frijda, 1987; Ortony and Turner 1990; Cornelius 1996). Oatley sees two primary components of an emotion: action readiness and phenomenological tone. Emotions are also usually accompanied by secondary components: conscious preoccupation, bodily disturbances, and expressions of various kinds. Two of these, conscious preoccupation and phenomenological tone, were not developed in either Frijda or Lazarus. *Phenomenological tone* refers to the general subjective sense of feeling associated with given emotions. *Mental preoccupation* refers to the fact that emotions tend to grab attention, often involving inner dialogues or thoughts (I would also include images), which tend to dominate during emotion episodes. Reports of subjects indicate that some components are not necessary for the emotion to be considered present and the percentages of components present over numbers of reported emotional episodes varies somewhat. Each basic emotion is tied to a particular juncture (like Lazarus' core relational themes and Frijda's action tendencies): thus, *fear* indicates a self-preservation goal threatened or a goal conflict; *anger* indicates an active plan frustrated; *happiness* indicates subgoals being achieved (epidemiology of these are reported in Oatley and Duncan 1994).

Complex emotions develop from the basic. By means of a careful examination of terms used for emotional experience, Johnson-Laird and Oatley classified the semantic structure of emotional vocabulary. They found that whereas basic emotions were occasionally experienced for no reason, most emotional experience arose "in relation to" some context. Emotion terms are used in relation to some event (gladden, frighten), to another person (love, hatred) or in relation to a goal (desire, craving). A complex emotion, "is a contextual emotion that has propositional content involving evaluation of performance in relation to a model of self" (Oatley 1992, p. 196). This evaluation may relate to goals (hope, despair), current state (pride, boredom) or past performance (nostalgia, remorse). It may also involve an evaluation of the self with respect to others, either with the focus on the self (embarrassment, shame) or on others (jealousy, sympathy).

One aspect of emotive experience that Oatley uniquely addresses is the subject of "moods." In his third postulate of his theory of emotions, Oatley states that "emotions are based on control signals that communicate pervasively within the cognitive system and tend to set up distinctive emotion modes. These modes can occur without any conscious semantic knowledge of their cause. They are referred to as moods when they become self-maintaining and remote from their initial cause" (Oatley 1992, 91). He considers moods to be emotional, in that they are based on the same kinds of readiness as the primary emotion modes. They are, however, not emotions proper because of their distance from the eliciting stimulus and their duration (Oatley 1992, 23-24). Moods tend to promote similar emotional experiences and mental operations and to disallow others. Oatley interprets this phenomena, called "mood congruence" by psychologists, neatly within his communicative approach to emotions.

Oatley also addresses the question of the apparent "irrationality" of the emotions, an issue raised by Chauncy against Edwards' interpretation of the Great Awakening. He gives this question two types of answers. He reviews the empirical evidence supporting the ideas that emotions are (1) noncausal by-products, (2) merely irrational intrusions, or (3) vestiges of phylogenetic history and finds them all wanting. Oatley then addresses rationality itself. Drawing from cognitive psychological material, Oatley argues that human thinking should be described as "drawing inferences from a mental model in the service of goals rather than as applying formal logic to problems" (1992, 152). People regularly hold irrational beliefs, reason illogically, and act inappropriately, and in somewhat predictable ways. Thus Oatley's first answer: rationality is not always so rational. It responds to salient material or scripts in light of a personally relevant goal or plan. Limited access to information and perspective and hard-wired habits of thought can prevent pure rationality from being attained in any given instance. Yet, as above, this is the very framework for the operation of emotion. They both operate in the context of active plans. Both are subject to the same limitations. Both can go awry. Then he turns to examine the functional approach to emotions. Emotions function to make ready a small suite of plans for action. They also serve to establish priority among elements in consciousness. Thus (his second answer), emotions have their own form of "rationality." Quite often it is not the emotion, but rather the related goals that invoke the irrational in emotions. (cf. also DeSousa 1987). It is through communication that one's goals are clarified.

One of Oatley's most significant contributions to emotions research, in my opinion, is his discussion of social or interpersonal emotions. He and Johnson-Laird write, "With the exception of fear, . . . most emotions of interest to humans occur in the course of relations with others. They are social emotions, and any theory of emotions must take this social dimension seriously, and not merely assume that relations with other people are an extension of the way we treat the physical environment" (Oatley and Johnson-Laird 1987, 41). Here, Oatley and Johnson-Laird's "communicative" theory shifts to a different level. Just as emotions serve, in intra-individual life, to manage transitions (junctures) within personal plans, so in inter-individual life, they serve to manage transitions in joint plans. Other humans serve, not merely as instruments of individual human plans, but as associates in cooperative plans. Conversation is the chief medium through which these plans are negotiated. But conversation can be misunderstood, degree of commitment to joint plans can be doubted, and joint plans can go awry, just as complications affect individual plans. Social emotions respond to these moments, just as individual emotions respond to changes in individual plan progress. Oatley identifies five principal aspects of the development of social emotions: attachment, social referencing, role taking, empathy, and temperament. Necessary to the process of mutual planning and the emotions that accompany, Oatley suggests, is the idea of the "self." Oatley's self is not a subjective identity, but rather is primarily social. Through one's model of the self one imagines actions cooperating with others. The model of self also contains an archive of interpersonal history. A model of the self enables one to take roles which embody conventions of social interaction, conventions which are laid out in mutually understood scripts. Like James Averill (discussed below), Oatley claims that emotions participate in these scripts; they are expected or permitted at different points and they are elicited when there is a change in mutual performance of a script. Social emotions function to renegotiate plans and relationships and to cause similar or complementary emotions in others. Emotion terms in conversation function to facilitate role adjustment, education, social comparison, and narrative.

Keith Oatley contributes to emotions research an emphasis upon the communicative function of emotions. While his approach bears similarity to that of Frijda and Lazarus, Oatley's information-processing model and interpersonal emphasis serve to complement their work with new insights. From Oatley one learns that emotions serve, in the individual, to communicate information necessary for the management of individual plans. Emotions serve, in society, to communicate information necessary for the management of mutual plans.

James Averill: The Social Dimension

James Averill was Lazarus' student. He worked with Lazarus on the cognitive dimensions of stress. Ultimately, however, Averill broke with the cognitivist school of his mentor. In doing so, he helped found the "social constructivist" school of emotions research (cf. Cornelius 1996). His work has had considerable influence on laboratory and cross-cultural research in emotions, and has stimulated much discussion in emotions theory. Averill has not written a monograph comparable to that of the earlier representatives. Nonetheless, a sufficient outline of his insights can be found in his 1980 articles on the constructivist view of emotions (Averill 1980a; 1980b) and in the introduction and conclusion to his book on anger (Averill 1982).

Averill defines emotions as, *"socially constructed syndromes (transitory social roles)* which include an individual's *appraisal of the situation* and which are *interpreted as passions rather than actions"* (Averill 1982, 6. Italics Averill's). To clarify Averill's approach, each of the elements of this definition will be developed.

First, Averill views emotions as *syndromes*. Borrowing from medical (and psychiatric) parlance, Averill understands syndromes as *"sets* of responses that covary in a *systematic fashion"* (1980a, 307; cf. 1980b 146). What Averill seeks to gain by this definition is distance from a slavish insistence upon one or two aspects of emotional experience as necessary and defining features of emotions. Thus action tendencies, physiological changes, appraisal patterns, bodily expressions and so on may all be typical of emotions, but none appears to be the defining feature necessary to identify an emotion *as* an emotion (notice the "family resemblance" approach here).

Second, these syndromes called emotions are *socially constructed*. Averill does not wish to deny the role that human biology plays in human emotions. He does, however, emphasize that the functional significance of emotional experience rests largely within the sociocultural system. The function of human emotions, what they intend to accomplish, is not found in analysis of the biological or even psychological system of human life. One discovers the *meaning* of emotions as one explores their role in societies and cultures. Societies *construct* these syndromes, by permitting, reinforcing, articulating some responses and ignoring, inhibiting, reinterpreting or rejecting others. Averill develops this theme greatly in his anthropological analysis of anger. Drawing from research in a variety cultures, he argues that the very experience of anger is defined by the cultural conditions surrounding it. He writes, "the social relationship determines not only the behavioral manifestation of the emotion, but the subjective experience of it as well" (Averill 1982, 64). Action tendencies, phenomenological tone, behavioral expressions are all "institutionalized responses" that have meaning only within a particular social context. Thus, while the social dimension may not be sufficient to define emotion, it is at least necessary.

Third, Averill takes his approach one step further, suggesting one look at emotions as transitory *social roles*. As the medical understanding of "syndrome" provided an appropriate metaphor for the multidimensional aspect of emotions, so the dramatic understanding of "roles" provides an appropriate metaphor for the interpersonal aspect of emotions. Like dramatic roles, an emotion is constituted by social rules and situations. Like dramatic roles, emotions do not exist as isolated events, but rather are interwoven with others to form a whole. An emotion is part of a larger story (a cultural matrix or "plot") which gives it meaning. Just as actors and actresses can choose when and how to enact a role so also persons are active participants in their emotions and not merely passive recipients. Similar to dramatic experience, involvement in the emotional role determines the nature and intensity of the emotional experience. Finally, emotional involvement, like acting, requires an understanding of the "plot," the cultural matrix, for meaningful experience (cf. Averill 1980b; 1990). These roles, then, function to regulate the dynamics of human relationships. Summarizing a set of studies exploring the causes and motives of anger in everyday experience, Averill writes, "the findings that anger is typically initiated by an appraised wrong, is directed toward a friend or loved one, and is constructively motivated are consistent with the notion that anger serves a positive social function by helping to regulate interpersonal relations" (Averill 1982, 183. cf Oatley 1992, 206-214).

Fourth, this syndrome or social role includes an *appraisal* of a situation. With this affirmation, Averill affirms the findings of the emotions research pioneered by Lazarus and others. However, even at this point, Averill emphasizes the social dimension. Just as the cognitivist research pointed to the previous arousal scholars to ask why situations were emotionally significant to some and not others, so Averill points to the cognitive scholars to ask what rules govern why some situations are appraised as emotively significant and others not. Averill conceives of emotions as a kind of "law-like" behavior, such that they operate by "rules." Rules of appraisal help determine the character of the object of emotional experience. Rules of behavior and feeling, help determine what is felt in emotion. Rules of attribution shape how a response is related to the self. Rules of prognostication evaluate the sense of time as relates to emotive experience. Averill's point is that "feeling rules of the above kinds . . . are largely social in origin. A person has not only the right, but in some cases even the obligation, to feel a certain way in appropriate circumstances" (Averill 1982, 23).

Finally, emotions are *interpreted as passions*. "Social roles" or "socially constructed syndromes" involving appraisal are insufficient to distinguish emotions from other non-emotional phenomena. Averill, therefore, identifies a third element which contributes to emotional experience, namely that they are "interpreted as passions." He takes this to mean that humans regard emotions, like perceptions, as happening to them, rather than as being intentional. He gives five primary reasons for such interpretations. Biological, social and psychological imperatives present a sense of "control precedence" (to use Frijda's term; cf. 1986). Systemic conflict or cognitive disorganization may also give the sense of being overcome by an emotion. Averill identifies three separate types of emotions which are associated with these different grounds of interpreting emotions as passions. *Impulsive* emotions represent "straightforward desires and aversions which are so automatic and compelling that they are not regarded as stemming from the self as agent" (e.g. grief, joy, hope, sexual desire). They are more often associated with the three imperatives. *Conflictive* emotions are based on the ground of systemic conflict and result from conflictive demands placed on the individual from society. Anger is a chief example of a conflictive emotion. *Transcendental* emotions are based on cognitive disorganization, involving a disruption of ego-boundaries. Anxiety and mystical experiences (defined similarly to Forman 1990) are examples of this third type.

Averill's research, and that of the social constructivist school, has amassed a fair amount of evidence for the influence of social factors upon various components of emotion (cf. Gergen and Davis 1985; Harré 1986; Cornelius 1996). Some of the research is cross-cultural or language analytical, aiming at isolating social influence. Other research involves laboratory research of everyday emotional experience as, for example, Labbot and her associates' exploration of laughing and crying during a film (reported in Cornelius 1996). Averill's contribution to research on the emotions has been to draw attention to a much neglected dimension to emotional experience, the social, and to demonstrate that this dimension does indeed play a significant role in the formation of human emotional experience.

Emotions as Schemas and Prototypes

"Emotion" itself is a category. This fact has significance for an understanding of the experiencer of emotions and for emotions research as such. For the experiencer of emotions the question concerns the nature of emotion process. Humans experience a vast quantity and variety of emotions as a part of daily existence. A part of this experience involves the evaluation of emotions themselves, the appraisal and regulation of emotion as it comes to awareness in the midst of experience. Thus humans sort, evaluate, summarize, store, and retrieve emotional experiences, emotional memories, and emotional summaries for use in comparing with subsequent experiences in light of an understanding of "emotions," and "emotion." How does this process take place? Some look to the notion of "script" or "schema" to help. The question for emotions research itself concerns the definition of an emotion. What should one place in the category "emotion" and why? Some look to the notion of "prototype" to help understand how "emotion" might be appropriately defined. Both issues are mentioned in the works of the representatives in the present study (on schemas and scripts cf. Frijda 1986, 382-83; Frijda and Mesquita 1994, 58; Lazarus 1991a, 140, 443; Oatley 1992, 204; on prototypes cf. Frijda 1986, 88; Lazarus 1991a, 37; Oatley 1992, 204,444; Averill 1982, 334). It will be helpful to examine the work of others who explore this aspect of emotions in greater depth.

Sylvan S. Tomkins, another one of the "grand old men" in current emotions research, suggested that the idea of script might be a very appropriate way of exploring the character of emotional experience (Tomkins 1978). For Tomkins, affect serves to amplify a situation in order to focus attention and action. His theory is complex and need not be described in detail here. Central to his theory is the idea that innate linkages between stimulus, affect, and response suggest that humans possess the possibility of organizing primitive scenes. These scenes can, furthermore, be *magnified*, that is they can be connected one scene upon another. Through autosimulation, imitation, and interaction new scenes are integrated with old, functioning either to magnify or attenuate previous experience. Emotions thus develop with a distinct backward look. Salient features of a repeatedly experienced scene are highly magnified and an established script is developed. Thus he looks to density, intensity, enduring effect,

sharpness of change, and frequency of affect in order to explore the
nature and development of emotional experience. Thus emotive
scripts serve to coordinate other operations in human experience. I
think that this function of emotion to coordinate elements of other
scripts and the like serves to link emotion research to the claims of
Medin and other categorization scholars. The selection and prioritiza-
tion of attributes, the development of interproperty relations, and the
cohesiveness of the "whole" within which attributes are evaluated
operates not merely in rational conceptualization, but also in a felt
sense of the whole created from the development of personal and corporate history. Thus attention, evaluation and response are guided
not merely by some conceptual "theory," or "world-view." Rather
the very notion of "theory" or "world-view" must be understood in
light of the developing affective sense of integration which contributes
significantly to the organization of experience. Some of these emotive
scripts, Tomkins suggests, serve to coordinate the very assembly of
the other scripts themselves (a communicative theory). He identifies
these central ones as "nuclear scripts." Nuclear scripts form one's
sense of meaning in life. His assessment of nuclear scripts may have
interesting application to religious emotional experience.

Howard Leventhal, in two articles (Leventhal 1980; Leventhal and
Scherer 1987), also approached emotion from the perspective of
schema research. He presents what he calls a "comprehensive theory
of emotion" in an essay contributed to *Advances in Experimental
Social Psychology* (Leventhal 1980). Following Dewey (1894, 1895)
and Neisser (1967) he situates emotion as part of an overall constructive process of experience that is divided into two stages (1) a perceptual motor stage, and (2) a decision action stage. He states that,
"emotional experience emerges in the first perceptual motor stage,
serving as one of two major sources of information for decision and
action. Decision, planning and action, however, can alter emotional
experience" (Leventhal 1980, 159). He identifies three *mediational
systems* that act and interact in contributing to emotional experience:
expressive motor processing, schematic processing, and conceptual
processing. The expressive motor mechanism is the generator of
emotion. It gives the sense of feeling to the subject. Schematic and
conceptual processing are two systems that attach particular types of
cognitive processing to emotion. Schematic (considered the more
important) "integrates specific situational episodes with autonomic,

subjective, expressive, and instrumental responses in a concrete, patterned, image-like memory system" (Leventhal 1980, 160). Conceptual processing corresponds to social labeling and attribution. As in the review of schemata research above, Leventhal, as Tomkins, understands emotional schemata as perceptual motor memories which serve to focus attention on salient stimulus features and generate anticipations for future experience.

Leventhal, along with Klaus Scherer applied this approach to the resolution of the question of the temporal priority of cognition or emotion (1987), suggesting that the inseparable interrelationship of schematic and conceptual processing necessitates appraisals and responses that are seen to be simultaneous. They describe the relationship between schematic processing and emotion as follows:

> The second, schematic, level of processing integrates sensory-motor processes with image-like prototypes of emotional situations. Schemata are created in emotion encounters with the environment and are conceptualized as memories of emotional experiences: They are concrete representations in memory of specific perceptual, motor (expressive, approach-avoidance tendencies and autonomic reactions), and subjective feelings each of which were components of the reactions during specific emotional episodes. (Leventhal and Scherer 1987, 10)

This integration occurs through a constant appraisal process of scanning of the environment called "stimulus evaluation checks." Conceptual, schematic, and sensorimotor processing assess different features of novelty, pleasantness, goal/need conduciveness, coping potential and norm/self compatibility. When stimuli are encountered that trigger schematic emotional memories (concerns?), emotions are elicited.

Tomkins, Leventhal and others, by linking research concerning the components of emotions to the findings of schema/script research, have illumined an understanding of the emotion process. Their presentations illustrate how emotional significance can develop around concerns, how the appraisal process can be conceived, and how various elements of emotional and cognitive experience may be united into a single process. Provided one does not attach oneself too rigidly to one model of information processing, one can benefit greatly from a recognition of the schematic tendencies of human experience.

As mentioned above, the discussion of prototype theory for emotions research itself concerns the question of the definition of "emotion." Averill's mention of emotions as *syndromes* as a means of avoiding identification of necessary and sufficient criteria for defining an emotion brings to mind the discussion above concerning category membership. Probably the most debated question in all of emotions research is the question, "what is an emotion?" While some search for a "key" defining feature (action tendency, physiological change, physiology plus attribution, and so on), others look to Rosch's research and suggest that one look at the category "emotion" prototypically. Discussion of the protypical nature of the category "emotions," and of the question of whether there are "basic emotions" in the same sense as Rosch's basic categories has stimulated some debate (cf. Averill 1982; Ortony and Turner 1990; Oatley 1992). Questions of prototypicality, basic categories, graded structure, and universality all appear as emotions are examined from this perspective.

Beverley Fehr and James Russell applied Rosch's methods to the category of emotions in a pioneering study (Fehr and Russell 1984). In this study they utilized (1) free listing of exemplars of the category "emotion," (2) generation of the superordinate from the basic category (e.g. Happiness is a/an _____), and (3) family resemblance analysis of attributes and substitution, in order to identify the prototypicality of certain emotion terms. Furthermore, in response to Gleitman, Armstrong and Gleitman's challenge to distinguish prototypical and "classical" concepts (1983), they compared emotions to other "prototypically" and "classically" defined concepts. They concluded that *emotions* should be understood as a prototypically defined category with fuzzy boundaries and that furthermore, that with regard to emotions, one is wise to distinguish between prototypicality of internal structure and fuzziness of boundaries, a distinction I addressed above as the difference between what a concept contains or encodes and one's sense of category membership. They suggest, however, that one not think of an emotion as a "thing," but rather as an *event*. In this manner the concept of an emotion might be helpfully viewed as a *script*, which makes similarity comparison more reasonable in the case of emotions.

Phillip Shaver and associates developed the "basic categorical" aspects of emotions (Shaver et al. 1987). Again using Rosch's approach to basic categories, Shaver and associates examined 213 emotion terms evaluating them for prototypicality and corresponding similarities. The result was that the emotions appeared to cluster into five major groups that, coincidentally, strongly resembled the "basic" emotions discussed by emotion theorists. They examined the contents of these basic level emotion-concepts further, concluding that "just as story readers construct generic story schemas and regular restaurant patrons construct restaurant scripts, observers and experiencers of emotion should, whether they are aware of it or not, construct basic emotion prototypes" (Shaver et al. 1987, 1072). A feature analysis of five basic emotions yielded a portrait of emotion process that greatly resembles that Frijda or Lazarus. Appraisal of a situation as significant triggers a variety of responses (action tendencies, conscious preoccupation, physiological changes, etc.). Two aspects of their research are relevant to the present study. First, they identified certain biases in the emotion process (e.g. the fact that people are not aware of their own narrow focus when describing personal experiences of emotion). These biases identified link the emotions research with an understanding of the heuristics and biases associated with categorization and judgment. Second, they suggest that prototypical analysis may be helpful in addressing the difficult subject of emotion *blends*, the fact that many emotional experiences appear not to be of a single emotion, but rather a combination or blend of more than one. I will address emotion blends later in the study.

Summary and Synthesis

Randolf Cornelius, in his recent review of empirical research on emotions (1996) sees the possibility of a "harmonic convergence" of emotions research in the future. Representatives from a wide range of approaches are finding themselves forced by the evidence to take account of each others' emphases. Those who stress biology must look again at the data concerning culture. Those who stress appraisal now acknowledge an irreducible physiological element in human emotion. The following summary will indicate what that convergence might look like, at least as far as the limits of my current purposes allow. As a synthesis of some of the most respected writers on emotions from current experimental psychology, I suggest that this summary may provide a "more empirically grounded" portrait of human affectivity, one which can inform a theory of Christian discernment with greater psychological specificity.

Thus far I have not addressed the issue of research methodology, but it would be appropriate briefly to draw attention to the diversity of method used to formulate this converging science of emotion. The study of human emotion encompasses a wide range of research methods, each of which is better equipped to measure different variables. Lazarus identifies a number of these variables in *Emotion and Adaptation* (1991a, 42-85; cf. also 1991b 831-32). He himself has mastered the use of laboratory or controlled experimental research for emotions study. Frijda has made excellent use of questionnaire research, and has utilized computers both for creating interactive surveys as well as for modeling emotive-relevant processes (cf. Sonnemans and Frijda 1994; Frijda and Swagerman 1987). Oatley has made use of semantic analysis (Oatley and Johnson-Laird 1988) in his research. Both Averill and Oatley have recovered the use of structured diaries to investigate subjects' perceptions of emotion episodes or events (Averill 1982; Oatley and Duncan 1994). When diverse experimental methods confirm similar findings the conclusions for the findings themselves are strengthened. Thus the fact that the compatible perspectives discussed above were developed using such diverse methods speaks well, I think, for the state of current research.

As I mentioned at the beginning of this section, my interest in this field regards not simply *emotions* but rather the broader spectrum of *affectivity*. As mentioned above, much ink is spilled in the scientific literature, determining what is or is not an emotion. In that process, operations which are not considered "emotions" are discarded from consideration even though they may be regarded as "affective" (e.g. Frijda 1986, 249-55). I understand "emotion" as the more narrow term, referring to particular identifiable patterns of affective operations. I will use "affectivity" as the more encompassing term to include emotions as well as other affective phenomena. Thus when I refer to affectivity or affective experience, I am speaking of a broad range of operations like mood, wish, desire, feeling, passion, urge, drive, intuition, hunch, wonder and others insofar as they are used not simply to indicate mental attitudes, states, inclinations that are not affective in the sense defined in the following paragraph. Unfortunately, many of the terms used for affective experience are also used more than one way in ordinary language. Thus when I speak of "wish" as part of affectivity, I am not referring to "wish" as mere preference, but rather that felt inclination toward something which may involve appraisal, phenomenological tone, mental preoccupation and so on. My interest, in not limiting my attention to the more identifiable (and more studied) emotions, is to include all those states or operations which have impact upon the character of Christian discernment.

But just what is affectivity? In light of the research reported above, it appears that affectivity is a system of somewhat interdependent operations, involving primary dimensions of human life (biological, psychological, social - and I would add ecological and spiritual). Averill's notion of an emotion as a "syndrome" in which action tendencies, physiological changes, appraisal patterns, bodily expressions and so on may all be typical of emotions, but none functions as the defining feature necessary to identify an emotion *as* an emotion, aimed at such an integration. However, his interest was on the individual "emotion" as such, whereas my focus lies in the consideration of the broader range of affective experience as an interrelated set of operations. By calling affectivity a *system* I acknowledge with Lazarus that there are distinguishable regularities or tendencies in human experience, regularities which can be observed and somewhat described. Regularities in brain mechanisms, facial movements, linguistic usage, social behaviors all can be observed with a degree of predictability to confirm the character of human emotion.[2] It is also a system of *interrelated operations*. The failure of emotion research to come to consensus concerning any "necessary and sufficient" criteria for category membership in "emotion," (or to come to consensus concerning the temporal priority of cognition or affect) while at the same time reaching significant consensus on the need to take into account divergent emphases, leads me to believe that one is safest to regard affectivity as a somewhat integrated nest of separate operations. A variety of cognitive, motor, hormonal, and social operations all combine to create affective experience. In affirming this integrative

---

[2] On an understanding of affective experience as involving regularities, see Frijda's understanding of emotions as "lawlike" (1988), Lazarus' "system" approach and "structure principle" (1991a, 39), and Shaver's description of a "patterned event" (Shaver et al. 1987, 1072).

approach to affectivity, however, I must make one point. It appears that affective experience, more than conceptual, has to do with human physiology. Laboratory research, questionnaires, diaries all point to the fact that emotions affect human bodies to a degree unmatched by other operations or systems (e.g. conceptual processing, mental imagery, intentional action). Furthermore these operations "have to do with" the *entirety of human experience* - biological, psychological, social, ecological, spiritual. They all contribute to making emotional experience what it is.

Affectivity is characterized by "heat," by changes in or qualities of action readiness, phenomenological tone, physiological processes and states, appraisals of situation significance, mental preoccupation, or similar tendencies.   Although regulatory mechanisms can control (somewhat) affective operations and although one may not always be attentive to these operations, affectivity usually arises with some perceivable accompaniment. The presence, quality and degree of each of the above components together determine *that* an experience is affective. They also indicate *what* affective episode may be active at any given moment. They not only indicate differences between major affective distinctions (e.g. between anger and happiness), but also between more subtle differences (e.g. the differences between a "crush," "falling in love," "lust," and "mature romantic love"). While these factors often gain their significance from social cues, they arise as felt phenomena. While I might not go as far as Averill in saying affectivity is "interpreted as passions" (in part because some affective phenomena are not emotions), some sense of passivity sensed is often present in affective experience.

As mentioned above, I include in my category of affectivity a variety of terms (without attempting to precisely define each): moods, sentiments, basic emotions, feelings, passions, reactions, desires and enjoyments, aesthetic emotions, empathy, transcendental emotions and the like. Many of these words can also be used in a non-affective way (e.g. "desires" can refer to preference, "transcendental emotion" can refer to a state of consciousness). My aim here is simply to give a general sense of the range of operations I am considering. Excluded are bodily states or sensations (e.g. physical pain), kinesthetic sense, attitudes, personality traits, determinative action or preference, cool thought.   The differentiation between affective and non-affective experience becomes somewhat complex in practice. Consider sexual drive, stimulation, and experience. On the one hand pure sexual stimulation is not an emotion, but a physiological reaction. Yet it is frequently associated with powerful emotions. Yet again, without affectively appropriate accompaniment, (and depending on the person, culture, situation) sexual stimulation can give rise to no emotion at all or to strong feelings of disgust, fear, or anger (consider the case of rape).

Affective operations usually follow a process involving stimuli, appraisal(s), feedback, responses, and effects. Frijda (1986), Lazarus (1991a, 37), Leventhal (1980) and others all emphasize this sense of *process* in affective experience.

As with categorization process, a subject comes to present affective experience already "given" in the sense described above by time and space. Cultural heritage, personal development, and cognitive/physiological structure precondition the human subject to receive or to reject certain stimuli in certain ways. Appraisal rules, expected phenomenological tone, permitted actions and action tendencies are pre-shaped prior to emotional experience and are further shaped by each consecutive experience (Tomkins 1978). Emotion schemata generalize and orient the subject to aspects of affective experience, both illumining and inhibiting aspects of the person-environment relationship. Emotions, like concepts, do not arise in a vacuum. Rather they are embedded.

Usually, affective operations are elicited by a stimulus or event. Outside of enduring moods and rare acausal emotional episodes (Oatley 1992, 23-24, 91-93), emotions appear to arise in response to situations confronting one. More precisely, emotions appear to arise in response to a configuration or constellation of the person-environment relationship or a juncture within cognitive process itself (Frijda 1986, 6; Lazarus 1991a; Oatley 1992). There is something about the way the perceived world (both "outer" and "inner" world) addresses the subject at a given moment that causes it to be affectively significant. That "something" in the way the perceived world is momentarily configured is *situational meaning*. A memory in the form of a mental image may arise in your mind stimulated by a passage of a history assignment - an image which reawakens feelings associated with that memory. Or a snarling mountain lion suddenly confronts you during a hike. In each case the perceived world is configured such to convey meaning or significance to that situation. It affords affective significance. Thus, more precisely still, affective operations are usually elicited by the perceived situational meaning present in a given space-time juncture. The significance of the person-environment relationship does not arise apart from the appearance of the situation or environment itself (bottom-up constraints). However the situation gets its meaning from the fact that it addresses a need, goal/plan, or concern (top-down constraints). I think it is best not to understand affectivity *merely* in the context of plan junctures, as Oatley. Some affective episodes are not best explained in terms of intentional plans. I prefer Frijda's term "concern" for most situations. It reflects the development of an area or issue of life that carries weight with a person. It indicates an area of sensitivity which can be touched. As Robert Burns asserts, however, "the best laid schemes o' mice and men gang aft a'gley" (Burns 1785), and therefore goals and plans should be included with concerns as contributors to situation meaning. Furthermore, I think it best also to include the term "needs." The threatening or satisfying of needs often brings emotional significance to a situation (e.g. Maslow's classic hierarchy of needs including physiology, safety, love and belongingness, esteem, and self-actualization; Maslow 1954). Frijda includes this in his understanding of "concern," but I think it best to make it explicit.

It is the appraisal of the situation in light of goal, concern, or need that transforms the situation into (or acknowledges it as) an emotionally relevant stimulus. All of the representatives emphasized the role of appraisal. By speaking of "appraisal" the literature indicates cognitive operations which play a significant role within the affective system, evaluating situations for affective significance. Appraisal evaluates a situation to determine its "core relational meaning" (Lazarus) or "situation meaning structure" (Frijda). Quite often these operations function by examining the situation "in light of" or in relation to (Oatley) certain factors. These factors are called "components" by Frijda and Lazarus. Leventhal and Scherer call them "stimulus evaluation checks" (1987). Factors such as relevancy (does this situation bear on life?), urgency (is it vital to deal with now?), valence (does the situation bring satisfaction or dissatisfaction?), coping potential (does it appear that this situation can be dealt with?), future expectancy (what do the prospects of this situation hold?), concern relevance (is this situation related to a particular concern?), object/subject evaluation (who is directly in view here?) and type of ego-involvement (how is the subject involved in the situation?) all serve to indicate the emotive significance of situations. Many of the rules for these appraisal functions derive from cultural context (Averill). Some scholars (e.g. Lazarus) see this appraisal process bringing increasing differentiation to emotional experience as the appraisal process develops. Hence appraisal operations help to determine both whether an experience will become affective and, if so, what form that will take. This is accomplished as the results of appraisal signal physiological changes, mental preoccupation, and other responses. The signalling of responses is accomplished through triggering prewired "affect programs" (Frijda) or developed "scripts" (Tomkins), or simply by broadcasting a general control message to individual mechanisms (e.g. the autonomic nervous system; cf. Oatley). If affectivity is viewed in light of appraisal, it could be said that affectivity functions *as* a kind of discernment, an evaluative process distinguishing between the significant and the insignificant.

Affective process also involves various feedback loops. Frijda's "regulation," Lazarus' "reevaluation" and "coping," and Averill's "norms" and "defenses" analysis (1980, 330) all describe some manner by which the developing emotion itself becomes part of the situation that is being addressed. It may seem rather complicated to think of a developing emotional experience as an integral part of the configuration of a situation, but evidence corroborates this point. Humans respond to the arising of an emotion just as to the arising of a situation in general. Feedback may address appraisal components (triggering reappraisal), action tendencies (e.g. inhibiting the list of possible actions available), or other aspects of the emotion process as such. Feedback may arise from a sense of coping potential (e.g. dealing with stress via problem or emotion-centered coping), from social norms (e.g. inhibiting how anger might be expressed or experienced), or other sources. One's ongoing categorization of affective experience triggers further affective operations, shaping the character of the original experience. Thus most responses to situations also include responses to the affective phenomena present as well.

Affective process usually culminates in the production of a set of responses. These responses are the "heat" mentioned above. Action tendencies, mental preoccupation, phenomenological tone, physiological changes, attention focus, enacted role, bodily expression and more appear as they are signalled through the appraisal process. I say "usually" to reflect the variants of emotion process noted by Frijda (1986). He writes, "Emotion in its typical form embodies the process in its entirety, from information uptake to overt response, with the part from appraisal to action readiness change as the trunk - that which is properly emotion. But subprocesses can be skipped, and the process can be interrupted at any point, thus producing the variants of emotional phenomena" (Frijda 1986, 461). For example a situation may arise which at the onset appears to be emotionally significant. But as the situation progresses, both the urgency and seriousness of the situation dissolve and, consequently, no physiological changes are signalled and action tendency communicates no heat. In the end, the response may become cool, goal-directed, unaffective action with respect to a matter of personal interest. Depending on intensity and duration of the affective experience, responses are usually aimed at adapting to the arising person-environment relationship in some fashion, both in terms of object-oriented action and in terms of subject-oriented action. As Lazarus mentioned, affective experience ultimately has effects. Initially it has the effect of backward-reinforcing schemata, thereby increasing the potential for their repetition in the future. Leventhal speaks of this in terms of the "magnification" of emotions. Short-term effects concern personal behavior and social functioning. Longer term affects concern health (e.g. impact of emotional experience upon immune system performance) and sense of well-being.

Affective processes need not be conscious but appear to be somewhat self-integrated. Lazarus in particular (1991a, 162-168) emphasizes the fact that appraisal need not involve conscious deliberation. Oatley's third and fifth postulates assume at least the same possibility (1992, 91,98). As for the self-integration of these conscious or unconscious operations, many emphasize the need for some kind of monitoring of the system as a whole - "its elicitation, its course, and its results, as well as of the relation of the emotional process to other processes of the system" (Frijda 1986, 459; cf. also Averill 1982). Tomkins uses the notion of "scripts" to illustrate how some affective operations can serve to monitor and coordinate other affective and cognitive processes. Oatley concurs and further concludes that this type of integration of operations requires the human to possess a "model of the self" which is used to image expected actions, responses, situations, and such.

There are some interesting similarities between affective and conceptual process. Figure 2 summarizes the stages of affective process as found in the representatives. By comparing the general shapes of conceptual and affective experience one can see that they both have a similar flow from pre-encounter "givens" to encounter, to evaluation, and ultimately to a response which, in turn, shapes the givens of subsequent encounters. Affectivity, like conceptual experience, has its background in the configuration of the moment before and it helps form the configuration of the moment following. Furthermore, both systems, affective and conceptual, are subject to biases, gaps, and lacunas. The self-absorbed defensive reaction, the cycle of addiction to romantic love affairs, the anxiety disorders that inhibit ordinary enjoyment of life, are all examples of the dysfunctioning of the affective system. Affective problems can appear at any stage or dimension of the system. Often mild affective disorders lie at the level of appraisal (e.g. the mis-evaluation of a situation as frightening or dangerous) as salient previous experiences may strongly reinforce certain schematic expectations without reasonable grounds. Other problems may appear at the level of social functioning, physiological dysfunctions, or a variety of other possibilities (cf. Lazarus 1991a, 437-465; Oatley and Jenkins 1992). And like conceptual process, affective process may be corrected. Attention, reappraisal, reeducation of concern all have been shown to affect the pattern of emotional experience.

Affective experience appears most commonly in social situations. Oatley and Johnson-Laird (1987; cf. Oatley 1992; Averill 1980a) are right to emphasize this point. With most affective experiences, one is not speaking about a neutral "environment," but a relationally-charged "society." It is in the context of *mutually* held plans, goals, concerns, needs that individual plans, goals, concerns, and needs, are sensed. Persons have the capacity to share, to some degree, these aspects of existence, just as humans have the capacity to share, to some degree, concepts and categories. Attachment, social referencing, role-taking, empathy and temperament all play an important part of affective experience. Becky Lynn Omdahl, in a series of studies (1995), has empirically demonstrated the capacity of people to share another's emotional situation by means of reconstructing emotional appraisal from verbal cues. Research in empathy has just begun to explore the processes by which affective sharing takes place, but there is strong indication that it does take place. It is for this reason, I think, that

Affirming the Touch of God

FIGURE 2:
HUMAN AFFECTIVE PROCESS

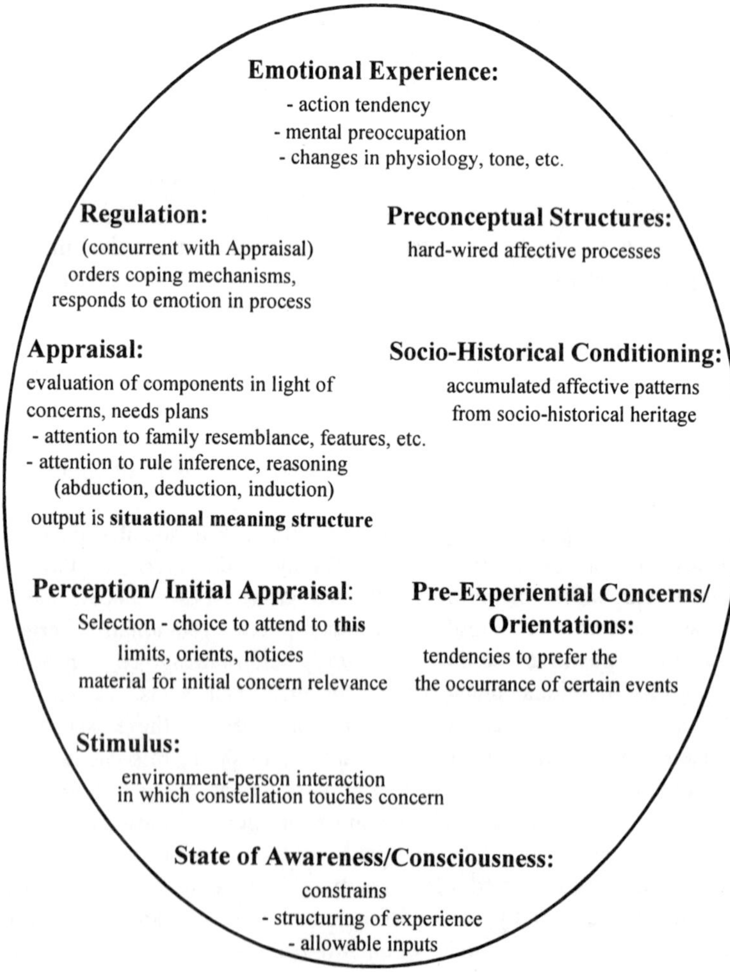

Emotional Experience:
- action tendency
- mental preoccupation
- changes in physiology, tone, etc.

Regulation:
(concurrent with Appraisal)
orders coping mechanisms,
responds to emotion in process

Preconceptual Structures:
hard-wired affective processes

Appraisal:
evaluation of components in light of
concerns, needs plans
- attention to family resemblance, features, etc.
- attention to rule inference, reasoning
  (abduction, deduction, induction)
output is **situational meaning structure**

Socio-Historical Conditioning:
accumulated affective patterns
from socio-historical heritage

Perception/ Initial Appraisal:
Selection - choice to attend to **this**
limits, orients, notices
material for initial concern relevance

**Pre-Experiential Concerns/
Orientations:**
tendencies to prefer the
the occurrance of certain events

Stimulus:
environment-person interaction
in which constellation touches concern

State of Awareness/Consciousness:
constrains
- structuring of experience
- allowable inputs

Averill's "social constructivist" approach can have any meaning. Averill's contention, that affective experience gains meaning orsignificance through culture, is echoed by most emotions research today (Lazarus 1988, 296; 1991a, 23-25; 349-84; 1991b, 825; Frijda and Mesquita 1994; Oatley 1992, 178-220). The centrality of the interpersonal dimension of affective experience is, needless to say, central to an account of Christian spirituality.

Like conceptual process, affectivity serves different functions. First, affectivity serves an *adaptive* function, to prepare the subject to respond to the environment or that which confronts. Frijda emphasized this point throughout his work. In this sense affectivity conveys the subject to the object. Second, affectivity serves a *noetic* function, conveying something of the object to the subject. Lazarus emphasized this function. Both psychologists (cf. Shaver et al. 1987; Leventhal 1980) and philosophers of emotion (Solomon 1976; Unger 1984) speak of emotions as a "kind of knowing." Lazarus distinguishes between *knowledge* and *appraisal*. Whereas knowledge provides information about the way the world works, appraisal provides information about the significance of the world. Both knowledge and appraisal are used in the affective system. My emphasis here is that the affective system itself (and not merely appraisal and knowledge sub-processes) has a noetic function. Moods, emotional reactions, feelings reveal something about the world. Whereas conceptual process (image and semantic) appears to be more oriented to conveying the *structure* of the environment, affectivity appears to be more oriented to conveying the *meaning* of the environment. Furthermore, by being more oriented to the meaning of the environment, affectivity is sensitive to (and conveys information concerning) aspects of the environment/situation that would tend to remain unnoticed by conceptual process. This leads me to the third primary function of affectivity, which I call the *semiotic* function. Affectivity functions to communicate or mediate both within and between persons. Oatley has emphasized this point in his "communicative" approach to emotions. The idea of the mediation of meaning is central to a communicative approach, whether it is conceived as the spreading of a broadcast control message through a neural network or between individuals in mutual planning. Averill (1980, 313-15; 1982, 23), Frijda ("situational meaning structure" and 1986, 453-79), Lazarus ("relational meaning"; 1991a, 132, 1991b, 824) and others (cf. J. Anderson 1995, Medin 1987) give "meaning" importance in their theories. The concept itself, however, is left relatively underdeveloped. Oatley presents the idea of communication, and something of shared meaning, but his presentation of the idea within information-processing models prevents a fuller understanding of the joining (and transmutation) of representation and enaction involved in semiotic mediation. I will address this point in the chapter on philosophy.

Just as cognitive operations play a part in the affective system, so also affective operations play a part in the cognitive or conceptual system. This was developed by Tomkins (1978) in terms of the use of emotive scripts to coordinate other types of scripts. In this sense affective operations serve as part of the "theory" within which categorization (and other cognitive operations) function. Reflection on conceptual cognitive process itself yields such observation. Consider the appearance of some phenomena to attention. As attention is given to a matter, there is an affective tone associated with that moment of consciousness. As perception develops to inquiry a different emotion is brought into service of the conceptual system. consider how inquiry feels. Thus, affectivity may serve to guide conceptual process through its entire journey. Just think of how a "hunch" feels. Think of what it is like to later reject that hunch. Consider what it feels like to finally gain solid evidence that something you thought is indeed the case. "Truth" is often confirmed in affectivity. Thus, significant shifts and changes in conceptual process are accompanied by (or triggered, guided by) contributions from affective operations. It is in this manner that one can speak of affective process playing roles in the *act* of categorization, and of Christian discernment.

Affective operations also play a significant role in determining the *subject* of categorization and conceptual process. The goals toward which categorization aims, the aspects of phenomena that are noticed as salient, the motivation to correct bias (or to ignore it), and the concerns or vested interests brought to categorization, are all shaped by one's affective history. "Disordered affections," to use the language of Ignatius, influences not merely the discernment of the divine but also the very categorization process itself.

Likewise affective elements participate in the formation of the *context* of human categorization and conceptual thought. Mood congruence has been demonstrated to influence conceptual assessment of events (cf. Oatley 1992, 92 and the bibliography mentioned). The context of social-emotive atmosphere also has been shown to influence conceptual process (Averill, 1982; Cornelius 1996). I think that the relationships between emotion terms and emotion experience cross-culturally (cf. Harré 1986; Gergen and Davis 1985) suggests that human conceptualization is also shaped by the cultural-emotive context surrounding the subject.

Finally, affective experience can serve as an *object* of categorization. I have already addressed this above in the discussion of regulation and of the prototypical and schematic categorization of emotion by the person experiencing emotion. Conceptual process can evaluate emotions themselves, noticing, identifying, understanding, comparing, and responding. It is this process that makes the Ignatian discernment of spirits possible.

Just as an affective system can be distinguished from a more conceptual system, there is also indication that the affective system may be distinguished from a system more related to deliberate action. Thus, Frijda, following Pibram and McGuinness' evaluation of brain function, speaks of an "effort system" which "is responsible for willful concentration and for the organization of response modes other than those habitual or natural as responses to the stimuli present" (1986, 388). Likewise in his essay on the "Laws of Emotions," Frijda ponders how the relationship of control of action by situational meaning structure and by deliberate intent are differentiated. He notes the common distinction between automatic and controlled processing questioning whether "this distinction illuminates the present context more than did the old distinction between Emotions and the Will" (1988, 357). His article develops this paradox between more and less control. Lazarus develops similar notions through a distinction between "motivation" and "emotion" (1991a, 171-72). Leventhal makes a similar assumption (1980, 168) distinguishing between separate "volitional" and "spontaneous" controls in the expressive-motor system. If it is indeed reasonable to posit another "volitional system," and a set of "volitional" operations, then one can also conceive the relationship of these operations upon the affective system. Once again, personal reflection informs one of the deliberate involvement in such affective processes as "nursing a grudge," or "cherishing a crush." I suspect it is volitional operations which are

called into play to enact much of the regulatory functions of affectivity developing from feedback loops.

Individual affective episodes can be plotted according to a multi-
factorial graph, yielding a portrait of the character of affective experience. Such factors might include valence (mentioned by all), intensity
(Sonnemans and Frijda 1994; Oatley 1992, 22) and duration and
development (Frijda 1987, 57; 1994, 475-76; Oatley 1992, 22). I
might also add "depth," referring to the level of script or concern
touched (perhaps on a scale from superficial to nuclear script/concern)
and "orientation" (something like object oriented vs. subject
oriented). Other factors could be identified for this kind of analysis.

It appears to me that so long as one does not consider "basic emotions" as some primitives from which all others either derive their
meaning or origin (cf. Ortony and Turner, 1990), it is reasonable to
assume that there are a small group of emotions which appear to
people as prototypical emotions and which correspond to near
universal "core relational themes." Though not conclusive, evidence
from physiology, facial expression research, and situation and
semantic analysis appears convergent. Affirmation of generally common emotional patterns need not deny the significant influence that
culture plays in the formation of emotional experience (as Averill,
1982, 326). The problem I find with emphasis on "basic emotions" is
that by focussing attention on these few emotions (twenty at most), a
vast range of more complex emotions are neglected. In light of the
cumulative nature of affective experience (especially mood congruent
arousal generalization cf. Frijda 1986) and the pervasive presence of
"blends" of emotions (cf. Omdahl 1995, 222-23), I think it is time
emotions research began to look outside the "basic emotions" for an
understanding of human emotional experience.

Without attempting to summarize the literature on emotional
development (cf. Frijda 1986; Lazarus 1991; Averill 1985), I will
simply say that it there are reasonable indications that emotions have
developed phylogenetically to accentuate an increasing dependence
upon appraisal and social factors. Ontogenetic development of affectivity generates an increasing differentiation of the affective system
over time, reinforced through significant contacts (usually parental)
and cultural forms.

Research on the positive emotions, aesthetic emotions and
empathy is woefully lacking. For example, Oatley lists "dysphoric"

and "negative" emotions in the index of *Best Laid Schemes* (1992). He does not list "euphoric" or "positive" emotions. Lazarus writes, "The positive emotions have been singularly ignored or de-emphasized historically, and it is not entirely clear why this should be so" (1991a, 264). The same is true for aesthetic emotions. Lazarus suggests that aesthetic emotions may not be one type but a variety of emotions "whose nature depends on the personal meaning imputed to aesthetic and religious experiences" (1991a, 294). Thus there is no central core relational theme, no set of appraisal components or action tendencies for aesthetic emotions, owing to their diversity. Frijda and Kerry Walters briefly discussed Frijda's "law of apparent reality" with regard to aesthetic emotions in *The American Psychologist* (Walters 1989; Frijda 1989). Frijda's law, asserting that emotions are elicited by events appraised as real, might appear problematic in the case of aesthetic emotions (using the context of artistic theater) in which the event is certainly not appraised as real. Frijda suggests that entry into the world of illusion proceeds by way of discounting (not ignoring) reality cues. We join with the actors, allowing our defenses normally present when reality cues indicate illusions to be set aside. In this way we allow ourselves to respond "as if" it were real. Frijda further distinguishes between the response to the character's fate in a work of art, and the response to the structure of the work of art as such. In the latter case he suggests that perhaps the form of the real, as a perfected ideal (such as the idea of grief, love or the like) may be the source of very deep emotions. Lazarus suggests that empathetic emotions reflect the same diversity mentioned with regard to aesthetic emotions. The emotion varies; the key is the sharing of another's affective experience. Lazarus writes,

> From this standpoint, empathy is not an emotion but either an *ability or disposition* to share another's emotions, and a *process* whereby this sharing occurs. It is, of course, a very important, prosocial ability and process, because it expresses the variable capacities of people to put themselves in the position of another's distress [note emphasis on negative emotions]. It is also emotional, without being an emotion, strictly speaking. Here the process of shaping the emotional distress is determined by another person whose distress is

being observed, not be the one who is empathizing (1991a, 289).

Frijda distinguishes this by speaking of the object components of "object fate" and "subject fate" (1986, 215). In both aesthetic and empathetic affective experience the object plays a more important role in determining the shape of the affective experience. Eleanor Rosch makes a suggestion related to the integration of psychological and meditative approaches to human experience, noting a weakness in the psychological approach. She states, "what the psychological paradigms lack, however, and could well use, is the account contributed by the meditative traditions of how people can go beyond the self monitoring and appraisal mode of feeling and acting to tap into their more integrated 'wisdom' mode" (Rosch 1997, 23). I would suggest that this "going beyond" self monitoring and appraisal is prefigured in aesthetic and empathetic affective experience.

Which leads to the consideration of religious emotions. If positive emotions are mentioned infrequently, and aesthetic or empathetic emotions even less, religious emotions are hardly mentioned at all. In describing the object component of "ego as constituent" (ego as contributing source of the situation appraised), Frijda mentions the existence of *ego-object fusion*, where awareness of object, as distinct from ego, disappears. He mentions that this occurs in mystic experiences (Frijda 1986, 214). He also refers to the component "value relevance" by mentioning that some "events appear to possess intrinsic positive or negative valences: they are good or bad with respect to a suprapersonal value, a suprapersonal basis for judgment" (p. 216, cf. also Frijda and Mesquita 1994, 67). Averill mentions the existence of a set of emotions called "transcendental emotions," which he divides into mystical experiences and anxiety reactions. Mystical experiences involve "a disappearance of self-identity and a sense of unity with some underlying reality" and are guided by "more encompassing categories of thought" (Averill 1980, 333-34). He develops the idea no further. Lazarus mentions religious experience along with aesthetic emotions. He also suggests, at the very end of *Emotion and Adaptation*, that "the only way we can rid ourselves of distressing emotions and attain peace of mind—assuming we might want to—is to renounce or change the very commitments on which they depend, a task that is difficult but facilitated by major losses or a conversion experience, which is a process we don't well understand. The reader knows that such renunciation is the goal of diverse spiritual movements" (1991a, 468). With this in mind, we turn to reflect on affectivity within the Christian tradition.

Christian Emotions

Just as one can speak of "aesthetic" and "religious" emotions, namely emotions which receive their distinctive character and meaning in the context of the aesthetic or religious objects to which they are related, so one can speak of "Christian" emotions, namely affective experience that receives its distinctive character and meaning within the context of the Christian religious tradition. Just as the Chinese affective sense of respect has its own distinctive phenomenal tone, action tendencies and the like because of the national culture which has formed that feeling, so also there are affective experiences which take on a distinctive character because of their millennia-long association with the culture of the Christian religion. Because distinctively Christian emotions are not discussed in the experimental literature, and because these particular emotions have a special place in discernment, it seems best to offer a few thoughts on the nature of Christian emotions in light of the a more empirically grounded understanding of human affectivity. With a more fully developed understanding of Christian emotions, I will be prepared to examine the full range of human affectivity with relationship to discernment.

First, Christian emotions, are, at least in part, a subspecies of religious emotions. As religious emotions, they exhibit properties similar to aesthetic or empathetic emotions (Lazarus). They also appear to involve significant alignments in terms of object components (Frijda). Likewise Rosch speaks about the meditative approach in terms of going beyond the self monitoring and appraisal mode. The convergence between these three is the emphasis upon Object-oriented rather than self-oriented process. In those emotions formed by the Christian religious tradition, as in religious emotions in general, appraisal, regulation, action tendency, and the other aspects of affective process are not merely guided by the significance for the self, but also respond to the significance of the Object in itself. Indeed, perhaps the "purity" of Christian emotions is a function of the degree to which this latter Object-orientation drives the affective experience. At times Christian emotional experience can involve an sense of the entire disappearance of self-identity, involving an experience of supreme unity with God. In these times, Christian emotions become Christian *transcendental* emotions, as described by Averill. Yet, while Christian emotions characteristically involve some shift in the self-object orientation of the affective process, most Christian emotions do not involve the complete loss of self-identity. Thus I think it best that one consider Averill's transcendental emotions as a subcategory of religious (and Christian) emotions.

Second, as a subspecies of religious emotions, Christian emotions are *Christian*. They are directed in some fashion to God as revealed in Jesus Christ and as known through the Christian tradition. I will prescind from theological and metaphysical questions until the chapter on philosophical theology. Here I simply want to emphasize, with Averill, the "embeddedness" of Christian emotions in Christian tradition. The appraisal rules concerning what is or is not religiously significant, the regulatory feedback controls that reveal what emotions may be experienced and how, the reinforcements concerning physiological changes, the expression modes and more are all to some extent defined by the culture (and quite often the subcultures) of the Christian tradition. Many of the emotions humans experience (or expect to experience) arise in the form of social roles taken on in the context of Christian culture. Not only what we think of our experiences, but to some extent, the very experience of the experiences is shaped by our exposure to the Christian tradition. I also suspect, however, that just as there are a few basic forms of affective experience which configure how humans relate to the natural, personal, and social worlds, so also there may be basic forms of experiencing the relationship to spiritual realities (for the philosophical debate on this issue cf. Zaehner 1957, Stace 1961, Katz 1978, Proudfoot 1985, Forman 1990; for an anthropological approach cf. Boyer 1995).

Third, I think one may assert, without injustice either to Frijda or to Paul Tillich (1951), that for the Christian, God is the Ultimate Concern. If there are "nuclear scripts" which bring order to other affective and cognitive scripts, then one's relationship with God may be *the* central script. To repeat my summary of Frijda above,

a *concern* is a disposition to prefer the occurrence of a given state of affairs. Concerns develop through the life-history of the subject. They are tied up in relationships, goals, and valued objects. They are often rooted in primary needs, desires or aversions. Some concerns are related to the general functioning of the subject as an organism. Some concerns are related to supra-personal values.

Stimuli become affectively significant as they touch a concern. Christian emotions arise as our Ultimate Concern is touched, as our "most valued Object," our "deepest need," our "supra-personal value," is addressed. The well-known Christmas carol "O Little Town of Bethlehem" proclaims, "the hopes and fears of all the years are met in Thee tonight." The expression of the joy heralded in the gospels reflects not simply a personal joy. In Christ, the eschatological hope has appeared. Personal, social, and cosmic "concerns" are addressed in the person of Christ. Some Christian emotions function primarily as a recognition of this Ultimate Concern. Other Christian emotions respond to the situations of life in light of this concern. Robert Roberts reflects this theme when he writes about the core concerns he calls "passions:"

> Emotion-dispositions are concerns, and concerns of a special type which can be called passions constitute our character, our inmost self. Passions differ from other concerns in determining a person's actions and emotions over relatively long stretches of his life, and roughly by being "higher" in the order of his cares. If an individual's passions are moral, they give him ethical character. If they are Christian, they give him Christian character (Roberts 1982, 19).

Fourth, I have mentioned in earlier chapters (and will develop in the following chapter) the idea the Christian God is a self-communicating God. Discernment often involves the evaluation of whether or not God is indeed self-communicated in a given event, under the assumption that a positive answer to the inquiry is possible. This gives rise to the possibility that the Holy Spirit can act as stimulus, or as an element of the "environment" to which affectivity responds. Assuming that the Holy Spirit can reveal and can communicate interiorly (and again, leaving the theological and epistemological issues for later), one may be able to perceive this divine self-communication much as one would perceive other interior events with affective significance. Frijda refined the notion of stimulus by saying that "constellations," "stimuli-as-signals of given modes of promise of concern satisfaction, or of threat thereto" elicit emotion. In this light one might think of the manner of the Holy Spirit's presence, in the context of a given situation, as the "constellation" giving rise to affective process. Some Christian emotions are responses to these stimuli in light of personal concerns.

Fifth, I suspect that at least a part of the "transformation of the passions" discussed in the Christian tradition involves a re-education of the subject vs. object concern informing the emotion. Appraisal must be taught to evaluate in light of the Other rather than the self.[1] This Other may include not only the divine, but also aesthetic value (the Good, Beautiful, etc.), and empathetic value (the other person). At times the transformation of passions will involve a "control" of action-tendency, mental preoccupation and the like through the formation of regulatory functions in light of the Other. At times the transformation of passions will involve an opening or release of passions which involves stimulated by the appreciation of the Other, a loosening of regulatory functions. At times the transformation of passions will involve the re-orientation or re-understanding of concern, change of plan, or satisfaction of need. Evelyn Whitehead and James Whitehead (1996) present a four-fold plan for entering "the way of the negative emotions" that illumines this approach. They speak of stages of *patience* (paying attention, improving the "acoustics"), *naming* (finding the correct name, naming the deep themes), *taming* (honoring the adversary, maintaining a sanctuary), and *living with passion* (nurturing our tiny desires, eating our shadow). Some distinctively Christian emotions appear in the context of this kind of transformation.

[1] By speaking of a re-orientation from self to Other orientation, I am not referring to a spirituality of "self-denial." Rather I am speaking in terms of emotions research concerning the two sources of affective elicitation. Where Other-orientation prevails, one's affective experience is driven primarily by the sense of the Other. For some, this Other-orientation may, indeed, facilitate a "self-denial" as traditionally conceived. For others an affective orientation results in a transformation which awakens a dormant self (cf. Dunfee 1982 and Hess 1997, 31-54.).

Sixth, following Oatley, it is wise to remember that most human emotions appear in interpersonal situations. Christianity is an interpersonal religion. Christian spirituality is characterized by a deeply personal dimension sensed in the divine-human relationship. The very notion of "covenant," a foundational concept in Christian theology, rests upon the understanding that the God-human relationship necessitates personal interaction, involving mutually shared plans and goals. However human limitations and biases, and the vagueness of the divine give ample room for "junctures" in these mutually held plans, both goal-fulfillment and goal-threatening junctures. The works of William Barry illustrate this dimension of Christian affective experience marvelously (e.g. Barry 1987a, 1989a, 1993). As one's covenant is shared not only with God, but also with other humans, the navigation of mutuality becomes more complex, and at times more affectively charged (cf. Unger 1984). Some Christian emotions arise as part of the management process of the goals and plans of the shared life of the divine and human.

Finally, based on the above, one can hypothesize a few "core relational themes" appropriate to a few central affective tendencies associated with the Christian tradition. Don Saliers develops some of these in *The Soul In Paraphrase* (1991). Ultimately, I suspect each distinct "Christian emotion" could be examined for distinctive phenomenological tone, action tendency, mental preoccupation, physiological change and so on—a task for future research in Christian emotions. Two appraisal components appear significant for Christian emotions. First is the appraised value of God. Whether God is seen as the direct stimulus of an affective experience, or whether a situation is appraised in view of the Ultimate Concern, the value of God is nearly always somewhere in the "blend" of Christian emotions. It appears most purely in the aesthetic emotion of worship. The second appraisal component is the assessment of the person-environment/God relationship. This appears as a sense of dependency, an affective recognition that God is God; one is derived from and, in a powerful sense at the mercy of, God. One finds an element of dependency, like worship, present in many Christian emotions. Praise and thanksgiving involve the presence of dual concerns: the sense of our needs, desires, plans, and the sense of the heart of God. Praise and thanksgiving regard God as the cause (blame) of our situation (appraisal). It is the awareness of the Ultimate Concern, and the shaping of our heart to this Concern, that enables the Christian to feel sincere thanksgiving in adversity as well as in prosperity. Petition and intercession also simultaneously involve both this sense of our need and God's concerns. At times our needs are primary and we pour out our concerns to God, fully aware of our dependence. At other times, God's own concerns are primary and we unite with these concerns (empathy) begging that "Thy kingdom come, Thy will be done" in justice, in revival, in peace. Sometimes we feel love, being appreciated by the Supremely valued Other. Sometimes we feel repentant, sensing the disappointment of the Supremely valued Other. Sometimes we experience revelation, a sense of new meaning, coherence, or "fit," which adjusts nuclear scripts and opens us up to new forms of life. In a manner such as this we can begin to conceive of distinctively "Christian emotions," those formed by the Christian tradition, in light of the findings of experimental psychological science concerning the human emotions.

Conclusions

We are now in a position to draw the insights of this chapter into a tentative whole. In the first section of the chapter we explored the nature of human categorization in an effort to clarify what an empirically grounded theory of discernment as *an act of knowledge* must take into account. We discovered that a theory of Christian discernment must acknowledge the influences that shape the discerner prior to a discernment event. We also found that discernment addresses regularities in the perceived world, regularities which can, to some extent, be mutually observed and shared. Furthermore, discernment involves a special type of categorization, evaluating the presence of one concept (*God*) in a variety of domains. A theory of Christian discernment must also account for the diversity of contexts, activities, and spiritual development of discerners and discernment situations. Discernment will differ for different people and at different times. A theory of Christian discernment must reflect carefully on issues of category membership, and must carefully relate rules of category membership (how one determines this is really *God*) to the variety of ideas associated with the concept *God*. A theory of Christian discernment would respect categorization as a *process*, often requiring the completion of stages for confident fulfillment. A theory of Christian discernment might see the development of connaturality as the increase of facilitation in noticing salient features related to discernment, and the classic works on discernment as shared "expertise" in a particular field. The expert tradition in Christian discernment indicates prototypes, salient features, rules and the like, all embedded within implicit theories of spirituality. These aspects of categorization appear to be well grounded in the empirical literature. As discerners become more familiar with the environment, the features, and the methods of discernment, they can feel increasingly confident that they are able to categorize *God* and *not God* in their experience. Finally, we learned that discernment, whether experienced or novice, functions as merely one element of an enactive mediation of experience.

In the second section of this chapter we explored the nature of human affectivity. We discovered that human affectivity involves the contributions of a number of domains: physiological, cognitive, social, and even spiritual. Affectivity includes, although is not limited to gross emotions. Affectivity, like categorization, also appears to follow a process often involving such stages as stimuli, appraisal, feedback and response. The affective system, like the conceptual, is shaped by culture and cognitive structure prior to any encounter. Affective operations arise as signals from the environment touch a concern. An appraisal process determines the situation to be concern-relevant, evaluating a variety of components in the situation relevant to one's concerns, needs, or plans. Changes in (and awareness of the changes in) physiology, action tendencies, phenomenological tone, conscious preoccupation, expression and such form the culmination of affective experience, and give affectivity its distinctive "feel." Its "meaning," however, is usually found in culture and in interpersonal relationships. Affective operations contribute to conceptual process, just as cognitive operations contribute to affective process. Affectivity, like conceptual process, serves to mediate between subject and environment. Distinctively *Christian* emotions are oriented in some form to their object and especially to the supreme Object, similar to the pattern in aesthetic emotions. In this manner God can be rightly understood as the Christian's Ultimate Concern. The various common Christian emotions (praise, repentance, etc.) can be understood in this light.

As an aside, it might be mentioned here that in my understanding, neither a facile hierarchical division between "emotions" (at the bottom), intellect, and will, nor a simple "libidinal energy release" model of affectivity can finally do justice to the empirical data of human affectivity. While it might be possible to identify "conceptual," "affective," and "volitional" systems in human experience, the taxonomic hierarchy stemming from Aristotle is simply without empirical warrant, and the mutual interplay of operations between systems demands that such assumptions as "emotions are irrational" be rejected as overly simplistic. Likewise, while I recognize the important role that elements like physiology, drive, and motivation have in human affectivity (especially when important concerns are touched), the integration of the cognitive and social dimensions in the affective system make many "energy release" models of human emotions appear to have missed the point. For similar reasons a model of feelings as "apprehensive-intentional responses to value" (cf. Tyrrell 1987) also may fall short of explaining the diverse functions and components involved in human affective process. While many writers in Christian spirituality have transcended these models (Ignatius and Edwards, for example), I suspect some re-conceptualization will be necessary in future reflection on affectivity in Christian spirituality.

The question that remains, in conclusion, is to consider what roles affectivity, as re-explored through current psychological research, might play in the process of discernment, as understood in light of categorization research. I demonstrated, in chapter two, that representatives from the history of Christian spirituality speak of human affectivity as participating in the process of discernment on a number of levels. Affectivity influences the *subject* of discernment, whether an individual taking the *Spiritual Exercises* or a body of Christian leaders trying to determine whether to promote revival meetings in a community. The *context* of discernment also possesses affective significance. The life of action amidst a Jesuit community, the dynamism of a national spiritual awakening each provide a unique affective context within which discernment is conducted. Furthermore, I showed that affective experiences could, in some conditions become an *object* of discernment. This was the case with regard to the "discernment of spirits" in individual spiritual direction as well as with regard to an evaluation of affective experiences arising from within a spiritual awakening. Finally, I showed that affectivity might play a part in the *act* of discernment, contributing to the evaluative process itself. I also used these same divisions to investigate the roles of affectivity within the process of categorization in general. In what follows I will present a few examples of the roles of affectivity in discernment as seen in light of the empirical material presented. I will present a more broad ranging application in the final chapters of the present study. My hope is that insights here presented will be sufficient to indicate how a "more empirically grounded" theory of Christian discernment might understand the roles which affectivity plays in the process.

With regards to the roles of affectivity in terms of the *subject* of discernment, a number of points may be made. First, one must acknowledge that each discerning subject (whether individual or group) comes to the discernment event with cultural, cognitive-structural, and developmental "givens." This is not only true of the concepts and categorization processes present, but also, as mentioned above, of affective patterns. What aspects of spiritual experience one is apt to notice or attend, what configuration of concerns (spiritual and personal/corporate) determine affective significance, what expressions of religious emotion are "permitted" (for example - (1) action tendencies like stillness, shaking, crying, laughing, or (2) phenomenological tones like the sense of loss of self-identity and merging with the divine, or (3) mental preoccupations like persistent mental imagery of nursing the infant Christ) are all, to some extent, given through our culture, cognitive structure, and (affirming the conclusions of Liebert 1986, 1992) development. At times these different "givens" can come into conflict, but they do so from the context of their having been given. Christian discernment must begin with what is given. This means that by understanding something of cognitive structure and culture, one can make reasonable judgments about general conceptual and affective patterns that may impact discernment in a given situation. It is helpful to recognize and review these at the onset of a discernment process. It also means that one cannot assume more of a discerner than what may be given. To expect the affective sensitivities of a contemplative from one raised in exuberant Pentacostalism (or vice versa), would be asking too much of a discerner.

This brings me to the second point, namely that an empirically grounded theory of Christian discernment must acknowledge the diversity of discerners and discernment situations. The *subject* of discernment is affectively unique in each situation. Not only are individuals and groups "given" in each situation, but also the goal-related activities relevant to the situation, the aims of and reasons for the discernment, the specific concerns associated with this situation, abilities to notice interior events, and the investment level of the discerner(s) in the discernment process itself all vary from situation to situation and discerner to discerner. Distraction of appraisal, patterns of regulation, and misattribution of experience are all affected by factors such as these. Discernment begins with discerners, and discernment theory will benefit by avoiding facile "cook-book" approaches whenever possible. Having said this, however, it must be acknowledged that many coming to spiritual directors in search of help, may need a simple outline to begin (as in some "First Week" work). I intend my rejection of simple models and formats as a principle for *discernment theory* as shared among spiritual directors and scholars of Christian spirituality.

I believe there is an affective component in many of the virtues commonly mentioned in discernment literature. The virtues of humility, submission, attentiveness, freedom, and sensitivity all carry with them an affective dimension. Indeed, as Aristotle suggests (1941 [iv bce], *Nichomachean Ethics* II.5-6; cf. also G. Hughes 1990) the virtues themselves may function as predispositions to respond affectively in certain ways in given circumstances. These predispositions to respond involve patterns of appraisal, regulation, and response generation. The preparation of the subject for discernment involves the education of these patterns. In some subjects there may be present patterns of affectivity which prevent perception of God's guidance or presence (Foley, 1991). Painful emotions, ignored or inappropriately attended, can stand in the way of recognizing and affirming what is from God (Whitehead and Whitehead 1996). Unconscious bias may stand in the way of effective freedom to choose the will of God (Rulla 1978; Meissner 1963, 1964a, 1964b). Dysfunctional affective patterns (Ignatius' "disordered affections") in a subject may need to be transformed in order to insure quality discernment. The growth toward "indifference," a chief virtue of Ignatian discernment, involves just such a transformation.

The transformation of affectivity in a discerning subject (not simply control), involves the re-orientation from self to Other. As mentioned above, the aesthetic/empathetic/meditational sense of the contemplation of the Other is distinctive of Christian emotions. J. J. Mueller, following the lead of Bernard Meland offers a three-step approach to what he terms "appreciative awareness." The first step is *opened awareness*. The event is allowed to disclose itself without preconceptions (notice the abandonment of self-concern here). The second step is *identification*, which involves a reciprocal relationship as event and person share representation and feeling. The third step is *discrimination*, which brings out what is present in the situation (Mueller 1984). Edwards emphasized the divine initiative in the transformation of affective sensibilities, enabling the regenerate believer to apprehend and to become oriented to the beauty and moral excellency of Christ. Ignatius emphasized the use of Gospel meditation to cultivate an appreciation for Christ. There is, I believe, increasing interest in the aesthetic dimension as related to matters of religion from the perspective of psychology (cf. Watts and Williams 1988; Mangan 1991). Work in this area offers much hope for the future. I believe discernment *of* God increases with the increased practice of attention *to* God.

Moving from aesthetic to empathetic affectivity, as this relates to the subject of Christian discernment, one can begin to talk of developing connaturality. As the Christian life matures, we become more familiar with, and more appreciative of, the "concerns" of Christ. A sharing of concern goes on between the divine and human, and one's concerns begin to be conformed to those of Christ. The developing sensitivity to the concerns of Christ (and the recognition of the counterfeits of these concerns) makes us more able to recognize, in the active presence of those concerns, the presence of God in a discernment situation.

Finally, affectivity is involved in the subject of discernment as a skill for discernment. The *Spiritual Exercises* aim at developing affective sensitivity in the discerning subject. Depending on the givens (for example, stage of affective development) and the circumstances of an individual discernment event (for example, a context of contemplative prayer), a variety of affective sensibilities may be helpful for the act of discernment. While they come into play (and will be discussed) in the *act* of discernment, as potentially developable *skills* they form an aspect of the subject of discernment as well. At times concerns or predispositions force a misattribution of impulses related to a discernment. Improved affective sensitivity (for example, the ability to distinguish consolation and desolation), can greatly aid in the recognition of what is or is not from God.

With regard to the *context* of discernment, only a few things need be said. I have already mentioned the more general context of the historical, cultural, social setting. These factors provide constraints upon the appraisals, regulatory functions, social roles and such, that affective process embodies. Discernment is performed *within* such settings. The options for one's own affective experience in discernment become available, at least to some degree, by observing the range of affective experience in the various sub-communities of the context, often by observing salient exemplars of various "ways of being" affectively. In the case of the Great Awakening, for example, one key discernment concerned whether a given affective trend was or was not of God (or at least, what elements of this affective trend are or are not of God). Affective experiences from a wide range of sentiment toward the Awakening presented a smorgasbord of "options" to the individual believer of the period, often complete with very salient exemplars of a few of the options. At times, the natural tendency to organize around the salient exemplar may distract a proper understanding of the category as a whole. In such a case, affective experience functions as a critical element of the context of discernment, as well as being the object of discernment.

Affective experience also functions within the context of discernment in a more narrow way. Mood congruent or incongruent affective experience influences the "atmosphere" in which Christian discernment is conducted. This includes both the accumulation of affective experience (arousal, appraisals, etc.) for the subject entering discernment, as well as the affective atmosphere of the immediate surroundings/situation. Cantor, Mischel, and Schwartz (1982) found this element of "atmosphere" to be a contributing factor to categorizing of everyday situations. Words like "frantic," "gloomy," "tense," "homey," and "charged" serve to identify aspects of this immediate affective context of discernment. Both in terms of the subject and the surroundings, one must remember that there is a tendency to evaluate toward prevailing mood. Good moods tend to cultivate positive evaluations of situations; bad moods produce negative evaluations. These kinds of affective-evaluative heuristics must be taken into account in a "more empirically grounded" theory of Christian discernment.

Affectivity can also function as the *object* of discernment. There are times when we want to know whether a particular affective experience (or set of them) is or is not "from God." In these times conceptual process (with the help of affective operations) evaluates the features of affective experience to determine its character. Both Ignatius and Edwards outlined reviews of one's affective experience: beginning, middle, and end. In this kind of review one examines affective experience, attentive to aspects of the experience that indicate its relationship to God. Discernment wisdom (expertise) points the believer to prototype experiences (e.g. "consolation without prior cause"), or individual features of affective experience (e.g. presence of tears - action tendency; frequent thoughts of love to God - mental preoccupation), or features of the surrounding atmosphere (e.g. examining whether one in moving toward or away from God). As the individual believer (or group) becomes more familiar with the discernment process, the discerner will begin to identify more and more relevant features of the affective experiences concerned. This will become one's own wisdom, gained not simply by communication but by experience. Increased attentiveness to affective experience will cultivate a certain level of expertise, causing the creation of a set of subordinate categories related to affective experience that are understood as many would approach basic level categories. Naming one's experiences can either help or hinder this process. On the positive side, a clear distinction may be made in experience, for example, between the feeling of legitimate "guilt," stimulated by divine disappointment and the sense of "accusation," stimulated by demonic oppression. Salient exemplars, important features and helpful rules will be identified from the memories and scripts of the spiritual history of an individual or group. In some cases, however, the tendency to organize around easily recognized salient examples can lead one astray, as, for example, when intensity of emotional expression is mistaken for the sincerity, depth, or divine origin of affective experience (or for the lack thereof). In these cases one must be careful, as Edwards advises, to discriminate between those signs which are not certain and the "more certain signs" of a work of the Spirit of God.

As affective experience becomes the object of discernment, it also becomes the environment and potential stimulus for new affective responses. Concerns about one's own emotions (or lack thereof), begin to play a part in the discernment process concerning affective experience. Regulatory scripts play a part here, and the evaluation process can get very complex. But it is important for a "more empirically grounded" theory of Christian discernment to recognize that one is not only dealing with emotions, but also with people's concerns, plans, expectations, needs, relative to those emotions themselves.

Finally, I suggest that affective experience also plays a part of the *act* of discernment itself. Affective experience, especially in its noetic and semiotic functions serves to mediate between the environment and the subject. Also, moving closer to the object-orientation of aesthetic, empathetic, and religious emotions, one finds that there is a much richer grasp of the object in view. Furthermore, I suggested above that affective operations contribute to the motion of cognitive process itself, signalling key shifts and developments of the process and coordinating cognitive and affective scripts. For these reasons, it seems reasonable to expect that affective operations play a significant part in the act or process of identifying what is, or is not, from God. Affective operations mediate the environment in a way not accomplished by conceptual process (and therefore complementary to conceptual process). Watts and Williams (1988) give an illustration of this kind of knowing in terms of the common "tip of the tongue" phenomena discussed in cognitive psychology. After much discussion in a group of people trying to recall someone's name, you happen upon the correct name, and you know it is the correct name. "You know you've 'got it' because it feels so completely different from all the near misses with which you've been struggling," they write (Watts and Williams 1988, 48). In situations of discernment, affective operations will tend to highlight aspects of the situation that conceptual process may be able to articulate only with great difficulty. Affective operations also, because of their focus on meaning, tend to notice aspects of the situation that may go unnoticed by conceptual process. This is especially true of Christian discernment, where affective orientation (as in aesthetic or empathetic emotions) possesses a heightened sensitivity to the key element involved in the discernment process (namely, God). Thus one can expect that discerners may be able to notice key features of the divine presence or guidance in situations because of affective components recognized in the situations, components that may go unnoticed by conceptual processes. Finally, I might suggest as illustration of the role of affectivity guiding conceptual process in discernment the common reference to the feeling of "peace" as a confirmation that one has concluded a discernment. This affective peace signals the shift in conceptual process, indicating that one has finally reached an adequate discernment.

Many more examples of these principles could be given. Nonetheless, the above are sufficient, I believe, to demonstrate how the findings of experimental psychology can validate and amplify an account of Christian discernment as an affectively-rich act of knowing. I have brought increased empirical specificity to the operations involved in Christian discernment, and in so doing have grounded both a descriptive account of discernment (what actually goes on when people actually discern) and elements of a normative account (what must be involved in the best possible discernment) in the insights of empirical research. However, the empirical grounding of a theory of Christian discernment is only part of the increased specificity desired. Empirical insights must be held together in a coherent whole, a whole which can unite the theological and the psychological, the philosophical and the spiritual. Furthermore, Christian discernment functions not only as a human act, but as a graced human act with relationship to the divine. Thus, we must also begin to address the presence and activity of God in discernment. Throughout this chapter I have prescinded from important questions of the nature of meaning, of divine revelation, and discussion of important philosophical questions. It is to these questions that I turn in chapter four.

Chapter 4

American Philosophy and Christian Discernment: A Development of the Foundational Theology of Donald Gelpi

This study seeks to illumine the understanding of Christian discernment. I hope to demonstrate that insights from experimental psychology, when interpreted with the help of a philosophically-sensitive model of human experience, can provide valuable resources toward making sense of Christian discernment. The findings of empirical psychology regarding human categorization and affectivity, summarized in the previous chapter, provided a measure of empirical grounding regarding the operations involved in Christian discernment. The exploration of categorization and affectivity was able to confirm my approach to discernment as an affectively-rich act of knowing insofar as that approach was able to interpret discernment within the constraints imposed by the findings of experimental psychology. I was also able to amplify and enrich that approach by supplying more detailed information about the discerning process and by suggesting a number of specific ways in which affective operations might participate in the dynamics of Christian discernment comprehended within that approach.

The present study intends, however, not merely to provide a theory of Christian discernment with empirical grounding, but also to suggest a clear and coherent conceptual framework within which the empirical material related to discernment can be intelligently

Affirming the Touch of God

understood. I have accomplished this in part through the suggestion of an overall definition which is able to encompass the diverse phenomena of Christian discernment: namely that Christian discernment can be beneficially understood as the affectively-rich act of coming to identify and know in a given situation, in light of one's Christian faith tradition, that which is significantly related to God. The working definition has been able to comprehend data from classical "discernment literature" in the history of Christian spirituality, from current scholarly research on Christian discernment, and from empirical psychology. My approach at present, however, lacks sufficient philosophical and theological specificity necessary to provide the clarity and coherence required of a theory of Christian discernment as an act of knowing. Hence I turn, in the current chapter, to the field of philosophical theology as found in the work of Fr. Donald Gelpi, S.J.

In 1996 Gelpi was asked to give a lecture to a gathering of people involved in the Roman Catholic charismatic renewal. His topic: "Discernment and the Varieties of Conversion." His aim: to reflect on the relationship between discernment and a construct of conversion. Gelpi has been developing a unique approach to Christian conversion for over twenty years. In this lecture, Gelpi was asked to bring insight to an understanding of discernment by exploring discernment through the eyes of his developing construct of conversion. He did so by elaborating three theses. Two of these theses serve to introduce some of the key issues of the present chapter. With the first, that *the charism of discernment endows natural prudential reasoning with docility to the illumination of Christ's Holy Breath* (1996, 6), Gelpi suggests that by a specific act of God's grace (the charism of discernment) particular mental operations (prudential reasoning) are changed in particular ways (endowed with docility) with relationship to God's self-communication (to the "illumination") through the agency of third person of the Trinity (of Christ's Holy Breath). He identifies prudential reasoning with the deliberation over possible courses of action (cf. Gelpi 1988b, 99-146; Dewey 1938). Deliberation reflects on actions in the light of ideals and principles. By gathering relevant facts, appreciating them in their context, and removing negative projections that might "skew its appreciative grasp," prudential reasoning begins to understand ways in which elements within a situation might contribute to the resolution of the problematic character of a situation (whether speculative ethical, or pragmatic). Having clarified the nature of prudential reasoning, Gelpi introduces his audience to the ministry of the Holy Spirit (called the "Holy Breath"). While "sanctification," the transformation enabling the believer to live out the life of sharing, forgiving, loving envisioned by Christ, describes the primary way in which one relates to the Breath of Jesus, "charismatic empowerment" names a second way. Through charismatic empowerment, gifts or "charisms" are given to different members of the church. These diverse charisms contribute to the shared faith consciousness of the community as a whole by enriching or enabling different aspects of community life. These gifts orient particular mental operations God-ward, thus giving them a responsiveness, a "docility" to the "Divine Breath's inspirations" (Gelpi 1996, 11). Thus the charism of discernment brings to the speculative, ethical, and pragmatic deliberations of the believer and believing community an orientation to God as revealed through the inspirations of the Holy Breath. In this way, "discernment helps faith communities distinguish between true and false accounts of its story and between life-giving and death-dealing hopes" (Gelpi 1996, 10).

Gelpi introduces his construct of conversion more directly in his second thesis: that *"the five forms of conversion provide the discerning heart with a tool for diagnosing the causes of personal and communal fragmentation and for identifying the ideals and principles needed to heal that fragmentation."* Gelpi suggests here that personal and communal breakdown arises within identifiable dimensions or realms of human experience. "Discernment," Gelpi writes

seeks to understand what kinds of "spirits," or impulses motivate personal and communal behavior. It distinguishes "good spirits" from "bad" ones. "Bad spirits" render personal and communal living problematic through disintegration. The presence of a "bad spirit" also betrays the absence of conversion in some realm of human experience." (1996, 15)

These five realms of human experience (affective, intellectual, moral, socio-political, religious) reflect areas of life within which one may turn from irresponsible to responsible action. The acknowledgement of the possibility of this kind of transformation (called "conversion") in each of these areas presents to discerning deliberation a matrix of ideals and principles in the light of which problematic situations can be evaluated (for example, the possibility of affective conversion invokes the ideal of healthy emotive experience). Furthermore, the ability to identify these realms in practice can aid discerning deliberation to identify particular kinds of personal or communal disintegration (naming the "bad spirit"), thereby facilitating the understanding of the disintegration present. Thus awareness of the five forms of conversion function as a "tool" for the discerning evaluation of problematic situations.

Within his presentation of these two theses concerning discernment and conversion, Gelpi introduces many of the issues of the present chapter and of any theologically/philosophically sensitive account of Christian discernment.   Indeed, as I shall show, a deeper understanding of the synthesis that underlies Gelpi's theses requires the exploration of a number of key theological and philosophical themes. For example, Gelpi mentions the self-communication of God and the ministry of the Holy Spirit in his first thesis. The roles of particular cognitive-affective operations involved in the discerning act of knowing are described in both theses, as "prudential reasoning," or "deliberation" (elsewhere discussed as "judgments of feeling"; Gelpi 1993, I, 130-31). The transformation of both self and community are addressed both in terms of the work of the Spirit (a charism), and in terms of personal responsibility (conversion). Attention to the "true" and the "false" (or the "good" and the "bad") is mentioned in both theses.

Philosophical theology should, in terms of the present study, provide an account of Christian discernment with a few essential ingredients: (1) it should articulate an overall approach to human experience that coheres with the findings of experimental psychology, (2) it should provide the framework for a concrete integration of the scientific material with an authentic Christian faith-perspective, (3) it should speak of the divine such that it can interpret the dynamics of discernment experience, (4) it should establish the epistemological principles upon which discernment as an "act of knowing" can be considered, and (5) it should include sufficient reflection on human affectivity (cf. Gelpi 1988b 122-25; 147-70; 1994-95 1.130; 1997, 274; Whitehead 1929, 5-14). As shown in the sample of Gelpi's reflections on discernment above, all of these are pursued in Gelpi's thought. Thus, having introduced a measure of empirical specificity to a theory of discernment in the previous chapter, I am now ready to explore the North American theological-philosophical synthesis of Donald Gelpi in order to introduce a measure of theological and philosophical clarity to an account of Christian discernment.

I am employing the field of philosophical theology at this point in my study in order to serve two general functions. First, I am using philosophical theology as a form of *analytical and critical discourse* (Schneiders 1998, 6). I hope to reflect on aspects of the Christian experience of God—specifically elements of the process of discernment—through the categories of philosophical theology. In so doing, as Schneiders suggests, I limit or "relativize" my approach to the phenomena of Christian spirituality to the categories developed in the work of the North American foundational theology of Donald Gelpi. Second, I am using philosophical theology to cultivate the possibility of a wider community of inquiry. By linking reflection on Christian experience to fundamental transcendent categories and specific theological categories (Lonergan 1972, 281-91), I intend to use the language of philosophical and theological discourse to form a conceptual framework within which to understand discernment. In so doing, I hope to "universalize" an approach to Christian experience in the sense of making it more accessible to ongoing dialogue within philosophical and theological communities.

In moving from psychological to theological and philosophical reflection, I also shift in emphasis from the descriptive to the normative account of Christian discernment. While I presented insights beneficial both for an explanation of what people actually do when they discern as well as for an explanation of what people ought to do in order best to discern, most of the emphasis has so far been on the descriptive side. But as I begin to speak of the use of these operations in the context of a specific faith perspective (the language of theology), and as I begin to reflect upon the use of self-controlled operations chosen in order to transcend bias and to insure that the discerning act of knowing is indeed an act of *knowing* (the language of philosophy), the emphasis will shift to the normative side. Not to say, of course, that theological and philosophical reflection fail to provide insight concerning what people actually do in discernment. I am speaking merely of a shift in emphasis.

The work of Donald Gelpi is especially relevant for such an investigation. Since the beginning of his writing career in 1959, Gelpi has made a conscious effort at the integration of philosophical and theological thought. He has taught and written in both fields. His thorough appropriation of North American philosophy within the framework of traditional Christian theology helps to make his work especially valuable for developing a theory of Christian discernment that is sensitive both to the old and the new. He has also made a conscious effort to integrate the affective dimension into his work, not only in terms of the content of his work but also in his theological method. As I shall show, Gelpi's "categoreal system" (Gelpi's term) coordinates well with the empirical data explored in the previous chapter. One does not feel like one is "forcing" the data into the framework or vice versa when correlating material from various disciplines within Gelpi's system. Furthermore, Gelpi has written extensively enough to provide a fairly comprehensive approach to the issues at hand. Nearly all of the key themes mentioned in previous chapters are addressed in Gelpi's work. It is for these reasons that I have chosen to utilize Gelpi's work to assist the mediation of a philosophically sensitive understanding of Christian discernment.

In the present chapter my aim is simply to summarize Gelpi's philosophical/theological synthesis and to use it to illustrate aspects of Christian discernment. After a brief review of the development of Gelpi's thought, I will present the primary philosophical categories of Gelpi's system. Next, I will review Gelpi's approach to two primary theological issues relevant to discernment, namely the questions of the self-communication of God and the work of the Holy Spirit. From there I will move to a discussion of the nature and transformation of the person and the community, Gelpi's construct of conversion. At that point I will be prepared to address an issue which Gelpi does not develop at length with relationship to discernment but which I believe carries significant weight, namely the clarification of an epistemology of Christian discernment. I will draw upon both Gelpi and his sources in North American philosophy in an effort to articulate a few logical steps necessary to develop an account of the reliability and limits of Christian discernment as an affectively-rich act of religious knowing. I will then close the chapter by bringing Gelpi's approach to Christian discernment, rooted in the synthesis just presented, into dialogue with the other philosophical accounts of discernment reviewed in chapter one. My aim here is not to give a full analysis of Gelpi's theology of Christian discernment, but rather to demonstrate the advantages of his synthesis for a philosophically sensitive account of Christian discernment as an affectively-rich act of knowing. In the fifth chapter of this study I will develop Gelpi's system further as I synthesize both psychology and philosophical theology within an independent model of human experience and Christian discernment.

The Development of Gelpi's Thought

Fr. Donald Gelpi's thought may be best introduced by introducing a number of adjectives appropriate to the man and his thought. First, Gelpi is a *Catholic Christian*. Born and raised in New Orleans ("that most Catholic of southern cities" 1993, I, 23) Gelpi was a regular participant in Mass and a student at a Catholic High School. Gelpi has maintained faithful association with the Christian faith and with the Roman Catholic tradition since. His writings explicitly reflect this association. They are usually explicitly directed to address particular contexts within the Catholic tradition (for example, compare Gelpi 1976 with 1993). Second, Gelpi is not merely a Catholic, but also a *Jesuit*. Entering the novitiate in Louisiana in 1951, Gelpi's training and interests express the dynamic that has driven Jesuit scholars since Ignatius encouraged his band of followers. His approach to religious life is that of an "active" religious (1969; 1970; 1988a, 169-202). His appreciation for the *Exercises* finds its way into many of his works (1966a, 238; 1971, 39f, 180f; 1987 [1978] 140f, 247). The bold, comprehensive character of his philosophical/theological synthesis betrays the vision of the "greater" (*magis*) so characteristic of Jesuit life. Third, Gelpi is a *foundational theologian*. In the work of Bernard Lonergan, and particularly in Lonergan's description of foundational theology as that theological specialization which attempts to articulate the nature of conversion in all its forms, Gelpi has found an academic "home." While he revises Lonergan in numerous points (cf. 1988b; 1994, 107-117), he does so from within the field of foundational theology, the critical analysis of conversion. His association with this field requires of him the use of philosophical, theological, biblical, historical, and psychological analysis. All are integrated into Gelpi's approach to foundations (cf. 1978/87; 1994-95). Gelpi has also been watered by the *charismatic* stream of Christianity. Since 1968 the charismatic experiences have significantly contributed toward his personal spirituality (1987 [1978] 11-12; 1993), and his reflections on these themes have born fruit in articles and books directly related to the work of the Spirit and charismatic experience (1970; 1971; 1982; 1985; 1988c). Finally, Gelpi is a *North American*. A personal realization of the differences between American and European practice of religious life when transferred to Europe stimulated a significant "religious conversion" for Father Gelpi (1993, I, 24). Gelpi's response to the Vatican's encouragement to inculturation fueled his co-foundation of the John Courtney Murray group, a collection of Catholic scholars seeking to explore Christian theological thinking from a North American idiom. The same interest energizes his own North American philosophical/theological synthesis.

Gelpi foreshadows his North American philosophical synthesis as early as his *Discerning the Spirit* (1970, esp. 236-38), where he applies elements of Peircean pragmatic logic to the development of a theology of religious life. This approach is also reflected in his *Pentecostalism: a Theological Viewpoint* (1971, 120). However, it was not until his first foundational work, *Charism and Sacrament*, that Gelpi began to systematically present the philosophical framework that was to underpin his theological thought from that time on (1976, 5-13). By this time he had systematically read through the works of all the major philosophical thinkers in North American history from Jonathan Edwards through Alfred North Whitehead. As Gelpi himself notes, the model presented is ultimately dependent upon no single author but rather "is a conflation of a number of different themes in American philosophical thought" (1976, 25n3). In *Charism and Sacrament* it is simply presented as the model for interpreting charismatic and sacramental experience. Though his next book, *Experiencing God*, follows *Charism and Sacrament* chronologically, it logically precedes the earlier work. In *Experiencing God* Gelpi articulates and defends at length the synthesis which undergirds his theological thought. He does so in the form of a theological anthropology (1987 [1978], 1-121). Aware that philosophical conflation is a dangerous enterprise, Gelpi is careful in his foundational writings to indicate precisely when and where he divides company with his predecessors and to demonstrate how consistency is maintained in his system. Though his terminology has changed over the years, the concepts which form Gelpi's primary categoreal system have developed in continuity with his early foundational writings. He has re-articulated this synthesis in many of his works (cf. 1985, 23-

42; 1988a, 1-66; 1994, 121-157). In the outline of Gelpi's thought which follows, I will refer primarily to the presentation given in his more recent writings, though I will refer to earlier works insofar as they provide depth regarding particular points undeveloped in later writings.

Primary Philosophical Categories

Gelpi's central philosophical category is the category of *experience*. The notion of "experience" has served uniquely as an organizing category throughout the history of North American philosophy (1988a, 11-19; cf. Smith 1992a). Examining philosophical questions with a view to experience brings an emphasis to the dynamic aspects of persons, things, ideas, and events. Some use the term "experience" to refer to practical knowledge gained by long term exposure (wisdom gained from experience). Others refer to "experience" more technically, referring to knowledge rooted in human senses or to a stage/state of consciousness prior to critical/conceptual involvement. Gelpi, following Alfred North Whitehead (Whitehead 1929, 182-94) gives the term a transcendental sense. In Gelpi's use of "experience" objects and subjects are not separate but rather stand within each other as elements of the same experience, as each participates in making an experience precisely what it is (1994, 2-3). In Gelpi's system, one does not simply *have* an experience: one *is* an experience, a developing union (Whitehead would use the term *concrescence*) of evaluations, actions, and tendencies (1985, 20-24; 1994, 126).

Gelpi calls his model a "triadic, realistic, communitarian" model of experience (1994). Though Gelpi's realism and communitarianism are vital elements of his philosophical synthesis, they are more appropriately discussed further below. By "triadic" Gelpi joins with philosophers whose constructs are framed around three primary categories (like Orestes Brownson, Francis Ellingswood Abbot and Josiah Royce; cf. 1997, 144f, 170f, 192f, 247). By utilizing a triadic, rather than a dyadic, model, Gelpi significantly revises the experiential framework of Whitehead. His support for this revision is found preeminently in the work of Charles S. Peirce. Gelpi's categories correspond to the various terms which Peirce uses for *Firstness*, *Secondness*, and *Thirdness* in his writings (e.g. Peirce, W 2.49-

59; D. Anderson 1995, 37-40).[1] The importance of a triadic frame-work in Gelpi's system cannot be overstated (cf. 1994, 121-57). It forms the source of his realism and his communitarianism.

"Values" make up the first primary category of experience (1993, I, xii; also called "quality" 1976, 1987 [1978], 1985; and "evalua-tions" 1988a). Whereas Peirce left his understanding of Firstness rather vague (D. Anderson 1995, 39; CP 1.418), Gelpi sees in values or evaluation a broad continuum of "feelings" which arise to partially constitute experience (following Whitehead 1929, 251-328). Gelpi identifies the realm of value, in human experience, with the appearance of any of a range of evaluative responses. Sensations, emotions, images, and inferential thought all are to be found on this continuum of evaluative responses. Just as the precise configuration of various kinds of attractions and repulsions (evaluative responses) shapes the nature of subatomic "reality," so human experience is shaped in the First, by a configuration of evaluative responses. Their appearance, to any degree and in any form, in conjunction with the other two categories forms the character of human experience. I shall review the elements of this evaluative continuum below.

Gelpi's second category is called "Action" (1993; also called "fact" 1976, 1987 [1978], 1985; and "interactions" 1988a). Gelpi's understanding of action draws from Peirce's Secondness (at times called "facts," CP 1.419) to identify the realm of resistance, of the concrete, of the matter to which evaluative response conforms or interacts. Rather than speaking of "objects" out there (and "subjects" in here), Gelpi prefers to see various elements joining to form a developing experience. Gelpi writes of this second category (here called "facts"), "Facts are, then, irreducibly relational. They do not exist 'in themselves and in nothing else.' They are the brute opera-tional impact of one entity upon another, the situational interplay of action and reaction" (1987 [1978], 76). Action is not, then the object of experience, but rather the presence of interactive reality.

[1]1. When referring to the works of Charles S. Peirce, I will use the abbreviation CP to refer to the *Collected Papers of Charles S. Peirce* (Peirce 1931-58) along with the associated volume and para-graph numbers. The abbreviation W will refer to the newer collection of the *Writings of Charles S. Peirce: A Chronological Edition* (1982-), along with the volume and page numbers.

With the addition of "general tendency" as a third category, Gelpi breaks company with Whitehead (1993; also called "law" 1976, 1987 [1978]; and "tendencies" 1988a). Whereas Whitehead conceived of reality merely as the momentary and constantly changing concrescence of fact and evaluation, of percept and concept, Gelpi, following Peirce, recognizes a third element in experience (CP 1.420). Tendency is simply the inclination to react or respond efficaciously and evaluatively in a particular way. Evaluation or action do not simply arise—they arise with a tendency, an inclination, to exist/process. Though tendencies are emergent entities, developing and decaying; though they are organic realities, whose complexity may wax or wane; they are nonetheless *habitual* realities, whose reality can be identified in the very manner in which the evaluative response and action join. As Gelpi writes, "They are the causal principles from which both actions and evaluations proceed" (1987 [1978], 77). This third category carries the sense of the general, of signification, of "thisness"—as opposed to the mere "suchness" of evaluation or the mere "thatness" of interaction—with it.[2] Gelpi summarizes his understanding of the third category (here called "law") and its relation to the others:

Laws, however, endow experience with a triadic structure both because they introduce a third kind of variable into experiential development and because they are habits of activity that link one fact to another in intelligible relationships. The law operative in water explains, for example, why it boils at one temperature and freezes at another. Laws differ from facts: Facts are concrete, while laws are generalized tendencies to certain kinds of reaction and growth. Laws differ from qualities: Qualities are inefficacious, while laws are the efficacious ground of action and evaluation. (1987 [1978], 77)

[2]When I speak of the "thisness" of tendency, I am not speaking of the character of experience which presents a vague something to me—which would refer more to action than tendency. Rather I am speaking of the character of experience which presents a real thing before me, a "this" which appears as a named or identifiable "this." It is tendency which enables human experience to identify "this" as this and not as a mere "that" or an experience of "such."

The all-encompassing category of *experience* and the three constructive categories of *evaluation, interaction, tendency*: these are the primary categories upon which Gelpi builds his philosophical theological system. It is this dynamic, triadic model of experience itself which gives Gelpi his character as an alternative to classical substance philosophical models. It is the inclusion of the category of tendency which gives rise to Gelpi's realism and which gives Gelpi his particular character as an alternative to contemporary process models of theology.

Two Theological Issues

In order to examine Christian discernment as an act of knowing that which is related to *God*, especially insofar that this is discerned in the context of the ordinary, ongoing life of the individual believer or community of faith, two important theological themes in Gelpi's thought should be reviewed. These theological themes address aspects of discernment unaddressed in the previous chapters of the present study. The first, the question of the self-communication of God, known as the doctrine of "revelation," addresses possibility of conceiving the discernment of something "from God," and of understanding the discernment process as graced by God's communication. The second, the doctrine of the Holy Spirit, explores the ministry of the third person of the Christian Trinity, whose activity makes God discernable to believers, and who graces that discerning process.

Revelation

Within the question of discernment as a knowing of something "related to" or "from" God, lies the question of God's own self-communication or revelation. From the side of the human discerner, one can ask what capacities, structures, etc. are present such that God can be discerned (or the question of the "conditions for the possibility of religious knowledge"). Yet, the same question can be asked from the side of the divine. What about God makes divine self-revelation possible such that what is "related to" or "from" God may be in some sense discernibly manifest? The former is the question of religious epistemological psychology; the latter is the question for theology.

This latter question could simply be answered in the negative, namely with the strictly agnostic answer that one can know nothing of God's existence, character, or communication. However, in the Christian tradition, and especially within the "discernment writings" in the history of Christian spirituality, God has been understood in some sense as a self-communicating God.

Gelpi, following Christian tradition on this point, affirms the self-communicating nature of God but he interpret's God's self-revelation in the light of the symbolic structure of experience. Just as many theologians adopt the term "Being" to identify the essential aspect of the divine, so in Gelpi's North American system God is portrayed as a triadic "Experience" (1985, 83-100; cf. Peirce CP 4.536). The mutual interpenetration, procession, and communication between the Father, Son, and Spirit forms the foundation of God's communicability to humans. Experience is transactional, interactive. Within the divine experience one can identify transactions (interactions) within the Godhead itself as well as transaction with God's creatures. Gelpi writes, "Because the divine experience is symbolic in its structure, it enjoys *communicable significance*. It is not only intelligible but supremely so" (1985, 94. italics Gelpi's).

The divine experience enters human experience, then, as activity, as an interaction, as a force impinging upon the evaluative responses of human experience. "Any divine act of self-revelation must be initially conformed to the capacity of the human mind to grasp it. If, then, God is to reveal Himself to human beings," Gelpi writes, "it must be by becoming concrete, enfleshed, incarnate. Since, however, the realm of matter resides in the realm of space and time, God's self revelation must be historical" (1987 [1978], 114). The supreme expression of this "enfleshment" is found in the incarnation of Jesus. And thus the revelation of God finds its concrete historical embodiment in the God/Man Jesus Christ (1985, 151-79; 1988b, 111-13; 1994, 149-55; 1994-1995). However, after Jesus' ascension, both Father and Son remain unavailable as concrete, interactive elements in historical experience. Therefore, "present experience of the reality of the Christian God begins, then, in a conscious encounter with the Holy Breath of Jesus, the divine Spirit, the sanctifying *Pneuma*, the *Ruah* of God and of His Christ" (1985, viii).

The Holy Breath

In order to make some sense of discernment in a Christian context, and especially in the context of Gelpi's charismatic foundational theology, it is essential to mention his understanding of the person and works of the Holy Spirit. Gelpi is eager to dispel misconceptions of the Holy Spirit caused by the development and consequent misunderstanding of the term "spirit." Rather than follow many traditional substance treatments of spirit which distinguish between "tangible" matter and "intangible" spirit, Gelpi wishes to stress the nature of God's Spirit as "force doing work" (1985, 11, 45-47). For this reason Gelpi refers to the third member of the Trinity as the *Holy Breath*.[3]

As mentioned above, Gelpi emphasizes the nature of the Breath of God as efficacious "force." He associates spirit with vectoral feelings, tendencies of action (1987 [1978], 156). At the same time, he views the Holy Breath as a principle of enlightenment, as the "mind" of God, as the divine interpretant, who mediates or interprets God within and without the Godhead (1985, 56f, 84f; 1994, 150). Gelpi draws upon biblical, historical, and experiential sources to defend the dynamic character of the Holy Breath. Gelpi associates the Holy Breath, in terms of his primary philosophical categories, with tendency or law. He writes,

> Laws are dynamic forces. And the laws which shape personal growth are living laws. For real persons live. When predicated of the divine Breath, the term "law" connotes, therefore, supreme vitality. As a legal entity, a self, the divine Breath is experienced by believers as a *life force*. And as co-creator, co-redeemer, and co-sanctifier with the Father and Son, She is also perceived in faith as a *life source*. (1985, 87)

Humans perceive the work of the Breath through the arising of certain elements within experience. In explaining how this takes

---

[3]Gelpi also ambitions a recovery of the feminine character of God through his re-appropriation of the doctrine of the Holy Spirit. For this reason Gelpi refers to the Holy Breath with the feminine pronoun (cf. 1987 [1978], 194f., 1985, 215-38; 1988c, 98-114).

place, Gelpi invokes the category of "transmutation." Transmutation conceives change on aesthetic and relational terms. The integration of a novel element with an experience requires the adjustment of its entire relational structure, just as the addition of a new color to a painting requires one to see it in relationship to all the other colors and of they to it (1976, 69; 1988a, 48-58). At the core of Gelpi's understanding of transmuting grace lies the conviction that dynamic orientation toward God is not to be found *a priori* in human subjectivity but rather "each self must acquire such an orientation either by fixing its personal beliefs on purely rational motives concerning the reality and nature of God or by responding positively and graciously in faith to some event of divine self-revelation" (1988a, 84). In such a situation the revelatory event together with the faith transmute the psyche by "building into it a wholly new habitual orientation toward a self-revealing God" (1988a, 85). This transmutation of experience is seen in a variety of different ways. In general, the gracious work of the Holy Breath functions to bring a docility, or yieldedness, to God (1976, 29; 1985, 155), often fostering a sense of repentance or a sense of openness/appreciation with relationship to God. She actively transforms all aspects of human experience; every moment of the evaluative continuum is subject to Her touch (1971, 165; 1985, 59; cf. 1998b).

One means by which the Breath of God effects the re-orientation of life is by the "gifts" of the Breath. Gelpi produces from the Scholastic division of gifts of sanctification (*dona Spiritus Sancti*; rooted in medieval reflection on Isaiah 11:1-2) and the gifts of service (*gratiae gratis datae*; rooted in reflection on the Pauline list of charisms in 1 Corinthians 12), a synthesis of traditional and charismatic theologies of the transformation of life. Gelpi identifies the gifts of sanctification with an "ongoing docility to the Holy Breath in putting on the mind of Christ" (1993, I, 117-118). Just as Jesus was responsive to the leading of the Holy Breath as he lived out and died for the vision of a sharing community of "little ones," so human faith, hope, love, and justice are elevated and perfected through the work of the Breath of Christ today. The Pauline gifts of service provide the church a "matrix of grace," an environment of different but valuable expressions of God's own experience, that nurtures individual believers and strengthens the community as a whole (1993, I, 56-155).

The Holy Breath takes the initiative in Christian conversion (1976, 56; 1988b, 23), and one tends to feel this iniative as an "impulse" arising in experience (1976, 14-15, 47, 52, 63; 1985, 87, 159). Gelpi also refers to these impulses of the Breath as promptings, inspirations, movements, invitations, or as a "call" (1971, 165, 179, 203, 227, 230; 1972, 93; 1985, 161). In his revision of sacramental and charismatic theology, *Committed Worship*, Gelpi includes "within the Breath's charismatic inspirations both occasional inspirations and more or less permanent calls to service" (1993, I, 118). The Holy Breath introduces the mind of Christ to the experience of the believer such that it is experienced as a force, an action, which transforms human experience. Thus, in terms of Gelpi's primary categories discussed above, Gelpi understands the work of the Holy Breath to involve the initiation of elements arising within experience, elements which arise with interactive force and which introduce tendencies into human experience that render it particularly oriented toward God and which enable mutual service to others by means of a manifestation of the divine mind through one another.

This brief look at Gelpi's understanding of God's self-communication and the Holy Breath paint a portrait of a God who is manifest directly within the experience of the individual and community, thereby giving Christian discernment its meaning. Since the Holy Breath functions as to reveal through human experience a God who possesses communicable significance and intelligibility, Christian discernment from the side of the divine becomes conceivable. First, there is an identifiable point of contact between God and humans, namely the historical experience of people and humanity in general. This makes the *recognition* of that which is related to God possible. Second, the God who is revealed is recognizable *as God* by the tendencies occurring within God, expressed and experienced within the historical experience of persons and communities. Furthermore, by the gracious transformation of personal and communal life, the very process of discernment itself can be seen as a gift of God. But to understand this better, one must understand more of the nature and transformation of person and community.

Persons and Communities

In order to provide an account of Christian discernment, one must not only grasp the divine who is discerned and who graces that process, but one must also understand something of the human doing the discerning. This grasp of the human must be supported both by empirical findings and philosophical coherence. As I mentioned above, philosophical reflection should assist an account of discernment specifically by articulating an overall approach to human experience that coheres with the findings of experimental psychology and by providing the framework for a concrete integration of the scientific material with an authentic Christian faith-perspective. I will pursue these issues in the present section by means of an exploration of Gelpi's thought concerning the nature and transformation of persons and communities. I will begin with a presentation of the "evaluative continuum," a philosophical construct which is vital to Gelpi's understanding of both individual and community life. This will bring me to a discussion of freedom, autonomy, self, and person, the themes necessary to define the individual person. Then I will mention briefly something of the nature and consciousness of community. With these themes in place I can then present the dynamics of Gelpi's central theme, conversion.

The Evaluative Continuum

Gelpi expresses his understanding of dynamic movement of human experience by means of a model of the "evaluative continuum." Drawing from a number of sources (Whitehead, Peirce, Dewey, Charles Hartshorne and Lonergan), Gelpi seeks to provide a synthetic account of the development of human experience. The continuum begins with sensation. External senses of sight, touch, and so on combine with proprioception, visceral sense and the like to produce "the first complex realm of human evaluative response" (1994, 127). Sensation is already affectively tinged (1987 [1978], 85-86), but the synthesis of affective and conceptual operations is even more pronounced as bare sensation passes to the moment of perception. Both sensation and perception bring with them a sense of, as Whitehead suggested, "presentational immediacy." Aspects of what is present are brought forward in perception for further evaluation as attention focuses on specific dimensions of sensed and perceived experience. In this manner "this" (as defined above) is noticed out of a wide array of sensational data. Gelpi, is careful to avoid presenting perceived objects as separate "things," grasped either by an "objective" or "subjective" knowledge. Rather perception is "the first phase of a transaction between my bodily processes and their sustaining, disintegrating environment" (1987 [1978], 82; following Merleau-Ponty 1962; Hartshorne 1945).

Imagery provides the next step in Gelpi's evaluative continuum. Imagery serves as a transition between perception and intuitive/rational thinking. Affective grasp of tendencies can either be clarified or confused through the influence of imagery. Gelpi's earlier writings often addressed the nature of affective experience at this point in his presentation of the evaluative continuum (1987 [1978], 87-94). His later works discuss affectivity throughout his description of the evaluative continuum (e.g. 1994, 126-131). I will discuss Gelpi's understanding of affectivity below. Imagery—remembered, reconstructed, imagined or archetypal—enhances and clarifies initial sensations and perceptions which are developed further forward in later stages of evaluative process (1994, 127). The developed functions of imagery and symbol are especially seen in the formation and use of language.

Gelpi mentions human categorization in his presentation of the evaluative continuum. He mentions it after "image" and before "inferential thinking." He writes,

> Abstract universal concepts result from definition. We intend
> defined terms to apply to all members of a given class of
> things. Our abstract classifications of things express human
> purposes. They seek to expedite our dealings with the realities
> around us by allowing us to anticipate the way in which they
> may be expected to behave. (1985, 28)

Though Gelpi does not mention it here, his presentation of categorization reflects the understanding of inquiry found in the thought of John Dewey (cf. 1988b, 101-103; Dewey 1938). In this perspective "definition" and "class membership" are not seen as bounded sets; rather they function as a part of "human purposes." The development and application of categories is part of an instrumental, interactive encounter with the tendencies and forces that are part of human experience.

Gelpi's most recent foundational writings tend to address "thinking," the next moment, by means of a distinction between different types of thinking (cf. 1993, I, 130-32; 1994). "Intuitive thinking" is more affectively driven. It "engages the interplay of feelings and images in order to grasp reality" (1994, 127). Intuitive thinking overlaps with scientific and historical/scholarly thinking. Scientific thinking (or "hypothetical" or "controlled experimental thinking") is divided into Peirce's three forms of logical inference: abduction, deduction, and induction (1994, 129; addressed below). Scholarship, historical thinking, and criticism blend inference and intuition to provide accounts of aspects of reality where controlled experimentation is impossible. Finally, "strictly normative thinking" functions to measure human experience by standards known by the subject to be binding (1994, 129-30). Needless to say, conditioning and affective elements shape all of evaluative processes such that none are "purely rational" (1994, 130).

At the same time, for Gelpi, human conceptual process is also not merely an irrational, instrumental attribution of concept to percept. Rather in a triadic perspective, evaluative responses grasp real tendencies. This is the foundation stone of Gelpi's realism, which I shall address in more detail below. For Gelpi, as for his mentor C. S. Peirce, generals, laws, concepts, definitions, are not mere creations of the mind. Rather, "if the human mind takes time to think clearly about events by invoking the pragmatic maxim, the world will teach it how to think realistically about the cosmos through the way in which events behave" (Gelpi 1997, 229; cf. 1994, 121-57; Peirce, W 2.193-273). Thus while concepts and categories are always subject to conditioning and revision, they ideally—and to some extent really—grasp true reality, the tendencies and habits that make experience what it is. I will show that for Gelpi affectivity participates in this grasp of reality (1988b, 82), even reality that cannot be "conceptualized" (1988b, 81).

Gelpi insists that affectivity is central to this evaluative continuum. Indeed, in *Experiencing God*, he refers to this continuum as an "affective continuum" (following Whitehead 1929). By reference to an affective continuum, Gelpi maintains that virtually every level of evaluative process, from the simplest sensation to complex thought is suffused with emotion (Gelpi 1987 [1978], 85-97). Emotions are situational and cumulative. As situational they express the ways in which self and environment interact; as cumulative they change or transmute one another creating temperaments and affective biases

(Gelpi 1987 [1978], 91-93). Affectivity is ruled by metaphor, synchronicity, and free imaginative association rather than by logical inference (Gelpi 1987 [1978], 93). Language, especially metaphor and lyric, forms a bridge from affectivity to inference, "between literature and logic" (Gelpi 1987 [1978], 94; cf. 1988b, 63ff). While his earlier works present a development from vague feeling-oriented operations to more logical inferential operations, in his later works Gelpi is increasingly explicit about the mutual presence of affective and inferential operations throughout the evaluative continuum (1988a, 92; 1988b, 42,115).

For Gelpi, aesthetic experience and affectivity are intimately connected. Gelpi has been interested in the philosophy of aesthetics from his earliest writing to the present (1959; 1987 [1978], 143-47; 1988a, 19-22; 1988b, 55-59; 1998b). Drawing from a variety of North American thinkers, as well as from his Jesuit roots in Ignatius, Gelpi has forged the outlines of a Christian aesthetic consistent with traditional theology and North American idiom. "The sense of beauty always engages the sympathetic emotions," he writes (1987 [1978], 141). In the example of Gelpi's thought on discernment presented above Gelpi suggested that discerning deliberation acts in light of ideals and principles. These ideals and principles are formed, by means of aesthetic operations (following Peirce CP 1.573-615). Thus Gelpi affirms Edwards' insistence that Christian conversion is bound up in the transformation of one's affective attunement to divine beauty (1998b).

For Gelpi, the affections also play an important part in religious experience. As will become clear, conversion to God touches affectivity first (1976, 23). Like Tillich, Gelpi holds that human experience becomes religious when it begins to touch on matters of "ultimate concern." By ultimate concern Gelpi means not simply a matter of intellectual importance but also a matter which drives deep affective satisfaction (1976, 23; 1987 [1978], 107-110; on "satisfaction" cf. Whitehead, 1929). The charisms of the Holy Breath frequently transform affective experience (e.g. 1976, 70ff). I shall develop this further in the account of conversion.

Most important for the construction of an epistemologically sensitive theory of discernment, Gelpi contends that emotions are "never purely subjective experiences" (1987 [1978], 91). In Gelpi's categoreal system evaluative responses—*all* evaluative responses—

make one simultaneously present to one's self and one's environment. Gelpi writes, "In other words, the way in which the organism gears itself affectively to deal with diverse situations reveals the way in which the dynamic, legal tendencies in both the self and its environment are presented initially and vaguely within experience" (1987 [1978], 91; cf. 1987 [1978], 117n41; 1985, 41; 1988b, 58). The semiotic nature of human experience[4] gives affectivity a "spacio-temporal symbolic" dimension, an emotional interpretant that mediates reality (1985, 40,84; cf. Peirce CP 5.475-76). Thus Gelpi insists that affectivity "grasps reality" (1988b, 82). Since the grasp of reality is fixed in judgment, Gelpi makes frequent reference to "judgments of feeling" or "intuitive judgments" (cf. 1988b, 53,81-82,87; 1993, I, 130). These judgments are "voiced" in lyric, in prophecy, in art, and in the "naturally prudential and charismatic judgments of discernment" (1988b, 87-88; 1993, 130).

Gelpi's presentation of the evaluative continuum usually ends with a discussion of decision and action (1987 [1978], 99; 1993, I, 133-34). Decision finally fixes the evaluative process and impacts the environment again with a final act or "fact." It is the development of decisions that form the self.

Gelpi claims that the spectrum of evaluative responses makes us present to ourselves and to our world. Evaluative response, from the least visceral sensation to the most abstract thought pattern, join with raw "interactions" in habitual "tendencies" to create the experiences we are. His construct of the human evaluative continuum presents a model of human experience that unites his primary theological and philosophical categories to a dynamic approach to cognitive-affective process and human experience in general. The similarities between Gelpi's evaluative continuum—moving from sensation through perception and image through judgment and actions which in turn re-

---

[4]The triadic nature of human experience (value, act, tendency) corresponds with a triadic structure of signification or "semiotic" structure involving Sign (value) which signifies something about Objects (act) through the mediation of Interpretants (tendency) (CP 2.274). The word "dog" acts as a Sign (an evaluation) referring to furry four-legged Objects (actual interactions) by facilitating in one's mind an image of these creatures (called an Interpretant - a tendency to respond in a particular way).

form the self—and the accounts of categorization and affective process already presented in the previous chapter should be obvious. A summary chart of this continuum can be found in Figure 3.

Selves and Persons

We have seen that an analysis of discernment must address the questions of the nature of the self and personal meaning. Both the philosophical and psychological material reviewed thus far has drawn attention to related questions. Might the discerning individual compare a sense of self, either a "fundamental innermost attitude" (Rahner) or a sense of existential identity formed by the history of a person (Spohn) with an object of choice? Do people store a socially developed model of the self which is used to imagine discerning options (Oatley)? Should we perhaps minimize emphasis on some sense of "self" in discernment and instead focus on relevant features of the discernment situation itself (Hughes)? Whence comes the "meaning" in the situation meaning structures that elicit emotions (Frijda) or in the theories which hold categories together with meaning (Medin)? The views of self, person and meaning are so diverse in both the philosophical and psychological literature that an attempt to evaluate compatibility between this material and Gelpi's approach would be futile. Instead one must look for the measure of coherence, consistency, adequacy, and applicability in Gelpi's system.

Gelpi's philosophical understanding of the self builds upon his account of tendency, freedom, and autonomy and leads to his concept of the person. For Gelpi the "self" need not refer to human existence. Gelpi defines a self as "an autonomously functioning tendency to act or respond in some way" (1994, 132; cf. 1985, 36). By "autonomy" Gelpi refers to the capacity of a self to initiate activity. Amoebae encircle and ingest food; sunflowers turn and face the sun; bees coordinate the building of a hive. Gelpi gives the example of chemicals absorbed into the human body. They have autonomous existence until they become part of the human body. Then those molecules cease to have autonomous existence. They are no longer independent "selves," but rather have become part of the "self" that is the human. Autonomy is enacted within a range of freedom determined by the kind of evaluative responses a given act terminates. Selves do not subsist in bodies as in substance philosophy. They emerge from their

FIGURE 3:
GELPI'S EVALUATIVE CONTINUUM

Decision and Action:
terminates evaluative continuum;
reinforces or inhibits tendencies
forms the self

Deliberation:
evaluates possible courses of action

Judging:
inferential (induction), judgments of feeling

Thinking:
intuitive, historical, scholarly. . .
scientific (abduction, deduction)

Imagination:
memory, imagery, archetypal . . .

Perception:
Already affectively tinged

Sensation:
actions impact experience with force

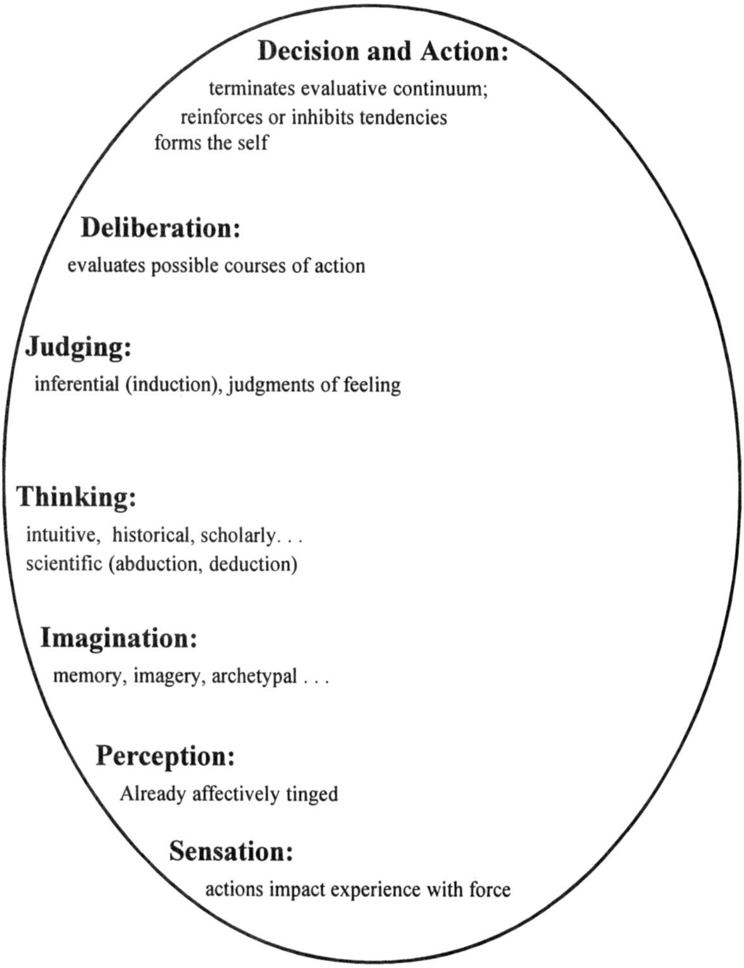

bodies. Neither do selves exist "separate" from their environment. Rather "every autonomous self creates itself through interaction with its world" (Gelpi 1994, 132). Bodies anchor selves in this world (1994, 133; cf. 1987 [1978], 84f). The limits of embodiment in time, space, culture and the like defines the range of freedom a given self might possess. "Persons, however," Gelpi writes, "differ from other selves in their capacity to convert, i.e. to assume self-conscious responsibility for their own personal growth and development in some real of experience" (1994, 133). Elsewhere he identifies persons with the possession of self-understanding and the capacity to act out of that self-understanding (1994-95, Vol. 2). for Gelpi, a personal self is an "emergent process" (1976, 46; 1987 [1978], 97), inexistent with its world (1976, 89-90). Gelpi's person is not the "transcendent subjective self oriented to Being" of Transcendental Thomism (1988a, 69-97; 1994, 90-120). But neither is it the "absent" self of some eastern traditions (1987 [1978], 355-73). Gelpi's refutation of both positions lies in his unique understanding of tendency: the human person is real, yet discovered not simply within subjective experience but rather developed and affirmed in the course of life. In this respect, his approach to the self of discernment is most similar to the philosophical position of William Spohn, also cohering with the psychological insights of Oatley (especially, as will be shown, when the communal dimension is included).

Consequently, for Gelpi, "meaning" is not something necessarily inhering in objects or events. Situations possess "significance" as they arise with particular tendencies. Meaning, however, develops from the evaluative responses given to situations. As the autonomous self integrates evaluations, interactions, and tendencies within itself, it tends to reinforce or to shed certain tendencies. The reinforcement or shedding functions to endow situations with meaning. Gelpi writes,

Evaluative responses are interpretive symbols, for they endow events with meaning. Meaning is the evaluative disclosure of relationship. But events signify in their own right; for every decisive act expresses and reveals the law or self that initiates and grounds it. Because events signify, they too are symbolic in their structure; but they are expressive rather than interpretive symbols. For the significance they express needs interpretation in order for them to become meaningful. (1985, 40)

Thus decisions continually "redefine the emerging self" (1987 [1978], 108; cf. p. 98; 1985, 90f) in the context of an ever developing horizon of meaning. Seen in this framework, Frijda's "situation meaning structure," which arises as the fruit of emotional appraisal, serves largely to indicate the significance of the situation. As the process of affective experience continues, however, the evaluative responses elicited/selected (action tendencies, mental preoccupation, etc.) endow the situation with meaning. Through decisions (autonomously chosen evaluative responses) the elements of experience are reharmonized into a new synthesis. Gelpi, following Whitehead, refers to this synthesis as "satisfaction." One experiences partial satisfactions continually; ever increasing levels of satisfaction are experienced as greater degrees of synthesis are attained. Ultimate satisfaction exhibits a religious character. Therein, for Gelpi, is meaning to be found.

For Gelpi, the self searches for meaning by integrating evaluations, interactions, or tendencies into itself. The divine is revealed to the self as an interactive force entering experience. The personal self of discernment then, is the person always on the edge of decision, formed by the past and forming oneself by this decision at this moment. If the active force of the Holy Breath is consented to in faith, or if the discerning self fixes belief in God, personal experience itself is transformed. Emotions are healed, reflection is governed by faith, and actions are governed by religious norms. As I will show, the forms and dynamics of Christian conversion merely spell out the dynamic interplay of the divine-human relationship as a meaning-full habit of interactions.

Community

Gelpi's construct of the person is inseparable from his understanding of the community. This understanding of community is rooted both in his theological and philosophical development; it plays an important role in his understanding of conversion and in his epistemology. Theologically speaking, Gelpi's understanding of the Christian Trinity and his understanding of society are mutually supporting constructs. In *Divine Mother* Gelpi presents a case for a social understanding of the doctrine of the Trinity, concluding that although (1) the divine persons are not persons in the identical way that humans are, nevertheless (2) the mutual self-donation of the divine persons defines the evaluative shape of the divine experience, and (3) the mutual self-donation of the divine persons explains the divine unity (1985, 140-141). By "mutual self-donation" Gelpi refers to the way in which the members of the Godhead give themselves to one another in love. Likewise Gelpi understands the community to share in this many-in-oneness of the Godhead. Thus Gelpi asserts that "the sharing of the charisms in community creates the matrix in which Christians learn individually and collectively to put on the mind of Christ" (1985, 202). I illustrated Gelpi's affirmation of this theme with relationship to an understanding of the gift of discernment presented at the beginning of this chapter.

Philosophically speaking, community is a necessary ingredient for personhood. After giving his definition of personhood with relationship to the capacity to convert, Gelpi asserts that "conversion presupposes, then, the relational character of persons; for responsibility means social accountability to other persons; and social accountability demands the capacity to respond to other persons as persons (1994, 133). Elsewhere Gelpi writes, "Human persons become fully personal only through relationship with other persons" (1994-1995, 2.178). Human "selves" interact and evaluate in a fundamentally social environment. Just as bodies anchor selves in this world, communities nurture people in the world. Communities of persons, "constitute the most significant and sustaining forces in the human environment" (Gelpi 1994, 133).

Gelpi draws upon the philosophy of Josiah Royce to emphasize the formation and maintenance of community consciousness (Gelpi 1987 [1978], 237-240; 1976, 101-103; cf. Royce 1968 [1918], 253-260; Oppenheim 1969). His summary of the development of community consciousness is worth quoting at length:

> Community consciousness grows through a . . . complex process of corporate historical reappropriation and self-direction. Communities become initially conscious of themselves as communities by reaching a consensus about the significance of the events that found them and of the history that links them to those events. Consensus about its historical origins endows a community with a shared sense of identity; but shared consciousness grows as a community decides on the

basis of its historical sense of identity the kind of community it
ought to become and then mobilizes the gifts of all its members
to transform that future into a reality. (Gelpi 1994, 135)

It should be obvious that both the historical identification of the community and the development of the community through a process of
endowing significant situations with meaning through evaluative
responses parallel Gelpi's understanding of the formation of the individual self.

Thus the community coming to discernment comes as a people in
the image of the Triune God, many-in-one. Just as with individuals
coming to discernment, the community comes on the edge of decision, rooted in a sense of self arising from its own history and defining itself with each evaluative response. It is this same community
that forms the context of an individual discernment; the shared history, values, and hopes of the community shape the range of freedom
within which each individual identifies that which is significantly
related to God. Thus in Gelpi's thought both person and community
are seen in necessary and constant interaction. Conversion involves
responsibility for both dimensions.

Conversion

In his early writings "conversion" does not function as a central
category (cf. 1966a, 219-220; 1972). By the publishing of *Charism
and Sacrament* in 1976, however, Gelpi had assimilated the thought
of Bernard Lonergan and his presentation of conversion is much more
nuanced. Indeed, *Charism and Sacrament* expresses a legitimate and
significant development of Longergan's approach to conversion. For
Lonergan, conversion exemplifies deliberate decision about one's
horizon, about the frameworks within which one lives. Lonergan
originally posited three levels of conversion: intellectual, moral, and
religious, reflecting different spheres of existence within which
deliberate decisions are made (Lonergan 1972). Lonergan only very
late (indeed, after Gelpi's published use of the phrase; cf. Lonergan
1977; Conn 1988) suggested the possibility of an "affective" conversion. As Gelpi's thought evolved he came to speak of five different
kinds of conversion and of seven dynamics within the converting

process.[5] I will use the presentation in *Committed Worship* (1993) to summarize his current approach to conversion.

Gelpi defines conversion as "the decision to pass from irresponsible to responsible behavior in some distinguishable realm of human experience" (1993, I, 17). Conversion comes in five forms: affective conversion rejects irresponsible resistance to facing one's disordered affectivity and commits one to cultivating emotional health; intellectual conversion involves a turn from "irresponsible acquiescence of received beliefs to a commitment to validation of beliefs in adequate frames of reference and in dialogue with other truth seekers"; moral conversion turns from "irresponsible choices to a commitment to measure choices against appropriate ethical norms"; sociopolitical conversion turns from "unreflective acceptance of institutional violations of human rights to a commitment to collaborate with others" for appropriate reform; religious conversion turns from ignorance or opposition to God to acceptance in faith (Gelpi 1993, I, 17).

Gelpi divides conversion into "natural" and "graced." He labels conversion "natural" when the decision toward responsibility is made apart from any explicit reference to religious reality. By speaking of *natural* conversion, Gelpi, following Lonergan, acknowledges that humans decide to adopt certain stances which transform their way of being. I have already noted that for Gelpi, decisions derive their character from the evaluative responses they terminate. Thus "natural" decisions engage only created realities and prescind from the historical self-revelation of God. Each developing self exists as "the habitual incremental repository of decision" (1985, 30-37). In human experience, this activity engages what Gelpi calls strictly normative thinking, the establishment of an "ought" which governs thought,

---

[5]In the mid-seventies Gelpi explicitly developed Longeran's construct and introduced two "dynamics"—ways in which one type of conversion shapes another—to the model. By 1982 the list of dynamics had been increased to three (Gelpi 1982). In an article on "The Converting Jesuit" (1986) Gelpi introduced a fifth form of conversion (socio-political - foreshadowed in 1987 [1978], 255) and increased the number of dynamics to seven. With slight revisions it is this form which has remained as the primary structure for Gelpi's understanding of conversion.

value, and behavior. Conversion, then, is the human decision to terminate an evaluative process by initiating a habit of evaluative response, especially with regard to particular spheres of activity. Natural conversion acts apart from any conscious interaction with the divine. Conversion is gracious when it responds to the self-communication of God. Gelpi writes:

> When God touches us and we respond in faith, we act graciously. When we interact with created realities in oblivion of God's gracious action in history, we act naturally. If grace functions in our environments but we ignore its presence inculpably, we still respond only naturally. When we deliberately resist the offer of grace, we sin. (1993, I, 28)

The interaction of graced and natural expressions of the various forms of conversion gives rise to a variety of conversion "dynamics," ways in which one form of conversion conditions another. Evaluative responses shape the interactive possibilities and tendencies of the experiences humans are and can be. A decision to adopt a horizon of responsibility (a strictly normative frame of reference) with regard to sociopolitical institutional reality, for example, initiates a world of new perceptions, understandings, feelings, and actions. Gelpi identifies seven critical "dynamics," or ways in which the forms of conversion interact:

> (a) Affective conversion animates intellectual, moral, religious, and sociopolitical conversion. (b) Intellectual conversion informs affective, moral, religious, and sociopolitical conversion. (c) Moral conversion helps orient affective, intellectual, religious, and sociopolitical conversion to realities and values that make ultimate and absolute claims on human behavior (d) Religious conversion mediates between affective and moral conversion. (e) Affective, intellectual, moral, and religious conversion authenticate sociopolitical conversion by supplying it with personal norms that help measure institutional responsibility. (f) Sociopolitical conversion authenticates affective, intellectual, moral, and religious conversion by deprivatizing them. (g) Religious conversion transvalues affec-

tive, intellectual, moral, and sociopolitical conversion. (1993
I, 33-34)

One example of the value of recognizing such dynamics for a theory
of discernment must suffice for the present. Consider the example of
Steve given at the beginning of chapter one. Steve's progress in relationships with women began with an intellectual conversion. He
rejected his irresponsible acquiescence in the belief that God would
simply send him a mate. Instead, he made a commitment to the validation of beliefs in a more adequate frame of reference (maybe God
was interested in *his* desires). This intellectual conversion, in turn,
informed his ongoing affective conversion in that it permitted feelings
to arise and be considered as part of the communication of divine will
that had not previously been allowed. Needless to say, this also
served to complicate his problem somewhat in that now he was
required to develop a skill of interior awareness in order to navigate
the relationship (affective conversion) as well as his sense of "God's
will" in the situation (religious conversion). In this manner Steve's
discernment is illumined by understanding the dynamics of conversion. I shall address these dynamics further below as they shape the
construction of a theory of discernment. There it will be necessary to
give more explicit account of such terms as "animate," "inform,"
"mediate," "authenticate," and "transvalue." For the present it is sufficient to grasp the basic structure of Gelpi's understanding of conversion which forms a theological category giving shape to the entirety of
his philosophical/theological synthesis.

Conclusions

Again, philosophical reflection should assist an account of discernment by articulating an overall approach to human experience that
coheres with the findings of experimental psychology and by providing the framework for a concrete integration of the scientific material
with an authentic Christian faith-perspective. In summary, I think it
is fair to say that Gelpi's account of the human person and community
can serve as a valuable asset toward the construction of a
philosophically-sensitive account of Christian discernment. Gelpi's
presentation of the evaluative continuum is quite compatible with the
findings of empirical science. His account of affectivity interprets

that dimension with an adequacy not provided in earlier models of "faculty psychology" (1976, 168; 1987 [1978], 133-36; 1994, 90-120) or in some current "turns to experience" (1994). Gelpi's account of self and meaning provide a framework which is able to interpret the various concerns expressed in both philosophical and psychological literature. His account of community consciousness is capable of interpreting the social dimensions of affectivity and categorization. Furthermore Gelpi integrates this account of person and community consistently within the framework of a Christian faith-perspective. At points I have noted specific insights that Gelpi's construct brings to discernment reflection. I will develop Gelpi's synthesis further in the following chapter insofar as it bears on a theory of Christian discernment.

The Epistemology of Christian Discernment

"Indeed, out of a contrite fallibilism, combined with a high faith in the reality of knowledge, and an intense desire to find things out, all my philosophy has always seemed to me to grow." (C.S. Peirce CP. 1.14)

Throughout the course of this study I have had occasion to draw a distinction between a *descriptive* account of Christian discernment, which seeks to explain what people actually do when they discern, and a *normative* account of Christian discernment, which seeks to explain that which people ought to do when they discern in order for their discernment to accomplish that which it aims. Aware that human experience is subject to heuristics and biases that hinder the relationship of evaluative responses to the environment, a normative account of categorization suggests actions (for example, the inclusion of "family resemblance" approaches toward category formation) for the improvement of human identification. When the categorization deals with the confident identification of that which is significantly related to God, then a normative account must suggest actions which cultivate the improvement of religious identification.

I have also, throughout the course of the study, approached discernment as an *act of knowing*. Discernment has been revealed as a process of coming to "know" that which is from God. I have stated that discernment aims not merely at the awareness of the presence or guidance of God but at the awareness of that presence or guidance *as* the presence or guidance of God. Thus far I have prescinded from careful analysis of just what is meant by this "knowing," other than to draw some parallels with the operations involved in human categorization. Furthermore, as "Christian" discernment, I have referred to discernment as an act or process of *religious knowing*. Although I have addressed the possibility of religious knowing from the side of the divine in the analysis of divine self-revelation and the work of the Holy Breath, in terms of the human, I have merely described the evaluative continuum within which the knowledge and discernment of the divine can be found.

It is necessary, then, in order to construct a normative account of Christian discernment, to establish something of a normative account of religious knowing, that is to suggest those self-controlled actions by which discerners can be more sure that their discerning acts actually approximate that which is intended, namely the identification of that which is from God. Furthermore, as an exploration of discernment as an *affectively-rich* act of knowing, this normative account must address the roles that affective operations play in this process. To accomplish this is to construct something of an affectively-sensitive epistemology of Christian discernment. Thus, in the present section, I move from an account of the conditions for the possibility of religious knowledge to an account of the reasonable warrant or grounds for identifying religious knowledge as *knowledge*, and of the roles which affectivity plays therein.

The problem of the verification of religious knowledge has consumed the reflections of philosophers from a wide variety of perspectives (cf. Flew and Macintyre 1955; Plantinga and Wolterstorff 1983), and I cannot begin to address all of the issues needed to treat this subject fully. On these matters Gelpi is a faithful follower of North American philosophers Charles S. Peirce and Josiah Royce. In *Experiencing God*, Gelpi presents his position on many of these points in a series of fourteen criteria for "adequate propositional access to experience and to God." In developing Gelpi's thought on these matters I will be developing the *realist* and the *comunitarian* aspects of Gelpi's triadic, realistic, communitarian approach to experience. I will draw both from Gelpi's criteria and from the more detailed discussion found in Gelpi's sources to develop an account of the epistemology of Christian discernment insofar as it addresses five questions: (1) Is knowledge even possible? What grounds the legitimacy of the categorization process itself? (2) How are cognitive bias and faulty heuristics transcended in self-controlled, logical thinking? (3) How does affectivity function in the mediation of "knowledge," and in what does that mediation consist? (4) What reasonable grounds are there for the formation of the belief, in a given situation, that one has correctly identified that which is significantly related to God, grounds for regarding the fruit of discernment as "knowledge," warranting action *as if* God were discovered? (5) What kind of certainty or assurance does the process or act of knowing called discernment promise to provide?

1. Is knowledge even possible? What grounds the legitimacy of the categorization process itself?

The article on "Universals" in the *Encyclopedia of Philosophy* divides up the parties with regards to the nature of categories and universals in the following schools: realism, conceptualism, nominalism, and resemblance theories. The author closes the article by stating that "questions about universals are questions about generality, and generality is the essential feature of all words, not just those that might be plausibly called names" (Woozley 1967, 206). The question of generality is the heart of the issue of categorization. Is generality identifiable? Gelpi, following C.S. Peirce, divides up the philosophical camps somewhat differently. He divides between "nominalists" of classical and conceptualist varieties, and "realists." The dividing point for Gelpi is the question "whether laws and general types are figments of the mind or are real" (1994, 4; cf. Peirce CP 1.15-26). Soon after this statement, Gelpi criticizes Schillebeeckx's construct of experience for its conceptual nominalism, recommending a study of Peirce to Schillebeeckx. He affirms Peirce's claim that the scientific mind grasps real tendencies (and generality). Gelpi refers the reader to Peirce's 1903 lectures on Pragmatism. In these lectures one finds the core of Peirce's (and Gelpi's) realism.

The epistemological core of these lectures—and Peirce's chief refutation of nominalism—is to be found in Lecture IV, on "The Reality of Thirdness," § 1, on "Scholastic Realism" (Peirce CP 5.97-119). In this point in the lecture, Peirce predicts that a dropped rock will fall to the ground, pointing out that he *knows* that it will fall to the ground. Humans know this because of past experience. He offers two (and only two) hypotheses concerning falling stones:

(1) the uniformity with which those stones have fallen has been due to mere chance and affords no ground whatever, not the slightest for any expectation that the next stone that shall be let go will fall; or
(2) the uniformity with which stones have fallen has been due to some *active general principle* in which case is would be a strange coincidence that it should cease to act at the moment my prediction was based upon it. (CP 5.100, italics Peirce's)

One may reply that the idea of an active general principle is forced upon us by our human categorical framework, expressing an epistemological agnosticism on this question. Nevertheless, Peirce's point still holds for the *reality* of the situation. No matter what one thinks about the situation these are the only possibilities. Peirce reminds them that a thousand such inductions are being verified daily and that one "will have to suppose every one of them to be merely fortuitous in order reasonably to escape the conclusion that general principles are really operative in nature" (CP 5.101).

Peirce moves from this point to discuss the centrality of perceptual judgment. He finds, in perceptual judgment, the first principles of all human reasoning, an affirmation which is repeated in the following lecture. He argues from geometric examples to demonstrate that a perceptual judgment involves generality. Peirce concludes, "Thirdness [tendency, law] pours in upon us through every avenue of sense" (CP 5.158).[6] Peirce ultimately argues that we perceive more than we sense, that real generality—in addition to sense impressions—is grasped in human perception inferentially.

While Gelpi does not develop Peirce's argument concerning perceptual judgment in detail, the affirmation that real generals are

---

[6]One can recognize the importance of this point in Pierce's lecture in that he uses this very point to form his critical second "cotary prooposition" (5.181) which helps to form the basis of his restatement of the "pragmatic maxim," (5.195-205) a central expression of Peirce's fundamental position.

unavoidably given in perception (for Gelpi—both perceptual and affective judgment; 1994, 15) grounds, for Gelpi, the acts of categorization and knowing as such. It is this point that is the foundation of Gelpi's "realism." Gelpi does not, however, in affirming a realist metaphysics, succumb to a naive "objectivist" epistemology. Indeed, he condemns epistemological dualisms which separate subject and object such that they cannot be properly interrelated. Gelpi, following Josiah Royce's transcendence of "mystical" and "realist" [naive realist] approaches, affirms that *(1) Adequate propositional access to experience will be possible only in a speculative framework that transcends the limitations inherent in both introverted and extraverted* [sic] *theories of the real* (p. 232; Gelpi's italics here and throughout; cf. Royce, 1976 [1899]).

Gelpi holds to a dynamic and critical realism. As *dynamic* Gelpi sheds the essentialist understanding of subject and object affirming that what is known in knowing are the vectoral tendencies present in experience rather than a substantial "thing." As *critical* Gelpi maintains that the real generalities which appear in perceptual judgment are not always obvious to the human mind. Rather, as I will develop below, self-controlled, cooperative effort is necessary to achieve knowledge. "But," as Peirce encourages—and which is really the important point, "the saving truth is that there is a Thirdness in experience, an element of Reasonableness to which we can train our own reason to conform more and more" (CP 5.160). I have identified the kinds of Thirdness or tendency involved in religious knowledge in the sections above. They are to be found in the historical and "real" tendencies appearing through religious events and religious communities. The touches of the Holy Breath, as elements of experience revealing tendency or law are no less "real" than the elements of experience presented in sensual perception (cf. Alston 1991). Thus, *(13) Adequate propositional access to God is possible only in faith, i.e., in conscious response to the divine act of self-revelation incarnate in Jesus and illumined by the action of the Holy Breath* (1987 [1978], 245).

In chapter three I was careful to demonstrate the implicit agreement among experimental psychologists that the perceived world possesses some kind of identifiable regularity. Whether one speaks of a "correlational structure" of the environment, of "affordances," of "repeatable patterns," or simply of "regularity," the fact of the matter is: tendency happens. And tendency happens in such a way that humans can and do identify it. The possibility of categorization, of human knowledge, and of Christian discernment lies in this fact.

2. How are cognitive bias and faulty heuristics transcended in self-controlled, logical thinking?

Gelpi's realism is tempered by his falliblism, or his humble expectations concerning the acquisition of knowledge. These two positions must be seen as two sides of the same sword. With the one Gelpi parries "nominalists" of one sort or another. With the other, Gelpi thrusts against the claims of the Transcendental Thomists. The reality of the general introduces the ideal possibility of knowledge; it does not mean, however, that humans have a priori orientation to infinite knowledge or Being. In the previous chapters I suggested that human reasoning is subject to a variety of biases and heuristics rooted in habit, salience and interest rather than logical clarity. Gelpi, following Peirce, acknowledges these tendencies in human reasoning. This acknowledgement forms the heart of Gelpi's "contrite falliblism," and shapes his approach to the normative use of inferential thinking. It forms an essential component in a normative account of Christian discernment.

The roots of this falliblism for Gelpi and for Peirce lie in an important critique of Kantian logic accomplished in Peirce's early studies. Peirce was a devout student of Kant's first *Critique*. Peirce was especially interested in the connection between Kant's understanding of logical propositions and his categories. By careful examination of Kant's logic, worked out in the drafts of his "New List of Categories," Peirce finally came to the conclusion that

> even the most fundamental, practically indubitable, general premises presupposed in these inferences—such as, for instance, that there are real things, that they affect our senses, and the like—hold only a priori relative to the cognitions for which they are presupposed. However as truth claims they are "fallible," like the entire corpus of knowledge to which the finite human being can attain, and therefore they are subject to confirmation by experience. (Apel 1981, 36; cf. also Murphey 1961, 55-94; Peirce W 2.49-58)

Gelpi makes repeated mention of the fact that Peirce saw through Kant's transcendental method, and that consequently the fruit of such a method yields not universally valid insights about the way the human mind works but revisable hypotheses concerning human cognition (1987 [1978], 234; 1988a, 94n8; 1994, 30-34).

Peirce's insights concerning Kantian logic developed alongside his own reformulation of the forms of logical inference. Acknowledgement of the nature and role of Peirce's forms of inference form an important foundation of Peirce's—and Gelpi's—epistemology. Peirce discovered that induction could be defined syllogistically as the inference of the major premise of a syllogism from its minor premise and conclusion. This led him to inquire whether he could find a form which inferred the minor premise from the major and the conclusion. This he found in Aristotle's *Prior Analytics* (Apel 1981, 39). The result of this discovery was the distinction between "hypothesis" (also called abduction or retroduction), deduction, and induction (cf. W 1.256-302). Hypothesis argues to a case; deduction to a result; induction to a rule or law. Final validation of the objects of inferential judgments are to be found in induction, for deduction concludes only what must be the result if certain conditions obtain. Whether these results do, in fact, arise is a matter of inductive observation. Here again is Peirce's emphasis on Thirdness being revealed in perceptual judgment. The consequence of this understanding of the logical forms for an understanding of fallibility and self-corrective thinking is this: reality is determined only insofar as it is confirmed by inductive observation, only insofar as one's representations conform to the actual behavior, the actual tendencies present in experience. Again, Peirce's is no naive realism, but rather a critical realism which sees its realism as an ideal to be reached through careful attention, and, as I will show, cooperative action.

Gelpi repeatedly reviews and refers to these forms of inference in his works (1976, 9-10; 1978-87, 94-96; 1988a, 50; 1994, 129). While not explaining the existence of cognitive bias or faulty heuristics, a careful understanding of the limits of human reasoning, even within its more self-controlled forms, serves to temper expectations concerning the fruits of a realistic epistemology and provides a sense of the ideal cognitive matrix from which bias and heuristics arise. Gelpi, in agreement with Peirce, proposes that, *(3) Adequate propositional access to experience must rest on a sound insight into*

the laws of inference and therefore on the conscious personal profes-
sion of a contrite logical falliblism (1987 [1978], 234).

Peirce begins directly to address the subject of bias and heuristics
in an article entitled, "The Fixation of Belief" (W 3.242-257), a well-
known article Gelpi outlines in his presentation of the criteria for adequate propositional access to experience (1987 [1978], 235-36).
Peirce suggests that "we are, doubtless, in the main logical animals,
but we are not perfectly so" (W 3.244). He notes in particular that
"most of us are more sanguine and hopeful than logic would justify,"
a suggestion confirmed by recent cognitive research (Kahneman,
Slovic, Tversky 1982). Peirce recognizes the presence of habits of
mind that guide human judgment. He calls these habits "guiding principles" of inference, noting that familiarity frequently grounds these
principles. He discusses the nature of doubt and belief, noting the
sloppy admixture of ordinary thought and clear logic in human
inquiry and concluding that "settlement of opinion is the sole object
of inquiry" (W 3.248). Peirce then describes four different common
methods of settling opinion or "fixing belief" in conditions of doubt.
The first, the method of *tenacity* holds to received judgments in spite
of evidence to the contrary, remaining safe within familiar belief.
The method of *authority* allows others—state, Church—to determine
and enforce the fixation of belief. Problems associated with this
method leads one to investigate a third method of fixing belief: the *a
priori* method or the method of reason and taste. However, as one
discovers that this method offers little beyond the method of authority, one finally passes to the fourth and final method, the method of
scientific investigation. Peirce asserts the fundamental hypothesis of
the scientific method as follows:

> There are real things, whose characters are entirely independ-
> ent of our opinions about them; those realities affect our senses
> according to regular laws, and, though our sensations are as
> different as our relations to the objects, yet, by taking
> advantage of the laws of perception, we can ascertain by
> reasoning how things really are, and any man, if he have suffi-
> cient experience and reason enough about it, will be led to the
> one true conclusion. (W 3.254)

Peirce does not presume that the method of science is universally
"better" than the other methods of fixing belief. Each has its own

particular convenience and advantage in different situations. The advantage in the method of science is providing greater assurance that one's beliefs will conform to the facts of the case. To choose the method of science is to initiate evaluative responses that require self-control and discipline.

In his later writings, Peirce gives an important expansion to his understanding of the method of science. Science here does not simply involve sufficient experience and reason, but also requires include the *mutual* investigative determination of truth (cf. CP 5.549-69). This point develops logically from Peirce's falliblistic realism. If real tendencies are present and can be perceived, and yet any individual perception is subject to bias and error, this difficulty is minimized by including in the investigation a variety of perceptions. Gelpi affirms this Peircean expansion first by proposing that *(5) Adequate propositional access to experience is mediated by personal commitment to shared inquiry* (1987 [1978], 236). He develops this insight further by insisting on the presence of diverse personality types in shared inquiry and upon the need for repentance and healing among those individuals to ensure adequate propositional access to experience (claims *(7)-(9)*, 1987 [1978], 240). Gelpi's *communitarian* approach is tied to the realistic and triadic elements at this point.

Profession of fallibism, acknowledgement of the function of logical inference, and personal commitment to shared inquiry all indicate that for Peirce, and for Gelpi, faulty heuristics and cognitive bias are transcended (to the degree possible) through choices that create and maintain "strictly normative" frames of reference. Peirce came to his understanding of the "normative sciences" late in his career. However, his conception of the normative sciences formed an important organizing principle for the thought of the mature Peirce (D. Anderson 1995, 40-56). This notion was based upon the idea that reasoning was self-controlled activity, and that as such logic governed how one "ought" to think in order that one's thoughts would conform to the nature of things. In this sense logic is seen as a special case of ethics, norms governing intellectual behavior. For Peirce, the norms for intellectual behavior (logic) are thus a subset of the norms for behavior in general (ethics), which is, in turn, a subset of the establishment of the valuable in itself (aesthetics cf. CP 8.239-240). This, for Gelpi, involves conversion, the fundamental decision (and the maintenance of the decision) to take responsibility for a given area of experience whether affective, moral, or intellectual. Thus, faulty heuristics and biases are transcended by intellectual conversion, the choice to allow one's reasoning be governed by appropriate rules of inference (1987 [1978], 205-255; 1993, I, 25). This converting choice itself is shaped and transmuted other forms of conversion: for example it is well known that the affective disorder of sexual addiction seriously influences one's inferential behavior regarding sexual issues. In terms of religious knowledge Gelpi confirms this in his claim that *(12) Adequate propositional access to God demands the willingness to subject abductive religious propositions to deductive clarification and to historical verification through shared systematic inquiry into the ultimate meaning and purpose of human religious experience* (1987 [1978], 245).

It seems to me that Gelpi moves beyond Peirce, especially in his more recent writings, in identifying a number of "types of thinking." His differentiation of "intuitive," "scientific," "historical/scholarly/critical," and "strictly normative" thinking (1994, 127-130) does not indicate methods of thinking ruled by faulty heuristics, as in Peirce's "Fixation." Rather he appears to indicate various legitimate spheres of reasoning each of which are ruled by distinct systems of self-controlled thinking. While the traditional understanding of abduction, deduction, induction accurately describe scientific thinking (and Gelpi lists them at that point, 1994, 129), other methods and operations more clearly illumine the dynamics of other types of human reasoning. Probably in order to indicate the breadth of human thinking, Gelpi differentiates these various types. Transcending bias would, therefore, require the adoption of frames of reference and rules of self-controlled thinking appropriate to each of the types of thinking, especially in the context of shared systematic inquiry. This kind of transcendence of bias would be cultivated with the kind of shared inquiry Gelpi envisions.

Since *(10) Propositional access to God is the inferential schematization of a personal encounter with the Holy. Since such an encounter is an instance of human experience, the normative principles governing adequate propositional access to experience in general also govern adequate propositional access to God* (1987 [1978], 240), the transition from self-controlled thinking in general to self-controlled thinking in religious matters is no great mystery. As will be discussed below, Christian discernment involves a variety of different types of thinking, but especially prudential and intuitive thinking. The transcendence of bias in Christian discernment will demand then, the cooperative, self-controlled thinking of a community integrally converted within themselves and to the things (tendencies) of God. Hence, *(14) Adequate propositional access to God is mediated only by active, prayerful participation in the shared activity of that universal, charismatic, community that is the living Church* (1987 [1978], 245).

To err is human. One can expect bias, faulty heuristics, ignorance, even willful prejudice. Human belief is fixed by means of a variety of frameworks and cognitive-affective operations. Thus an ideal realism must be accompanied with a concrete falliblism. This is true not only for knowledge-in-general, but also of the act of knowing known as Christian discernment. A normative account of knowing and discernment asks how these biases and heuristics can be transcended. How can people move beyond failures to achieve, with greater reliability, the aims of Christian discernment? Gelpi's Peircean construct would first encourage intellectual conversion, the choice to allow one's reasoning be governed by appropriate rules of inference. This choice is itself shaped and transmuted by the other forms of conversion. Thus for Gelpi, bias and heuristics are first transcended by continually growing in integral conversion. Second, bias is transcended through a commitment to shared inquiry. Gelpi's triadic and therefore realistic system is fruitless without the communitarian component. By gathering people together of different temperament, different perspectives, and different histories, to examine carefully the question, one insures greater possibility of moving beyond personal prejudice and identifying perceptions that correspond with the actual state of the environment. Third, one must adopt self-controlled actions which are appropriate to the kinds of thinking needed in any specific case. Whether one is talking about scientific, historical, or intuitive thinking, one must become acquainted with the operations associated with the proper function of each of these types of thinking and apply them when the situation calls for it. Needless to say, different discerning situations will require different types of thinking. Finally, discernment as an act of *religious* knowing requires that bias be transcended through association with the things and people of God.

3. How does affectivity function in the mediation of "knowledge," and in what does that mediation consist?

Having established reasonable grounds for the process of categorization itself and for the correction of bias and heuristics that enable that process to achieve its intended (albeit ideal) aim, I must now clarify, within a study of discernment as an *affectively-rich* act of knowing, how affectivity functions within the process of acquiring "knowledge." Gelpi details his initial thoughts concerning the nature of affectivity in *Experiencing God*. However, it is in his reformulation of foundational method in *Inculturating North American theology* that his understanding of the role of affectivity in mediating knowledge is most clearly developed. The later reformulation seeks to respond to Lonergan's understanding of foundational method in light of Gelpi's completion of three works in foundational theology (1988b, 25; cf. 1976; 1987 [1978]; 1985). After "trying out" Lonergan's method in these three works, Gelpi became convinced (1) that Lonergan was in the main correct that foundational method had much to offer the goal of developing an inculturated theology, (2) that Lonergan's account of human experience was flawed in fundamental ways, especially with regard to the role of affectivity, and (3) that a revised understanding of the role of affectivity in human experience would necessitate a revision of one's understanding of the aim and process of foundational theological method itself. *Inculturating North American Theology* is Gelpi's effort to make those revisions.

Gelpi's primary affirmation, which I have noted above in my review of his understanding of affectivity, is that affectivity grasps reality. Comparing the approaches of process theologian Bernard Meland with Bernard Lonergan, Gelpi affirms that, "Meland understands more clearly than Lonergan that human affectivity grasps the real as such. . . . He has seen that we should never characterize human affectivity as merely subjective, but as a way of perceiving a situation" (1988b, 58). Affectivity performs two "perceptual functions." First, it provides a vague initial interpretation of the kinds of tendencies which are shaping experience. They are not blind "reactions," but rather "they mediate cognitively between sensory images on the one hand and memory and imagination on the other" (Gelpi 1988b, 60). This statement agrees substantially with what has been learned in the previous chapter concerning the role of affectivity in coordinating other operations. Second, affections perceive reality. I take this to be Gelpi's way of affirming the role of appraisal in emotion as mediating between situation and concern. "Nevertheless," Gelpi writes, "affections . . . do more than perceive reality. They pass judgment upon it" (1988b, 60). Affectivity communicates the particular grasp of the tendencies in experience by taking the character they do. Judgments of feeling (aesthetic judgments, hunches, discernment) do not operate inferentially, but rather intuitively. The artistic hunch that one's sculpture is finally "just right" immediately grasps the synthesis of tendencies in the patterns of shapes in sculpture and the tendencies within the artist. A good artist learns to be attentive to these hunches, for they tend to grasp the way things are. Affective judgments exhibit no more (nor no less) fallibility than inferential judgments. Furthermore, like inferential judgments, they transpire consciously and unconsciously (Gelpi 1988b, 61).

Affectivity combines with image to create "appreciative consciousness." Memories, fantasies, archetypal images all reflect, shape and combine dynamically with affective operations. Through language, Gelpi suggests, affective insight is finally reshaped into communicated perceptions. Gelpi finds this communicated "voice" of appreciative insight in four forms: the voice of prophecy, the lyric voice, the narrative voice, and the voice of discernment (1988b, 62-75). Thus Gelpi affirms that one way affectivity mediates knowledge is by the shaping of image and appreciative consciousness, which in turn, is expressed in prophecy, lyric, narrative, and discernment. Hence, for example, a theological method which wishes to respect the role of affectivity in terms of its contribution to a grasp of the real (in this case, adequate propositional access to God) will do well to respect the use of theological methods involving prophecy, lyric, narrative, and discernment.

Gelpi claims, therefore, that affectivity functions in the *act* of knowledge to mediate the tendencies of reality to the human experience itself. Affectivity also functions to form the tendencies of the one in whom affectivity and knowledge arises. I refer to this as the role of affectivity in the *subject* of knowledge. Gelpi recognizes that affective predispositions (habits, tendencies) form in people and that these patterns seriously affect the ways in which reality is perceived. Enlightened or disordered hope can make the difference at times between adequate access to experience and misjudgment. Gelpi speaks of learning to "differentiate true from false hopes and adequate from inadequate ones" (1988b, 86). Likewise one must learn to resolve dialectical conflicts among appreciative perceptions of the real. If, as Gelpi claims, access to experience is *social* and, at least in part, *affective*, then it will be necessary to clarify contradictory affective judgments, just as it is necessary to do so with inferential judgments. This will require the implementation of sound literary, artistic, psychological, ethical, and religious norms, as well as the employment of an analysis of the relative adequacy of appreciative frames of reference (1988b, 87-89; cf. 1959). Finally, the insights of affectivity must be coordinated with the insights of inference in order to bring a coherent grasp of the tendencies which confront one (1988b, 89-90).

Bernard Lonergan claimed that "genuine objectivity is the fruit of authentic subjectivity" (Lonergan 1972, 192). Accordingly, he affirmed a set of postulates which summarized his five stage epistemology (Experience, Understanding, Judging, Acting, Transformation) and encouraged people toward the integral conversion necessary for objective knowledge. He named them: be attentive, be intelligent, be reasonable, be responsible, and be loving. In *Experiencing God*, Gelpi moves one step further, to propose that *(11) Adequate abductive propositional access to experience and to God is mediated by the free play of affectivity and by conscious sensitivity to the intimations of heuristic passion* (1987 [1978], 242). Ten years later, in *Inculturating North American Theology*, Gelpi specifically refers to Lonergan's postulates and, in light of his affective revision of Lonergan's epistemology and method, expands the list. Gelpi adds, "be repentantly appreciative . . . be imaginative . . . be tasteful, prudent, and discerning . . . coordinate the perceptions and judgments of your heart and head" (1988b, 97).

This intentional integration of affectivity into a theory of knowledge, such that adequate propositional access to God requires affective sensitivity, will have important consequences for a philosophically-sensitive account of Christian discernment. I will indicate the directions that these consequences might take in terms of the subject, context, object, and act of discernment. In terms of the *subject* of discernment, affectivity serves as a major factor shaping the possibility of adequate propositional access to God. I have already mentioned the effect which affective conversion might have upon discernment through the healing of disordered affections, and how the deprivatiza-tion of affectivity in socio-political conversion might shape the dis-cerning process. Religious conversion itself transvalues affective con-version and mediates between affective and moral conversion, trans-forming self-confrontation into repentance before God and awakening the heart to an aesthetic vision of the excellency of the gospel. In so doing, religious conversion shapes the orientation of the affections within the context of discernment and, in turn, transforms the dynamics of discernment itself. The transformation of the affective aspects of prudential judgment through religious conversion (cf. Gelpi 1998b, 456; 1996, 1-10) brings a docility, a yieldedness, to the Holy Breath that functions both as a gift and as a "skill" related to the prac-tice of discernment. As docility is cultivated and greater range of affective sensibilities are awakened, the "discerning heart" can recog-nize more of the self-communicating tendencies of the divine.

For Gelpi, the *context* of discernment is formed by those elements which unite to make the present experience what it is. Context, including affective context, does not exist separate from experience as something "out there" or "past" which shapes the individual, but rather stands *within* experience. Whether one looks to immediate con-text or broad historical/cultural context, the context of experience forms the shape of the precise "feeling," or the configuration of evaluative elements in any given moment. It helps define the "free-dom" and the "self" who exercises that freedom.

Affections can function as an *object* of discernment. There are times, for example in the evaluation of the character of charismatic experiences, where affective experiences serve as the object of dis-cernment in the sense that they are the "matter" which one wants to evaluate (cf. Gelpi 1987 [1978], 343). There are also those times, as when discerning one's form of life, when the "matter" is the calling or form of life expressing the will of God (cf. Gelpi 1976, 200-202). In this case affectivity may form the *immediate* object, as Gay delineated, with the pattern or tendency of the affective evaluations serving as the *mediate* object, and the next mediate object being the will or guidance of God. The tendencies of affective evaluation pre-sent in experience then serve as signs of the presence or guidance of God in experience which serve to indicate an appropriate choice of life.

Finally, Gelpi's works give most emphasis to the role(s) of affec-tivity in the *act* of discernment. Christian discernment is clearly associated with "intuitive thinking," and "judgments of feeling" (Gelpi 1993, I, 130). Affectivity grasps reality, Gelpi claims. And this grasp of reality is transvalued through the influence of religious conversion. Affectivity is involved in the act of discernment in the sense that discernment is practiced in prayerful docility to the Holy Breath (hence arises the possibility of affective impulses of the Breath participating in the process; cf. Gelpi 1970, 310). But affectivity also is involved in evaluating the tendencies which lie outside the specifically religious aspects of a discernment situation. Thus, for example, an affective sense of grief at injustice "grasps" realities which may inform a discerned call of life, apart from any specific "impulses" of the Holy Breath indicating a particular call. Affective conversion also animates the other forms of conversion, supplying the discerning act with a drive and orientation that guides the hunches, suspicions, possibilities, and convictions toward its particular end. Other aspects of the relationship between affectivity and discernment in Gelpi's system could be identified. The above are sufficient to suggest (1) the adequacy and applicability of Gelpi's system in terms of its ability to interpret the experience of Christian discernment, and (2) the convergence and complementarity of Gelpi's philosophical/theological framework with the historical and psychological material already presented in the previous chapters.

4. What reasonable grounds are there for the formation of the belief, in a given situation, that one has correctly identified that which is significantly related to God, grounds for regarding the fruit of discernment as "knowledge," warranting action as if *God were discovered?*

I have phrased the question in terms of "reasonable grounds for the formation of a belief" (or warranted belief) in order to speak to questions of philosophical epistemology. I have phrased the question in terms of warranting "action *as if* God were discovered" because in a Peircean system what one regards as "knowledge" is that on which one is willing to act. Thus positive identification of that which is *God* is "known" when one is willing to act on the assumption that God is present. While Gelpi himself has not directly spoken to this question, I think that a "Gelpian" response can be provided by the synthesis of the material presented above.

First, discernment belief, belief that in a given situation one has achieved the aims of discernment and actually identified that which is significantly related to God, is grounded in the character and communication of God's historical self-revelation through Christ and through the Holy Breath. Gelpi's portrait of the experience of God and the interactions of God with God's creation warrants the assumption that the "related to" or "from" God could actually derive thence. I shall call this proposition the communicability of the divine.

Second, the nature of human experience itself in this Breath of God gives reason to assume the possibility of discernment belief and grounds its reliability in practice. A triadic understanding of human experience, involving the union of actions, evaluative responses, and tendencies, makes possible the reception and comprehension of the divine as an interactive element within experience, as a "force" doing work. I shall call this proposition the receive-ability or response-ability of the human person.

Third, the nature of human knowing gives reasonable warrant to accept the possibility of discernment belief. Gelpi's triadic, realistic, falliblistic, communitarian theory of knowledge provides reason to think that self-controlled, integrally converted, shared inquiry, shaped by rules of operation appropriate to the material at hand (note Gelpi's emphasis both on docility to the Holy Breath and intentional use of psychological, ethical, and doctrinal sources) is capable of positively identifying the character of the tendencies arising in a personal or corporate experience as being "from God" or not. Since real tendencies appear in perceptual judgment, both affective and inferential thinking can grasp something of the tendencies that impinge on life. Through attentive, intelligent, reasonable, responsible, loving inquiry; by being repentantly appreciative, imaginative, tasteful, prudent, and discerning; by coordinating the perceptions and judgments of heart and head; the Christian person or community is capable by the very nature of knowing to grasp something (albeit fallibly) of the reality that is God. I shall call this proposition the possibility of real knowledge.

Fourth, insight into the forms and dynamics of conversion ground access to discernment belief. The forms and dynamics of conversion yield norms by which bias and faulty heuristics present in a discernment situation can be transcended. For example, negative self-image rooted in emotional scars from childhood hurts can seriously affect one's ability to recognize God's invitation of love in the context of discerning a call of life. Dynamic (a) states that affective conversion animates intellectual, moral, religious, and sociopolitical conversion. Gelpi writes, "one form of conversion animates another when it endows the latter with emotional zest and enthusiasm, creativity, imaginative flexibility . . . and an ecstatic absorption in beauty that engenders genuine self-forgetfulness" (1993, I, 34). Healing of one's emotional scars can serve to enable the discerner to become aware of impulses of the Holy Breath that otherwise would have been unnoticed or brushed aside.

Likewise narrow intellectual paradigms can frequently hinder discernment. For example, in the context of communal discerning prayer for someone who is suffering from illness, one may consider that all illness is a manifestation of the presence of a demonic spirit in the person. Another may think that sickness is the consequence of sin. Another may brush all this aside and presume that sickness is simply (and merely) a matter of physiology. Intellectual conversion informs religious conversion (b), encouraging one to take responsibility for the frames of reference that govern the expression of one's ministry to others. In so doing, intellectual conversion introduces a broader sense of perspective to the discernment situation and measures the relative adequacy or inadequacy of different frames of reference. Even the felt sense of "we are missing something here," or "now we have got it" in discerning charismatic prayer is shaped by the intellectual conversion of those present.

Again, Gelpi notes that sociopolitical conversion authenticates the other forms of conversion by deprivatizing them (f). As one is nourished in the mind of Christ through sociopolitical conversion, one's own growth in affective conversion is altered through the introduction of the felt sense of grief and pain over injustice and oppression of the weak. This transformation of affectivity will, in turn, influence one's personal discernment of God's presence and activity in culture, in the Church, and in one's own personal life.

Thus, every form of conversion will enhance other forms of conversion contributing to the adequacy of propositional access to God in each discernment situation. It is in this sense that, as was mentioned at the start of this chapter, the five forms of conversion can provide the "discerning heart" "tools for diagnosing the causes of personal and communal fragmentation and for identifying the ideals and principles needed to heal that fragmentation" and "sound principles for humanizing the Christian and for Christianizing the human" (Gelpi 1996). Furthermore, as the "discerner" is expanded from individual to community, and from community to Church, blending different personality types, different gifts, and different perspectives in a mutually supporting inquiry, insofar as these larger groups are themselves increasingly integrally converted, the adequacy of discerning access to God develops even more, bringing ever clearer discernment and greater propositional access to God. Thus discernment belief is grounded by the degree of integral conversion in each discernment situation. For this reason, the warrant for belief that an individual or group has, in fact, identified that which is (or is not) significantly related to God, would depend to some extent upon an assessment of the level of integral conversion present in the discerning individual or group. Here Gelpi's epistemological framework and theology of conversion converge with conventional discernment wisdom. I shall call this the principle of converting correction.

Fifth, the ability to differentiate tendencies *as* tendencies makes discernment belief possible, warranting that belief in particular situations. The "criteria" of discernment, whether affective (is it attended with a sense of peace?), social (does it flow from love for others?), doctrinal (does it acknowledge the truth incarnate in Jesus Christ?), or the like are names for tendencies which signify to some extent the presence or activity of God. These tendencies will appear in many forms, since discernment situations come in many forms. There are tendencies of interactions which identify criteria of discernment (for example in situations of cultural evaluation) and there are tendencies of evaluative response which identify criteria of discernment (for example in Ignatius' rules for the discernment of spirits). Thus discernment only has significance, and can only have functioned in history, because certain tendencies of evaluative response or interaction can be *identified as tendencies.*

I am talking here about the realm of tendency, habit, manner, real generality. Cumulative associative perceptual judgments, judgments of what is the case rooted in shared inquiry and careful, self-controlled analysis, identify tendencies which others can recognize. It is the fact that "consolation," for example, *can* be named that is important. Whether one actually does so or not is less important than the intuitive recognition of the dynamic tendency. Ignatius recognized spiritual tendencies in his times of meditation and only later was able to name them. The Thirdness or real tendency present uniquely in every discerning situation validates the criteria as a norm. At the same time, it is the understanding of tendencies as *merely tendencies* that grounds discernment as an art and not a rigid science. It may be one of the weaknesses of the "manual tradition" of Christian spirituality (cf. Tanquerey 1930) that it can communicate a reduction of discernment and the spiritual life to necessary and sufficient interpretations of the signs of the presence of God. It is often through a recognition of the number of criteria met and the strength of that fulfillment that discernment belief is identified. Thus the overlap of tendency with tendency reflects a kind of "family resemblance theory" of categorization guiding Christian discernment. This approach to discernment involves rational comparison (cf. Gelpi's encouragement toward the use of a variety of resources; 1970, 309), yet often is finally expressed as a "judgment of feeling." Thus it is the character of the divine tendencies *as tendencies* and *as merely tendencies* that grounds discernment belief in the particular situation. Discernment belief is warranted in any given situation insofar as there are divine tendencies present and recognized as such. I shall call this the principle of the particular tendency.

Ultimately, therefore, discerning access to the divine derives its warrant from the revealed character of God and in the history and life of the Church. Divine tendencies are divine tendencies only insofar as they communicate God. A Peircean epistemology is grounded only in the way the universe works and in the capacity to conform one's minds thereto. In the case of Christian discernment, "the way the universe works" involves the presence of tendencies which have their origin in divine reality. It is the divine experience interacting with human experience in real generality that makes discernment possible. Yet, at the same time, the recognition of the divine experience as identifiable tendency is only possible within the context of the developing interaction of divine and human. For, to some extent, the recognition of divinely inspired impulses is shaped by the developed experience that we are. As individuals and communities decide to act upon certain signs of the presence of God, they reinforce evaluative responses and "criteria" are established. Thus as the breadth of time and space and conversion expands, the Church expresses an ever increasing "expertise" concerning the tendencies which may be associated with the divine. Thus discernment belief finds its warrant, in the ultimate sense, from the infinite *tendency* of the divine in *interaction* with the expanding *evaluative response* of the converting world. While Gelpi does not directly address the grounds of Christian discernment in the manner I have here presented, I think this presentation has faithfully interpreted Christian discernment within the framework of Gelpi's foundational synthesis.

This brings us to the final epistemological question regarding discernment: the question of certainty.

5. What kind of certainty or assurance does the process or act of knowing called discernment promise to provide?

Gelpi himself addresses this question only in the contexts of his early evaluations of charismatic renewal. Gelpi closes the book *Discerning the Spirit*, with some reflections on discerning prayer designed to cultivate the reevaluation of the forms of life chosen by religious individuals and communities. He offers a few comments on the charismatic renewal and upon the means by which divine intervention should be evaluated. Upon noting the need to be open considering the influence of a variety of factors involved in perceived interventions of God, Gelpi concludes that,

> any judgment concerning whether or not this or that event is the result of a divine response to prayer will be at best a probable one when it is the result of objective critical reflection. One can at best decide that when the circumstances and consequences are weighed against legitimate rules for discernment of spirits . . ., it is not unreasonable in the light of the Christian revelation to believe that this event truly comes from God. (1970, 325)

Likewise, in *Pentecostalism: A Theological Viewpoint*, Gelpi addresses the degree of certainty which the believer possesses concerning the divine source of charisms and the state of the soul of a person expressing these charisms. Since humans do not have access to the source of another's charism *directly*, that source must be *inferred* from the life and ministry of another. Again, Gelpi's notes the variety of factors that can be involved in the expression of

Pentecostal phenomena. He states that "the conclusions of such an evaluation at the very most yield only probability that the phenomena in question proceed, at least in part, from divine influence" (1971, 203). I think this probabilism is in keeping with the "falliblism" of all of Gelpi's later foundational writings. The limitations of human cognition and incomplete conversion, and the scope of the material weighed in Christian discernment make it very difficult to give "absolute" certainty to discernment belief. Rather, as Gay affirms (1959), one has, in Christian discernment, a "moral" certainty. One has reason to act upon the belief that in a given situation the presence or guidance of God has been identified.

Conclusions: Interpretations of Discernment

This chapter has attempted to provide a theory of Christian discernment with greater theological and philosophical specificity by employing the categories of the philosophical theology of Donald Gelpi as means of interpreting Christian discernment. I have shown that Gelpi's foundational theology provides a conceptual framework which adequately interprets the findings of empirical psychology within a larger framework capable of comprehending divine self-communication and the motions of the Holy Breath. His emphasis on the affective dimension appropriately complements the psychological, philosophical, and theological issues surrounding the interpretation of Christian discernment as an affectively rich-act of knowing. Furthermore Gelpi's system provides fundamental insights for constructing a reasonable epistemology upon which the reliability of Christian discernment can be understood. It remains to suggest how Gelpi might respond to the other theological and philosophical treatments of discernment, summarized in chapter one.

First, Gelpi's system appears to support the conclusion drawn from the philosophical and theological literature, that discernment can be helpfully explored as an affectively-rich act of knowing. Gelpi himself defines discernment slightly differently depending on the context in view. For example, when speaking of the discerning prayer related to one's goals, purposes and aspirations, Gelpi states that "the process of personal spiritual discernment is, then, nothing else than the effort to penetrate and to assimilate his [Christ's] salvific vision" (1970, 308). In his summary of the Pauline charisms Gelpi asserts that "the gift of discernment seeks to authenticate impulses which claim to be Spirit-inspired and Spirit-led by evaluating their genesis and consequences against religious, ethical, and psychological criteria" (1976, 91). Still later in his *Inculturating North American Theology*, Gelpi speaks of discernment as an affectively-sensitive and therefore needed "voice" in foundational theological method. Speaking of both "natural discernment" and the "charismatic discernment of spirits," Gelpi argues that "both forms of discernment draw upon an appreciative insight into reality in order to make judgments about how to deal with it practically" (1988b, 74). This last definition brings one closer to the portrait of discernment presented in the lecture reviewed at the opening of this chapter, that of graced deliberation in the context of problematic situations. In spite of the differences in these definitions, terms like "authenticate," "make judgments," "distinguish between true and false" (1996, 10, mentioned in chapter 1), suggest that one is not far wrong in exploring discernment as an act of knowing, or even categorizing ("distinguishing," "authenticate"). I have already addressed the centrality of affectivity.

Second, it is worth noting, in response to all of the philosophical literature reviewed in chapter one, that Gelpi broadens the range of discernment much beyond the arena of moral choice. The subject of discernment appears in one form or another throughout Gelpi's works. From his doctoral dissertation on Ralph Waldo Emerson's method of "spiritual discernment" (cf. 1991), to his works on the discernment of a way of life in religious orders (1966b; 1970), to his "discernment wisdom" in the context of the charismatic renewal (1971; 1972; 1976) to the more systematic presentation of discernment in his foundational works (1976; 1987 [1978]; 1985; 1988a; 1988b; 1993), Gelpi has addressed discernment as it relates to a variety of situations and settings. As was noticed in Gelpi's presentation at the beginning of the chapter, discernment is not defined so much by its particular context (whether speculative, moral, or pragmatic), but by the kinds of evaluative responses (prudential or deliberative thinking) employed in the process. This expanded range of discernment consideration functions not so much to correct the other philosophers treated above.[7] It does, nevertheless, serve to increase the scope within which discernment can be philosophically considered.

[7]The philosophers reviewed give no indication of intentionally limiting discussion of discernment solely to moral choice. They simply never develop reflection on discernment beyond this arena.

Gelpi has summarized and responded to the theology of Karl Rahner on numerous occasions (see especially 1966b; 1988a, 67-96; 1994, 90-120), and this is no place to detail Gelpi's response to Rahner's system in general. I will only address one point with regard to a philosophy of discernment. I find that an application of Gelpi's system to Christian discernment serves Rahner's own aim of grounding Christian discernment in a "supernatural logic." As mentioned earlier, Rahner's article aimed at the key question of how the particular will of God can be known (and known to be known). Rahner's own search for "indubitable criteria" attempted to set forth necessary first principles for this supernatural logic underlying Christian discernment. Essays responding to Rahner's approach, however, demonstrated that Rahner's criteria of transcendental awareness of God present in pre-reflective consciousness was more dubitable than Rahner had hoped. Gelpi himself addresses the dubitability of this criterion in his own response to Rahner's transcendental method (1988a, 67-96; 1994, 90-120). I have shown, however, that a careful application of Gelpi's epistemology, founded in the logic of C. S. Peirce and Josiah Royce, is capable of supplying the very first steps of the supernatural logic of discernment Rahner envisaged. Gelpi's system, however, accomplishes this apart from the transcendental method and the faculty psychology of Rahner. Gelpi's system roots orientation to God, not in a pre-reflective awareness of God present in the pure desire to know (which Gelpi would call an unverified hypothesis concerning the nature of human experience), but rather in the ongoing interactions of experience, in the events and communities of Christian life. I have already addressed the difficulties with traditional formulations of faculty psychology in previous chapters; Gelpi's responses to Rahner confirm these concerns.

Gelpi's system also affirms Luigi Rulla's interest (building on Lonergan's model of knowing) in joining the psychological to the spiritual, emphasizing the role unconscious aspects of disordered affectivity shaping the discernment process. Gelpi addresses conscious and unconscious aspects of affective conversion repeatedly in his works (especially in 1987 [1978]; 1993; 1994-1995). Indeed, his account of conversion in these works treats of the healing of the fear, anger, shame, and guilt that plague human life at some depth. However Gelpi's revisions of Lonergan's psychology and epistemology enable Gelpi to give a much fuller account of the role of affectivity in discernment (beyond the mere apprehension of values).

Gelpi also fulfills Gerald Hughes' interest in relating discernment to a clear understanding of prudential thinking. This was seen in his recasting of prudential thinking in the light of John Dewey's understanding of "deliberation." However Gelpi's understanding of the evaluative continuum, his treatment of the transformation of prudential thinking through conversion, and his acknowledgement of discernment as a "judgment of feeling" enables Gelpi, I believe, to provide a more adequate integration of the affective and inferential dimensions of discernment than Hughes. In this I believe Gelpi moves beyond Aristotle (and perhaps Ignatius) in developing a fully integrated "process theology" which grounds his understanding of discernment.

On the whole, Gelpi's approach appears most similar to the brief article of William Spohn. Indeed, Spohn, with Gelpi, is also a member of the John Courtney Murray Club, a group of scholars attempting to voice Christian theology within a North American idiom. Nonetheless, Gelpi's system gives Spohn's historical and affective interests greater logical and systematic specification, much as Peirce's logic provides the grounds for the mature Royce's philosophy of religion.

Thus the North American philosophical-theological synthesis of Donald Gelpi offers both greater breadth and increased philosophical specificity to an account of Christian discernment. His triadic, realistic, communitarian construct of experience provides a coherent account of the individual and community capable of interpreting the findings of experimental psychology within the context of an authentic Christian faith-perspective. Gelpi's realistic, fallible, communitarian epistemology has been able to provide necessary steps toward an epistemology of Christian discernment as an act of knowing. Furthermore, his sensitivity to affectivity has brought to this exploration a sense of discernment as an affectively-rich act of knowing. With elements of empirical and philosophical specificity in place, I am now prepared to draw the insights concerning Christian discernment together into a synthetic whole.

Chapter 5

An Account of Christian Discernment as an Affectively-Rich Act of Knowing

In the previous two chapters, this study critically analyzed Christian discernment in light of the cognate disciplines of experimental psychology and North American philosophical theology. Through an exploration of the findings of experimental psychology, I provided a measure of empirical grounding to an account of Christian discernment by identifying specific cognitive and affective patterns that shape the character of the discernment process. I suggested a number of roles which affectivity might play in the discernment process. This analysis illumined the descriptive account of discernment, which addresses what people actually do when they discern. I noted, however, that both experimental psychology and discernment wisdom suggest that humans possess the capability to transcend bias and fallacy, making possible the move from a merely descriptive account of Christian discernment to a normative account, one that identifies self-controlled behaviors that increase the likelihood of discernment actually accomplishing that which it aims to accomplish. I further suggested that important insights for a normative account might be found in logical rather than merely psychological analysis, in the analysis of those self-controlled actions which foster the attainment of that at which discernment aims. For an exploration of Christian discernment, however, this logical analysis must show itself sensitive to both theological as well as philosophical and psychological issues.

Therefore I turned, in chapter four, to an examination of the thought of North American philosophical theologian Donald Gelpi. Through this examination, I provided a measure of theological and philosophical specificity to an account of Christian discernment. This specificity was accomplished by using the thought of Gelpi to present a consistent and coherent account of divine-human communication and of the means by which one can reasonably determine access to God. I demonstrated that Gelpi's categoreal system coheres well with the findings of experimental psychology, enabling the interpretation of psychological material within the context of a faith perspective. By using the insights of both Gelpi and his intellectual mentors, I was able to sketch the outlines of an epistemology of discernment indicating the kinds of self-controlled behaviors (patterns of thought, feeling, relationship, conversion, and the like) that increase the likelihood of discernment correctly identifying that which is (or is not) from God. Once again, I emphasized the roles which affectivity plays in this process. Finally, I brought Gelpi's thought into dialogue with other philosophical reflections on discernment, indicating the values of Gelpi's system for constructing an account of Christian discernment.

In the present chapter I move, by means of constructive interpretation, to draw the study together into a whole. The chapter divides into two parts. Part one serves to integrate insights presented in chapters three and four into a revised version of Gelpi's account of Christian experience. Part two then calls upon this account of Christian experience to interpret discernment, exploring the questions of Christian discernment traditionally presented in the literature of Christian spirituality. In so doing I hope to provide a more empirically grounded and philosophically and theologically sensitive account of Christian discernment. The following chapter will then take this account and apply it to two common contexts of the practice of Christian discernment today.

A Model of Human and Christian Experience

This part seeks to draw insights from experimental psychology and North American philosophical theology into a single coherent theory of human and Christian experience, one which can provide a framework for an account of Christian discernment. I will proceed in this part by commenting on a working definition of human experience, namely that *human experience is the somewhat integrated arising of various mental-biological operations or systems of operations, ordinarily occurring within an identifiable pattern or process, developing in time and space within the context of a web of relationships.*

Operations and Systems

In chapter three I identified both particular regularities in mental-physical process called *operations* (such as image-retrieval, concept recognition, event appraisal, or hormonal activation) as well as distinguishable sets of interrelated operations called *systems*. I named at least two classes of operations and accompanying systems. *Cognitive* operations exhibit a special sensitivity to the structure of the environment. Inquiry, judgment, insight, deduction, comparison, synthesis and other similar operations fall into this category. I included many of the individual components of category formation and retrieval here. As a number of discrete operations cooperate to enable a particular way of acting that highlights verbal or spatial process with this sensitivity to the structure of the environment, one can recognize a *cognitive system*. It must be remembered, however, that the cognitive system employs a variety of operations, affective as well as cognitive. *Affective* operations are especially sensitive to the meaning of environment-person relationship and more heavily involve physiological processes (hormonal activity, heart rate, galvanized skin responses and the like). Feeling, attraction, action tendency, excitement, mood, reaction, and the host of labels for individual emotions fall into this category. The *affective system* incorporates both affective and cognitive operations within a unique means of adapting to the confronting environment distinct from the cognitive system. I also suggested the possibility of a third system: the *volitional system*. This system appears to be more sensitive to deliberative action or self-control. I identified volitional operations involved in the regulative stages of the affective system in events such as "nursing a grudge."

Donald Gelpi's foundational theology gives explicit recognition to the distinction and integration of affect and inference in human expe-

rience.   While not developing these categories in the detail summarized above, Gelpi carefully distinguishes affect from inference,
each of which functions by different rules of operation.   Furthermore,
Gelpi repudiates a hierarchical "faculty psychology" which fails to
recognize the integration and equal role of various operations and
systems in human experience.   While not necessarily speaking of
"will" or "volition" as a separate system of operations, Gelpi's
understanding of autonomy contributes to the grasp of this aspect of
human experience.   For Gelpi, a self exists as a combination of
evaluative and decisive habits, as the "habitual, incremental repository
of decision" (1985, 37).   However, the key element of a self is
autonomy, the capacity to initiate action or evaluation.   In human or
personal experience this ability to initiate action arises within the context of finite freedom, self-understanding, vital continuity and relational existence.

It seems reasonable, based upon the information gained thus far,
to posit two primary and one subsidiary systems within human experience.   Affective and cognitive systems and operations cooperate to
form central human patterns of adaptation to our confronting environment.   The volitional system is less understood.   It appears more tied
up with each of the other systems, albeit with the emphasis upon
autonomy or self-control.   Whereas affectivity and cognition respond
to some extent to the confronting "out there," the sole object upon
which the volitional system acts appears to be the process of human
experience itself: for example the choice to attend to *this* perception,
the decision to take *this* action, the election to cultivate *this* desire.
Volition is thus the autonomous contribution to the motion of affective or cognitive process.   As such volition may be less an independent system itself but rather arises as the development of affect or cognition insofar as they fall under the autonomy or deliberation of the
human person.

I use the phrase "somewhat integrated" to reflect the ambiguities
within human experience.   Aside from the various dis-integrations
labeled in the Diagnostic and Statistical Manual of Mental Disorders,
there are a host of more subtle ways in which affect, cognition, and
volition may be working disharmoniously.   Thoughts and feelings
arise with apparently no relationship to one another and at times
human experience appears to be a random presentation of mental
events.   Indeed, some scholars have gone so far as to view human

experience as simply the activation of independent operations, mini-mizing the existence of an integrated "self" (Gardner 1983, Ornstein 1986). It seems appropriate to me, given the evidence presented, to recognize both the cooperation of systems and operations in human experience, necessary for survival, and yet to acknowledge the incomplete nature of that cooperation, by use of the phrase "somewhat integrated."

Experiential Process

Human experience ordinarily follows a recognizable pattern; it "flows" in a particular direction. Gelpi identified a number of stages in an "evaluative continuum": experiencing (involving both sensation and perception), imagining, thinking (both intuitive and rational), judging (both logical inference and judgments of feeling), deliberat-ing, deciding and acting (cf. 1994, 126-132). Likewise, in chapter three I showed that both human categorization and affectivity do not arise *ex nihilo* but rather appear within the context of cycles of human experience. The similarity with which these cycles are identified in the experimental literature can be observed merely by comparing the order of the table of contents of a variety of standard textbooks in cognitive psychology. These experiential cycles identify both pre-perceptual factors constraining the nature of a given conceptual or affective event (such as structures "hard-wired" into human neurology or physiology, conditioning, world-view, and state of consciousness) as well as those stages associated with particular operations (such as stimulus, perception/appraisal, storage and retrieval, inquiry and refinement, regulation, decision and action, emotional experience). My own synthesis of the philosophical and experimental material identifies six separate stages in experiential process.

I associate the first stage with bare consciousness or *Being aware*[1] itself. Consciousness—at least "ordinary" consciousness—involves the presence of human experience as given within the context of a few existential variables of awareness: range (open, restricted), intensity (dull, alert), energy (relaxed, tense), and level (conscious, uncon-

---

[1]Throughout this and the following chapter I will refer to these stages by the use of capitalization (thus Being aware, Experiencing, Understanding, and so on).

scious). Our state of consciousness, changing constantly with the movements of the predisposing variables (for example, whether focused and intense or open and relaxed) constrains the possibilities of what can be sensed and perceived. The condition of bare awareness also indicates the forms which structure experience, thus not only affecting *what* is experienced, but *how* it is experienced. One can also understand human experience analogically as waves upon the ocean of consciousness. In this sense consciousness is not merely a "stage" or human experiential process, but is rather the raw material upon which all of human experience arises. Gelpi addresses consciousness at points in his work (e.g. 1987 [1978], 83-85; 1994, 135), but does not make it a primary part of his evaluative continuum. It is explored in some of the experimental psychological work, especially as it seeks to interact with philosophical insights (Varela, Thompson, Rosch 1991; Rosch 1996, 1997; Mangan 1972; Palmer 1999).

The second stage is characterized by *Experiencing*. I include in this stage all which is discussed in the experimental literature as stimulus, sensation, perception, and initial memory processing. Gelpi similarly speaks of sensation and perception at this point in the evaluative continuum with imagery serving as a transition between this and the following stage. I have already noted the active character of this stage of human experience, involving selection, pattern recognition, evaluation and more.

From Experiencing, one moves to *Understanding*. I here include that which Gelpi's later work labels "thinking" in its various types. In terms of the experimental literature, this stage includes much of what cognitive psychology discusses under conceptual processing, general knowledge, and language processing and emotions research discusses under appraisal and regulation. As noted earlier, human experience is noetic-adaptive. We seek to adapt ourselves to that which confronts us, and in so doing, that which confronts us is to some extend mediated to us. This noetic mediation receives a heightened focus at this stage as humans make sense of their world.

I associate the fourth stage with *Judging*. At this stage, human experience moves from the question of "what is the case?" to "is it really the case?". To use Peirce's divisions of logic, where abduction and deduction are primary in Understanding, deduction and induction play central stage in Judgment. Experimental psychological literature also addresses patterns of human judgment. Problem solving research addresses phenomena common to understanding, judging and deciding/acting. Affective experience completes appraisal and concern processing and moves toward emotion formation at this stage.

Judging moves toward *Deciding* and *Acting*. Psychological research involves an entire spectrum of studies on decision-making. Likewise Gelpi places emphasis upon decision and action as the termination of the evaluative continuum. At this stage there is an investment, an entrustment, of the person in the judgment previously made, either through the formation of a personal belief or in the taking of an action, effectively impacting the confronting environment. In a similar manner, affective experience achieves the expressive stage at this point, giving rise to action tendency, phenomenal feelings, mental preoccupation, physiological changes and the like.

Finally, the fruits of decision and action, in turn, bring the person to a stage of *World view adjusting*. While Gelpi speaks of frames of reference among which world view would number, he emphasizes decision as the termination of the evaluative continuum and does not include world-view adjustment as a separate stage of the evaluative continuum. He does, however, mention that every action reinforces or shapes the nature of who we are as developing selves (1994, 132). It is within the transition between decision/action and world-view formation that conversion, the decision to take responsibility for a given area of life, takes place. In experimental psychological literature one hears of this stage in terms of feedback loops and conditioning due to experience. Theory theory in categorization research might speak of theory revision at this point as well as the establishment or reinforcement of scripts and schemas. World-view adjustments, in turn, shape the character of consciousness through interaction with pre-existing accumulated knowledge/habits and socio-historical conditioning. This interaction of world-view and pre-existing conditions, face the confronting environment creating a new person-environment relationship and the cycle of human experience begins again.

Again, I mentioned that human experience "ordinarily occurs" within this process or pattern. By "ordinarily occurs" I simply mean that there is a general tendency of human experience to flow in a predictable direction, frequently passing through recognizable stages on its way. Empirical analysis of human categorization alone—not to mention studies of other aspects of human experience—gives ample evidence that ordinary human cognition does not necessarily follow an ideal logical structure. Often human experience functions more efficiently within a finite universe by taking short-cuts. We frequently "jump to conclusions," bypassing Understanding and moving directly to Judging. Likewise we "leap without looking," moving directly from Experiencing to Acting without Understanding or Judging. Many of the heuristics and biases discussed in the literature on judgment and decision-making involve the neglect of the use of particular operations or entire stages of experiential process due to the prominence of some salient feature of the environment or of the experience as developing. Much of the time, this neglect or misuse of an operation is simply due to normal patterns of experiential organization. But, in addition, operations at each stage can be dysfunctional. Awareness may be either mindful or repressive; we may be either attentive or closed in our Experiencing; our Understanding may be either intelligent or biased; our Judgments may be reasonable or invalid; our Decisions may be either responsible or irresponsible; our World view adjustments may reflect both a yieldedness to reality or a hardening from reality. We may live wise or foolishly. It is precisely at this point where the possibility of volition or self-control has central relevance. At any stage in human experience, there may be need for the volitional system to initiate patterns within the process, thus shaping the development of the process itself. Yet this action of human volition is achieved within the context of a variety of constraints from within and beyond us. In addition to breaks in the process due to finitude or dysfunction, there are times where process is interrupted due to "supreme function." To borrow a phrase, truth happens. In this way constraint, autonomous volition, and the forces of reality interact, giving rise to the mysteries of human life, and to the transformation of conversion.

The Web of Relationships

We have recognized Gelpi's understanding of conversion as the decision to take responsibility for a "sphere of life," giving rise to a variety of different conversions (affective/psychological, intellectual, socio-political, religious, moral). Furthermore, we have also acknowledged the variety of lenses through which affectivity can be viewed in the empirical material (social, physiological,

phenomenological and so on). This gives rise to the value of reflecting on the context and nature of human relationships. Others discuss
these aspects of human experience as "dimensions" of human experience (cf. Barry 1992, 28). I, however, wish to emphasize the essential relatedness of human experience. Human experience, apart from
multiform relatedness, simply does not exist. In this sense inter-
relatedness becomes a necessary, though not sufficient, condition for
human experience. Indeed, just as some have viewed individual
operations as the primary reality and the personal self as the mere
contiguous collection of these operations, so also others have looked
at human society or the ecosphere itself as the primary reality and
individual selves as merely particular components of this larger, more
fundamental reality (cf. Sessions 1995; Drengson and Inoue 1995).
For the purposes of this study I will emphasize relatedness insofar as
it gives context and definition to personal experience. Our relationships make us who we are; our thoughts, feelings, choices only arise
within the context of a complex network of "others" to whom we
relate.

These "others" to which we are necessarily related impact us at the
Experiencing stage of human experience, serving as perceived causes
of our experiencing such and such. They provide the contents: the
objects, the environment, the world of our experience. Having
entered our experience these "others" serve to form the material from
which our memories, thoughts, images, feelings, decisions and such
are formed. As one moves to Deciding and Acting, these others of
our relatedness are once again confronted as the world, objects,
environment *upon which* we act. Each of the spheres of relatedness
contain realities that possess autonomy and thus real identity. Thus a
particular human society has its own "self" and its own "life." The
precise impact of each relational sphere involves the combination of
(1) the introduction of a configuration of experience arising within
consciousness (within a precise setting and state) along with (2) the
activity of cognitive and affective operations and systems developing
in certain patterns, resulting in (3) images, feelings and the like
which, in turn, shape belief formation re-organization and personal
transformation.

The "others" of our relatedness can be grouped variously. I
choose to think of humans as having relationship with four separate
spheres. First, humans exist in relationship to *nature*. Human expe-

rience is physical, chemical, biological, zoological, ecological. The force of gravity, the composition of soils, the presence of bacteria, the behavior of plant and animal life and much, much more all shape our existence. One's geographic and historical location enable particular relationships with various natural forces. A thirteenth century American teepee-dweller and a dweller of the concrete jungle of a twentieth century Urban ghetto are exposed to different diseases, possess different hopes, raise families differently, and express worship to God differently in part because of the differences in relationship to nature. While Gelpi might see this aspect as part of the socio-political dimension, I choose to identify a separate *ecological* conversion which expresses the fundamental responsibility for relationship with nature. Just as socio-political conversion deprivatizes the other forms of conversion in light of our fundamental relatedness to human society, so ecological conversion will further deprivatize human life in light of a much larger community of relatedness within which we have our being.

Second, humans experience a relationship with a *self*. Human experience is deeply psychological. Our own thoughts, feelings and choices can become the objects of our own thoughts feelings, and choices. As our developing experience is comprehended as a somewhat unified whole there arises within our experience a perceived "self" with which we have to do. The patterns of self-relationship are often the stuff of clinical psychology, although in the experimental material I presented a variety of approaches to self-understanding and relationship. As persons take fundamental responsibility for thoughts, feelings, and choices, forms of conversion are introduced (*intellectual, affective, moral*) which transform the relationship to the self. It is even possible to think of significant transformations of our understanding/action with regard to certain neglected stages of human experience: for example a conversion bringing significant sensitivity to one's states of awareness. Those who speak of *psychological* conversion appear to me to be referring not simply to the transformation of disordered affectivity but rather are speaking of the transformation of the relationship to the self as a whole (cf. Doran 1977).

Third, humans experience relationship with *other humans*. Thus, human experience is interpersonal, social, economic, political, and fraternal. Often some of the deepest elements of our experience arise from relationships with other people. The fundamentally social aspect of affective life is emphasized in the research of Averill and Oatley. As one takes fundamental responsibility for our relationships with other people, especially in the context of the wider "selves" of institutional society, then one enters into *socio-political* conversion.

Finally, humans experience relationship with the *transcendent*. While not emphasized in experimental psychological literature (yet cf. Fowler 1981), it is nonetheless appropriate in this study to reflect the perspective of Gelpi and the history of Christian spirituality that humans relate to forces beyond those measurable by standard experimental means. Discernment literature frequently speaks not only of interaction with God, but also of angelic and demonic forces—however one may wish to understand these today. I have addressed, in chapter four, the conceivability of the human perception of the Holy Breath acting as a force within experience. It is the character and self-communication of God through Jesus Christ and the Holy Breath that forms the first grounding principle of Christian discernment as discussed in chapter four. From this foundation one can begin to understand the possible dynamics of a developing relationship with the transcendent realm as such. As fundamental responsibility is taken for relationship with God *religious* conversion is experienced.

The dynamics of conversion outlined by Gelpi flow from the ways in which the spheres of human relatedness mutually affect each other as well as from the development of human responsibility and transformation as applied to each sphere. As I have outlined this model of human experience, one would be able to identify more than seven dynamics, for as new stages of experience are identified and more spheres of relatedness are named and the permutations of transformation increase exponentially (for example, one might say that ecological conversion contextualizes affective, intellectual, moral, religious, and socio-political conversion by both localizing and globalizing them).

Human experience "develops" within this web of relationships. It should be obvious by now that I, with Gelpi, do not consider human experience or the human "being" to be a static reality. When I say that people arrive at any present moment as "given," I mean that the "givenness" of the present moment summarizes the trajectory of a person as shaped thus far and identifies the possibilities for becoming in the next moment. Persons are developing selves, identifiable by virtue of the real tendencies inherent in each experience, but developing in time and space insofar as they are merely tendencies and not reified "things." The insights of developmental psychology have much to offer at this point, for by acknowledging the collective insights of this field we realize that our thoughts, feelings choices, Experiencing, Awareness, relatedness and so on are framed, experienced, and structured differently at different points in our development. Not only are we different people because of our temporal and historical location, but we are different people within ourselves because of our developmental location in the context of these spheres of relationships.

Human experience not only develops within the context of this web of relationships, but the function and dysfunction, the awkward finiteness, even the original and personal sinfulness of humankind are lived out in the context of this web of relationships. Hence, social bigotry, ecological neglect and abuse, personal woundedness, and spiritual rebellion are all thus addressed by various forms of conversion both natural and graced. Self-controlled activity or divine grace may effect transformation of any element or stage of human experience with particular focus upon one or another sphere of human relatedness. In this way, one might experience a particular enlightenment (graced) while reading the passage in Romans 8 concerning the travail of the earth bringing new Understanding with regard to one's relationship to nature.

Needless to say, the above model is not only a model of human experience, but also a model of human knowing. I have spoken of human experience as adaptive, as enactive, as semiotic, and as *noetic*. Human experience is noetic insofar as it grasps something of the real tendencies that are present within the web of relationships within which human experience consists. Following Gelpi's lead I understand human experience to lead toward a more or less adequate grasp of reality. Proximately, and with contrite falliblism, knowledge is acquired through the ordinary patterns of individual human experiential process involving both affective and cognitive systems. Volitional action brings a measure of self-control to our knowledge acquisition processes, enabling the avoidance of bias. Adequate access to reality is increased as the experience of others is brought into dialogue. Finally—and to draw this line of argument to its logical conclusion—knowledge is ultimately established through an infinite integration of experience.

I have summarized and synthesized the previous chapters into a working model of human experience and knowing. This model emphasizes (1) the place of operations and systems of human mental-physical activity, (2) that activity as arising within a process often following a recognizable pattern of stages, and (3) the fundamental relatedness of human experience. A diagram illustrating this model is presented in Figure 4. It is this model which will be used to develop a more empirically grounded and philosophically sensitive account of Christian discernment.

Consequences of the Model of Experience for Descriptive and Normative Accounts of Christian Discernment

Before I proceed to an account of Christian discernment as traditionally discussed, it will be valuable to summarize a few of the key consequences of the model of human experience as presented above for the formation of an account of Christian discernment in general. In each of the preceding chapters I have submitted the topic of Christian discernment to descriptive or critical analysis by means of historical, psychological, and philosophical/theological research, indicating insights and implications which may be brought to bear upon an understanding of Christian discernment as an affectively-rich act of knowing. Without reiterating the details of those insights and implications, I wish here simply to summarize and to draw attention to those implications which derive especially from the model as presented above.

First, Christian discernment is a similar set of operations, a similar question, applied to diverse circumstances. This point has been made since the first chapter. Discernment involves the evaluation of phenomena to determine what is significantly related to God. It is this evaluation-in-order-to-confidently-categorize character of discernment that gives it its unifying similarity in such a wide variety of settings. I identified this common structure in the different types of discernment presented in Ignatius' *Spiritual Exercises*. A similar structure was noted in the different contexts of Jonathan Edwards' works on discernment. In chapter three, I identified this set of operations more precisely as a special type of categorization, one which evaluates the quality of experience. As an act of categorization, one can expect that discernment in all its diverse settings will take the

FIGURE 4:
A MODEL OF HUMAN EXPERIENCE

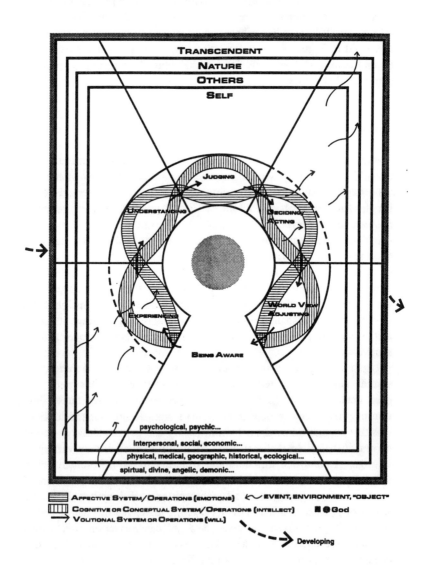

character of a process and will involve conceptual associations and designations of category membership. As an experiential process it will bear similarity to the stages of human experience listed above, beginning in bare Awareness, arising in Experiencing, moving through Understanding and Judging, expressed in Acting, and reintegrated through adjustments to World-View. One can expect affective and conceptual operations involved in categorization and in addressing spiritual reality to be active in Christian discernment. The use of prototypes, similarity comparisons, graded structure, and a range of exemplars will play a part in designating what is, or is not, from God.

Nonetheless, this common set of operations is applied to a variety of different circumstances. The configuration of impact arising from one's network of relationships varies with time and space. Yet each may need evaluation with regard to spiritual character. Similar sets of operations may be applied to a wide range of relational configurations. A prophetic utterance in a congregational meeting, a potential strategy for political involvement, a personal spiritual experience, options for career choice, all can be the objects of the Christian discernment.

Second, the Christian discerner comes to an act or situation of discernment as an existential "given." This identifies the *subject* of Christian discernment. Discernment ushers forth from a person or community as both formed and forming. I emphasized this point in my review of both categorization and affectivity research. Gelpi made this point as well in terms of an emphasis on the non-static or developing nature of selves and persons. Human experience varies in state from one moment to the next. The givenness of each individual at each individual moment involves the accumulation and integration (to whatever level accomplished) of all that is brought to and through each self up to that point. For this reason, as noted above, discernment will differ from person to person. Developmental history, personal background, genetic inheritances all will constrain the capabilities for each individual to notice, recognize, or respond to aspects of the discerning process. One person may have been raised in a culture where careful attention to inner movements, such as those involved in the recognition of consolation and desolation, was ignored or even discouraged. This background will present difficulties for classic Ignatian discernment. Similarly, the act of discernment will be approached differently by the same person in different situations. Increased maturity, familiar circumstances, positive affective atmosphere all will contribute to the likelihood of a given discernment process actually identifying that which is related to God.

It is because of the accumulated "givenness" of each individual in each discernment situation that there is such value to the advance preparation of the discerning subject. This was emphasized by Ignatius in his insistence upon the transformation of disordered affections and on the development of spiritual appreciation and connaturality. I also mentioned this point from the perspective of categorization research, noting that discernment process should be expected to improve with experience and through association with the expertise of past discernment wisdom. I noted as well the affective component to the classic virtues associated with Christian discernment, demonstrating the value of the re-orientation from self to Other (as in aesthetic and empathetic emotions) for re-forming habits and tendencies of awareness, understanding, and response related to discernment process. Gelpi emphasizes this point in his stress upon the need for increasingly integral conversion, a major factor in determining adequate propositional access to God. The value of preparation is also implied in the encouragement to cultivate affective skills in preparation for discernment. The development of appropriate affective sensitivity and "docility," to use Gelpi's term, is a valuable pre-patterning of accumulated experience that helps to form the discerner such that in a given discernment situation the subject's givenness and the discernment situation and process are increasingly compatible.

Third, discernment is carried out within real person-environment relationships. The configurations of human relationships, the objects and material of discernment, appear in experience with a sense of force, of impact upon the perceived world. They also appear with a sense of quality, an "evaluability," or more specific to the topic at hand, a "discernibility." Finally, elements of the person-environment relationship within which we conduct discernment arise with real tendency. As mentioned in chapters three and four, it is the real tendencies of the perceived world, insofar as they are perceived as confronting and as discernible, that give rise to discernment in the first place. By this we identify the *objects* of discernment. I have noted this above under the concept of "configurations" of relationships.

Throughout this study I have used the categories of Robert Gay (1959) to distinguish between the various objects involved in discernment. I expand upon Gay's framework by identifying four separate "objects" of discernment. First, relational configurations (alternative choices, experiences, trends and such) arising with discerning significance, become what I call the *focal objects* of discernment: they are what the discernment is "about." Another way of looking at it is to say that the discernment situation itself, summarized into a single question, is the focal object of discernment. We say we are discerning God's presence or guidance with regard to *this*. For example, in an Ignatian election the vocational decision among alternatives would be the focal object of discernment. The universes that come under examination in order to proceed in an act of discernment are called the *immediate objects* of discernment. The immediate object of discernment is that to which we look, the "immediate" aim of attention, in order to resolve the discernment question. In an Ignatian Second Time election, dependent upon the discernment of spirits, affective motions form a significant immediate object of discernment. In a Third Time election (which confesses little presence of significant affective motions) the thoughts, plans, and projected futures of the subject become the immediate objects of discernment. The character, tendencies, and trajectory of the immediate objects of discernment, then, become the *mediate objects* of discernment. While the focal object identifies *why* we look, and the immediate object defines *at what* we look, the mediate object identifies *for what* we look. We are trying to notice patterns, signs, signals that will point to the *next mediate object* (or the aim) of discernment, namely God's presence, activity, or guidance. The aim or next mediate object defines what we see when discernment is complete. As mentioned above, the presence of an affection itself can serve as an object of Christian discernment: either as the focal object (is this emotion from God or not?), or as the immediate object (affective movements providing signs of the divine presence with relationship to some other focal object).

When the person-environment relationships are not the focal objects of discernment, they function as constraints upon the situation and process of discernment—in short, as the *context* of discernment. The primary context of Christian discernment is the divine-human relationship. Following Gelpi, I assume that discernment is fundamentally grounded upon the self-communication of God. Dynamics of the relationship with God, therefore, form a significant part of the context of determining what, in one's experience is significantly related to God (circular as it may seem to think that God is centrally involved in determining what is from God and what is not). Christian discernment is both a self-controlled and divinely graced movement of human experience. Furthermore, in one sense the habits of experiential process themselves, as accumulated in the subject, form another context of a given discernment act, for these habits constrain the possible means of perceiving, evaluating, and responding to a given situation. By so constraining they form a piece of the context of the act of discernment. Category systems learned in the past (for example the increased valuation, common in charismatic circles, upon confirmation of personal calling through a "prophetic word") form scripts or schemas which shape the way discernment proceeds. One can recognize another context in the surrounding relationships with other people. These relationships touch on key concerns related to discernment situations and affect the way options in discernment are perceived. For example, I noted the range of affective options which serve as the context of discernment involving affective perception or expression. These three: the subject, context, and objects of discernment, I call the *horizons* of discernment.

Fourth, Christian discernment functions as an affectively-rich process of knowing, aiming at the knowledge of that which is significantly related to God. This specifies the *act* of discernment itself. I mentioned above that this model of human experience is also a model of human knowing, for human experience seeks to adapt and respond noetically and semiotically to that which confronts it. Christian discernment is therefore the process of human experience itself, with attention to certain operations and sets of operations (for example, the operation of category attribution), as it attends to certain presenting configurations of person-environment relationships. As an act of knowing which aims at identifying that which is significantly related to God, operations related to categorization take center stage in the knowing of Christian discernment. Indeed, as noted above, this aspect of discernment identifies a common element of discernment in all its varied situational contexts. As an act of categorization, one can expect discernment to suffer from all of the complexities associated with categorization in general. Indeed, because of the subtle, affective operations central to Christian discernment, one may expect the categorization processes associated with discernment to be especially complex. For this reason one may expect to find people lost on discernment "rabbit trails," enamored by "false criteria," and deeply in need of the wisdom of expertise. I think this factor has created the need for help supplied by the classic statements on discernment in the history of spirituality.

As an act of knowing, however, discernment is subject to volitional controls. We can initiate tendencies and patterns of thought and action which, in turn, increase the likelihood of discernment achieving its aim—the confident identification of *God*. Thus, as an act of knowing, discernment can subject itself to epistemological principles, principles which govern adequate access to reality—here to the reality of God. I reviewed these principles in chapter four, noting the role of God's self-communication, of the triadic nature of human experience, of the nature of human knowing (the rules of a holistic logic), of the dynamics of conversion, of the presence of tendencies *as* tendencies, and finally of the character of God and the Church. Thus while, as an act of human knowing, discernment is subject to all the foibles of human knowing, it also can subject itself to the controls which attempt to minimize the danger and consequences of these foibles, and to the mysterious moments when clarity simply appears. The process of Christian discernment for the individual/community, is, then, the identification of and appropriate adaptation to the tendencies present, confirmed with the developed and developing categories of the community of discerning believers. As I have mentioned previously, this process of knowing yields adequate, though not infallible access to the (R)reality which confronts and communicates.

As an affectively-rich act of knowing, I have affirmed throughout this study that affective operations and the affective system as a whole play a significant role in the act of discernment (as well as with relationship to the subject, context, and objects of discernment). Important portions of God's self-communication enter human experience from the Holy Spirit as affective forces. Gelpi referred to these as "impulses." These impulses enter experience with real Thirdness or regular, identifiable tendency. The prayerful "docility" necessary for good discernment involves an affective sensitivity. Both Ignatius and Edwards emphasized the perception of the "manner" or trajectory and character of affective experience as an important element of discerning what is from God. Affectivity meditates between the subject and environment, revealing the nature of the person-environment relationship—and in so doing mediating something of the character of the environment itself. Affectivity gives a richer grasp of some aspects of reality through judgments of feeling, judgments not possible apart from the affective system. These aspects (especially those that regard aesthetic and empathetic emotions) are especially significant for spiritual matters. Affectivity also contributes something to the nature of cognitive process, thereby guiding the dynamics of categorization (and the categorization of Christian discernment) on to its aim. Thus affectivity provides clues for awareness of when "I have it." As Gelpi asserts, affective conversion animates the other forms of conversion.

With this summary of the nature of Christian discernment as integrated with the above model of human experience I have presented a basic understanding of the subject, context, objects, and act of Christian discernment. I am now prepared to give an account of discernment in terms of its presentation in the literature of Christian spirituality.

A General Account of Christian Discernment

In chapter one I listed a number of issues or questions that have gained attention from reflective works on Christian discernment, questions regarding the nature of discernment as a gift or virtue, the understanding of *spirits* in the phrase "discernment of spirits," the nature of God's "will," and so on. Most books on discernment will offer something to say about basic principles of discernment, the preparation or qualities of the discerner (or characteristics of a discerning group), models of discernment to avoid, the basic process of discernment, attending to God's presence and movements in individuals and/or groups, criteria by which God's presence or movement is recognized (cf. Kelsey 1978; Larkin 1981; Green 1984; McKinney 1987; Johnson 1990; Barry 1990; Farnham, Gill et al. 1991; Lonsdale 1992; Wolff 1993; Willard 1993; Carthusian 1995; Mueller 1996; Morris and Olsen 1997). My aim in this section is not to give a comprehensive treatment of all these issues and questions but rather to present a sketch of some of the more common issues as understood in light of the model of human experience and implications for Christian discernment outlined above.

Definition

I have already established a working definition of discernment that has provided the study with an interpretant for the diversity of discernment practices and situations. I stated that discernment is the affectively-rich process and act of coming to identify and know in a given situation, in the light of one's Christian faith tradition, that which is significantly related to God (or significantly not related to God). This definition incorporates elements of definitions found elsewhere, yet it draws attention to the character of discernment as an act of knowing and categorizing ("identify"). I have shown that this interpretant serves well to explain the nature of Christian discernment as described historically and as specified both empirically and philosophically. This definition has guided the study thus far and will serve to guide the account of Christian discernment that follows.

The Need for Discernment

The need for discernment is a common theme in discernment literature. The character of human experience itself, addressing diverse forces impacting human life emphasizes the need of discernment. Awareness of the complex context of spiritual warfare fuels the pleas for discernment in both Ignatius and Edwards, as it does in some today (cf. Sneck 1981). Yet the complexity of the Christian walk, and the need for discernment, arises not merely from the presence of evil and good "spirits," but also because of the diversity of relationships which influence human experience. A single impulse may have portions of the perceived whole arising from psychological defense mechanisms or from medical conditions, as well as from spiritual forces. William Barry writes, "discernment is necessary not only because of the possible influence of the evil spirit, but also because of the multidimensionality of human experience" (Barry 1992, 34).

The need for discernment is also mentioned with relationship to contemporary uncertainties (Green 1984). For example, Kathleen Fischer (1988, 114) writes: "Discernment is more important than ever in a world where women and men are increasingly aware of the reality of oppression. It needs to be rethought in this new context." This study affirms this assessment of the present need for discernment. As our surroundings change—and they are changing more rapidly than any time in history—the operations connected to identifying the presence and guidance of the divine are essential to the navigation of person, community, and planet. Many traditional habits of discernment process (for example, God's will is to be identified with the desires of one's superior) simply are not workable in twentieth century life. As Fischer suggests, major areas of life must be reconsidered with regards to their impact upon our ways of identifying and knowing that which is significantly related to God. Significant changes in our relationships with nature, self, others, force a rethinking of our own relationship with God and the means by which that relationship is discerned. For this reason, authentic Christian discernment is especially valuable today.

Discernment: Gift or Virtue

The question of whether the ability to recognize that which is (or is not) from God should be regarded as a virtue that can be fostered or must simply be received as a gift from God has received various emphases throughout the centuries. In light of the present study this question can be illumined by Gelpi's understanding of transmuting grace. Transmuting grace acts to reorder the natural elements that structure human experience "to a satisfaction they could never achieve in and of themselves: namely loving union with a God who has entered human history" (Gelpi 1988a, 86). Thus divine grace takes the ordinary operations and systems of human experience as I have described above (acting within process and within relationships) and infuses them with a fundamental Other-orientation, or with a sensitivity for Ultimate Concern. This is the orientation of aesthetic and empathetic consciousness discussed in chapter three. The capacity for discernment, in terms of the operations and systems of human experience, have always been there. Grace simply transvalues them such that they find their aim and ground anew in Christ. The ability to categorize and to feel emotion are part of the hard-wired equipment with which humans enter the world but as this equipment is touched by the Spirit of God it becomes sensitive to the things of God and affectively-informed categorization becomes spiritual understanding. This was precisely Jonathan Edwards' point in *Religious Affections*. In this sense discernment is a gift. St. Paul emphasizes the spontaneous work of the Holy Spirit in the midst of a gathered community to the end of mutual edification in Christ when he mentions the gift of discernment of spirits in 1 Corinthians 12.

As an ordinary set of operations in human experience, however, discernment is also subject to development apart from the gracious acts of God. Individual operations associated with Christian discernment (for example, clear thinking or the ability to attend to inner affective motions) can be cultivated, much as improvement of one's breathing can improve the performance of a gifted singer. Furthermore, the systems and stages of human experience are subject to the transformations of what Gelpi terms natural conversion, the taking of responsibility for key areas of life. Insofar as we can respond to the re-orienting grace of God with intentions and actions of our own, Christian discernment thus becomes a virtue as well as a gift. In this way, both natural and graced conversions contribute to the character of discernment as expressed in the Christian community.

Types of Discernment

We have already mentioned the variety of contexts or situations under which and toward which discernment is conducted. Common settings of discernment give rise to the identification of particular "types" or "kinds" of discernment. Jules Toner gives indication of this variety, stating that, "there are manifold kinds of spiritual discernment: discernment of true and false doctrine, of true and false prophecy, of true and false mystical experiences and of different degrees or stages of mystical experience, discernment of what is truly God's will for one's free choice among alternative courses of action, to name only a few" (Toner 1995a, 11). As I have mentioned above, these kinds arise from the tendencies involved in the relational configurations which confront us.

Basic Theological Principles

A variety of key theological principles are emphasized in works on discernment: for example, God's involvement in human history (Green 1984; Barry 1990), God's self-communication and ongoing dialogue with human persons (Willard 1993; Lonsdale 1992), God's constant loving invitation to God's people (Farnham, Gill et al. 1991; Lonsdale 1992), and the character of God's will (Friesen 1980;

Johnson 1990; Costa 1993). In chapter one I drew attention to Robert Gay's emphasis in the interior work of God's grace (Gay 1959) and to Karl Rahner's theological starting point for discernment found in the manifest presence of God within unreflective consciousness (Rahner 1963; Rahner 1964). In chapter two I drew attention to Ignatius' principle and foundation for the discerning work of the *Spiritual Exercises,* namely that "human beings are created to praise, reverence, and serve our Lord our God" [23] and Edwards' primary principle of the discernment of religious affections in the transforming work of saving grace. In chapter four I developed Donald Gelpi's understanding of a few key theological points, particularly his understanding of revelation or the self-communication of God, of the work of the Holy Breath, and of the dynamics of conversion. While all of these points deserve recognition in some form a few deserve special attention here.

First, discernment as an *act of identifying and knowing* depends upon the possibility and character of God's discernibility. Thus the doctrine of God's revelation or self-communication is central to a theological foundation of Christian discernment. How one understands God's self-communication—whether as unthematically present in human consciousness and only brought to awareness in times of "consolation without prior cause," or as the effecting of perceived forces or impulses within experience, or as circumscribed within the text of scripture, or as discovered only in the praxis of action with and for the oppressed of the world—is of critical importance for the theory and practice of discernment.

Second, discernment as an act of knowing and especially as an *affectively-rich* act of knowing, brings one face to face with reflection upon the Holy Spirit. Present access to God is gained especially throough the affectively-rich ministry of the Holy Spirit. Furthermore, it is often within reflection upon the work of the Holy Spirit that discussion of discernment—and especially the affective aspects of discernment—takes center stage. The documents of the second Vatican council affirm that, "the people of God believes that it is led by the Spirit of the Lord, who fills the earth. Motivated by this faith, it labors to decipher authentic signs of God's presence and purpose in the happenings, needs, and desires in which this People has a part . . ." (cited in Morneau 1982, 171). It is for this reason that some books on discernment regard themselves as commentaries on the ministry of the Holy Spirit (Toner 1982; Mueller 1996). William Yeomans writes, "The presence of the Holy Spirit in our hearts means that no one is devoid of certain basic elements of discernment" (1989, 3). The centrality of one's understanding of the ministry of the Holy Spirit for the understanding of discernment also means that one's position with certain disputed matters of doctrine concerning the ministry of the Holy Spirit may have significant consequences for one's practice of discernment. For example, the belief that the dispensing of the gifts of the Holy Spirit listed in 1 Corinthians 12 (including the gift of "discernment of spirits") ceased with the close of the canon of scripture or at some other time would likely affect one's understanding of the nature of the evaluation of a personal or communal sense of being "led by the Spirit" (cf. Sneck 1981; Parker 1996).

Third, discernment ought to be rooted in the theology of the character of God. If discernment is the identification of that which is *significantly related to God*, then discernment will be most improved with a thorough acquaintance with God, both personally and theologically. This was a central aspect of the Puritan understanding of discernment (cf. Bayly 1714 [1612?]), and I think ought to be to be today. The matter is especially complicated in current theological discussion, however, due to the thorough reconsideration of the Christian doctrines of God and Christ in light of feminism, deconstructionism and cultural/religious pluralism. The need for careful scholarship and converted hearts is especially needed in the development of the articulation of an understanding of God capable of informing an approach to discernment of that which is significantly related to God.

Finally, I will offer a few comments on the theology of "God's will" in light of the account of human experience and discernment presented above. Discussions of this subject range from assuming the ultimate aim of discerning is the "finding of God's particular will" for a person (Rakoczy 1980, 80), to denying the existence of a particular will in God (Friesen 1980), to identifying a number of "wills" in God (Johnson 1990). The implications of these differences in theory for the practice of discernment, especially within the context of life-choices, are significant. I have already noted the ambiguity of contemporary understanding of human "will." In terms of human experience, I think it is best not to see will as a separate and hierarchical "faculty." Rather, as discussed above, what is called "will" is the expression of autonomy within the limited freedom of a self. It is the movement/inclination of cognitive or affective process insofar as initiated by the self. To the degree that this is an adequate way of understanding the notion of God's will as revealed in scripture and tradition, one can view God's will as the movement of God's thoughts and feelings, as the direction of God's Spirit upon the earth variously expressed and perceived. Viewed in this way, phrases like "the lead-ing of the Spirit" (Parker 1996), "the perfect will of God" (Billings 1987), "following Jesus" (Sobrino 1979) and "doing what the Father is doing" (Blackaby and King 1994), can all be comprehended under a single interpretant. This intention or movement of God's mind and heart is expressed differently to different individuals and groups as appropriate to the ongoing relationship—God's will is not something "out there" believers are supposed to discover but rather is an intimate part of a sincere relationship with God (a point continually reiterated in discernment literature)—and is perceived by different means and with different intensities. It is for this reason that one can distinguish three separate "times for the making of an election" all of which are aimed at the designation of the will of God for a free choice of action.

Preparation

The topic of the preparation of the discerner is common in discern-ment literature. I have already discussed the value of preparation for discernment in light of the givenness of each self within a discernment situation. Since human experience begins each moment as an accumu-lated and developing self, good preparation builds tendencies into experience that increase the likelihood of discernment achieving that to which it aims: namely, the identification and knowledge of that which is significantly related to God. Some of this preparation comes simply from the act of "gaining experience." The authors of *Listening Hearts* write, "Discernment cannot be reduced to any rules of thumb. Rather, the ability to discern develops from living the life of the Spirit, a process of growth involving an ever-greater integration of desires, feelings, reactions, and choices with a continuing commit-ment to abide in Christ" (Farnham et al. 1991, 25). This "ever-greater integration," as per the epistemological framework presented above, involves an intentional sympathetic openness to diverse per-spectives. David Landegent writes of the necessity of this kind of preparation for discernment in the context of evangelical Christian factions of "the right" and "the left":

> It is incumbent upon Christians to listen not only to the prophets who scandalize society, but also to the ones who scandalize us. A Christian on the left must not only applaud Jim Wallis but also discern what it is in the message of the Moral Majority that irritates (should I say, scandalizes) him or her. Christians on the right should do the same. For it is in those areas in which we are easily provoked that we ourselves may be fleeing the scandalous Word of the Lord.
>
> We must examine our ears periodically to make sure they can hear God speak through unlikely channels. Discerning the spirits means more than distinguishing what kind of spirit is at work in the prophet. It also means distinguishing what kind of spirit is at work in us (Landegent 1983, 5).

The topic of preparation is also often discussed under the heading of "qualities of good discerners." Lists of qualities or virtues pertaining to discernment serve to remind potential diserners that the identification of that which is from God is not simply the product of a discernment procedure but rather flows from discerning *people*. These lists address skill development with relationship to the operations associated with discerning categorization as well as with the spheres of relationship associated with the various discerning situations (cf. Rakoczy 1980, 40ff; Byron 1974). Likewise the purifying of "disordered affections" so important to Ignatian discernment is aimed at transforming patterns of mis-appraisal, inappropriate regulation or concern habits, and the like. Similarly Edwards' articulation of the "less certain signs" in his works aimed at correcting patterns in his readers—patterns rooted in affectivity as well as cognition—of action tendency responding to revival phenomena. By preparing themselves with a clearer understanding of the "less certain" and the "more certain" signs of God's work, Edwards' readers would be capable of initiating new tendencies of thought and feeling in the context of revival phenomena and not merely be subject to the action tendencies associated with salient, but less significant features of the revival.

The preparation of the discerner also arises through education. By acquainting oneself (speaking of individual or community) with the great writings on discernment in the Christian tradition one gains from the expertise of centuries of confident categorization. The nuances of particular categories can be illumined by reading or hearing about key discerning categories or processes in the Christian tradition. Consider, for example, Thomas Merton's description of the experience of "indifference," the yielded desire for God's will present in spite of personal preference, contained within his account of traveling to the Abbey of Gethsemani, where he hoped to enter:

> It was a strange thing. Mile after mile my desire to be in the monastery increased beyond belief. I was altogether absorbed in that one idea. And yet, paradoxically, mile after mile my indifference increased, and my interior peace. What if they did not receive me? Then I would go to the army. But surely that would be a disaster? Not at all. If, after all this, I was rejected by the monastery and had to be drafted, it would be quite clear that it was God's will. I had done everything that was in my power; the rest was in His hands. And for all the tremendous and increasing intensity of my desire to be in the cloister, the thought that I might find myself, instead, in an army camp no longer troubled me in the least.
>
> I was free, I had recovered my liberty. I belonged to God, not to myself: and to belong to Him is to be free, free of all the anxieties and worries and sorrows that belong to this earth, and the love of the things that are in it. (cited in Barry and Connolly 1982, 112)

By educating ourselves with the discerning processes of the Christian tradition, we tap into the expertise and increase the likelihood of quality Christian discernment.

Hindrances to and Errant Models of Discernment

Just as the preparation of the discerner addresses the operations and relationships associated with discernment and discernment situations, so the "hindrances to discernment" frequently mentioned often refer to neglect of operations, gaps in the process, and dysfunctions of system integration. Many of these are affective in character. Bob Mumford lists selfishness, stubbornness, disobedience, insincerity, impatience, self-sufficiency, and pride as key hindrances to divine guidance (1971, 58-64). Rakoczy mentions aiming discernment at the trivial, lack of recognition of the diversity of philosophical approaches, lack of inner freedom, pride, bad will, willful ignorance of the facts, absence of prayer and a selective reading of the times (1980, 52-53). Margaret Goldsbury identifies a variety of factors that affect the integrity of discernment, naming physiological factors, psychological factors, theological factors, and spiritual factors (1989). These lists of hindrances show, as my epistemological reflections have made clear, that quality discernment is a function, at least in part, of integral conversion (on this cf. also Dubay, 177, 146-56).

Whereas lists of hindrances to discernment generally involve a personal gap in operation or system, discussions of "errant models" involve the institutionalization of these gaps: incomplete criteria assumed, operations neglected as a matter of course, habitual inattention to key aspects of the relational configuration built into the expectations of discernment process. Dunne's refutation of both the "discovery" and the "decision" model (1974), Rahner's careful avoidance of the dual dangers of situational ethics and formal moral theory (1963), and Willard's characterization of "message-in-a-minute," "it's all in the Bible," and "whatever-comes" models of discerning God's guidance (1993, 53-56) all respond to specific gaps in integral conversion especially as existing within the relationship configurations associated with discernment. Quite frequently, these gaps arise as discernment is made into a formula rather than assuming, with Mumford (1971, 33) that "learning the skill of receiving guidance is learning to walk in intimate fellowship with God."

Who Discerns?

This question is especially significant within contexts of communal discernment, such as community guidance within religious orders, assessing community strategy for social action within interdenominational bodies, and the evaluation of prophetic utterances within charismatic communities (McKinney 1987; Sheeran 1983; Sisters of the Holy Names of Jesus and Mary 1991, Spohn 1973; and the articles in *Catholic Charismatic* June/July 1978; on this question in general cf. Belloso 1978). Nevertheless, communal participation in individual discernment is also encouraged in discernment wisdom and in some communities the involvement of the community in the discernment of the Lord's guidance related to individual decisions has been or is very important (cf. Benedict 1975 [574?]; Palmer 1988). The issue brings up sensitive questions related to the relationship between charism and authority. In terms of the present study two comments on this subject deserve mention. First, the strength and authority of discernment is increased as the community of discerners expands. This should be obvious from my discussions of categorization and philosophy. Adequate access to reality—and therefore to confident judgment of that which is significantly related to God—is found within the increasingly converted and enlarged community. While involvement of large numbers of individuals in a small matter of personal discernment is neither realistic nor necessarily helpful, I think discernment is at its best when the movement of God is identified by the mind of a body of believers. Second, the best configuration of participants in the discernment process depends upon the relational configuration surrounding the discernment situation. Balance of expertise in the spheres most concerned with the discernment (including both those who best know the individual(s) involved in the discernment and those who are most familiar with God), diversity of perspective and personality, blend of cognitive and affective systems, recognition of the presence of bias, significance of discernment situation for individuals, giftedness of persons, and authority of persons to effect change or decisions in contexts related to the discernment must all be weighed with regard to the selection of participants in a discernment process. These factors are present (albeit less consciously considered) even within the context of informal personal discernment informed by a few close friends.

The Nature of "spirits"

The question of the nature and character of the "spirits" referred to in the phrase "discernment of spirits," has been a topic of much discussion in recent literature on discernment (cf. Wink 1984; Upkong 1989; Price 1980; Rakoczy, 1980; Sweeney 1983; Toner 1982). Much ink has been spilt either defending or demythologizing the spirits identified in Christian discernment. My contribution here is the simple offering of a "Peircean suggestion." In a Peircean framework reality is not "thingness" but rather Thirdness, the regular tendencies which can be manifest in perceptual experience, whether affective or cognitive. Just as the Holy Spirit can be understood as a force doing work in the midst of human experience, so evil or good spirits can be comprehended as forces which operate habitually in recognizable ways with a degree of autonomy. With this understanding of reality a first step may be made toward reconciling traditional "real beings" models, Jungian "archetypal" models, and other psychologically or socio-politically based models of spirits.

The Basic Process of Discernment

While all will agree that "there is no canonized way to conduct spiritual discernment" (Houdek 1996, 115), most outline some basic structure of the process of discernment to aid those learning to discern. Furthermore, these outlines consistently reflect key stages, operations, and even the general "flow" of human experience as presented earlier in this chapter. This can be seen even in Ignatius' description of the aim of the Rules for the Discernment of Spirits, "rules to aid us toward *perceiving* and then *understanding* . . . the various motions which are caused in the soul: the good that they *may be received*, and the bad that *they may be rejected*" [313 emphasis mine].

Though a discernment situation does not arise *as* a discernment situation at the stage of Being aware, one's state of consciousness does affect whether and how a discernment situation is viewed. It is for this reason that Ignatius warns his followers not to make a significant change in a time of desolation [318]. The influence of the desolation upon one's state of consciousness make clear evaluation difficult. I have also noted that one's current awareness is shaped by an accumulation of the past, indicating the value of preparing consciousness for discernment.

A discernment situation arises as the stage of Experiencing moves to Understanding. *Something* arises in our experiencing, some phenomena—a prophetic utterance, a trend in church life, a set of alternatives for personal choice. It arises as significant enough to draw perception into focused attention (initiating a certain amount of affective energy in the attention), yet vague enough to trigger other affections related to the ambiguity. The phenomena must be related to faith. At some point a question is raised: where is God in this? Is this significantly related to (or significantly not related to) God?

Another type of discernment arising at this stage is the ongoing noticing, knowing and responding appreciation of God (or rejection of sinfulness) of everyday living, which arises at the level of perception. I
would not call the latter a *discernment situation*, though it is a legitimate type of discernment (cf. Ignatius' "finding God in all things").
A discernment situation appears at the point of inquiry (the first part
of Understanding), when the question of divine relationship is posed.

The next step in the process of discernment involves both gathering information and preparing one's heart and mind to discern. These
activities order oneself for Understanding. It is helpful to pay conscious attention to gathering information, as it is so easy to think of
religiously significant matters as beyond the need of such mundane
processes as gathering information. To neglect this simple operation,
however, can lead to ignorance of important facts related to the discernment situation. All kinds of facts are helpful at this stage: people
involved, potential impacts, needs, feelings (cf. Sisters of the Holy
Names of Jesus and Mary 1991). It is also at this time that a basic
analysis of the situation in light of the concerns of scripture and the
church tradition is made, in order to weed out unnecessary discernment situations. It is also at this time that discerners begin to prepare
their own hearts for this particular discernment situation. This is the
time for recognizing and admitting our own concerns, for recognizing
our own affective preferences. This is a key time for cultivating
indifference, for recalling to ourselves the principle and foundation of
discernment in God's love for us and our lives created for God's service, and for cultivating a vision for the kingdom of God in our lives.
Through this kind of "First Week" and "Second Week" preparation in
the face of a discernment situation we foster the connaturality so
beneficial to Christian discernment (Sullivan 1980; Spohn 1983, 51).

As the process of discernment develops it begins to involve a
"paying attention" to a variety of different sources from which indications to the presence or guidance of God may be noticed. The signs
of God's presence or activity depend to some degree upon the type of
discernment in view. God's confirming voice concerning a choice or
judgment may be found through profound spiritual experiences (such
as a First Time election, cf. Ignatius, *Spiritual Exercises* [175]),
through impulses arising through the operations and systems of human
experience (cf. Johnson 1990) or through scripture or the church, or
through ordinary conversation with others or reflection on our own

stories (Farnham et al. 1991). At this point a kind of "just listening" becomes involved in discernment (Willard 1993, 214), or in communal discernment, often a time of prayerful reflection is introduced (McKinney 1987). This waiting around and paying attention is important, for it focuses discernment upon sensitivity to the Spirit of Christ rather than methods of categorization that might come naturally ("judging a book by its cover") but are not rooted in integral conversion. This stage of the discernment process may involve a bit of "play" with the information related to the discernment as imagination, comparison, "feeling as if," and other operations are incorporated into the discernment process. If we can speak of "creative regression" in discernment (Parker 1996, 117-144), it appears most visible at this stage.

As information related to the discernment is collected, Understanding of the discernment situation begins to shift to a specific Judgment. At times our own conversion is addressed in the process of discernment and the discernment situation itself becomes secondary. If, however, the situation remains a matter of focus (guided by affective interest and shifts in cognitive inquiry) people usually employ specific criteria to sift and evaluate the information gathered. Lists of criteria in discernment literature abound (cf. Mumford 1971; Schmidt 1976; Sobrino 1979; Morneau 1982; Rakoczy 1980; Sheeran 1983; Sheets 1983; Barry 1989b; Morris and Olsen 1997) and space does not permit a thorough evaluation of discernment criteria here. Nevertheless a couple of comments should be made about criteriology in light of the current study.

First, as with the question of who should discern, the criteria of discernment are governed in part by the relational configurations within which discernment is being conducted. Discernment of major communal decision should involve paying attention to the sense of mutual agreement (and not mere superficial uniformity—note the need for affective sensitivity) in the midst of the group as a criteria indicating the direction of the Holy Spirit. Evaluation of the source of a unique and frightening spiritual experience would employ the criterion of spiritual tone to assist the discernment process (here the frightening tone would be evaluated by its character: what kind of "frightening" is experienced in terms of mental preoccupation, action tendency, etc., as well as by its trajectory: is the subject a believer progressing/regressing in the Christian faith?). Since each discerning situation is slightly different, the category *of God* must be understood within some kind of loose family resemblance theory, that increases in specificity with the degree of familiarity with discernments of a particular kind.   Situation appropriate criteria will also be accompanied by process appropriate criteria (rooted in the clarification of the "kinds of thinking" needed), such as the sense of peace that indicates that the desired end has been found and no significant questions are left hanging.

Second, contra Hughes (1990) and following Spohn (1983), I think it is perfectly appropriate to see affectivity itself as providing certain important criteria to the discernment process. With Gelpi and the research on affectivity, I would affirm the ability of the affective system to mediate something of that which confronts us in ways that the cognitive system cannot. Judgments of feeling are simply rooted in different operations and perceptions than cognitive judgments. Consequently, conditions of the affective system itself can provide indications about the presence and guidance of the divine self-communication. Experience, including affective and spiritual experience, is semiotic, that is it signifies and mediates something of its source through the character of the experience itself. By noticing, understanding, and evaluating the presence, character, and trajectory of affective experience in light of the history of expert category delineation and attribution found in discernment literature such as found in Edwards' or Ignatius' works, one can confidently assess the movement of God within human experience. Indeed, the careful discernment of affective experience can often be a more certain sign of the activity of God than the changes in circumstances commonly called "open doors" (a biased heuristic of discernment related to the salience of personal circumstances).   A balance of situation appropriate criteria and process appropriate criteria will include a generous measure of affectively-rich criteria in virtually any discernment situation along with those rooted in cognitive operations.

Discerning evaluation culminates in a judgment, an election, a decision. Whereas Gelpi, following good pragmatic logic, identifies the point of discernment with the confident establishment of a response to the discerning situation, I give emphasis just slightly prior to this, in the confident categorizing Judgment *that* something is or is not from God. While this judgment is quite often most clearly known in the knowledge of the precise nature of response to the situation, I think there are times when confident discernment that some phenomena is or is not of God does not always bring with it a clear knowledge of response. At times practical wisdom must follow clear discernment. In any case, discernment is finally expressed in Decision and Action. In situations of communal discernment this is often called "implementation."

Still, discernment does not end with implementation or action but the very act of discerning implementation serves to reorder or reinforce existing habits and tendencies of the individual or group. Feedback loops inform and adjust the World-view of the discerner, shaping the self that returns to discern anew. Finally, the discernment itself is confirmed in the ongoing life of those who discerned.

Certainty

How certain can one be, after a discernment process, that one has actually identified that which is significantly related to God? How sure can one be that this choice, this evaluation, this trend is indeed the expression of God's will, presence, or guidance? I have already addressed this question in chapter four. According to the epistemological principles developed above we cannot expect epistemological certainty, but rather move forward in response to probable judgments of moral certainty. This moral certainty increases in reliability as the sense of the activity of the Spirit heightens (as in a First Time election or within a case of consolation without prior cause) or as the discerning community expands in diversity, conversion, and number. Ultimately certainty in discernment depends upon the character of God and the development of God's people (cf. Toner 1991, 274-315; Orsy 1976, 68).

Integration of operations and systems: the roles of affectivity in Christian discernment

This brings me to the question of the roles of affectivity in Christian discernment. It should be obvious by now that I do not see discernment as either predominantly rational evaluation (as Friesen 1980; Hughes 1990) or simply as "heart as opposed to head" revelation (the emphasis of Jean Pierre de Caussade 1989 [1861] at times inclines this way). Rather discernment is, as Jan Bots writes, "founded on the interplay of intellect and feeling, in which both are completely integrated" (Bots 1982, 64; cf. also Larkin 1981, 59). Furthermore, I understand discernment as a type of knowing especially interested in categorization. Jules Toner writes of the Ignatian discernment of spirits:

> To understand a motion once we are in touch with it means at least three things: (1) discerning the characteristic features by which it is distinguished from other motions; (2) discerning its direction, what consequences it tends to effect in one's own or another's spiritual life; (3) discerning its origin, what spirit is prompting this motion. (Toner 1995a, 13)

Each of these operations, and especially (1) and (3), are categorizing operations. This same categorizing character of discernment is, I think, found in virtually all types and contexts, and is pursued by means of a process similar to that outlined above.

I suggested in chapter three that particular "Christian" emotions, those oriented to the realities of the Christian faith, can be explored in terms of distinctive phenomenological tone, action tendency, mental preoccupation and the like. Appraisal of the value of God and the person-environment situation (including assessment of the felt presence of God) will lead to distinctions between affective experiences of worship, thanksgiving, repentance, petition, empathetic sharing of the "heart of God," and other emotions. Affective experiences such as these will play a special role in discernment.

In previous chapters I have suggested ways in which affectivity plays a part in Christian discernment. Data from the history of Christian spirituality, from empirical research in emotions, and from North American philosophical theology all indicate that affectivity participates significantly in every aspect of Christian discernment. I outlined this participation in terms of the ways that affectivity may shape the subject, the context, the objects, and the act of discernment. But really the matter is more complex than this.

First, as discussed in chapter three, what I refer to by the term "affectivity" includes more than that studied within the field of "emotions" research. Moods, sentiments, reactions, aesthetic emotions, empathy, and more are all included in my understanding of the affective system and category of affective operations. Even particular operations or sets of operations such as concern retrieval, appraisal, mental preoccupation, and action tendency are best understood as interdependent parts of affectivity. I mentioned in chapter three, for example, the role of "nuclear scripts," and their relation to concerns and the Ultimate Concern of emotions responding to the realities of the Christian faith. Thus any single operation or combination of operations or type of affectivity may influence discernment in various ways and times. For example, a person with habitual fearful appraisals may negatively anticipate some types of profound spiritual experience, which will, in turn shape this person's process of discerning a path of personal spirituality.

Furthermore, as outlined above, the act of discernment is not a simple event but rather a developing process, a process which can never be definitively prescribed without violating the very character of that process. The fact that the act of discernment is a developing process means that affectivity (in all its complexity) potentially affects discernment differently at any given stage of that process. In addition, since discernment is conducted interactively within relationship to God (as well as other forces) the nature of the process and the affective factors involved are never entirely within our control or comprehension. Fearful disposition may affect discernment at the pre-experiential stage of World-view and expectations; it may also play a part in the actual point of Judgment of that which is from God. In light of the unconsciously held salience of anxious appraisals, spiritual experiences seen in others may simply seem too frightening and "out of control" to accept as being from God. God might also break into a discerning process "out of nowhere" with a powerful First Time experience of such love and kindness that dissolves all anxiety and identification of that which is from God becomes absolutely clear.

The roles of affectivity in Christian discernment, or the ways in which affectivity contributes to or shapes Christian discernment, can, therefore, be explored in terms of three interconnecting sets of factors. First, we can examine the categorizing *process* of discernment itself, loosely following the stages of human experience. Second, we can look at the aspects, operations, and types of *affectivity*, each of which can have a unique influence upon human experience and Christian discernment. Finally, we can explore the *horizons* of discernment within which the influence of affectivity is in view: that of the subject of discernment, that of the context of discernment, and that of the objects of discernment (in the act of discernment the element of the subject is in view).

With this framework, one can, for example, reflect upon the ways in which mental preoccupation (an aspect of affectivity) with the child Jesus in terms of the focal object of discernment (namely this preoccupation is that which one is trying to evaluate—is this person's/group's preoccupation with something of God or not?) affects discerning categorization at the stage of Understanding (a moment within the discerning process) within the context of someone's or group's devotional experience. This would involve examination of and reflection on the patterns of categorization and the factors which are involved in the categorization of tendencies of mental preoccupation in people, especially with regard to spiritual concerns. Thus one would explore root concerns and factors which are associated with this person's/group's constant obsession with devotion to the child Jesus in an effort to determine whither this preoccupation arises from divine initiation or whether other personal, social, or spiritual forces are predominant. Affectivity plays the role of the focal object in this case, namely that which one is trying to evaluate. If the person doing the discerning is also experiencing this preoccupation, then this mental preoccupation aspect of affectivity plays not only a role as an object of discernment, but it also shapes the subject of discernment. If this experience of preoccupation is part of a community obsession, then the same aspect shapes the context of discernment as well. Certainly other aspects of affectivity would be involved in the discernment of whether or not this preoccupation is significantly related to God or not. Mild feelings of anxiety may arise as the discerner wonders if the cultivation of this kind of experience is legitimate. Additional discoveries about the person or group in question related to their experience may elicit emotional reactions (especially if the discerner is also the experiencer). If the "discerner" is a committee called upon to investigate this behavior, the dynamics of group feeling will also contribute to the affective forces guiding discernment in this case. Attention to intuition and imagination (both affectively-rich operations) at the stage of discerning Understanding may reveal aspects of God's presence or activity in this situation that help to secure a confident judgment.

Likewise one might consider the multiple roles of "mood" in Christian discernment. Mood is a condition of the subject of discernment insofar as our affective condition at any moment is cumulative. Research in emotions indicates that the affective energies of a moderate length of time (or even long season in some cases), leave residues upon their experiencers, increasing the likelihood of similar affective responses. Thus there is a sense in which happiness breeds more happiness (mood congruence). A discerner approaching discernment from a generally relaxed, warm mood full of trust will approach the process of discernment differently than if the cumulative mood was anxious, hurried and forced. The range of Awareness, the openness to Experiencing, the freedom of "play" at the stage of Understanding are all significantly affected by the mood of the discerner. Factors may shift the mood of the discerner, thus shifting the conditions under which discernment proceeds and, in turn, affecting the reliability of the judgment that something is or is not significantly related to God. Mood can also contribute to the context of discernment, the relational configurations within which discernment is conducted. The mood of a corporate gathering in a time of communal discernment (e.g. discernment in an uninterested leadership team), the general trends of larger spiritual movements (e.g. discernment in the midst of a great awakening), or even the political climate of a nation (e.g. discernment in the face of impending governmental collapse) can all affect the dynamics of discernment. Even the geographic environment of a discernment process offers something to a discernment situation. It is for this reason that people so often "get away" to a different physical space for the purpose of discerning significant personal decisions. Mood can also serve as an object of discernment, either as something which is evaluated for whether of not it derives from God or as an indication of the work of God with regard to other areas of life.

One can also explore the dynamics of the traditional Ignatian understanding of "consolation" within this framework. Ignatius identifies consolation in his Rules for the Discernment of Spirits as follows:

> *The Third*, about spiritual consolation. By [this kind of] consolation I mean that which occurs when some interior motion is caused within the soul through which it comes to be inflamed with love of its Creator and Lord. As a result it can love no created thing on the face of the earth in itself, but only in the Creator of them all.

Similarly, this consolation is experienced when the soul sheds tears which move it to love for its Lord—whether they are tears of grief for its own sins, or about the Passion of Christ our Lord, or about other matters directly ordered to his service and praise.

Finally, under the word consolation I include every increase in hope, faith, and charity, and every interior joy which calls and attracts one toward heavenly things and to the salvation of one's soul, by bringing it tranquility and peace in its Creator and Lord.

Ignatius is not trying to give a "necessary and sufficient" definition of the category of spiritual consolation here. Rather he is indicating the range of prototype experiences which one may expect to find within this category. In this definition a few matters are of note. First, virtually every significant aspect of affective experience is mentioned in this description: phenomenal experience (soul inflamed with love), action tendency and physiological expression (tears), mental preoccupation (attracted toward heavenly things), mood (tranquility and peace), and habits of appraisal (hope), belief (faith), and action (love). Any and all aspects of emotional experience and expression can arise as primary components of spiritual consolation. I suspect the range and diversity exists in part because of the range of relationship configurations of nature, self, others, and transcendent that are present in different instances of consolation. Second, all of these aspects of affective experience are perceived as positive, as experiences one might like to have, even the experience of repentant tears. Third, spiritual consolation involves a perceptible change in these positive affective operations. Consolation is an *increase* in joy, a motion *caused*, a call and *attraction* to the divine. The evaluation of the change becomes even more important in the evaluation of the specious consolations of the Second Week. Finally, a single concern unites all of these aspects of affective experience, namely the person of the Creator and Lord. Consolation is clearly Other-oriented, even when it involves "grief for its own sins." Consolation involves the heart being drawn toward Someone in aesthetic and empathetic affectivity. This Other-centeredness gives consolation its character as "spiritual" and even "Christian" consolation.

The affective movements known as spiritual consolation most frequently arise within the process of Christian discernment as the immediate object. Since these movements arise with real tendency they can be recognized for their character and patterns. It is for this reason that Ignatius can present a range of prototypes as listed in his Rules. It is then the "principle" of the affective movement which is the mediate object of discernment. This pattern or trajectory, or tendency, in turn, points to the next mediate object or aim of discernment, that which this particular experience as directed signifies, namely the presence or guidance of God. The subtle characteristics of affective experience are examined by the discerner in comparison with previous experiences of consolation and information on consolation given by the expertise of the Christian tradition (integrating both affective and conceptual skills). This comparative reflection, in turn, helps to identify the semiotic significance of the affective experience for the discerner's grasp of (Understanding and Judgment) and response to (Action) the presence or guidance of God.

It should be clear from the above examples that the possibilities of ways in which the affective system and affective operations are involved in the process of Christian discernment are nearly endless. Affectivity, in all its forms, operations, and expressions, can be present at any point in discernment process and with relationship to subject, objects, or context. For this reason it is impossible to delineate all of the "roles of affectivity in Christian discernment." As systematic presentation of all possible lines of influence is impossible, I have here only indicated a few possible roles of affectivity by means of the examples above. A chart illustrating the permutations of the three related factors of discernment process, aspect of affectivity and affective association is presented in Figure 5. Because of the inherent complexity of the matter, perhaps the best way of grasping the dynamics of the interplay of affectivity and discernment process will be found in the actual practice of Christian discernment. We turn to a couple of examples of this practice in the final chapter.

FIGURE 5:

FACTORS IN THE DISCERNMENT PROCESS

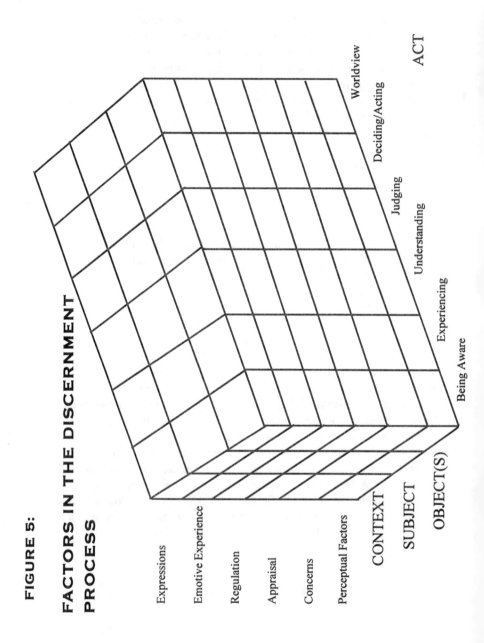

Chapter 6

The Practice of Christian Discernment as an Affectively-Rich Act of Knowing

Having presented a summary account of Christian discernment in light of the present study, I am now prepared to demonstrate the value of a more empirically grounded and philosophically sensitive account of Christian discernment by means of an application of these findings to the actual practice of Christian discernment. Therefore, in this chapter I will make a few applications of the results of the study to two common settings of Christian discernment. The first will be the setting of spiritual direction, in which a spiritual director seeks to assist another in recognizing and following the Spirit of God. The second will be the setting of the pastoral evaluation of charismatic or affectively-rich trends that pass through church communities on occasion. As mentioned in chapter one, I have chosen these settings because of their similarity to the issues of Ignatius' and Edwards' works, and for their relevance for individuals and communities today.

Discernment in Spiritual Direction

The practice of spiritual direction has blossomed over the past two decades. The 1998 membership directory of Spiritual Directors International, an organization founded in 1990, lists 2810 members worldwide. Spiritual direction has also blossomed in terms of the contexts of its practice, making its way out of the preserve of Roman

Catholic religious life to touch people from a wide variety of religious traditions and life-situations. The development of spiritual direction in recent years has forced a reappropriation of the practice in light of new circumstances. The fruits of this are expressed in a number of works on spiritual direction published in the past two decades (Leech 1977; T. Edwards 1980; Carroll and Dyckman 1981; Barry and Connolly 1982; Neufelder and Coelho 1982; Culligan 1983; Nemek and Coombs 1985; Guenther 1992; Houdek 1996). Specialized studies related to particular aspects or contexts of spiritual direction were published contributing to the reappropriation of spiritual direction in contemporary contexts (May 1982; Fischer 1988; Barry 1992; Johnson 1991; Liebert 1992). Part of this reappropriation has been a reexamination of the nature of Christian discernment as understood within the context of spiritual direction.

The ministry of spiritual direction has been described variously in the literature. Margaret Guenther uses the images of hostess, teacher, and midwife to drive her reflections on spiritual direction (Guenther 1992; cf. also Fischer 1988). Kenneth Leech and Tilden Edwards use medical and interpersonal images, reflecting on the traditional notions of the "cure of souls," or the "physician of the wounded soul" and the "soul friend," or "spiritual friend" (Leech 1977; T. Edwards 1980). Barry and Connolly offer one of the better definitions of spiritual direction asserting that:

> We define Christian spiritual direction, then, as help given by one Christian to another which enables that person to pay attention to God's personal communication to him or her, to respond to this personally communicating God, to grow in intimacy with this God, and to live out the consequences of this relationship.

Key elements of this definition include the *help* to another, in terms of the other's *relationship with God*, expressed in *life*. Writings on spiritual direction take great care to distinguish spiritual direction from the practice of counseling/therapy or sacramental ministry (Leech 1977; T. Edwards 1980; Guenther 1992). Whereas therapy is problem-centered and sacramental ministry focuses upon the impartation of the Gospel, spiritual direction centers around ongoing care for another which attends to one's experienced relationship with God or to one's life insofar as it is lived in relationship to God.

Writers on spiritual direction unanimously affirm that discernment is a critical, if not *the* critical, aspect of spiritual direction. Henri Nouwen's definition of spiritual direction, offered in the introduction to Leech's *Soul Friend*, states that, "spiritual direction is direction offered in the prayer life of the individual Christian. It is an art which includes helping to discern the movements of the Holy Spirit in our life, assisting in the difficult task of obedience to these movements, and offering support in the crucial life decisions that our faithfulness requires" (Leech 1977, vi). Likewise, Kathleen Fischer writes in *Women at the Well*, "Discernment is not simply one moment in the spiritual direction process. All of spiritual direction is discernment, since the goal of both is to help us become as closely attuned as possible to God's purposes for us, thereby discovering our own happiness as well" (Fischer 1988, 113). Frank Houdek writes, "Discernment is perhaps the most important aspect of the director and directee relationship" (Houdek 1996, 113). In this regard I recall the phrase given by Elizabeth Liebert at the first lecture of a course on discernment: "at the core of applied spirituality or spiritual formation is spiritual direction and at the core of spiritual direction is discernment."

Though I have never seen it articulated in just this way, it appears to me that there is, within the emphasis on discernment in spiritual direction, a distinction between two interconnected types of discernment. I call it the difference between Discernment and discernment(s). The big Discernment in spiritual direction is the general noticing, evaluating, celebrating, responding with relation to God's presence in the overall life of the directee. It is the finding and following of the path of God in the ongoing life of the directee, the recognition and celebration of the presence of God in all things in the life of the directee, the perseverance through that which is and is not from God *in* God. The small discernment(s) of spiritual direction are the individual evaluations of particular "discernment situations." *This* experience, *this* choice, *this* image of God are explored as to whether or not each in particular is or is not significantly related to God.[1] Particular discernment(s) and the big Discernment inform each other as general path sheds light on the particulars and the particulars accumulate to forge a path. Nevertheless, it can be helpful to keep

---

[1] I will use capitalization henceforth to distinguish between these two types of Christian discernment considered in spiritual direction.

these types of discernment distinct at least in theory for the sake of being clear what it is one is discerning in any given moment in spiritual direction. Therefore directors might want to ask themselves, "how much of this particular situation and how much of general path is under discernment at this point in the director-directee relationship?"

The discerning of spiritual direction is unique insofar as it employs co-discerning process. The directee's knowledge of and response to that which is from God is "the point" of spiritual direction. Yet at the same time, the discerning expertise of the director plays a significant part of "the reason" for spiritual direction. The result is a very delicate relationship between director and directee. Like the good midwife, the good spiritual director may gently offer advice concerning what may be happening but only within the understanding that the directee is the one who must "give birth" in the end. Consequently, in spiritual direction, one must think of a primary subject (the directee) and a secondary subject (the director) of discernment. As affectivity and process merge within the work of each subject in the context of Discernment and discernment(s), the strengths and weaknesses of each will influence the final one process of discernment which flows from the spiritual direction relationship.

The literature on spiritual direction, like literature on discernment already reviewed, appears implicitly to comprehend discernment as an affectively-rich act of knowing. References to Discernment as "attunement" or "alignment" with God imply knowing when one is or is not in tune or aligned (T. Edwards 1980; Barry 1992). Likewise, descriptions of the many particular discernments encountered in spiritual direction portray them as occasions where one endeavors to ascertain whether this calling, this experience, this relationship is of God (Leech 1977; Fischer 1988). The theme of the value of affectivity appears commonly in writings on spiritual direction, often with the aim of correcting a Western overbalance of cognitive process (T. Edwards 1980, 41; Barry 1992). The frequent mention of the values of helping the directee learn to attend to affective experience (Barry and Connolly 1982), of hearing and legitimizing another's affective experience (Fischer 1988), of assisting the directee to name inner experience (Liebert 1989), and of giving the directee a safe environment to express and explore affective experiences (Guenther 1992) give to spiritual direction—and the acts of discernment contained therein—a warmly affective atmosphere.

What can an increasingly empirically grounded and philosophically sensitive account of Christian discernment provide the practice of discernment as found within the world of spiritual direction? That is the question I address here. As the following will indicate, I think the application of empirical and philosophical specificity to discernment as practiced in spiritual direction largely serves to confirm that which good directors intuitively understand. Just as the work of Elizabeth Liebert, by articulating the implications of developmental psychology for the practice of Christian discernment (Liebert 1986, 1992), provided greater specificity to the implicitly held canon among spiritual directors that certain types of prayer and discernment should only be encouraged among those directees who were "ready," so the present study offers greater specificity to spiritual directors' already live interest in paying attention to the horizons of discernment, paying attention to affectivity, and paying attention to the process of discernment itself.

Paying Attention to the Horizons

In my account of human experience in the previous chapter I asserted that human experience arises as a patterned activation of systems and operations within a matrix of relationships. These relationships help to form both the nature of the self in experience and the environment in which and toward which human experience exists. In my general account of Christian discernment, I identified the subject, context, and objects of discernment in terms of these relationships. I identified these as the "horizons" of discernment. In terms of the work of a spiritual director, attention to these horizons means paying attention (1) to *who* is coming to you for help in discernment (subject), (2) to *whence* the Discernment/discernment arises (context), and (3) to *what* is being discerned (objects).

In terms of the subject, the *who* of discernment, the findings of this study would support development of sensitivity to the affective and categorization habits of the directee. While spiritual direction is probably not the place for the completion of a battery of psychological tests on affective history and conceptual patterning, the spiritual director would do well to integrate insights from experimental psychology into to the framework with which the director views the directee (this same suggestion has been made with reference to developmental awareness; cf. Liebert 1986, 1992). Likewise, this would not involve a systematic analysis of every permutation of, for example, the roles of each aspect affectivity in a given discernment situation. Rather the acquisition of some familiarity with the ins and outs of human categorization and affective experience will serve to enable the director to draw attention to features in a directee's discerning process that may deserve notice. I have emphasized the fact that each discerner comes to the discernment situation as given. Personal and cultural history, genetic inheritance, medical conditions, preparation for discernment, all serve to shape the real person who comes to God and to the director for help. I think possibly the fruit of this study is to place in the mind of the director a set of questions which serve to inform the direction process of this person as given, questions which again are not systematically pursued, but inform the director's view of the directee. How does this person categorize her world in general? What is salient for her? Are there prototype experiences of God to which all others are compared (for better or for worse)? Are there disordered affections present in the directee which may significantly affect the discernment process? What concerns or appraisals underlie these? What degree of empathetic connaturality does the directee possess toward the things of faith? What range of concerns might she share with the Gospel? To what significant conversions does she give testimony? Is she capable of noticing key inner experiences? Where has God been active in her life in the past? At what level of subtlety? These and similar questions—again, the possibilities are endless—will shape the perspective of the director informed by a more empirically grounded account of discernment.

Attention to the context of discernment, to the *whence* of discernment, will involve a sensitivity to the surrounding relational configurations from which the person and discernment arises. Does the religious background of this directee emphasize certain ways of determining God's will (for example the use of "fleeces")? Does his cultural background foster or inhibit the recognition of inner experience? What charisms does his church community provide that are especially relevant expressions of God's grace for the directee at this point in time? Might geographic and ecological factors affect this person's discernment (for example, should the director send him to the country for a retreat?; might a relationship with an animal foster his faith at this time?)? Are there patterns of affective appraisal that might strongly influence his discernment of a matter (for example, "if it's wild, it's wrong")? What realistic range of affective options does the directee possess in the midst of this discernment? The attention to context will also be sensitive to the more immediate context of mood and the immediately surrounding affective atmosphere. What kind of mood is being provided to the directee by his own season of life, by his home environment, by key relationships? As a good host(ess), the spiritual director also provides important contributions to the atmosphere of discernment by the manner in which the director conducts the spiritual direction sessions.

Attention to the objects of discernment, to the *what* of discernment, will involve taking a broad perspective concerning the Discernment/discernments of the directee. Objects come in all kinds, as noted above. Issues only become questions of discernment (or focal objects), however, when the question, "is this from God?" is identified for the directee with sufficient energy to activate the operations involved in discernment process. One relevant question at this point is the question of why *this* issue or situation, of all situations, stimulated the question of discernment for the directee. What concerns are in view? In what aspect of the situation does doubt about association with God (giving rise to the question "is this from God?") rest? What does this reveal? Is this a discernment object which is likely to draw the directee into fundamental conversion(s) or is it simply a situation of categorization and action? If the focal object is an experience, it may be helpful for the director to trace the beginning, middle, and end of the experience mentally. Note, if appropriate, the relationship between immediate, mediate, and next mediate objects involved. Take into consideration salient or prototypical aspects of the experience. Might the character and trajectory of the directee's experience be a sign of the activity of God or of another spirit?

Paying Attention to Affectivity

As mentioned above, current spiritual direction literature emphasizes the value of welcoming experience of and reflection upon affectivity within the context of the spiritual direction relationship. The research on psychology and discernment as found in the present study only offers greater specificity to this welcome, drawing attention to the various operations, forms, points of influence, and horizons influenced by affectivity in a given discernment situation. I have discussed the key horizons above and I will discuss the points of influence when I address attention to process. Here I simply note the value of attending to various affective operations in the context of spiritual direction.

Affective experience arises for the most part with the junction of a concern and a person-environment relationship. This junction provides the stimulus that activates the affective system. When important affective experiences arise within the context of a Discernment/discernment (which can happen at any point in discernment process) it may be helpful for the director to reflect upon the concern(s) and the relational configuration which may underlie the rise of affectivity. Of special import is the orientation to Ultimate Concern related to religious affectivity. To what extent is the affective experience driven by attention/attraction to the Supreme Other? To what extent is the directee capable of this? Lack of development in shared concern with God, does not, however, preclude the possibility of spiritual direction and discernment. God seems to be quite gracious about working within the framework of our own self-oriented concerns. Indeed, writings of some masters of Christian spirituality indicate that ultimately the distinctions between self-concern and Ultimate Concern join (Bernard of Clairvaux 1987 [1130?]).

Affective experience also involves an appraisal of the person-environment relationship producing a sense of situational meaning. Factors involved in the appraisal (relevancy, urgency, valence, coping potential, future expectancy, concern relevance, object/subject evaluation, and type of ego involvement) are evaluated as the form and degree of affectivity is established. The process of appraisal itself is a form of discernment, a judgment of feeling sorting the significant from the insignificant. I mentioned in chapter three that breakdowns in the affective system often appear with faulty appraisal (for example, inappropriate evaluations of dangerous due to previous salient experiences of fear). I also mentioned the re-orienting of negative emotions in the context of the Christian faith (cf. Whitehead and Whitehead 1996). If the directee is capable, and it is appropriate, the director can gently cultivate improved appraisal patterns by providing structured environments either within or outside the spiritual direction session to "try on" new ways of appraisal with regard to discernment issues. With regard to a discerning election of life-choice, it might mean taking some time to imagine options with Christ nearby. Other habitual patterns of misappraisal (such as Ignatius' "disordered affections") may be addressed within the bounds of spiritual direction by allowing discussion of disordered affections to become part of the bringing of self to God (Houdek 1996, 62-78) or by assisting the directee through a season of meditation on these disordered affections (cf. Howard 1999, 72-87).

Regulatory operations can also influence the development of discernment. Tendencies toward certain actions might be inhibited by regulatory functions originating from personal or cultural history. The onset of strong experiences (of negative or positive valence) may activate coping mechanisms, which, in turn, transform the impact of the experience. Gerald May identifies a number of these as they relate to spiritual experience in terms of the classic "defense mechanisms" of depth psychology (May 1982, 70-73).

Emotional experience, such as action tendencies, mental preoccupations, physiological changes, enacted roles and the like, are of great importance to discernment. Emotional experience is the most noticeable "stuff" of desolation and consolation. Often this noticeability of emotional experience gives the signals that some spirit is active in the directee's life.

In actual practice the spiritual director will frequently find himself or herself working backwards through components and stages of affective process. In this manner awareness of particular action tendencies, mental preoccupations or other forms of emotional experience (for example, tendencies to shed tears) may lead to reflection concerning the appraisal(s) which gave rise to the experience (perhaps a sense of the beautiful excellence of the Savior - worship). This in turn will lead to reflection on the concern and person-environment relationship which may have given rise to this particular appraisal at this particular time (the Spirit of God may have stimulated an enlightening of the directee's heart through the hearing of a song). By attention to the configuration and movement of relationships leading to the appraisal and the emotional experience, one may be able to pinpoint the source of the action of the Holy Spirit. Through this process of backward reflection—examining the end, the middle, and the beginning—a director and directee may find significant help in recognizing the ways that affectivity influences the process of discern-

ment, and in so doing may more clearly identify that which is significantly related to (or significantly not related to) God.

Paying Attention to the Process

Attention to the horizons and the affective movements in discernment emphasizes the empirical portions of the study and primarily
applies descriptive aspects of an account of discernment. By looking
at the subject, objects and context of a given Discernment/discernment
and by attending to the ways in which affectivity might be present the
director learns what may be expected in the discernment as actually
practiced by the discerner. Attention to the process, however, moves
more directly toward application of normative aspects of an account of
discernment. By seeing horizon and affectivity as part of a process is
to discover what can be encouraged in discernment: what to notice,
what to introduce, what to reinforce, when to wait, when to act.

Attention to process involves two foci. The first is more descriptive. It is the watching of how things are going, following the relationships, stages and systems of human experience as they develop in
light of the discernment situation. The second involves the application of the epistemological framework presented above, attending to
the grounds of truth insofar as they may be realized in this situation.
The aim of the spiritual director in this regard is to foster, whenever
and however appropriate, the discernment process most likely to yield
adequate access to the confident knowledge that something is or is not
significantly related to God. I will illustrate this by reference to the
grounds of discernment achieving its expressed aim as outlined in
chapter four.

First, discernment is grounded in the self-communication of God
through Christ and the Holy Spirit. The possibility of discerning that
which is significantly related to God assumes that God can be significantly related to human experience in such a way that this relationship can be recognized. Indeed, this ground of discernment implies
not only the discernability of God but also the possibility of God's
activity within the midst of the discernment process. While introducing an unavoidable element of circularity into the epistemology of discernment theory, the dependence upon the grace of God even within
the act of identifying whether something is or is not of God is
emphasized by many writers on discernment. Gelpi calls this depend-

ence "docility" to the Breath of God within the process of discernment. The application of the self-communication of God through Christ and the Holy Spirit in the context of spiritual direction appears as directors bring their directee's *to* Christ and the Holy Spirit. This involves teaching them to assume and live under a core belief in God's active presence and self-communication (Guenther 1992; Willard 1998). Involved in this is the act, whenever and wherever appropriate, of pointing out the diverse vehicles through which God's self-communication is perceived and especially of empowering use of those vehicles which might have special significance for the directee (explored in terms of personality type in Michael and Norrisey 1984 and Thomas 1996). It also involves bringing them to Christ, encouraging time with God such that God can communicate within and into the directee's discernment situation. To modify a colloquial saying, you can't make a horse drink, but you sure can bring it to water.

Second, discernment is grounded in the nature of human experience and knowing. Discernment, with all its foibles and potentials is rooted in ordinary human experience. The fact that experience arises as evaluable makes experience discernible in the sense that we can notice the quality of experience. That experience arises as confronting us, as *there*, makes possible the perceived objects of discernment as facts or actions of experience. Yet the arising of experience with real tendency is what makes experience discernible in the sense of identifying the something as actually the case, something which has been before and can be observed again. The tendencies of our feelings and thoughts and the autonomy which we take over them (or choose not to take over them), our Awareness, Experiencing, Understanding and so on, our relationships with nature, ourselves, others, and the transcendent, all arise with real tendency, offering the means by which access to reality can be obtained. The value of a firm grasp of the triadic nature of experience as Evaluation, Act, and Tendency brings to spiritual directors a belief in an authentic, yet fallible realism. The firm possession of this belief is passed on to the directee in terms of both a confidence that discernment can reach its aim—God can be found—and in a sincere acceptance of the partiality of the very achievement of that aim.

Practically speaking, the systems, stages, and relationships of human experience will probably receive the most attention by spiritual directors in discernment. Operations may be missing from a discernment process, (for example those who consider attention to affectivity as being too "subjective"); application of operations within distinct stages of discernment may be dysfunctional (for example, a directee, unaware of the possibility of passive "dark nights" may Understand a dryness in prayer to be simply a sign of sinfulness in her life), and in such cases the reliability of discernment is lessened thereby. Likewise, the oversalience of some event (for example the characteristics of a significant growth experience years ago) may lead to limited prototypes for discerning evaluation. False criteria at the stage of Judging (for example the belief that God's call must be confirmed by miraculous signs) or hardening of motive at the stage of Acting (an unwillingness to follow God's call) can also short-circuit the reliability of the discernment process. Problems within patterns of relationships with nature (like medical conditions), self (as with strong negative self-image), others (for example, a dysfunctional situation at work), or the transcendent (as in the case of oppression by an evil spirit) will have the potential of seriously affecting a discernment and may need to be addressed by a spiritual director when appropriate. Attending to the process of discernment, however, does not simply mean the correction of difficulties. Noticing patterns, correcting errors, introducing tendencies, reinforcing aspects of the discernment, and just simply waiting are all involved in attending to the process of discernment in the context of spiritual direction.

Third, discernment is grounded in the dynamics of integrated conversion. While spiritual directors cannot provide the grace needed for the transformations of religious conversion and its impact upon the other forms of conversion, they can draw attention to this activity when it is noticeable and relevant. Spiritual directors can also provide a gentle nudge toward conversion when they see that directees are ready, as a means of placing them in the space where God can accomplish the work of grace. Furthermore, spiritual directors can foster the taking of responsibility involved in the forms of secular conversion. Lack of conversion can cause serious gaps in the discernment process (for example when lack of socio-political conversion brings with it the assumption that "what the Father is doing" involves only evangelistic concerns, consequently limiting options for discernment of vocation). At times, directors must simply accept the fallibility of each discernment subject and the partiality of each discernment process, aware of the dangers which attend a directee's shallow discernment. At other times spiritual directors may have opportunity to provide the right word at the right moment, stimulating ongoing conversion in the directee's life.

Fourth, discernment is rooted in the presence of tendencies *as* tendencies. The ability to differentiate tendencies as tendencies makes discernment possible. The fact that one can, in discernment, recognize in contemporary experience some qualities that can be identified as *God*, indicates that there is some measure of continuity, some real tendency in God that can be noticed, understood, and accepted as tendency to be a certain way. This is the condition for the possibility of discernment criteria. Criteria identify what particular tendencies to keep in view. The discerning subject or spiritual director serves as a lookout, attending to "what is there" in the directee's experience but also attending to it with an informed understanding of what to be looking *for*. This is the realm of the mediate object which identifies pattern, character, presentation, trajectory and the like as they serve as signs of God's presence. The patterns which are watched for are often linked to their signification in the writings on discernment by means of the enumeration of a set of criteria the fulfillment of which indicates relationship to God (or significant non-relationship to God).

This relationship between tendency and criteria can be illustrated by reference to a few specific sets of criteria. Jon Sobrino, in his *Christology at the Crossroads* states, "the disciple living today . . . does possess one ultimate criterion for correct discernment: i.e. Jesus himself (1978, 129). The affirmation of Jesus as the ultimate criterion is common to discernment literature and Sobrino develops his understanding of this affirmation in an article published the following year entitled "Following Jesus as Discernment" (1979). He identifies discernment as "the particular quest for the will of God, not only to understand it but also to carry it out" (Sobrino 1979, 14). The type of discernment in view here is, therefore, the elective discernment of alternative actions. Sobrino encourages the reader to consider how Jesus himself discerned in view of his understanding of the Father as a "prototype" of the structure of every Christian discernment. Sobrino suggests four criteria that arise from reflection on Jesus' own discernment: (1) partial incarnation in history - choosing a particular spot in history, with the poor and oppressed, from which to act, (2) effective praxis of love - seeking not only to announce good

news but to bring it about, (3) praxis of socio-political love - a love
that applies to all segments of society, a love that becomes justice, (4)
openness to a conflictive love - which in standing *for* must also stand
against. The important thing to note about Sobrino's criteria here is
the structure of his argument. He is suggesting that Jesus' activity
can serve as a "prototype," comparison to which helps to identify
actions which are "God's will." Discernments of actions which
exhibit concern for or flow from partial incarnation in history, effective praxis of love and so on can be reasonably judged as discernments which have identified the will of God. Conversely discernments which ignore these criteria are not basing their discernment on
important tendencies of God.

Barry and Connolly, in their *Practice of Spiritual Direction*, offer
a loose list of "criteria for evaluating religious experience" (1982,
101-118). This list includes (1) comparison with other experience,
(2) quality of the dialogue with God, (3) peace, (4) fruit, (5) developing sense of the reality of God as someone who is not directly within
the directee's control, (6) "Is it like God?". In each case a tendency
associated with God is acknowledged and used as the basis of evaluating the experience of the directee. By comparing current experience
with a touchstone experience of the divine (assuming God's tendencies at are consistent), one can at times notice significant similarities
or difference that provide clues to the source of the current experience. While this criteria can sometimes lead one astray, for God can
change ways of acting toward someone, certain aspects of the experience which may be characteristic of God may be able to be identified
in two very different experiences. Thus one simply recognizes (or
fails to recognize) the God so clearly communicated in an earlier
experience. The sense of peace, so frequently mentioned in discernment literature, flows from our understanding of the way God works,
God's tendencies. Even though God may speak through a frightful or
painfully revealing experience, if the directee is someone moving
from good to better it is likely that God's self-communication will be
attended by a deep sense of peace, even when accompanied with other
negative emotions. The criterion about a developing sense of God as
not within the control of the directee simply acknowledges the character of God (tendency) as sovereign. Experience which comes from
God leads one to acknowledge God's sovereignty. Finally, the ques-

tion, "is it like God?" boldly affirms an entire range of tendencies as part of God's ways. Thus Barry and Connolly write,

The Fathers of the Church describe Christians as imitators of God. They would bear other people's burdens and not use any power and wealth they might have to make other people serve them—not because such behavior conflicts with rational morality, but because it is not the way God acts" (1982, 113).

Michael Sheeran explores the dynamics of the corporate discernment of congregational decisions within Friends (or Quaker) communities in his *Beyond Majority Rule* (1983). In this book, he outlines a set of criteria drawn from the early history of the Society of Friends which served to indicate to a traditional meeting that a leading of the Spirit (or sense of the Holy Spirit concerning a matter) was indeed from God. This list includes such criteria as (1) the place of the cross, (2) the Scripture, (3) the submission of openings, (4) the fruits of the Holy Spirit, and (5) silent, unadorned speech. These criteria served to wean out leadings which were self-serving (hence the criteria of the cross, of the submission of openings and of unadorned speech), and indicated tendencies which were characteristic of God. Harmony with the Scriptures is frequently named as an important criterion in discernment literature, for the scriptures reveal in writing something of the way God is and acts, such that contemporary leadings, choices, or experiences can be compared accordingly. The fruits of the Spirit are also commonly listed as criteria. They indicate the tendencies of human experience to be expected when led by the Spirit.

One might also conjecture a set of criteria provided by various forms of conversion. Thus inquiry concerning affective conversion might lead one to ask questions of a psychological, emotional, and aesthetic nature concerning the person or group doing discernment. Regard for intellectual conversion might lead one to ask questions about the adequacy of frames of reference from which a discernment is made. Sensitivity to moral conversion might lead one to explore whether judgments, deliberations, decisions are being made in the context of the rights and duties of others or with a view to the common good. Interest in religious conversion might lead spiritual directors to examine whether discernment is being made with explicit reference to the historically revealed God, or in view of the ideals of the kingdom of God, or within the context of the living community of God. Sensitivity to socio-political conversion might explore discernment in terms of its impact upon (or ignorance of) institutional realities. Likewise sensitivity to ecological conversion would explore the same in terms of our relationship with nature.

No list of criteria is failsafe. Both Barry and Connolly and Sheeran note the weaknesses of their own criteria listed. A necessary and sufficient definition of "from God" cannot be found, and the experts on discernment are well aware that one must access some loose kind of family resemblance theory of categorization when dealing with discernment. The criteria are helpful indicators of constant and recognizable tendencies. Nevertheless, each case is unique. Good spiritual directors, informed by philosophical sophistication, will be attentive to the process of discernment by paying careful attention to the criteria being used by directees. Both situation appropriate criteria (like the comparison of experience, if the focal object is an experience) and process appropriate criteria (like the sense of peace) must be wisely applied to increase the likelihood of discernment achieving its aim.

Discernment is ultimately grounded in the character of God and the development of the Church. I have mentioned something of the character and tendencies of God. These tendencies, however, can only be perceived in interaction with human experience. As the tendencies of God and the experience of God's people develop, directees gain and communicate an accumulation of knowledge and experience of God. This is the expertise of discernment wisdom, a wisdom which is never final, but always growing in light of new situations (cf. Fischer 1988, 113-132). This developing discernment wisdom does, however, give some sense of the growing awareness of the tendencies of God, tendencies which can be noticed and understood in the lives of directees today. Good spiritual direction, therefore, will seek to be informed by and thus to participate in the accumulated wisdom of discernment literature. In this manner the infinite tendency of the divine, in interaction with the expanding evaluative response of the converting world may forge an ever-increasing knowledge of how and where one might recognize that which is significantly related to God. Spiritual directors would do well to join with this movement.

I have shown how a more empirically and philosophically sensitive model of discernment can be applied in the world of spiritual direction. It is applied by encouraging directors to pay attention, to notice, introduce, correct, and to wait in light of the realities of what is going on. By paying attention to the horizons of discernment, to the dynamics of affectivity, and to the process of discernment, informed by the insights of experimental psychology and North American philosophy, spiritual directors can better lead their directees toward Discernment/discernments which achieve their aim: the identification and knowledge of that which is significantly related to God.

Revival or Enthusiasm: Discerning Affective Trends in the Church

The second setting of the practice of Christian discernment within which I will apply the model of discernment presented is the setting of the pastoral evaluation of affective trends within the Church. Since the earliest centuries of the Church, Christians have recounted powerful emotional experiences of God arising from the dynamics of corporate encounters with God. Revivals, awakenings, movements and trends have swept through the Church and have stimulated the transformation of individuals and congregations. Indeed, the charismatic movements of the twentieth century have grown large enough to be considered by some to be a third force in Western Christianity alongside Protestantism and Roman Catholicism. Large movements such as the Jesus People movement or the charismatic renewal (Riss 1988), and smaller developments such as Promise Keepers events or Cursillo groups have had significant impact on the affective aspects of the faith of those touched by their fire. Affectivity notwithstanding, group experience of God, like human experience in general, is multidimensional. Sociological factors, psychological factors, natural factors, and spiritual factors all contribute to the phenomena of revitalization movements (cf. McGloughlin 1978; Albrecht 1989).

Revitalization movements and other affectively-laden trends or religious expressions can stimulate some of the finest expressions of heart-felt love for God. At other times they can become the vehicles of unbridled emotionalism—or worse. Because of the potential for good or ill, and because of the powerful influence these movements periodically carry with them, Christians, and particularly church leaders, are occasionally called upon to discern the character of a particular expression. Recommendations or warnings must be issued if needed. Pastoral care must be given both to those who are receiving from this trend as well as those who are not. The intensity of the experiences and the momentum of the trend may touch people at very deep levels of concerns, both those who receive and those who don't. Consequently people affected by affective trends—and even bystanders—may find a great deal of emotional energy associated with the movement itself, feeling either deeply touched and a deep sense of loyalty to this expression and things associated with it, or deeply offended by things that happen therein, or deeply threatened by the same. Thus both the passionate call for discernment from all sides—for there are always sides taken—as well as the real need for discernment are especially strong in times of affective trends.

Though every situation is unique and each trend brings its own complexities, the sides taken in the context of affectively-laden movements and expressions can be loosely associated with the labels given the two camps that formed in the context of the Great Awakening in America: New Lights supporting the pursuit and expression of affectivity in the context of these trends, and Old Lights critical of these trends. New Light sentiment has been expressed in Protestantism in the writings of Jonathan Edwards as well as in the works of John Wesley (e.g. 1984 6:304-313 and Vols. 1-4), Charles Finney (1979), Richard Lovelace (1979), John White (1988), D. Martyn Lloyd Jones (1987), and William DeArteaga (1996). Classic Old Light statements include Charles Chauncy's *Seasonable Thoughts* (1743), Jessie Penn-Lewis' *War On the Saints* (1991 [1912]), and Ronald Knox's *Enthusiasm* (1994). Moderate expressions appear in all varieties, as seen for example, in Jonathan Edwards' moderate New Light position with regard to the Great Awakening. The general question parties on all sides claim to be addressing is the question of discernment: Is this trend significantly related to God (or significantly not related to God)?

In the present study I will examine the pastoral discernment of affective trends by means of a case study. I will apply the insights of the study thus far gained to the discernment of a single affective trend known as the "Toronto Blessing," mentioned in chapter one. Since its onset in 1994, the Toronto Blessing has touched millions of people. It has been reported in many major newspapers and magazines. I have personally witnessed the effects of this movement while on pastoral staff at a local congregation, and therefore can speak of this movement from personal experience and from interviews collected both at the time and thereafter. After reviewing the history of the Toronto Blessing I will offer reflections on the practice and malpractice of discernment of affective trends as it pertains to the current study in the context of the Toronto Blessing.

The History of the Toronto Blessing

Though the movement known as the "Toronto Blessing" was preceded by a variety of different influences, and indeed can be understood as a fire started from sparks taken from some of these influences, it was in Toronto's Airport Vineyard Church on January 20th, 1994 that the "Toronto Blessing" started. Randy Clark, pastor of the St. Louis Vineyard church was invited by John and Carol Arnott of the Airport Vineyard to visit and lead a series of healing and renewal meetings. Clark and the Arnotts had recently received powerful fillings of the Holy Spirit after a season of spiritual dryness. The meetings surpassed the expectations of the sponsors and they decided to extend the renewal to nightly meetings. The nightly meetings have continued up to the present. Christian leaders from all over the globe and from virtually every Christian denomination have come to Toronto, experienced some powerful encounter, and have returned to their home to "spark" similar phenomena elsewhere (Riss 1995).

The Toronto Blessing has received a good deal of press attention in part because of the kinds of emotional/physiological phenomena associated with it. *National and International Religion Report*, July 11, 1994 stated that "Consistent reports describe a state similar to drunkenness, including shaking with laughter, crying, slipping into a trance, and falling to the floor. Repentance, warm feelings of love and peace, the 'return of the prodigals,' and a number of salvations also have been reported" (*National and International Religion Report* 1994, 1). The preponderance of experiences of laughter has given the Toronto Blessing the label "the laughing revival" (Doucet 1994; Ostling 1994). These emotional-physical phenomena have also stimulated many controversies surrounding the Toronto Blessing. As with revitalization movements in the past, sides have been taken concerning the discernment of the Toronto Blessing. As I mentioned in chapter one, a variety of evaluations of the movement have been published. Some consider the movement a great work of God (Chevreau

1994; Arnott 1995; DeArteaga 1996). Others consider it a mixed blessing, containing both wonderful aspects but also dangerous and harmful aspects as well (Beverley 1995; The Theological Commission of the Charismatic Renewal in the Catholic Church of Germany 1996). Others are more critical of the movement, denying its legitimacy as an authentic revival, seriously concerned with behaviors characteristic of the movement, and/or are convinced that the movement is a delusion originating from evil spirits rather than from God (Smith 1994; Hanegraaff 1997). Each of these evaluations claims to be rooted in good principles of discernment (many of them offering commentary on Edwards' own principles). My purpose in the present study is to use the Toronto Blessing and its interpretations along with the insights of the present study to offer reflections on how we discern affective trends.

Preliminary Considerations in Discernment

A few reflections appear even as one begins to consider the discernment of an affective trend such as the Toronto Blessing. These reflections relate to questions addressed in discernment literature under the heading "preliminary considerations." The first of these is the need for the clarification of the discernment question. I noted above that a situation becomes a discernment situation at the point when the question, "is this of God" becomes clear to the discerner with sufficient energy to move experience on to inquiry and resolution. However, just what we mean by a question such as "is the Toronto Blessing of God?" depends upon the focal object of the question as well as the context within which or the audience for whom the question is intended. I think some confusion of writing and pastoral care has arisen in part because of the lack of clarity of this issue. First we must ask, when we seek to evaluate the "Toronto Blessing," precisely what are we looking at? What is the phenomena, the range of relational configurations around which our discernment will focus? Beverley (1995), for example, limited his analysis to events observed in Toronto itself. The significance of the Toronto Blessing as a *movement*, however, is not found in the events of the Airport Vineyard; rather it is found in thousands of congregations and small group meetings throughout the globe. For example, much ado has been made about the phenomena of animal sounds expressed at the meetings. In the Vineyard Christian Fellowship of San Francisco, however, where for months the church held nightly meetings attended by hundreds of people, this particular phenomena was almost non-existent throughout the duration of San Francisco's season of impact by Toronto (this was the case for a number of congregations outside Toronto). As The Theological Commission of the Charismatic Renewal in the Catholic Church of Germany, wisely states, "It is therefore necessary to avoid speaking of the "Toronto Blessing" as a single entity; indeed one must discriminate carefully between its various dimensions and expressions. Some similar events in communities and groups are even independent of 'Toronto' or stand in a very loose connection with 'Toronto'" (1996, 27). Hanegraaff's association of Toronto, the Vineyard Association, the prophetic movement, and the Word of Faith movement was much too facile, failing to recognize the significant differences between expressions and communities surrounding the Toronto Blessing (1997). For example, Hanegraaff published his book-length critique of the Toronto Blessing *after* the formal disassociation of Toronto from the Association of Vineyard Churches without his mentioning the circumstances surrounding that break, circumstances which clearly reveal nuances which must be considered in an evaluation of this type. The specification of the focal object under consideration is critical to insure a reasonable discernment of whether *this* is of God. Furthermore, clarification of the discernment question also entails clarity concerning what we mean by "of God." For example, the very identification that this trend or movement is indeed "of God" may not confirm that it should be called "revival." Thus John Wimber, founder of the Vineyard movement wrote of Toronto that "what many people in our churches are experiencing is *not* revival. But it is the only thing that becomes revival" (Wimber 1994).

One must also keep the context or intended audience and purpose in mind when the discernment question is being made. When we ask "is the Toronto Blessing of God?" whose interests are in view? Is the question posed by leadership of congregations as a means of evaluating the movement *in general* with respect to general expressions of recommendation or concern (much as Edwards' inquiry concerning the character of a "work of God" in general in *Distinguishing Marks*)? If so then the discernment process must be conducted with the broadest possible considerations in mind. Is the question asked in light of giving recommendations of participation of specified kinds to some particular individuals or congregations? Then the discernment process must be conducted in light of these aims, and the question for the participant must be a question of elective personal action rather than blanket evaluation of a movement. The church leader is, in this case, providing wise advice to individuals or a community of discerners who then must ask for themselves in light of your advice, "Lord, would you be pleased with my participation in this certain expression or dimension of the Toronto Blessing?" The same is true for those who are not simply considering participation in the movement in general (for example, attending meetings) but also for those who are considering exploring particular experiences of God (such as falling, laughing, and the like). As with all emotions, human volition plays a part in the regulation of tendencies to different emotional experiences. At times, we give ourselves "permission" to feel certain things. Questions of "do I permit/cultivate this particular experience?" or "how do I respond to this experience I had last night?" will involve the question of whether the Toronto Blessing is of God, but they must do so with particular sensitivity to the audience and intention of the question. It is unwise to draw, from the assumption that the Toronto Blessing is (or is not) from God in general, the simple conclusion that all should seek to pursue (or to avoid) all that flows therefrom. Though the questions are mutually involved, I suggest that the discernment of the relationship of the movement to God in general should be distinguished from questions of individual participation or response.

A second question of preliminary consideration is the question of who should discern. To some extent this follows from the specification of the question. Who is asking the question and for whom? Is this a question of formal leadership making policy for a body of believers? Then appropriate authority should be involved in the discernment process. Is it a matter of general recommendation to a group of people? Then respect must be given to the primary role of the elective discernment of individuals in light of leadership wisdom. Leadership should not even subtly connect valuations of spiritual health to an individual's association with affective trends in cases of general advice. Is this a matter of personal spiritual direction regarding the pursuit or response to God's work in an individual? Then the issue concerns the ordinary co-discernment of a spiritual direction relationship. The collecting of discerners with regard to affective trends should pay careful attention to the insights outlined above concerning the value of an expanded and integrally converted community. This aspect was demonstrated to me in the literature reviewed by the nuanced and clear approach to discernment found in the paper by The Theological Commission of the Charismatic Renewal in the Catholic Church of Germany as compared with some of the other books written by individuals. As mentioned above, affective trends have a tendency of touching us at core concerns, accentuating the biases of those who evaluate these trends. Hence one finds even more reason for careful discernment being accomplished by teams of believers drawn from different perspectives, experiences, personalities, and charisms.

A final question with regard to preliminary considerations is the issue of the preparation of the discerners. The serious need for intense, deep, and prayerful preparation of discerners in the context of the evaluation of affective trends should be obvious in light of what has been said. I think that the reaching of "indifference" among those who discern affective trends is especially difficult. Because of this, there is all the more reason to insist upon a thorough preparation of those involved in this type of discernment. We must openly admit our prejudices, our lack of conversion, our biases, our power issues which might contribute to a faulty discernment of a movement like the Toronto Blessing and allow Christ to cleanse these "disordered affections" as much as possible through the process of prayerful preparation for discernment and through the co-operation of the people who discern. The cultivation of connaturality is a complicated issue in the case of affective trends. Advocates on either side of the Toronto Blessing have passionately argued their position under the banner of Christ's kingdom. Indeed it is the identification of the particular cause with core Christian values that gives such energy to each side. In this sense I would applaud the published evaluations of the Toronto Blessing on their fervent concern for the things of God. Perhaps I might only encourage humility and greater care in the association of particular evaluations with these kingdom concerns. With regard to the preparation of the mind, I suggest discerners, in order to discern correctly at the "information gathering" stage of discernment, should gather a variety of different types of information. Insider and outsider information must be integrated as a whole. I find many evaluations of the movement to over-rely on testimonies from one perspective. Beverley's "Snapshots of the Toronto Blessing" (1995, 16-22) provided a valuable composite picture of the phenomena. Again, my recommendation is to avoid journalistic or "talk show" attack or defense of affective trends, which often serves to exacerbate bias without appropriate information or preparation, but rather to encourage the collaborative discernment of fellow leaders concerning a matter of significant import to the Christian community. From this context, a wide variety of information from a wide variety of people and perspectives can be integrated into a mature discerning process. Or perhaps I should say that the process might be enabled to take place under the leadership of mature discerning people.

The Criteria of Discernment

In terms of issues related to the process of discernment itself, I will address one point of great importance and which draws from the material presented in chapter two. This is the question of criteria or "signs" of a work of God. I have mentioned above that criteria identify the real tendencies of the character or work of God which can be recognized with consistency in human experience. The God who inspired the Scriptures will tend to act in harmony with their principles. The Spirit of Christ will exalt Christ in the Church. Evaluators of the Toronto Blessing from all sides appeal to specific criteria to defend their position. What is more, nearly all appeal to the works and criteria of Jonathan Edwards to defend their different positions. Selective use and misapplication of Edwards' works, and misunderstanding of Edwards' context and the contexts of the Toronto Blessing, have resulted in a Jonathan Edwards quoting match that leaves Beverley crying out, "Where Is Jonathan Edwards When You Need Him?" (1995, 76). My aim here is to offer a few comments on the use of Edwards in three books on the Toronto Blessing (Hanegraaff 1997, Chevreau 1994; Beverley 1995) as a means of exploring the designation of situation-appropriate and process-appropriate criteria for discerning the presence of God in affective trends.

Guy Chevreau had both pastoral background and a Th.D. in historical theology from Wycliffe College, Toronto School of Theology, when he found himself attending the January 1994 meetings of the Airport Vineyard. In time Chevreau found himself on the floor weeping,

"Wailing, if the truth be told, for something like forty minutes. While there were no conscious, cognitive pictures, or images, memories or impressions, a long-standing bitterness and resentment was lifted in the process. That, and a sense that I had been released a little further into a new sense of God's sovereign authority and providential care over my life" (Chevreau 1994, 15).

Guy Chevreau became a regular receiver of the Toronto Blessing from that point on. His experience led him back to a review of church history, which, in turn, led him to the writings of Jonathan Edwards. Chevreau spends a good third of his book, the first published book-length defense of the Toronto Blessing, commenting on the works and context of Jonathan Edwards (1994, 70-144). He quotes at length from the works of Edwards and from Sarah Edwards' journals recorded in Sereno Dwight's "memoirs of Jonathan Edwards." Again and again, Chevreau draws attention to the fact that phenomena such as people were experiencing in the context of the Toronto Blessing are not uncommon, but were rather received and approved by none other than the founder of American evangelicalism himself. He weaves reflections on the experience at Toronto into his quotations from Edwards with phrases like, "As is stressed repeatedly at the Airport Vineyard, Edwards recognizes that God's work is unique in each individual, 'in the degrees both of awakening and conviction, and also of saving light, love and joy, that many have experienced . . . Some having been seized suddenly, others awakened gradually'" (1994, 92).

Chevreau correctly applies Edwards' criteria of less-certain signs found in *Distinguishing Marks* to the phenomena at Toronto. "Both Edwards and the pastors at the Airport do not take exception to the manifestations;" writes Chevreau, "what they are saying is 'Draw no conclusions, based *only* on the manifestations, either way, pro or con'" (1994, 102). He reviews four of Edwards more certain signs from *Distinguishing Marks* but makes no application to the circumstances at Toronto. He documents the debates between Edwards and Chauncy which led to the publication of Edwards' *Some Thoughts Concerning the Present Revival.* Comparing Edwards' concern to approve revival phenomena while desiring errors be corrected with the policy of the Airport Vineyard, Chevreau writes that, "Very much aware of the truth of Edwards' insights here, the pastors at the Airport

Vineyard continue to try to manage 'wild fire' as it breaks out. While welcoming the Spirit's transformative work, the more exuberant manifestations are neither highlighted nor trophied; rather the question is asked repeatedly: 'Tell us more about your relationship with Jesus'" (1994, 117). He reviews a few of Edwards' critiques of the Awakening and problems associated with the friends of the revival from *Some Thoughts*, faithfully interpreting Edwards' thoughts on censuring, spiritual pride, and extremism. It does not enter Chevreau's mind (or at least, his book) at this point to consider whether at times the friends of the Toronto Blessing may be guilty of the same sins as the friends of the Great Awakening. He notes correctly that through the end of his writings Edwards was unashamed of the manifestations appearing in the revival meetings.

What I found disconcerting in my reading of Chevreau, however, was his near neglect of *Religious Affections*, which was published by Edwards to address difficulties related to the friends of the revival, difficulties Edwards felt so concerned about that he felt they had the potential to short-circuit the power and longevity of the move of the Spirit. Missing the important context, in *Religious Affections*, of the discernment of *saving* works of God (or transforming works, as opposed to the merely common works), and of *that* connection, in turn, with profession of faith and Edwards' baptismal stance (discussed in chapter two of the present study), Chevreau fails to see the possible applications of *Religious Affections* to Toronto. He reviews Edwards' emphases on the value of affections, giving only two pages to Edwards' "more certain signs" and making no application to the events of the Toronto Blessing.

Here is my point. I think Chevreau may be correct in his claim that Edwards' would not be concerned with the presence of unusual manifestations in the context of revival meetings. Unfortunately, however, proof that one need not be concerned with the phenomena does not give sufficient evidence of whether the Toronto Blessing ought to be regarded as a work of God, nor does it guide the leadership concerning the care of people experiencing manifestations in the context of that movement. To argue whether or not the work was a work of God, Chevreau would have had to apply the "more certain signs" found in *Distinguishing Marks* to the Toronto Blessing, something he probably assumed but failed to explicitly document (documentation Edwards was careful to provide in his works). Furthermore, even if he were to demonstrate that the Toronto Blessing was a work of God in general, this does not mean that everything experienced within that movement is to be regarded as "transformative" (Chevreau 1994, 117). I have seen many people get "blasted" by the Spirit in a time of renewal prayer only to get so caught up in the repeated experience of God's *invitation*—overjoyed to be a part of the Spirit's work—that he or she loses track of attending to the transforming *response* that the invitation-experience may be leading the person into. The warning of *Religious Affections* is this: just because you might experience something powerful (even "from God") in the context of a genuine move of God, don't think that you or others are necessarily transformed (the "Brown" case is, to me, a clear case of a powerful divine invitation with no transformation; cf. Beverley 1995, 96-97; Hanegraaff 85-86). Failing to heed Edwards' warnings, Chevreau leaves his readers assuming that because the Toronto Blessing is a work of God, they can just lie back (or fall back) and trust themselves to be transformed by the Spirit. Indeed, this is often precisely what happens. Nonetheless, to cultivate Christian experience without moving to the next steps of personal discernment and response is to leave the believer nowhere to go. It can result in spiritual elitism, factions, and the degeneration of the very revival the leaders intend to promote.

Hank Hanegraaff, the nationally syndicated radio "Bible Answer Man" and president of Christian Research Institute, found himself growing increasingly concerned with reports of a revival in Toronto that bore great similarity to non-Christian cults. Hanegraaff distributed a cassette tape more clearly articulating the concerns already popularized through commentary on his radio program (Hanegraaff 1995). The cassette message mentions Edwards but does not develop his thought. Two years later Hanegraaff published a book further arguing his case. Hanegraaff's book, *Counterfeit Revival*, begins with the query, "What can Heaven's Gate, Waco, and Jonestown have in common with a church near you?" (1997, inside cover). In this book, he greatly expands his treatment of Edwards, giving it a central section of the book identifying the "Lying Signs and Wonders" of the Counterfeit Revival. His concern at this point is the use of Edwards to support the phenomena of the Toronto Blessing by the movement's promoters. To quote Hanegraaff, "The most disturbing deception of all is that the leaders of the Counterfeit Revival have co-opted one of the church's true spiritual giants and dishonestly claimed him for their own" (1997, 82). With this concern in mind, Hanegraaff moves to apply Edwards' principles to the Counterfeit Revival.

He divides his treatment of Edwards into two chapters. The first, titled "A Great Apostasy," applies Edwards' "less certain signs" of a work of the Spirit found in *Distinguishing Marks* to the Counterfeit Revival. In the following chapter, "A Great Awakening," he applies the five more certain signs of the same work. What is striking about Hanegraaff's presentation of Edwards' material, in particular his application of the "less certain signs," is that he applies these signs, which give no proof whether a movement be of the Spirit or not, to show evidence that indeed the Toronto Blessing is a counterfeit revival. That is to say that while he acknowledges the intent of Edwards' signs in principle (1997, 83), in practice Hanegraaff applies Edwards' signs precisely opposite of the manner in which Edwards intended. For example, whereas Edwards goes to great lengths to argue that the fact that a movement gives rise to very extraordinary phenomena can *not* be used as evidence that the movement is *not* of God, Hanegraaff spends his entire discussion of this sign presenting (perhaps "ridiculing" might be more accurate) cases demonstrating the extraordinary nature of the phenomena associated with events at Toronto. Rather than confirming Edwards' contention that extraordinary phenomena are not legitimate evidence that a work is not of the Spirit (Edwards' emphasis in *Distinguishing Marks* is clearly on this side, as discussed in chapter two), Hanegraaff suggests, quoting Dr. Nick Needham, that perhaps there is "something sinister" about the phenomena at Toronto (1997, 83-87). In a similar manner in his discussion of Edwards' second sign, that "a work is not to be judged of by any effects on the bodies of men," Hanegraaff devotes his discussion to a comparison of the bodily effects of *true* revival (which bodily effects he selectively recounts from Edwards' works), with those found in the "Counterfeit Revival" at Toronto (1997, 87-88). Once again, Hanegraaff has missed Edwards' point entirely, namely that discernment of a work of God *cannot* be judged true or false by means of bodily effects. Likewise in his discussion of Edwards' fifth sign, that "'Tis no sign that a work that appears and is wrought on the minds of people, is not from the Spirit of God, that example is made use of as a great means of it" Hanegraaff spends his discussion of this point portraying the silliness of the use of examples like Benny Hinn and John Wimber found in the Toronto Blessing (1997, 93-94). Edwards' point was that real human examples, no matter how silly, do not demonstrate that a work is not of God. Hanegraaff attempts to apply Edwards' sign to show evidence that the Toronto Blessing is clearly *not* a work of God. Hanegraaff consistently applies Edwards in this manner throughout every one of the nine signs given by Edwards to show criteria which *ought not* to be used to argue that a work *is not* a work of the Spirit. He has missed Edwards' point entirely. Furthermore, when Hanegraaff moves to the discussion of the more certain signs of a work of the Spirit, he resorts to selective quotation and characterization to accuse the leaders of the Toronto Blessing of diminished Christology, disrespect for the Scriptures, doctrinal error, and egocentric love, as Beverley notes (Hanegraaff 1997, 103-116; cf. Beverley 1995). Once again, rather than fairly evaluating the Toronto Blessing based upon the general tendencies which ought to be expected of a work of God in general, Edwards remains misunderstood and the reader is not led into careful and prayerful discernment based on appropriate use of appropriate criteria.

James A. Beverley, in his "investigative report" of the Toronto Blessing, noting the confusions over Edwards' Calvinism and cessationism, suggests that perhaps both sides have made too much over Edwards. He suggests with Ian Murray that perhaps Chevreau has betrayed Edwards' emphasis in making too much of physical manifestations. He wonders if it might not be best to leave Edwards aside. "In the end," Beverley writes, "we must each do our own analysis and not be too burdened by the ghosts of Edwards or Chauncy" (Beverley 1995, 82). I'm not so certain this is the best course of action. Edwards has done his descendants a great favor by identifying features of affective trends which, in their salience, have a tendency to focus attention inappropriately, inclining the categorizations of these trends to be based upon tendencies which are not essentially related to God, but rather are often simply accompaniments of the movement. Furthermore, Edwards articulates in his revival works those positive tendencies of God which are to be expected in revival contexts, both with regard to the work in general as well as those specifically savingly transforming works which are experienced by individuals in the context of a work of the Spirit. Indeed, Beverley's own list of "ten tests for truth" (1995, 26-28) bears a great deal of similarity to the particulars discussed in Edwards' own lists. Edwards also has the sensitivity to distinguish between the evaluation of the event in general and the question of individual participation and response, discussed above. Rather than recommending the abandonment of Edwards-discussion (and while I myself have my own places of disagreement with Edwards), I would encourage a more careful and thorough discussion of Edwards with regard to his wisdom for the Toronto Blessing. I will offer my own application of Edwards' positive criteria of a work of God to the Toronto Blessing below.

On Emotions in the Context of Affective Trends

Affective trends affect people. They affect them affectively. As such, good discernment of affective trends, informed by a more empirically grounded understanding of human experience such as that presented in the present study, will be sensitive to the dynamics of affectivity in the context of affective trends. This sensitivity is necessary to the clear sight of the work of God as it arises within human experience, even the human experience of affective trends. Here I will simply offer a few comments in light of the insights of the current study.

First, those who come to a revival meeting or charismatic prayer group or the like come as existentially "given." Each person comes into contact with a trend as a unique individual. One may come to an evening meeting in a series of evening meetings such as is common for meetings associated with the Toronto Blessing as a Pentecostal habitual experiencer, an "experience junkie," as some say. Another comes for the first time, complete with who knows what kind of expectations. Another comes for the second time. The previous night he was "blasted" by the Spirit. Another comes in caution. The last time she came to a meeting like this, she had a negative experience. Still another has been coming for weeks and still has yet to experience anything of significance. Nonetheless, he is sincere about his desire to pursue God and doesn't want to miss the opportunity for "something more." Another comes having felt something slightly the night before but didn't "go with it" because she was very self-conscious about the other people around her. She doesn't want to "fake it" but also feels that there is some element of her pressing into the experience in order to actually make contact with God. Still another just wants to fit in with the crowd, to fit in with all the excitement that is going on. He wants experience, wants the relationship with God that the others are talking so much about. Another is an introvert, shy of big groups, of loud noise, of unpredictability. Meetings like these are unpleasant or fearful. Another is neither introvert or shy but still used to being in control. While not pathologically controlled, he is just the kind of person who just does not "let go" too easy. Still another may come having experienced something the night before but doesn't quite know what to make of it. She doesn't understand what is happening either in the event or in her relationship with God. Still another is "right in the flow" of the event, having experienced and prepared to meet God wherever God might be found this night. The variety of concerns, appraisals, accumulations of tradition and experience present in any given meeting is truly vast. Affectivity has already affected those who come to a meeting before they ever arrive. Scripts are formed and followed by each of these types of people. They do not change easily. In these ways affectivity helps form the givenness that forms the gathered meeting each night.

Affectivity also influences each point of the meeting, in the relational configurations that surround the experience and throughout each stage of the development of emotional experience. In addition to one's previous experience and the expectations that precede the meeting itself, one must also consider the effect that a person's day may have on the meeting (did you have a fight with the boss?), or one's situation in life in general (are they on the verge of a divorce?). What heart desires are primary as the person enters the gathering? One must also consider the nature of the atmosphere or mood of the gathering. Are there problems with the sound system? What is the music like? What do the speakers say? How do the messages speak to the hearts of the people? Include as well the affective significance of the initial impulse toward emotional experience or expression. What stimulates this impulse? Toward what actions does it tend (do you feel inclined to cry, shake, fall, kneel, sit in contented silence, or other tendencies?)? What strength does the impulse arise with? Some impulses arise as only a light inclination toward a feeling or action. Others are so strong they can hardly be resisted. Are there appraisals, thoughts, images, or similar phenomena associated with the impulse? To what do these point? And then there is the role of regulation (might you, should you, do you want to, express, control, ignore, or

resist this impulse?). Perception and response to the impulse depends
to some degree on orientation. Is she moving from good to better or
better to worse? What kind of quality does the impulse itself have, as
presented in the context of the gathered meeting? And then there is
the development of the experience itself. Does the experience itself
change, fading or increasing in intensity or quality? Are there new
elements introduced to the experience from the outside (as, for example, when people may offer some prayer for you in a gathering, or
may lay a hand on you in blessing, or when someone next to you falls
down and bursts out in hysterical laughter). The collective experiences of all those gathered create a sense of the development of both
the "outside" and the "inside" experience, as anything from a
sustained period of holy silence to an exuberant hour of song and
dance capture the gathered assembly as a whole. This progression of
experience, in turn, produces feedback and informs world-view even
as the encounter develops.

At times people won't feel a thing in these meetings. The
dynamics of the *lack* of affective experience must thus become as
much a part of our understanding of affectivity as an understanding of
its presence. The lack of affective experience in the context of affective trends occurs for a variety of reasons. Personal history, cultural
history, or personality may predispose the lack of affective experience
either in general or in the context of meetings of this type. Some element of the meeting itself may predispose someone toward lack of
experience ("this music just does not do a thing for me," or "big
gatherings put me on edge"). Avoidance or resistance to God may
result in the refusal to respond to God's invitation to realize the
Gospel within. It may be that relationship with God has reached an
awkward plateau and is "on hold" until someone is ready to face
something. Perhaps a person has been harboring serious unconfessed
sin in his life, creating a separation between himself and God. Perhaps affective experience in these meetings is simply *not* what God is
doing in someone's life. For example, God is doing quiet repentance
in his life and these meetings are all about boisterous joy. Or perhaps
God simply wants this person "dry" for some reason (as in some passive dark night). It may also be that God actually *is* doing something
and one simply does not notice it, either because God's work is very
hidden or because of a lack of noticing skills or attention to God (perhaps his attention is on the extra-ordinary, causing him to fail to

notice God in the ordinary). At times, we may be put off by the leaders, their message, their style, particular actions. A variety of factors are involved in both the experience of emotion and the experience of the lack of emotion in the context of an affective trend. The variety of factors involved in a person's experience needs to be respected by leaders within revitalization movements. These dynamics are complicated even more by the factor of the meeting being a large gathering (Harris 1989). For example, I think John Arnott's presentation of reasons for not experiencing under the simple headings of fear and pride (Arnott 1995 102-133) too easily places the blame for not "receiving" from the Toronto Blessing upon the individual attendee. In this light I would encourage greater, rather than less freedom of expression: freedom to be silent, to wait, to watch, freedom not to experience (without the subtle judgment that one is "hard to receive").

And if this meeting is, in fact, an expression of God's moving, then one expects that God will "show up" and manifest God's presence in the hearts of those who come, in the midst of all the diversity of people and situations. During the peak of the Toronto Blessing I was regularly helping at the nightly meetings at the church where I was on staff. I was also leading a directee through a Nineteenth Annotation version of Ignatius' *Spiritual Exercises*. As I reflected on the dynamics and fruit of both environments, I was impressed with a few similarities. First, both environments approach renewal with the assumption of God's love, the belief in coming to this meeting, this exercise, that God desires to reveal himself to me today. Furthermore, both environments also expect that God's self-communication will be experienced affectively. In the nightly meetings this expectation is present, for example, in the way the meetings are introduced and in the placement of "catchers" behind people during prayer so that if they fall they will not injure themselves. In the *Exercises* this expectation is present in the "prayer for what I desire." But the *Exercises* go one step further. The *Exercises* do not merely expect that the Spirit will be active in this exercise, it also encourages the expectant prayer that the retreatant will experience certain types of emotions. Another similarity is affectively-sensitive attention to the atmosphere. In a nightly "renewal meeting," as it was called where I served, the music, the placement of chairs, and the lighting were all arranged to foster wholehearted coming before and receiving from God. Likewise Ignatius encourages retreat directors to pay careful attention to the atmosphere of the retreatant's room during the different Weeks in order to cultivate the particular experiences desired. In sum, in both environments, the participant feels discouraged if nothing is experienced. Both environments appeared to be means of God's communicating deep invitations to conversion.

One aspect of the discernment of what is "from God" in the context of affective trends is the role of the meeting leader: the pastor, worship leader, prayer team member. The leader must "cultivate" but not "manipulate" the experience of others. This takes a good deal of sensitive discernment. We must first watch our own motives. How do we need people to respond for our *own* sake? How much of our own dreams, sense of fulfillment, ego, and the like are tied up in the events of these meetings? We must be aware that people can easily feel manipulated. We must be as gentle and as tender as possible. This is especially true of large gatherings. We must be attentive to individual persons as much as possible, noticing how they tend to respond. Leaders of the meetings must also focus on the response of the heart rather than upon outward affective expressions. All agree on this point, though how it is expressed in practice differs widely.

Leaders must arrange for the pastoral care of individual participants in these gatherings. They must arrange places and times for people to talk to others about their experiences and to process them if they want. Is someone moving from good to better, from bad to worse? I have seen people who are regressing in their faith go to a meeting, experience a powerful shaking-up inside (and outside), and assume from the experience (without counsel) that because they had a powerful experience of God that all is fine with their faith. Leaders need to assist others not only in *having* an experience of God, but also in *understanding* and *responding* to that experience. Are some in need of comfort, challenge, nurture? Furthermore, there is also need for ministry to those who *don't* receive. They need to ask them where they *do* find God (perhaps in silent awareness, in personal relationships, in study of the Scriptures, in action). Perhaps leaders can open windows of grace for these people. They need to give them the freedom to return and see what God might have for them tomorrow—as well as the freedom not to return, either without any sense of judgment.

Some of these areas are sufficiently difficult to monitor in the midst of all the excitement of these types of meetings that I would suggest the leaders appoint close friends or a committee to review each evening for signs of perceived manipulation or for other "danger signs." Discernment informed by a clear understanding of the dynamics of human affectivity will be sensitive to these kinds of concerns. While not addressing the question of *whether* a particular affective trend is or is not "of God," leadership that is sensitive to the dynamics of affectivity as presented above will help to maintain the authenticity of a genuine move of God.

Some Personal Conclusions

I have utilized the phenomena of the Toronto Blessing as a way of reflecting upon the discernment of affective trends in the Church. I have explored a few issues of preliminary consideration, the use of criteria to evaluate a move of God, and some aspects of affectivity which influence the character of an affective trend. I offer a few thoughts here as a means of bringing these reflections on the practice of discernment in the context of affective trends to a close.

One must differentiate between the discernment of the movement in general, the discernment of individual experiences, and the discernment of particular aspects of the movement. Each requires a different type of discernment and, consequently, different discerners, criteria, and operations. The discernment of a movement in general requires the broadest range of perspectives, information, and criteria. For the evaluation of a work of God in general, one is only examining whether this trend or movement is significantly related to God in some way. We need not ask whether the experiences of the meetings are especially saving or transforming (for example, by looking merely for numbers of "converts" to determine the divine source of a work). This would be narrowing our discernment question to an inquiry concerning *what kind* of work God is doing in this movement or trend. Likewise discussions of whether a trend should be legitimately labelled a "revival," or "renewal," or "awakening" is similar to discussion of different types of spiritual consolation. While this discussion may have some value, the primary concern is the confident discernment of the presence or activity of God at all; and we must not think that consolation must be of one particular form in order to be genuine consolation.

I have not treated the discernment of individual experiences in the context of an affective trend with any depth because I have discussed similar matters in my treatment of spiritual direction. Edwards' signs in *Religious Affections* can serve as very helpful tools for self-examination by pastoral ministry or renewal meeting participants. However, these signs were written specifically as signs of the specifically *saving* or regenerative work of God, perhaps even more specifically as preparatory to the public profession of faith in the context of the baptismal rites of the period. One must pay careful attention to the context for appropriate transfer of sense and meaning from Edwards' situation to that of today.

The discernment of different aspects of an affective trend involves the identification of those features of a movement (genuine or not) which are the virtues, the charisms of a movement. What specific practices, what attitudes, what tendencies introduced by this movement express the heart of God, that appear to be "from God"? Likewise, we also discern that which Edwards calls "imprudences and irregularities." We look carefully at a movement (even a genuine move of God) and identify aspects of this move which are not "from God." For leaders in the movement this becomes a discernment of elective action, "Should we introduce, continue, reject or change *this* particular aspect of our leadership of the movement?" For participants it involves a discernment of selective *reception*, "How should I respond to *this* particular aspect of the meeting tonight?"

I am convinced that far too little time and attention has been given to the careful and prayerful discernment of affective trends. Due to the intensity with which they confront us, we frequently react rather than discern. Perhaps this cannot be avoided in light of the need for statements *right now*. Nevertheless, I long for teams of leaders from diverse perspectives to devote themselves to extended bipartisan co-discernment (not debate) of affective trends, developing mutually originated criteria, and resulting in "pastoral letters" being published with recommendations for leaders and participants. Documentation of healing stories, prophetic utterances, and numbers of people changed can be investigated in the context of the prayerful pursuit of that which is truly from God. Stories of all kinds can be collected and heard. Part of the process-appropriate criteria I look for in a discernment of affective trends is the breadth of discernment team and the sense of agreement among the team as the process ends. Perhaps

Hanegraaff's recent meetings with the Brownsville Assembly of God and Toronto's reuniting with the Canadian Vineyard show signs of this co-operation.

So, is the Toronto Blessing "of God" or not? As should be obvious by now, the question is not all that simple. For what it is worth, however, I offer a few of my final reflections after reviewing the research and my own personal experience. As I write, it is now about five years after the peak of the influence of the Toronto Blessing among the congregation I served in San Francisco. As I reviewed the material for this section of the chapter I intentionally read the literature critical of the Toronto Blessing first, because I was more familiar with supporting arguments. Then I read Beverley's more "moderate" approach. Finally I read literature from the friends of the Toronto Blessing. Each reading took me back to personal memories, interviews, e-mailed stories, and discussions with leaders. As I read the "critical" literature I was reminded of the "imprudences and irregularities" of the Toronto Blessing. I made a list of them. There were presumptuous prophecies given in the context of the Toronto Blessing, and too much was made of them. There were exaggerated stories; we should vow never to publish or proclaim healing stories without careful documentation first and never claim, in our excitement, more than what is plain to be seen. I grieve the name-calling from both sides: friends of the revival labeling opponents "pharisees," while opponents calling leaders in the Toronto Blessing "counterfeit."

There has been elitism among participants; there really were people who thought better of themselves because they were especially easy to receive—meaning they shook alot or something similar when prayed for. While some would fault the Toronto Blessing for an elitism of the leaders, I would state the opposite. To me the "blessing" of the Toronto Blessing has been the way it has been spread through ordinary pastors, pastor after pastor, congregation by congregation without the necessity of the "big person up front." At times the focus has been upon the power or anointing of the leader, but the predominant practice has been to choose lay people from the local setting to act as prayer teams who minister the Spirit to those who attend the meetings. The presence of "catchers" is difficult to assess. On the one hand it can serve to manipulate the congregation into particular responses. But on the other hand, if there is a real expectation that people might collapse, it is simply a matter of safety to respect this possibility. In spite of all the talk about not emphasizing the manifestations, there was too much emphasis on the manifestations. Perhaps this is inevitable in light of the unusual nature of people's experiences, but at times I felt that leaders went too far in drawing attention to them.

One of my primary concerns with this movement was that it appeared to "stay at the top." Many simply got hooked for long periods of time enjoying the sense of feeling God's love for them without asking where this communication of God's love was taking them. But again, perhaps that is just what God wanted. Why can't we take long seasons of our lives just to enjoy the love of Jesus Christ? At times, the Toronto Blessing led to a mentality of needing to "go somewhere" (like Toronto) where a splash from the stream of God could be found only to neglect the digging of deep wells to retrieve the vast amounts of water hidden below. Then, of course, there was the failure of follow-up. The assumption that this was a movement of God led to the additional assumption that everything (or nearly everything) experienced therein was of God (or perhaps God mixed with my own emotions). There was little encouragement or training in the processing of these experiences through discernment, wisdom, and maturity. These were the imprudences of the Toronto Blessing as I experienced it.

As I read through Beverley's more moderate approach I began to remember the good things about the renewal, the sincerity of the participants, the growth in relationship to God I saw among many, the times of worship. I returned to Jonathan Edwards' five criteria of a general work of God. First, a move of God brings an increase in the esteem of Christ. I remembered Christ being proclaimed among the homeless, and the same homeless given a home (spiritually and physically) through this movement. I remembered the emphasis in preaching, time and time again on the love of Jesus. I especially remember this esteem for Jesus expressed in the worship songs highlighted in this season. Second, a move of God operates against the interests of Satan's kingdom. I remember the confessions I heard from those I interviewed. I remembered the restored marriages, the healed relationships, the freedom to pursue the things of God released. Third, a move is accompanied by a greater reverence for the Scriptures. It is true that biblical preaching was not a high point in the Toronto Blessing and at times an anti-intellectual message was communicated. But many people found a new love for the Scriptures in this movement. There were times during this season when I was unable to attend meetings because of the necessity of schoolwork. I would be home studying the Scriptures and I would find myself shaking and tingling with admiration for the beauty of God's communication. Fourth, a move of God operates to lead persons to the truth and out of error. Again, there was not a lot of doctrinal sophistication expressed through the Toronto Blessing (although it stimulated some serious discussion of the nature of revival). What I saw most, however, was a large case of something similar to what William Barry calls the "affective principle and foundation" (Barry 1992, 63-64). Perhaps the affective grasp of a single fundamental truth is truth enough. The final sign of a work of God is love. While Hanegraaff may wish to talk of the counterfeit love among people present at a meeting (and I am aware of instances where serious conflicts were stimulated in the wake of renewal meetings), I can point to numerous instances where the love for one another grew stronger. Yet, in all honesty, probably love for neighbor was not the strong point of the renewal.

Indeed, it was love of God and the sense of being loved *by* God that were the strong points. And perhaps this is the proper first step. Barry, in his discussion of the affective principle and foundation quotes from psychiatrist Mackenzie to illustrate his point:

> The *enjoyment* of God should be the supreme end of spiritual technique; and it is in that enjoyment of God that we not only feel saved in the Evangelical sense, but safe: we are conscious of belonging to God, and hence are never alone; and, to the degree we have these two, hostile feelings disappear. (cited in Barry 1992, 63-64)

Barry himself comments further on this affective principle and foundation:

> This affective principle and foundation can be called the experience of having a spiritual identity, a real relationship to God. It is . . . the experience of being loved and lovely that precedes the experience of sinfulness, the experience of enjoyment and

oneness with God that enables a person to see the present state
of self and world as a fall from grace. (Barry 1992, 64)

Barry suggests that the establishment of this affective principle and
foundation may take some time. I might suggest that for many people
this affective principle and foundation was established in a very short
time through the means of renewal meetings.

When I turned to the books written by the friends of the Toronto
Blessing, it was this aspect, that of the realization of being loved by
God (perhaps *the* most fundamental truth in the Christian faith; cf.
John 3:16) that returned to me with full strength. I recalled e-mail
after e-mail, interview after interview, experience after experience
where this truth was brought home into the depths of someone's heart.
The theme is expressed very clearly in Chevreau's or Arnott's books
and I think it truly was the charism of the Toronto Blessing. This was
not a move of repentance or salvation or healing. It was a time for
realizing, and enjoying, the truth of God's special love for us given to
us through Jesus Christ and poured upon us through the procession of
the Holy Spirit. John Arnott writes in his chapter "God's Love: The
Bottom Line," "The greatest revelation I hear night after night is that
God has come to people by the power of the Holy Spirit and revealed
His love to them personally" (Arnott 1995, 23). This is my experience as well. In spite of the "imprudences and irregularities" I still
think that the Toronto Blessing was a special time when Jesus invited
us to see just how much God loves us. My hope is that through careful, collaborative discernment the character of genuine affective
trends, individuals' experiences, and the aspects of those trends which
are and are not of God may be more clearly recognized and
understood so that wise promotion of the kingdom of God may be
advanced.

Conclusions and Further Research

I set about this study in search of greater empirical and philosophical specificity within an account of Christian discernment. I defined
discernment as an affectively-rich act of knowing which seeks to
identify that which is or is not significantly related to God. By means
of the historical study of chapter two, using the writings of Ignatius of
Loyola and Jonathan Edwards, I provided a general description of dis-

cernment in its structural similarities and contextual diversity. I also introduced some of the key roles that affectivity plays in discernment in terms of the subject, object, context, and act of discernment.

In chapter three I turned to critical analysis, here with regard to the cognate discipline of experimental psychology. In this chapter I reviewed the findings of experimental psychology to date with regard to the operations involved in human categorization and affectivity. This chapter illumined our understanding of a descriptive account of discernment, that is our understanding of those operations ordinarily involved in the categorizing process of Christian discernment as one might expect under normal conditions. The chapter also provided much greater specification concerning the nature of affectivity and the roles which affectivity might play in Christian discernment.

In chapter four critical analysis was explored through the discipline of North American philosophical theology. I accomplished this through an examination of the thought of Donald Gelpi. Gelpi's thought provided the main lines of a framework of thinking which was capable of interpreting the diverse material from both empirical and religious sources. Furthermore, the move from empirical psychology to philosophy and logic offered developments of a normative account of Christian discernment, insights into actions that facilitate discernment actually achieving its aim of identifying that which is or is not significantly related to God.

The findings of empirical research and the insights of philosophical theology were then integrated into a single model of human experience in chapter five. It was this model that was used to formulate a general account of Christian discernment. Finally, in the present chapter, I applied this account of discernment, rooted in greater philosophical and empirical specificity, to two areas of discernment practice: that of spiritual direction and that of the pastoral evaluation of affective trends in the Church. This constructive interpretation demonstrated the value of an account of discernment sensitive to psychological and philosophical insights.

In the process of this study, I have made contributions to a variety of fields. First, I have contributed to the field of Christian spirituality by developing our understanding of Christian discernment. The integration of various contexts and types of discernment within the single interpretant of an "affectively-rich act of knowing," as well as the distinction between descriptive and normative elements of discussion about discernment, have served to provide means by which discernment can be more helpfully explored in future research. The study has also brought, as intended, greater specificity to the understanding of key elements of Christian discernment. An awareness of the processes of categorization by which *of God* or *not of God* are established and utilized has been presented with much greater detail and with clear links to empirical research. The awareness of such elements of discernment as "consolation," "connaturality," and "indifference" has been given greater specification in light of the findings of emotions research.

Second, through my historical description, this study has clarified patterns of Christian discernment common to Protestant and Roman Catholic alike. I have noted six different types of discernment present in the *Spiritual Exercises* of Ignatius of Loyola and two separate types in the works of Jonathan Edwards. Further, by clarifying the context and intention of Edwards' works on revival, I have further specified the character of Puritan discernment in the Eighteenth century.

Third, by exploring religious experience in terms of experimental psychology (I am thinking here particularly of cognitive psychology), this study extends that field into territories where it has not gone before. As mentioned above, experimental psychology, and cognitive psychology in particular, has avoided such spheres of discourse as aesthetic, empathetic and religious experience. Nonetheless people have religious experiences and they frequently do so complete with all of the systems of ordinary mental process. This study has offered suggestions concerning how operations discussed within the field of cognitive psychology can act upon religious objects and within religious spheres. In doing so the study has opened the doorway to further dialogue between the fields of Christian spirituality and cognitive psychology.

Fourth, by exploring the possibility of achieving confident identification of that which is or is not of God in the context of Christian discernment, I have contributed to the field of religious philosophy. The epistemological framework indicates both the real possibility and the fallibility of religious knowledge. As such it may be seen as a further step in the religious exploration of constructive postmodern philosophical thought.

Fifth, this study has contributed to the practice of spiritual direction. By providing greater specification of the nature of categorization and the roles of affectivity in discernment, the spiritual director can be better acquainted with what to expect from those who come to them for help in Discerning/discerning. Furthermore, by grounding Christian discernment in sound epistemological principles, the study provides spiritual directors means by which they can guide directees toward discernment processes that are more likely to achieve the aim of identifying and understanding that which is significantly related to God.

Finally, the study has contributed to the evaluation of affective trends within the Church. By applying insights from psychology and epistemology to this topic the study encourages a more prayerful, careful and co-operative approach to the evaluation of revivals, renewals and other revitalization movements. By clarifying the criteria of discernment the study points the way to valuable indications of God's work that have true consistency. By outlining some of the dynamics of affectivity found within the context of renewal meetings, the study has provided greater specification to understanding of the work of God in affective trends and gives the leaders of such movement perspectives with which the authenticity of such movements can be maintained.

Along the way this study has suggested a number of areas for continuing research, through which the understanding of Christian discernment can be further developed. First, there is a need for integrated biblical analysis of discernment. This may be done either thematically or by corpus. Studies of the evaluation of prophetic utterance, of the presentation of Jesus as "of God," of community or personal guidance, of the recognition of the sphere of the demonic, and other similar concepts need to be further explored. Explorations of Pauline or Johannine approaches to discernment could be pursued. These separate studies would then be brought together into an integrated, up to date study of biblical discernment. The interpretant presented in this study offers a fine framework from within which this study can be structured.

The historical study of discernment has advanced greatly over the past few decades but there is more work to be done. This is especially true with reference to Protestant studies. The relationship between authority and discernment is a significant issue at the time of the Protestant reformation, with segments of the reformation expressing distinct positions on this question. The Puritans and Pietists have a rich literature on discernment and little has been done to draw this literature into dialogue with ongoing discussion of discernment in the field of Christian spirituality. A variety of other figures can be mentioned for their value to the study of Christian discernment.

I suspect that some of the most needed research in the area of the theology of discernment will surround the doctrines of Christology and theology proper. By articulating those tendencies by which God revealed in Jesus Christ is known, we also articulate important criteria by which the church recognizes the presence and action of God. Much work has already been done in the area of pneumatology, and I think it is probably in dialogue with feminist, liberationist, scientific and pluralist thought concerning God and Christ that adequate criteria for discernment will be re-considered in the next generation.

A number of psychological studies of discernment might be pursued, developing from the work of the present study. Discernment can be explored by means of the more rigid experimental methods of cognitive psychology, or through survey/interview type research. There is a need for a broad-based descriptive study of Christian discernment, drawing from a wide range of denominations and locations. Gender-based or developmental-based studies could be conducted driven by the theory presented in this study. More studies of the discernment processes of particular communities are needed. The roles of affectivity can be explored in greater depth, exploring various factors of affective experience in terms of the subject of discernment, for example.

In terms of philosophy, I see a couple of interesting possibilities. Throughout my research on this topic I have had the suspicion that the clarification of the epistemology of Christian discernment has some contribution to make to the question of the "religious experience" argument for the existence of God. The demonstration that a contingent of experts from any religious tradition have established a means through religious experience by which that which is from God can be reasonably (though not infallibly) ascertained, seems to offer something to the problem of whether religious experience can provide evidence of the existence of God or not. This must be worked out with relationship to the ever-growing literature on this philosophical question. This study can be thought of as an analysis of Alston's notion of "overrider systems" (cf. Alston 1991). Furthermore, this study can be developed further by integration with other philosophical systems. For purposes of space, the present study was limited to North American philosophical systems. However, it will be necessary, in light of the epistemological principle itself, to view discernment in light of Russian, Native American, or Chinese cosmological and epistemological reflection.

Finally, exploration of the practice of discernment deserves attention. In the current study I applied the account of discernment to only two areas of the practice of discernment, those of spiritual direction and the evaluation of affective trends. Furthermore, the applications given were only presented in the form of sketchy outlines and suggestions. A much fuller application of an account of Christian discernment can be given these two areas, and not only these but also the discernment of prophetic utterances in congregational settings, the communal discernment of alternative actions, the personal discernment of elective vocation, the discernment of community socio-political strategies, and many other discernment settings.

Works Cited

Albrecht, D. E. 1989. An investigation of sociocultural characteristics and dynamics of Wallace's "revitalizaton movements": A comparative analysis of the works of four social scientists. Unpublished manuscript.

Alston, W. P. 1991. *Perceiving God: The epistemology of religious experience*. Ithaca and London: Cornell University Press.

Anderson, D. R. 1995. *Strands of system: The philosophy of Charles Peirce*. Purdue University Press Series in the History of Philosophy. West Lafayette, IN: Purdue University Press.

Anderson, J. R. 1995. *Cognitive psychology and its implications*. 4th ed. New York: W. H. Freeman and Company.

Anderson, W. E. 1980. Introduction to *Works of Jonathan Edwards*. Vol. 6, Scientific and Philosophical Writings. Edited by W. E. Anderson. New Haven, CT: Yale University Press.

Antoncich, Ricardo. 1975. The *Exercises* and the spiritual discernment of political options. Unpublished manuscript.

Apel, Karl-Otto. 1995. *From pragmatism to pragmaticism*. Translated by John Michael Krois. University of Massachusetts Press, 1981. Reprint, Atlantic Highlands, NJ: Humanities Press (page references are to the reprint edition).

Aristotle. 1941 [iv bce]. *Nichomachean ethics*. In *The basic works of Aristotle*. Edited by Richard McKeon. New York: Random House.

Arnott, John. 1995. *The father's blessing*. Orlando, FL: Creation House.

Aschenbrenner, G. A. 1983. Consciousness Examen. In *Notes on the Spiritual Exercises of St. Ignatius of Loyola*. The Best of the Review, no. 1., ed. David Fleming, 175-185. St. Louis, MO: Review for Religious.

Averill, James. 1980a. A constructivist view of emotion. In *Emotion: Theory, research, and experience*. Vol. 1. *Theories of emotion*, eds. Robert Plutchik and Henry Kellerman, 305-339.

_____. 1980b. The emotions. In *Personality: Basic aspects and current research*, ed. Ervin Staub, 133-199. Englewood Cliffs, NJ: Prentice Hall.

_____. 1982. *Anger and agression: An essay on emotion*. Springer Series in Social Psychology. New York, Heidelberg: Springer-Verlag.

_____. 1985. The social construction of emotion: With special reference to love. In *The social construction of the person*, eds. K.J. Gergen, and K. E. Davis, 89-109. New York, Heidelberg: Springer-Verlag.

_____. 1986. The acquisition of emotions during adulthood. In *The social construction of emotions*, ed. Rom Harré, 98-155. Oxford: Basil Blackwell.

_____. 1988. A Ptolmaic theory of emotions: A review of "The Emotions" by Nico Frijda. *Cognition and Emotion* 2, no. 2:81-87.

_____. 1990. Inner feelings, works of the flesh, the beast within, diseases of the mind, driving force, and putting on a show: six metaphors of emotions and their theoretical extensions. In *Metaphors in the history of psychology*, ed. D. E. Leary, 104-132. Cambridge: Cambridge University Press.

_____. 1993. Grief as an emotion and as a disease: A social-constructionist perspective. In *Handbook of bereavement: Theory, research and intervention*, eds. M. S. Stroebe, Wolfgang Stroebe, and R. O. Hansson, 77-90. Cambridge: Cambridge University Press.

_____. 1994. Aristotle meets the computer and becomes conflicted: A review of "Best laid schemes: The psychology of emotions" by Keith Oatley. *Cognition and Emotion* 8, no. 1:73-91.

Bakker, Leo. 1970. *Freiheit und Erfahrung: Redaktionsgeschichtliche Untersuchungen über die Unterscheidung der Geister bei Ignatius von Loyola*. Studien zur Theologie des geistlichen Lebens, Vol. 3. Würzburg: Echter Verlag.

Balthasar, Hans Urs von. 1980. Reflections on the discernment of spirits. *Communio: National Catholic Review* 7:196-208.

Barruffo, Antonio, Tomaso Beck, and Francis Sullivan. 1980. *L'azione dello Spirito Santo nel discernimento*. Rome: Centrum Ignatianum Spiritualitatis.

Barry, W. A. 1987a. *God and you: Prayer as a personal relationship*. New York: Paulist Press.

_____. 1987b. The kingdom of God and discernment. *America* 157, no. 7 (Sept 26):156-159.

_____. 1987c. Toward communal discernment: Some practical suggestions. *The Way: Supplement* 58 (spring):104-112.

_____. 1989a. *Seek my face: Prayer as personal relationship in Scripture*. New York: Paulist Press.

_____. 1989b. Toward a theology of discernment. *The Way: Supplement* 64 (spring):129-140.

_____. 1990. *Paying attention to God: Discernment in prayer.* Notre Dame, IN: Ave Maria Press.

_____. 1991. Discernment of spirits: A response to the spiritual crisis of our age. *Review for Religious* 50:103-109.

_____. 1992. *Spiritual direction and the encounter with God: A theological inquiry.* Mahwah, NJ: Paulist Press.

_____. 1993. *God's passionate desire and our response.* Notre Dame, IN: Ave Maria Press.

Barry, W. A. and W. J. Connolly. 1982. *The practice of spiritual direction.* New York: The Seabury Press.

Barsalou, L. W. 1987. The instability of graded structure: Implications for the nature of concepts. In *Concepts and conceptual development: Ecological and intellectual factors in categorization*, ed. U. Neisser, 101-140. Cambridge: Cambridge University Press.

Bayly, Lewis. 1714 [1612?]. *The practice of piety.* 51st ed. London: Daniel Midwinter.

Belloso, J. M. R. 1979. Who is capable of discerning? In *Discernment of the Spirit and of spirits*. Concilium, No. 119., eds. Casiano Floristán and Christian Duquoc, 84-94. New York: The Seabury Press.

Benedict of Nursia. 1975 [547?]. *The rule of St. Benedict.* Translated, with Introduction and Notes by Anthony C. Meisel and M. L. del Mastro. Garden City, New York: Image/Doubleday.

Benke, Christoph. 1991. *Unterscheidung der Geister bei Bernhard von Clairvaux.* Studien zur systematischen und spiituellen Theologie, Vol. 4. Würzburg: Echter Verlag.

Berger, Peter. 1967. *The sacred canopy: Elements of a sociological theory of religion*. Garden City, NY: Doubleday.

Bernard of Clairvaux. 1987 [1130?]. *On loving God*. In *Bernard of Clairvaux: Selected works*. Translated by G. R. Evans. New York: Paulist Press.

Beverley, J. A. 1995. *Holy laughter and the Toronto blessing: An investigative report*. Grand Rapids, MI: Zondervan.

Billings, Bob. 1987. Having a ball in the perfect will of God. *Fundamentalist Journal* 6 (September):23-24.

Blackaby, H. T. and C. V. King. *Experiencing God: How to live the full adventure of knowing and doing the will of God*. Nashville, TN: Broadman and Holman.

Boland, Paschal. 1959. *The Concept of* Discretio Spirituum *in John Gerson's "De Probatione Spirituum" and "De Distinctione Verarum Visionum a Falsis."* Washington, DC: Catholic University of America Press.

Bonhoeffer, Dietrich. 1963. *The cost of discipleship*. Translated by R. H. Fuller. New York: Macmillan.

_____. 1971. *Letters and Papers from Prison: The Enlarged Edition*. Edited by Eberhard Bethge, translated by R. H. Fuller, Frank Clarke, John Bowden, et al. New York: Macmillan.

Bots, Jan. 1982. Praying in two diections: A Christian method of prayerful decision-making. *Review for Religious* 41 (January-February):58-64

Boyer, Pascal. 1995. *The naturalness of religious ideas: A cognitive theory of religion*. Berkeley: University of California Press.

Boyle, M. O. 1983. Angels black and white: Loyola's spiritual discernment in historical perspective. *Theological Studies* 44 no. 2 (June):241-257.

Bourne, L., R. Dominiski, and E. Loftus. *Cognitive processes*. Upper Saddle Rive, NJ: Prentice Hall.

Brown, Roger. 1965. *Social psychology*. New York: The Free Press and London: Collier-Macmillan Limited.

_____. 1979. Cognitive categories. In *Psychology's second century: Enduring issues*, eds. R. A. Kasschau and C. N. Cofer, 188-217. New York: Praeger.

Buckley, M. J. 1973. The structure of the rules for discernment of spirits. *The Way: Supplement* 20 (autumn):19-37.

_____. 1975. The contemplation to attain love. *The Way: Supplement* 24 (spring):92-104

Burns, Robert. 1785 (publication date of collection not listed). To a mouse: On turning her up in her nest with the plow. In *My poetry book: An anthology of modern verse for boys and girls*, ed. Mrs. Huffard and Mrs. Carlile, 190-191. Winston Press.

Byrne, Lavinia. 1989. Asking for the Grace. *The Way: Supplement* 64 (spring):29-36.

Byron, W. J. 1974. Discernment and poverty. *The Way: Supplement* 23 (autumn):37-42.

Calvin, John. 1964 [1536?]. *Institutes of the Christian religion*. Translated by Henry Beveridge. Grand Rapids, MI: Wm. B. Eerdmans. References to this work are given by standard book, chapter, and paragraph numbers.

Canévet, Mariette. 1990. Se connaitre soi-meme en Dieu: Un aspect du discernement spirituel dans les "Confessions" d'Augustin. *Revue des Sciences Religieuses*. 64, no. 1 (January):27-52.

Cantor, Nancy, Walter Mischel, and Judith Schwartz. 1982. A prototype analysis of psychological situations. *Cognitive Psychology* 14:45-77.

Caraman, Philip. 1990. *Ignatius Loyola: A biography of the founder of the Jesuits*. New York: Harper and Row.

Carter, Howard. 1976. *Questions and answers on spiritual gifts*. Tulsa, OK: Harrison House.

Carthusian. 1995. *The call of silent love*. Carthusian Novice Conferences II. *Vocation and Discernment*. Cistercian Studies Series, No. 163. Kalamazoo, MI: Cistercian Publications.

Chacko, Jiji. 1996. *Test the spirits: A study in the discernment of spirits*. Bangalore, India: Sabu Paul.

Chan, Simon. 1998. *Spiritual theology: A systematic study of the Christian life*. Downers Grove: InterVarsity Press.

Chauncy, Charles. 1743. *Seasonable thoughts on the state of religion in New England*. Boston: Rogeers and Fowler for Samuel Eliot.

Cherry, Conrad. 1990. *The theology of Jonathan Edwards: A reappraisal*. Garden City, N.Y.: Doubleday, 1966. Reprint, Bloomington and Indianapolis: Indiana University Press (page references are to the reprint edition).

Chevreau, Guy. 1994. *The Toronto blessing: An experience of renewal and revival*. Toronto: HarperPerennial.

Clarke, T. E. 1993. Discernment: An Ignatian perspective on John Woolman's "Journal". In *Spirituality in ecumenical perspective*, ed. E. Glenn Hinson, 101-114. Louisville, KY: Westminster/John Knox Press.

Clebsch, W. A. 1973. *American religious thought: A history*. Chicago History of American Religion Series. Edited by Martin Marty. Chicago and London: University of Chicago Press.

Colacurcio, R. E. 1972. The perception of excellency as the glory of God in Jonathan Edwards: An essay towards the epistemology of discernment. Ph.D. diss., Fordham University.

Conroy, Maureen. 1993. *The discerning heart: Discovering a personal God*. Chicago: Loyola Press.

Cooey, Paula. 1989. Eros and intimacy in Edwards. *Journal of Religion* 69:484-501.

Cornelius, R. R. 1996. *The science of emotion: Research and tradition in the psychology of emotion*. Upper Saddle River, NJ: Prentice Hall.

Costa, P. M. 1993. *Direzione spirituale e discernimento*. Rome: Edizioni ADP.

Crampsey, J. A. 1989. Jesus and discernment. *The Way: Supplement* 64 (spring):19-28.

Culligan, K. G., ed. 1983. *Spiritual direction: Contemporary readings*. New York: Living Flame Press.

Culligan, Kevin. 1992. Saint John of the Cross and modern psychology. *Studies in Formative Spirituality* 13 (February):29-48.

Dalmases, Cándido de. 1985. *Ignatius of Loyola, founder of the Jesuits: His life and work*. Translated by Jerome Aixalá. St. Louis, MO: The Institute of Jesuit Sources.

Daniel, S. H. 1994. *The philosophy of Jonathan Edwards: A study in divine semiotics*. Bloomington and Indianapolis: Indiana University Press.

Darwin, Charles. 1998 [1872]. *The expression of the emotions in men and animals*. 3d ed., with an Introduction, Afterward, and Commentaries by Paul Eckman. New York: Oxford Univeersity Press.

Dautzenberg, Gerhard. 1971. Zum religionsgeschichtlichen Hintergrund der διακρισις πνευματων (1 Koρ 12,10). *Biblische Zeitschrift* 15:92-104.

————. 1975. *Urchristliche Prophetie: Ihre Erforschung, ihre Voraussetzungen im Judentum und ihre Struktur im ersten Korintherbrief.* Stuttgart: Verlag W. Kohlhammer.

Dawes, R. M. 1988. *Rational choice in an uncertain world.* Fort Worth: Harcourt Brace.

DeArtega, William. 1996. *Quenching the Spirit: Discover the REAL spirit behind the charismatic controversy.* 2d ed. Orlando, FL: Creation House.

deCaussade, Jean-Pierre. 1989 [1861]. *The Sacrament of the Present Moment.* Translated by Kitty Muggeridge. Glasgow: William Collins Sons, 1981. Reprint San Francisco: HarperCollins.

Delattre, R. A. 1968. *Beauty and sensibility in the thought of Jonathan Edwards: An essay in Aesthetics and theological ethics.* New Haven and London: Yale University Press.

DeNicolas, A. T. 1986. *Powers of imagining, Ignatius de Loyola: A philosophical hermeneutic of imagining through the collected works of Ignatius de Loyola.* Albany, NY: State University of New York Press.

deSousa, Ronald. 1987. *The rationality of emotions.* Cambridge: The MIT Press.

Dewey, John. 1894. The theory of emotion: (I) Emotional attitudes. *The Psychological Review* 1, no. 6 (November):553-569.

————. 1895. The theory of emotion: (II) The significance of emotions. *The Psychological Review* 2:13-32

————. 1938. *Logic: The theory of inquiry.* New York: Henry Holt.

Diadochus of Photice. 1967 [450(?)]. On spiritual knowledge and discrimination: One hundred texts. In *The Philokalia: The complete text*, eds. G. E. H. Palmer, Philip Sherrard, and Kallistos Ware, 1:253-296. London: Faber and Faber.

Dinjan, Dr. Fr. 1967. *Discretio: Les origines patristiques et monastiques de la doctrine sur la prudence chez saint Thomas d'Aquin*. Assen: Van Gorcum.

Discernment Pro Arte. 1997. Tools for discerning your path. World Wide Web site accessed 3/31/97: http://www.discernment.com/Service.htm

Doran, Robert. 1977. *Subject and psyche: Ricoer, Jung and the search for foundations*. Washington, D.C.: University Press of America.

Doucet, Daina. 1994. Renewal excites Canadian churches. *Charisma* (June):52-53.

Downey, Michael. 1997. *Understanding Christian spirituality*. Mahwah, NJ: Paulist Press.

Drengson, Alan and Yuichi Inoue, eds. 1995. *The deep ecology movement: An introductory anthology*. Berkeley, CA: North Atlantic Books.

Dubay, Thomas. 1977. *Authenticity: A biblical theology of discernment*. Denville, NJ: Dimension Books.

Dulles, Avery. 1965. Finding God's will: Rahner's interpretation of the Ignatian election. *Woodstock Letters* 94:139-152.

Dunfee, S. N. 1982. The sin of hiding: A feminist critique of Reinhold Neibuhr's account of sin and pride. *Soundings* 65 (fall):316-327.

Dunn, J. D. G. 1979. Discernment of spirits - a neglected gift. In *Witness to the Spirit: Essays on revelation, spirit, redemption*.

Proceedings of the Irish Biblical Association, No. 3, ed. Wilfrid Harrington, 79-88. Dublin: Irish Biblical Association.

Dunne, T. A. 1974. Models of discernment. *The Way: Supplement* 23 (autumn):18-27.

Dussel, Enrique. 1979. Discernment: A question of orthodoxy or orthopraxis? In *Discernment of the Spirit and of spirits*. Concilium, No. 119., eds. Casiano Floristán and Christian Duquoc, 47-60. New York: The Seabury Press.

Dunstan, G. R., ed. 1975. *Duty and discernment*. London: SCM Press.

Dupré, Louis and Don E. Saliers, eds. 1989. *Christian spirituality III: Post-Reformation and modern*. World Spirituality: An Encyclopedic History of the Religious Quest, No. 18. New York: Crossroad.

Dupré, Louis and J. A. Wiseman, eds. 1988. *Light from light: An anthology of Christian mysticism*. Mahwah, NJ: Paulist Press.

Dyckman, K. M. and L. P. Carroll. 1981. *Inviting the mystic, supporting the prophet: An introduction to spiritual direction*. New York: Paulist Press.

Edwards, Jonathan. 1834. *The works of Jonathan Edwards*. Edited by Edward Hickman. Reprint, Edinburgh and Carlile, PA: Banner of Truth Trust, 1987 (page numbers are to the reprint edition).

_____. 1948 [1745]. Miscellany 782 on "The sense of the heart." In Jonathan Edwards on the sense of the heart, Perry Miller, *Harvard Theological Review* 41/2 (April):123-146.

_____. 1972a [1741]. *The distinguishing marks*. In *Works of Jonathan Edwards*. Vol. 4, *The great awakening*. Edited by C. G. Goen. New Haven, CT: Yale University Press.

_____. 1972b [1737]. *A faithful narrative*. In *Works of Jonathan Edwards*. Vol. 4, *The great awakening*. Edited by C. G. Goen. New Haven, CT: Yale University Press.

_____. 1972c [1743]. *Some thoughts concerning the revival*. In *Works of Jonathan Edwards*. Vol. 4, *The great awakening*. Edited by C. G. Goen. New Haven, CT: Yale University Press.

_____. 1959 [1746]. *Works of Jonathan Edwards*. Vol. 2. *Religious affections*. Edited by J. E. Smith. New Haven, CT: Yale University Press.

_____. 1980. *Works of Jonathan Edwards*. Vol. 6. *Scientific and philosophical writings*. Edited by W. E. Anderson. New Haven, CT: Yale University Press.

_____. 1998 *Works of Jonathan Edwards*. Vol. 16. *Letters and Personal Writings*. Edited by G. S. Claghorn. New Haven, CT: Yale University Press.

Edwards, Tilden. 1980. *Spiritual friend: Reclaiming the gift of spiritual direction*. New York: Paulist Press.

Egan, H. D. 1976. *The* Spiritual Exercises *and the Ignatian mystical horizon*. St. Louis: Insititute of Jesuit Sources.

Endean, Philip. 1989. Discerning behind the rules: Ignatius' first letter to Teresa Rejadell. *The Way: Supplement* 64 (spring):37-50.

Farnham, S. G, J. P. Gill, R. T. McLean, and S. M. Ward. 1991. *Listening hearts: Discerning God's call in community*. 2d ed. Harrisburg, PA: Morehouse Publishing.

Farrow, Jo. 1989. Discernment in the Quaker tradition. *The Way: Supplement* 64 (spring):51-62.

Fee, G. D. 1994. *God's empowering presence: The Holy Spirit in the letters of Paul*. Peabody, MA: Hendrickson.

Fehr, Beverly and J. A. Russell. 1984. Concept of emotion viewed from a prototype perspective. *Journal of Experimental Psychology* 113, no. 3:464-486.

Finney, C. G. 1978 [1835]. *Revivals of religion.* Virginia Beach, VA: CBN University Press.

_____. 1979 [1845]. *Reflections on revival.* Compiled by D. D. Dayton. Minneapolis, MN: Bethany Fellowship.

Fischer, Kathleen. 1988. *Women at the well: Feminist perspectives on spiritual direction.* New York: Paulist Press.

Fleming, David, ed. 1983. *Notes on the* Spiritual Exercises *of St. Ignatius of Loyola.* The Best of the Review, no. 1. St. Louis, MO: Review for Religious.

_____. 1983b. The Ignatian spiritual exercises: Understanding a dynamic. In *Notes on the* Spiritual Exercises *of St. Ignatius of Loyola.* The Best of the Review, no. 1, ed. David Fleming, 2-18. St. Louis, MO: Review for Religious.

Floristán, Casiano and Christian Duquoc, eds. 1979. *Discernment of the Spirit and of spirits.* Concilium, No. 119. New York: The Seabury Press.

Foley, J. S. 1991. Feelings and the spiritual life. *Homiletic and Pastoral Review* 92 (November):29-52.

Forman, R. K. C., ed. 1990. *The problem of pure consciousness.* Oxford: Oxford University Press.

Fowler, J. W. 1981. *Stages of faith: The psychology of human development and the quest for meaning.* San Francisco: Harper and Row.

Friesen, Garry. 1978. God's will as it relates to decision-making. Ph.D. diss. Dallas Theological Seminary.

_____. 1980. *Decision making and the will of God*. Portland, OR: Multnomah Press.

Frijda, N. H. 1986. *The emotions*. Studies in Emotion and Social Interaction. Cambridge: Cambridge University Press/Editions de la Maison des Sciences de l' Homme.

_____. 1987. Comment on Oatley and Johnson-Laird's "Toward a cognitive theory of emotions." *Cognition and Emotion* 1, no. 1:51-58.

_____. 1988. The laws of emotions. *American Psychologist* 43, no. 5 (May):349-358.

_____. 1989. Aesthetic emotions and reality. *American Psychologist* 44, no 12 (December):1546-1547.

_____. 1994. Lazarus' labor of love. *Cognition and Emotion* 8, no. 5:473-482.

Frijda, N.H. and Batja Mesquita. 1994. The social roles and functions of emotions. In *Emotion and Culture*, eds. Shinobu Kitayama and Hazel Rose Markus, 51-87. Washington, DC: The American Psychological Association.

Frijda, N. H., Peter Kuipers and Elizabeth ter Schure. 1989. Relations among emotion, appraisal, and emotional action readiness. *Journal of Personality and Social Psychology* 57, no. 2:212-228.

Frijda, N. H. and Jaap Swagerman. 1987. Can computers feel?: Theory and design of an emotional system. *Cognition and emotion* 1, no. 3:235-257.

Fruchtenbaum, A. G. 1996. The Toronto Phenomenon. Article from *CTS Journal* 2 nos. 1-2 (spring-fall) and accessed 11/24/98 online from http;//www.bible.org/chafer/ctsjrnl/96a-02 [and 03].htm.

Futrell, J. C. 1970. Ignatian Discernment. *Studies in the Spirituality of Jesuits* 2, no. 2 (April):1-88.

Ganss, G. E. 1973. Thinking with the Church: The spirit of St. Ignatius' rules. *The Way: Supplement* 20 (autumn):72-82.

_____. 1991. Introduction and commentary to *Ignatius of Loyola: The* Spiritual Exercises *and selected works*, by Ignatius of Loyola. Edited by G. E. Ganss. New York/Mahwah, NJ: Paulist Press.

Gardner, Howard. 1983. *Frames of mind: The theory of multiple intelligences*. New York: Basic Books.

Gaustad, Edwin. 1957. *The great awakening in New England*. N.Y.: Harper.

Gay, R. M. 1959. *Vocation et discernement des esprits*. Montreal: Fides.

Geertz, C. 1973. *Interpretation of Cultures*. New York: Basic Books.

Gelpi, Donald. 1959. Artistic and prudential judgment. *The Modern Schoolman* 36 (March):163-177.

_____. 1966a. *Functional asceticism: A guidline for American religious*. New York: Sheed and Ward.

_____. 1966b. *Life and light: A guide to the theology of Karl Rahner*. New York: Sheed and Ward.

_____. 1970. *Discerning the Spirit: Foundations and futures of religious life*. New York: Sheed and Ward.

_____. 1971. *Pentecostalism: A theological viewpoint*. New York: Paulist Press.

_____. 1972. *Pentecostal piety*. New York: Paulist Press.

_____. 1976. *Charism and sacrament: A theology of Christian conversion*. New York: Paulist Press.

_____. 1987 [1978]. *Experiencing God: A theology of human emergence*. New York: Paulist Press. 1978. Reprint, Lanham, MD: University Press of America (page references are to the reprint edition).

_____. 1982. Conversion: the challenge of contemporary charismatic piety. *Theological Studies* 43:606-628.

_____. 1984. *The divine mother: A trinitarian theology of the Holy Spirit*. Lanham, MD: University Press of America.

_____. 1986. The Converting Jesuit. *Studies in the Spirituality of Jesuits* 18, no. 1 (January):1-38

_____. 1988a. *Grace as transmuted experience and social process, and other essays in North American theology*. Lanham, MD: University Press of America.

_____. 1988b. *Inculturating north American theology: An experiment in foundational method*. American Academy Studies in Religion 54. Atlanta GA: Scholar's Press.

_____. 1988c. *The Spirit in the world*. Wilmington, Deleware: Michael Glazier.

_____, ed. 1989a. *Beyond individualism: Toward a retrieval of moral discourse in America*. Notre Dame, IN: University of Notre Dame Press.

_____. 1989b. Conversion: Beyond the impasses of individualism. In *Beyond individualism: Toward a retrieval of moral discourse in America*, ed. Donald Gelpi, 1-30. Notre Dame, IN: University of Notre Dame Press.

_____. 1991. *Endless seeker: The religious quest of Ralph Waldo Emerson*. Lanham: University Press of America.

_____. 1993. *Committed worship: A sacramental theology for converting Christians.* Vol. 1. *Adult conversion and initiation*; Vol. 2. *The sacraments of ongoing conversion.* Collegeville, MN: The Liturgical Press.

_____. 1994. *The turn to experience in contemporary theology.* Mahwah, NJ: Paulist Press.

_____. 1994-95. Firstborn of many: A Christology for converting Christians, 3 vols. Unpublished manuscript.

_____. 1996. Discernment and the varieties of conversion. Unpublished manuscript of lecture presented at the Catholic Charismatic renewal.

_____. 1997. Varieties of transcendental experience: A study in constructive postmodernism. Unpublished manuscript.

_____. 1998a. *The conversion experience: A reflective process for RCIA participants and others.* New York: Paulist Press.

_____. 1998b. Incarnate excellence: Toward an American theological aesthetic. *Religion and the Arts* 214 (1998); 443-466.

Gergen, K.J. and K. E. Davis, eds. 1985. *The social construction of the person.* New York, Heidelberg: Springer-Verlag.

Gerstner, J. H. 1991. *The rational biblical theology of Jonathan Edwards.* Powhatan, VA: Berea Publications; Orlando, FL: Ligonier Ministries.

Giallanza, Joel. 1978. Spiritual direction according to John of the Cross. *Contemplative Review* 11, no. 3 (fall): 31-37.

Glass, A. L. and K. J. Holyoak. 1986. *Cognition.* 2d. ed. New York: Random House.

Gluck, M. A. and J. E. Corter. 1992. Information and category utility. Unpublished manuscript.

Gleitman, L. R., S. L. Armstrong, and Henry Gleitman. 1983. On doubting the concept 'concept'. In *New trends in conceptual representation: Challenges to Piaget's theory?*, ed. E. K. Scholnick, 87-110. Hillsdale, NJ: Lawrence Erlbaum.

Goen, C. G. 1972. Introduction to *Works of Jonathan Edwards*. Vol. 4, *The great awakening*. Edited by C. G. Goen. New Haven, CT: Yale University Press.

Goldman, A. I. 1986. *Epistemology and cognition*. Cambridge, MA: Harvard University Press.

Goldsbury, Margaret. 1989. Diminishing God's handiwork: Blocks to discernment. *The Way: Supplement* 64 (spring): 80-87.

Goleman, Daniel. 1995. *Emotional intelligence*. New York:Bantam Books.

Gopnik, Alison, and Andrew N. Meltzoff. 1997. *Words, thoughts, and theories*. Cambridge, MA: MIT Press.

Green, T. H. 1984. *Weeds among wheat: Discernment: where prayer and action meet*. Notre Dame, IN: Ave Maria Press.

Grossmann, Walter. 1988. Gruber on the discernment of true and false inspiration. *Harvard Theological Review* 81, no. 4:363-387.

Grudem, W. A. 1978. Gerhard Dautzenberg on 1 Cor 12.10. *Biblische Zeitschrift* 22, no. 2:94-102.

_____. 1982. *The gift of prophecy in first Corinthians*. Washington, D.C.: University Press of America.

Guenther, Margaret. 1992. *Holy listening: The art of spiritual direction*. Cambridge: Cowley Publications.

Gula, Richard M. 1997. *Moral discernment*. New York: Paulist Press

Gustafson, J. M. 1974. *Theology and Christian Ethics*. Philadelphia: A Pilgrim Press Book.

Halaska, Margaret. The model of discernment: The experience of a Franciscan. *Review for Religious* 43 (March-April):259-63.

Hambrick-Stowe, C.E. 1989. *The practice of piety: Puritan devotional disciplines in seventeenth-century New England*. Chapel Hill, NC: University of North Carolina Press.

Handy, Robert. 1986. Some patterns in American Protestantism. In *The study of spirituality*, eds. Cheslyn Jones, Geoffrey Wainwright, and Edward Yarnold, 474-76. New York, Oxford: Oxford University Press.

Hanegraaf, Hank. 1995. The counterfeit revival. Audiocassette. San Juan Capistrano, CA: Christian Research Institute International.

_____. 1997. *Counterfeit revival*. Dallas: Word.

Harré, Rom, ed. 1986. *The social construction of emotions*. Oxford: Basil Blackwell.

Harris, R. J. 1989. *A cognitive psychology of mass communication*. Hillsdale, NJ: Lawrence Erlbaum.

Hartshorne, Charles. 1945. *The Philosophy and Psychology of Sensation*. Chicago: University of Chicago Press.

Heider, E. R. 1972. Universals in color naming and memory. *Journal of Experimental Psychology* 93, no. 1: 10-20.

Hess, Carol Lakey. 1997. *Caretakers of our house: Women's development in communities of faith*. Nashville: Abington Press.

Hilton, Walter. 1981 [1390(?)]. A treatise on discernment of spirits, necessary for those who wish to lead spiritual life. In *Spiritual Classics*, ed. Charles Crawford, 97-110. New York: Crossroad.

Hoke, G. M. 1909. The spirit and power of discernment. *Methodist Review* 91:601-604.

Holbrook, C. A. 1973. *The ethics of Jonathan Edwards: Morality and aesthetics*. Ann Arbor, MI: University of Michigan Press.

Hood, R. W. Jr., ed. 1995. *Handbook of religious experience*. Birmingham, AL: Religion Education Press.

Hood, R. W. Jr., Bernard Spilka, Bruce Hunsberger, and Richard Gorsuch. 1996. *The psychology of religion: An empirical approach*. 2d ed. New York and London: The Guilford Press.

Hoopes, James, ed. 1991. *Peirce on signs: Writings on semiotic by Charles Sanders Peirce*. Chapel Hill, NC: University of North Carolina Press.

Houdek, F. J. 1996. *Guided by the Spirit: A Jesuit perspective on spiritual direction*. Chicago: Loyola Press.

Howard, E. B. 1999. *Praying the Scriptures: A field guide for your spiritual journey*. Downers Grove, IL: InterVarsity Press.

Hughes, G. J. 1990. Ignatian discernment: A philosophical analysis. *Heythrop Journal* 31:419-438.

Hughes, G. W. 1975. The first week and the formation of conscience. *The Way: Supplement* 24 (spring):6-14.

Ignatius of Loyola. 1959. *Letters of St. Ignatius of Loyola* trans. William J. Young, S.J. Chicago: Loyola University Press.

Ignatius 1991a [1558?]. *Autobiography*. In *Ignatius of Loyola: The Spiritual Exercises and selected works*. Edited by G. E. Ganss. New York/Mahwah, NJ: Paulist Press.

_____. 1991b [1544]. *Spiritual Diary.* In *Ignatius of Loyola: The* Spiritual Exercises *and selected works.* Edited by G. E. Ganss. New York/Mahwah, NJ: Paulist Press.

_____. 1991c [1548]. *Spiritual Exercises.* In *Ignatius of Loyola: The* Spiritual Exercises *and selected works.* Edited by G. E. Ganss. New York/Mahwah, NJ: Paulist Press.

_____. 1991d. *Selected Letters.* In *Ignatius of Loyola: The* Spiritual Exercises *and selected works.* Edited by G. E. Ganss. New York/Mahwah, NJ: Paulist Press.

_____. 1991e. *The Deliberation on Poverty.* In *Ignatius of Loyola: The* Spiritual Exercises *and selected works.* Edited by G. E. Ganss. New York/Mahwah, NJ: Paulist Press.

James 1961 [1902]. *The varieties of religious experience: A study in human nature.* New York and London: Collier MacMillan Publishers.

Jaquette, J. L. 1995. *Discerning what counts: The function of the* adiaphora topos *in Paul's Letters.* SBL Dissertation Series 146. Atlanta, GE: Scholar's Press.

John, O. P., S. E. Hampson, and L. R. Goldberg. 1991. The basic level in personality-trait heirarchies: Studies of trait use and accessibility in different contexts. *Journal of Personality and Social Psychology* 60, no. 3:348-361.

Johnson, B. C. 1990. *Discerning God's will.* Louisville, KY: Westminister/John Knox Press.

_____. 1991. *Speaking of God: Evangelism as initial spiritual guidance.* Louisville, KY: Westminister/John Knox Press.

Johnson, L. T. *Scripture and discernment: Decision making in the church.* Nashville, KY: Abingdon Press.

Affirming the Touch of God

Johnson, Mark. 1987. *The body in the mind: The bodily basis of meaning, imagination, and reason*. Chicago: University of Chicago Press.

Kahneman, Daniel, Paul Slovic, and Amos Tversky, eds. 1982. *Judgment under uncertainty: Heuristics and biases*. Cambridge: Cambridge University Press.

Katz, S. T., ed. 1978. *Mysticism and philosophical analysis*. New York: Oxford University Press.

Keane, P. S. 1974. Discernment of spirits: A theological reflection. *American Ecclestical Review* 168:43-61.

Kelsey, Morton. 1972. *Encounter with God: A theology of Christian experience*. Minneapolis, MN: Bethany Fellowship.

_____. 1973. *Healing and Christianity: In ancient thought and modern times*. New York: Harper and Row.

_____. 1976. *The other side of silence: A guide to Christian meditation*. New York: Paulist Press.

_____. 1978. *Discernment: A study in ecstasy and evil*. New York: Paulist Press.

Klug, E. F. 1962. The will of God in the life of a Christian. *Concordia Theological Monthly* 33, no. 8 (August):453-468.

Knox, R. A. 1994. *Enthusiasm: A chapter in the history of religion with special reference to the 17th and 18th centuries*. Oxford: Oxford University Press, 1950. Reprint, Notre Dame, IN: Notre Dame University Press.

Kosslyn, S. M. 1980. *Image and mind*. Cambridge: Cambridge University Press.

Landegent, David. 1983. Discerning the spirits. *The Reformed Journal* (September):5.

Lange, C. G. and James, William. 1967 [1922]. *The emotions*. N. Y,: and London: Hafner Publishing.

Lakoff, George. 1987. *Women, fire and dangerous things: What categories reveal about the mind*. Chicago: University of Chicago Press.

Larkin, E. E. 1974. The dark night of John of the Cross. *The Way* 14, no. 1 (January):13-21.

_____. 1981. *Silent presence: Discernment as process and problem*. Denville, NJ: Dimension Books.

Laurence, D. 1979. Jonathan Edwards, Solomon Stoddard, and the preparationist model of conversion. *Harvard Theological Review* 72, nos. 3-4 (July-October): 267-83.

Lazarus, R. S. 1984. On the primacy of cognition. *American Psychologist* 39, no 2. (February):124-129.

_____. 1991a. *Emotion and adaptation*. New York: Oxford University Press.

_____. 1991b. Progress on a cognitive-motivational-relational theory of emotion. *American Psychologist* 46, no. 8 (August):819-834.

_____. 1993. From psychological stress to the emotions: A history of changing outlooks. *Annual Review of Psychology* 44:1-21.

Lazarus, R. S. and Craig Smith. 1988. Knowledge and appraisal in the cognition-emotion relationship. *Cognition and Emotion* 2, no. 4:281-300.

Lee, S. H. 1973. Imagination and the Increasing Reality in Jonathan Edwards. In *Philosophy of religion and theology: 1973: Preprinted papers for the section on philosophy of religion and theology*, ed. David Griffin, 31-48. Tallahassee, FL: American Academy of Religion.

_____. 1988. *The philosophical theology of Jonathan Edwards*. Princeton, NJ: Princeton Univerity Press.

Leech, Kenneth. 1977. *Soul friend: The practice of Christian spirituality*. San Francisco: Harper and Row.

Letemendia, Felix and Croft, George. 1968. Phenomenology, psychiatry and Ignatian discenment. *The Way: Supplement* 6 (May):27-34.

Leventhal, Howard. 1980. Toward a comprehensive theory of emotion. In *Advances in Experimental Psychology*, ed. Leonard Berkowitz, 13:139-207. New York: Academic Press.

Leventhal, Howard and Klaus Scherer. 1987. The relationship of emotion to cognition: A functional approach to a semantic controversy. *Cognition and Emotion* 1, no. 1:3-28.

Levko, John. 1997. From discernment to deification with Athanasius. *Diakonia* 30, no. 1:5-20.

Lewis, Paul. 1994. "The springs of motion": Jonathan Edwards on emotions, character, and agency. *Journal of Religious Ethics* 22, no. 2 (fall): 275-98.

Libânio, J. B. 1977. *Spiritual discernment and politics: Guidelines for religious communities*. Translated by Theodore Morow. Maryknoll, NY: Orbis Books.

Liebert, Elizabeth. 1986. The process of change in spiritual direction: A structural-developmental perspective. Ph.D. diss. Vanderbilt University.

_____. 1989. Eyes to see and ears to hear: Identifying religious experience in pastoral spiritual guidance. *Pastoral Psychology* 37, no. 4 (summer):297-310.

_____. 1992. *Changing life patterns: Adult development in spiritual direction*. Mahwah, NJ: Paulist Press.

Lienhard, Joseph. 1980. On 'discernment of spirits' in the early church. *Theological Studies* 41 (spring):505-529.

_____. 1993. 'Discernment of spirits' in the early church. *Studia Patristica* 17, part 2:519-527.

Linville, P. W. and G. W. Fischer. 1993. Exemplar and abstraction models of perceived group variability and stereotypicality. *Social Cognition* 11, no. 1:92-125.

Littell, F. H. 1960. The work of the Holy Spirit in group decisions. *The Mennonite Quarterly Review* 34 (April):75-96.

Lloyd-Jones, D. Martyn. 1987. *Revival*. Westchester, IL: Crossway.

Locke, John. 1961 [1722]. *An essay concerning human understanding*. Edited by John W. Yolton. Everyman's Library. New York: Dutton (references to this work are by book, chapter, and section).

Lonergan, Bernard. 1967 [1949]. The natural desire to see God. In *Collection*, ed. Fred Crowe, 84-95. New York: Herder and Herder.

_____. 1958. *Insight: A study of human understanding*. New York: Philosophical Library. Reprint, New York: Harper and Row.

_____. 1972. *Method in Theology*. New York: Herder and Herder. Reprint, Minneapolis, MN: Seabury Press.

Lonsdale, David. 1992. *Listening to the music of the Spirit: The art of discernment*. Notre Dame, IN: Ave Maria Press.

Lovelace, Richard. 1979. *Dynamics of spiritual life: An evangelical theology of renewal*. Downers Grove, IL: InterVarsity Press.

_____. 1989. The anatomy of puritan piety: English puritan devotional literature, 1600-1640. In Dupré and Saliers 1986, 294-323.

Magill, Frank and Ian P. McGreal, eds. 1988. *Christian spirituality: The essential guide to the most influential writings of the Christian tradition*. San Francisco: Harper San Francisco.

Malatesta, Edward, ed. 1970. *Discernment of spirits*. Translation of the article "Discernement des Esprits" in the *Dictionnaire de Spiritualite* by Sr. Innocentia Richards. Collegeville, MN: The Liturgical Press.

Malley, B. E. 1996. The emerging *cognitive* psychology of religion: A review article. *Method and Theory in the Study of Religion* 8-2:109-141.

Mandler, G. 1984. *Mind and body: Psychology of emotion and stress*. New York: Norton.

Mangan, B. B. 1972. Meaning and structure of consciousness: an essay in psycho-aesthetics. Ph.D. diss. University of California, Berkeley.

Maritain, Jacques. On knowledge through connaturality. *The Review of Metaphysics: A Philosophical Quarterly* IV,4, no. 16 (June):473-481.

Martucci, Jean. 1978. "Diakriseis pneumaton" (1 Co 12,10). *Eglise et Théologie* 9:465-471.

Marty, François. 1958. Le discernement des esprits dans le Peri Archon d'Origine. *Revue d'ascetique et d'mystique*. 34 (July-Sept):253-74.

Maslow, A. H. 1954. *Motivation and personality*. New York: Harper and Row.

Matlin, M. W. 1994. *Cognition.* 3d ed. Fort Worth: Harcourt Brace.

May, G. G. 1982. *Care of mind, care of spirit: Psychiatric dimensions of spiritual direction.* San Francisco: Harper and Row.

McCallister, B. J. 1995. Cognitive theory and religious experience. In *Handbook of religious experience,* ed. R. W. Hood, 312-352. Birmingham, AL: Religion Education Press.

McCarthy, J. J. 1985. A discernment model for the ethics of birth control: An application of a narrative method with critical observations. Ph.D. diss. Graduate Theological Union.

McClain, G. D. 1995. Spiritual discernment and social justice. *Christian Social Action* (May):8-10.

McDermott, G. R. 1992. *One holy and happy society: The public theology of Jonathan Edwards.* University Park, PA: The Pennsylvania State University Press.

_____. 1995. *Seeing God: Twelve reliable signs of true spirituality.* Downers Grove, IL: InterVarsity Press.

McGinn, Bernard. 1993. The letter and the spirit: Spirituality as an academic discipline. *Christian Spirituality Bulletin* 1, no. 2 (fall):1-10.

McGloughlin, W. G. 1978. *Revivals, awakenings, and reform: An essay on religion and social change in America, 1607-1977.* Chicago History of American Religion Series. Chicago: University of Chicago Press.

McKinney, M. B. 1987. *Sharing wisdom: A process for group decision making.* Allen, TX: Tabor Publishing.

McNamara, William. 1977. *Mystical passion.* New York: Paulist Press.

Medin, D. L. 1989. Concepts and conceptual structure. *American Psychologist* 44, no. 12 (December):1469-1481.

Medin, D. L. and M. M. Schaffer. 1978. A context theory of classification learning. *Psychological Review* 85:207-238.

Medin, D. L. and W. D. Wattenmaker. 1987. Category cohesiveness, theories, and cognitive archeology. In *Concepts and conceptual development: Ecological and intellectual factors in categorization*, ed. U. Neisser, 25-62. Cambridge: Cambridge Univerity Press.

Meissner, W. W. 1963. Psychological Notes on the "Spiritual Exercises". *Woodstock Letters* 92:349-366.

_____. 1964a. Psychological Notes on the "Spiritual Exercises" II. *Woodstock Letters* 93:31-58.

_____. 1964b. Psychological Notes on the "Spiritual Exercises" III. *Woodstock Letters* 93:165-191

_____. 1984. *Psychoanalysis and religious experience*. New Haven: Yale University Press.

_____. 1992. *Ignatius of Loyola: The psychology of a saint*. New Haven: Yale University Press.

Merleau-Ponty, Maurice. 1962. *Phenomenology of Perception*. Translated by Coln Smith. London: Routledge and Kegan Paul.

Michael, C. P. and M. C. Norrisey. 1984. *Prayer and temperament: Different prayer forms for different personality types*. Charlottesville, VA: The Open Door.

Miller, Perry. 1948. Jonathan Edwards on the sense of the heart. *Harvard Theological Review* 41, no. 2 (April):123-146.

_____. 1981. *Jonathan Edwards*. William Sloane Associates, 1949. Reprint, Amherst, MA: University of Massachusetts Press (page references are to the reprint edition).

Morneau, R. F. 1982. Principles of discernment. *Review for Religious* 41 (January-February): 161-75.

Morris, D. E. and C. M. Olsen. 1997. *Discerning God's will together: A spiritual practice for the church.* Bethesda, MD: Alban Publications.

Mueller, J. J. 1984. Appreciative awareness: The feeling-dimension in religious experience. *Theological Studies* 45:57-79.

Mueller, Joan. 1996. *Faithful listening: Discernment in everyday life.* Kansas City, MO: Sheed and Ward.

Mumford, Bob. 1971. *Take another look at guidance: A study of divine guidance.* Plainfield, NJ: Logos.

Munitiz, J. A. 1988. Loyola's 'spiritual diary' I: Ignatius' idea of discernment. *The Month* 21 (June):719-724.

Murphey, Murray. 1961. *The development of Peirce's philosophy.* Cambridge, MA: Harvard University Press.

Murphy, Laurence. 1976. Consolation. *The Way: Supplement* 27 (spring):35-47.

Murphy, Nancey. 1990. *Theology in the age of scientific reasoning.* Cornell Studies in the Philosophy of Religion. Ithaca and London: Cornell University Press.

Murray, I. H. 1987. *Jonathan Edwards: A new biography.* Edinburgh and Carlile, PA: Banner of Truth Trust.

National and International Religion Report. 1994. Spiritual renewal spreading. July 11, 1994. Roanoke, VA: Media Management. Vol 8, no. 15:1-3.

Neisser, Ulric. 1967. *Cognitive psychology.* Century Psychology Series. New York: Merideth Publishing.

Nemeck, F. K. and M. T. Coombs. 1985. *The way of spiritual direction*. Consecrated Life Studies, Vol. 5. Wilmington, DE: Michael Glazier.

Neufelder, J. M. and M. C. Coelho, eds. 1982. *Writings on spiritual direction by great Christian masters*. Minneapolis, MN: The Seabury Press.

Nuttall, G. F. 1947. *The Holy Spirit in puritan faith and experience*. Chicago and London: University of Chicago Press.

Oatley, Keith. 1992. *Best laid schemes: The psychology of emotions*. Cambridge: Cambridge University Press.

Oatley, Keith and Elaine Duncan. 1994. The experience of emotions in everyday life. *Cognition and Emotion* 8, no. 4:369-381.

Oatley, Keith and J. M. Jenkins. 1992. Human emotions: function and dysfunction. *Annual Review of Psychology* 43:55-85.

Oatley, Keith and P. N. Johnson-Laird. 1987. Toward a cognitive theory of emotions. *Cognition and Emotion* 1, no. 1:29-50.

O'Malley, J. W. 1993. *The first Jesuits*. Cambridge, MA: Harvard University Press.

Omdahl, B. L. 1995. *Cognitive appriasal, emotion, and empathy*. Mahwah, NJ: Lawrnce Erlbaum.

Oppenheim, Francis. 1969. A Roycean road to community. *Proceedings of the Jesuit Philosophical Association* (April):20-61.

Orsy, Ladislas. 1976. *Probing the Spirit: A theological evaluation of communal discernment*. Denville, NJ: Dimension Books.

Ortony, Andrew and T. J. Turner. 1990. What's so basic about basic emotions. *Psychological Review* 97, no. 3:315-331.

Osherson, D. N. and E. E. Smith. 1981. On the adequacy of prototype theory as a theory of concepts. *Cognition* 9:35-58.

Ostling, R. N. 1994. Laughing for the Lord. *Time* (August 15):38.

Owen, John. 1965 [1674]. *The works of John Owen.* Edited by William H. Goold. Vol. 3. *The Holy Spirit.* Edinburgh and Carlile, PA: Banner of Truth Trust.

Page, Kirby. 1954. *How to find the will of God (and get power to do it).* Nashville, TN: Tidings.

Paivio, A. 1971. *Imagery and verbal processes.* New York: Holt, Reinhart and Winston.

Palmer, Parker. 1988. The clearness committee: A way of discernment. *Weavings: A Journal of the Spiritual Life* (July/August):37-40.

Palmer, Stephen. 1999. *Vision Science: Photons to Phenomenology.* Cambridge, MA: Bradford/MIT Press.

Parker, S. E. 1996. *Led by the Spirit: Toward a practical theology of pentecostal discernment and decision making.* Sheffield: Sheffield Academic Press.

Penn-Lewis, Jessie. 1991 [1912]. *War on the saints.* 9th ed. New York: Thomas E. Lowe.

Peters, William. 1979. Ignatius of Lyola and 'discernment of spirits'. In *Discernment of the Spirit and of spirits.* Concilium, No. 119., eds. Casiano Floristán and Christian Duquoc, 27-33. New York: The Seabury Press.

Pierce, C. S. 1931-58. *Collected Papers of Charles S. Peirce.* Edited by C. Hartshorne, P. Weis (volumes 1-6), and A. Burks (volumes 7-8). Cambridge, MA: Harvard University Press.

_____. 1982-. *Writings of Charles S. Peirce: A Chronological Edition.* Edited by Max Fisch. Bloomington, IN: Indiana University Press.

Plantinga, Alvin. 1993. *Warrant and proper function*. New York: Oxford University Press.

Plantinga, Alvin and Nicholas Wolterstorff, eds. 1983. *Faith and rationality: Reason and belief in God*. Notre Dame, IN: University of Notre Dame Press.

Poorman, M. L. 1993. *Interactional morality: A foundation for moral discernment in Catholic Pastoral Ministry*. Washington, D.C.: Georgetown University Press

Posner, M. I. and Steven W. Keele. 1968. On the genesis of abstract ideas. *Journal of Experimental Psychology* 77, no. 3, Part 1. (July):353-363.

Price, Leslie. 1980. What is meant by testing the spirits? *Journal of the Academy of Religion* 3, no. 2 (April):210-213.

Proterra, Michael. 1983. *Homo spiritualis nititur fide: Martin Luther and Ignatius of Loyola, an analytical and comparative study of a hermeneutic based on the heuristic structure of* discretio. Washington, D.C.: University Press of America.

Proudfoot, Wayne. 1985. *Religious experience*. Berkeley: University of California Press.

_____. 1989. From theology to a science of religions: Jonathan Edwards and William James on religious affections. *Harvard Theological Review* 82, no. 2 (April): 149-68.

Raabe, A. M. 1972. Discernment of spirits in the prologue to the "Rule" of Benedict. *American Benedictine Review*. 23, no. 4 (December): 397-423.

Rahner, H. 1953. *The spirituality of St. Ignatius Loyola: An account of its historical development*. Translated by F. J. Smith. Chicago: Loyola University Press.

_____. 1956. "Werdet kundige Geldwechsler": Zur Geschichte der Lehre des hl. Ignatius von der Unterscheidung der Geister. *Gregorianum* 37:444-483.

_____. 1968. *Ignatius the theologian*. Translated by Michael Barry. New York: Herder and Herder

Rahner, K. 1963. On the question of a formal existential ethics. In *Theological investigations*, Vol 2. *Man in the Church*. Translated by Karl-H. Kruger, 217-234. Baltimore, MD: Helicon Press.

_____. 1964. The logic of concrete individual knowledge in Ignatius Loyola. In *The dynamic element in the church*. Translated by W. J. O'Hara, 85-170. New York: Herder and Herder.

_____. 1987. *Foundations of the Christian faith*. Translated by W. V. Dych. New York: Crossroad.

Rakoczy, Susan. 1980. The structures of discernment processes and the meaning of discernment language in published U.S. Catholic literature, 1965-1978: An analysis. Ph.D. diss., The Catholic University of America.

Rifkin, Anthony. 1985. Evidence for a basic level in event taxonomies. *Memory and Cognition* 13, no. 6:538-556.

Riss, R. M. 1988. *A Survey of 20th-century revival movements in North America*. Peabody, MA: Hendrickson.

Rizzuto, Ana-Maria. 1979. *The birth of the living God: A psychoanalytic study*. Chicago: University of Chicago Press.

Roberts, R. C. 1982. *Spirituality and human emotion*. Grand Rapids, MI: Wm. B. Eerdmans.

Rosch, E. H. 1973. On the internal structure of perceptual and semantic caterogies. In *Cognitive development and the acquisi-*

tion of language, ed. Timothy Moore, 111-144. New York: Academic Press.

_____. 1977. Human categorization. In *Studies in cross-cultural psychology*, ed. N. Warren, 1:1-49. London: Academic Press.

_____. 1978. Principles of categorization. In *Cognition and categorization*, eds. E. Rosch and B. B. Lloyd, 27-48. Hillsdale, NJ: Lawrence Erlbaum.

_____. 1983. Prototype classification and logical classification: The two systems. In *New trends in cognitive representation: Challenges to Piagets theory?*, ed. E. K. Scholnick, 73-86. Hillsdale, NJ: Lawrence Erlbaum.

_____. 1987. Wittgenstein and categorization research in cognitive psychology. In *Meaning and the growth of understanding: Wittgenstein's relevance for developmental psychology*, eds. M. Chapman and R. Dixon, 151-166. Hillsdale, NJ: Lawrence Erlbaum.

_____. 1988. Coherences and categorization: A historical view. In *The development of language and language researchers: Essays in honor of Roger Brown*, ed. F. Kessel, 373-91. Hillsdale, NJ: Lawrence Erlbaum.

_____. 1992. The micropsychology of self interest. Unpublished manuscript.

_____. 1994. Categorization. In *Encyclopedia of Human Behavior*. Vol. 1. San Diego: Academic Press.

_____. 1996. The environment of minds: Toward a noetic and hedonic ecology. In *Cognitive Ecology*. Handbook of Perception and Cognition, 2d ed., eds. M. P. Friedman and E. C. Carterette, 5-28. San Diego, CA: Academic Press.

_____. 1997. Transformation of the Wolf Man. In *The authority of experience: Essays on Buddhism and psychology*, ed. S. Pickering, 6-27. Surrey: Curzon Press.

Rosch, E. H. and C. B. Mervis. 1975. Family resemblances: Studies in the internal structure of categories. *Cognitive Psychology* 7:573-605.

Rosch, E.H., C. B. Mervis, W. D. Gray, D. M. Johnson, and Penny Boyes-Braem. 1976. Basic objects in natural categories. *Cognitive Psychology* 8:382-439.

Royce, Josiah. 1976 [1899]. *The world and the individual*. First Series. Gloucester, MA: Peter Smith/Dover.

_____. 1968 [1918]. *The problem of Christianity*. The Macmillan company (1918). Reprint, Chicago: University of Chicago Press (page references are to the reprint edition).

Rutman, D. B. 1970. *The great awakening: Event and exegesis*. The Wiley Problems in American History Series. New York: John Wiley and Sons.

Ryle, James. 1993. *Hippo in the garden: A non-religious approach to having a conversation with God*. Orlando, FL: Creation House.

Saliers, D. E. 1991. *The soul in paraphrase: Prayer and the religious affections*. 2d ed. Clevland, OH: OSL Publications.

Sauer, Armin and Petra Horn. 1994. Trost und Trostlosigheit nach den "Geistlichen Übungen" des Ignatius von Loyola. In *Glaubend leben: Gerhard Ruhbach zum 60. Geburtstag*, eds. Hans-Jürgen Hoeppke and Armin Sauer, 104-115. Wuppertal and Zurich: R. Brockhaus.

Schmidt, H. P. 1976. Scheidung der Geister. In *Der Geist und die Geister*, eds. H. P. Schmidt, W. J. Hollenweger, and Horst Burkle, 5-38. Konstanz: Friedrich Bahn Verlag.

Schmidt, H. P., W. J. Hollenweger, and Horst Burkle. 1976. *Der Geist und die Geister*. Konstanz: Friedrich Bahn Verlag.

Schneiders, Sandra. 1982. Spiritual discernment in "The Dialogue" of Saint Catherine of Siena. *Horizons* 9, no. 1:47-59.

_____. 1989. Spirituality in the academy. *Theological Studies* 50:676-697.

_____. 1993. Spirituality as an academic discipline: Reflections from experience. *Christian Spirituality Bulletin* 1, no. 2 (fall):10-15.

_____. 1994. A hermeneutical approach to the study of Christian spirituality. *Christian Spirituality Bulletin* 2, no. 1 (spring):9-14.

_____. 1998. The study of Christian spirituality: Contours and dynamics of a discipline. *Christian Spirituality Bulletin* 6, no. 1 (spring):1-12.

Schweizer, Eduard. 1989. On distinguishing between spirits. *The Ecumenical Review* 41:406-415.

Sessions, George, ed. 1995. *Deep ecology for the 21st century*. Boston: Shambala. Distributed in the U.S. by Random House.

Shaver, Phillip, Judith Schwartz, Donald Kirson, and Cary O'Connor. 1987. Emotion knowledge: further exploration of a prototype approach. *Journal of Personality and Social Psychology* 52, no. 6:1061-1086.

Sheeran, M. J. 1983. *Beyond majority rule: Voteless decisions in the religious society of Friends*. Philadelphia, PA: Philadelphia Yearly Meeting.

Sheets, J. R. 1983. Profile of the Spirit: A theology of discernment of spirits. In *Notes on the* Spiritual Exercises *of St. Ignatius of Loyola*. The Best of the Review, no. 1, ed. David Fleming, 214-225. St. Louis, MO: Review for Religious.

Sibbes, Richard. 1973 [1635]. *The bruised reed and smoking flax*. In *Works of Richard Sibbes*. Edited by A. B. Grosart. Vol. 1. Edinburgh and Carlile: Banner of Truth Trust.

Simonson, H. P. 1982. *Jonathan Edwards: Theologian of the heart*. Grand Rapids, MI: Wm. B. Eerdmans, 1974. Reprint, Macon, GA: Macon University Press.

Sisters of the Holy Names of Jesus and Mary. 1991. *Momentum*. St. Anthony-on-Hudson, NY: General Chapter of the Sisters of the Holy Names of Jesus and Mary.

Smith, E. R. and M. A. Zarate. 1990. Exemplar and prototype use in social categorization. *Social Cognition* 8, no. 3:243-262.

Smith, J. E. 1959. Introduction to *Works of Jonathan Edwards*. Vol. 2, *Religious affections*. Edited by J. E. Smith. New Haven, CT: Yale University Press.

_____. 1981-82. Testing the spirits: Jonathan Edwards and the religious affections. *Union Seminary Quarterly Review* 37, nos. 1-2 (fall/winter): 27-37.

_____. 1992a. *America's philosophical vision*. Chicago: University of Chicago Press.

_____. 1992b.. *Jonathan Edwards: Puritan, preacher, philosopher*. Notre Dame: Notre Dame University Press.

Smith, S. S. and J. F. Kihlstrom. 1987. When is a schema not a schema?: The "big five" traits as cognitive structures. *Social Cognition* 5, no. 1:26-57.

Smith, Warren. 1994. Holy laughter or strong delusion? *SCP Newsletter* 19, no. 2 (fall):1-14.

Sneck, W. J. 1981. *Charismatic spiritual gifts: A phenomenological analysis*. Washington, D. C.: University Press of America.

Sobrino, Jon. 1978. *Christology at the crossroads: A Latin American approach*. Translated by John Drury. Maryknoll, NY: Orbis Books.

_____. 1979. Following Jesus as discernment. In *Discernment of the Spirit and of spirits*. Concilium, No. 119., eds. Casiano Floristán and Christian Duquoc, 14-24. New York: The Seabury Press.

Solomon, Robert. 1983. *The passions: The myth and nature of human emotion*. New York: Anchor Press/Doubleday.

Sonnemans, Joep and N. H. Frijda. 1994. The structure of emotional intensity. *Cognition and Emotion* 8, no. 4:329-350.

Spittler, R. P. 1980. Competent charismatic theology: A review of Donald Gelpi's "Experiencing God." *Agora* 3 (winter): 21-22.

Spohn, W. C. 1973. Charismatic communal discernment and Ignatian communities. *The Way: Supplement* 20 (autumn):38-54.

_____. 1983. The reasoning heart: An American approach to Christian discernment. *Theological Studies* 44:30-52.

Stace, W. T. 1960. *Mysticism and philosophy*. Philadelphia and New York: J. B. Lippincott.

Steele, R. B. 1994. *"Gracious affection" and "True virtue" according to Jonathan Edwards and John Wesley*. Pietist and Wesleyand Studies, no. 5. Metuchen, NJ and London: The Scarecrow Press.

Sullivan, Francis. 1980. Lo Spirito Santo e il discernimento personale. In . *L'azione dello Spirito Santo nel discernimento*, Antonio Barruffo, Tomaso Beck, and Francis Sullivan, 80-84. Rome: Centrum Ignatianum Spiritualitatis.

Sweeney, R. J. 1983. Christian discernment and Jungian psychology: Toward a Jungian revision of the doctrine of discernment of spirits. Ph.D. diss., Graduate Theological Union.

Sweitek, Günter. 1972. "Discretio spirituum": Ein Beitrag zur Geschichte der Spiritualität. *Theologie und Philosophie* 47:36-76.

Tanaka, J. W., and Marjorie Taylor. 1991. Object categories and expertise: Is the basic level in the eye of the beholder? *Cognitive Psychology* 23:457-482.

Theological Commission of the Charismatic Renewal in the Catholic Church of Germany, The. 1996. Concerning extraordinary bodily phenomena in the context of spiritual occurrences. *Pneuma: The Journal of the Society for Pentecostal Studies* 18, no. 1 (spring):5-32.

Therrien, Gérard. 1973. *Le discernement dans les écrits Pauliniens*. Etudes Bibliques. Paris: Librarie Lecoffre.

Thomas, Gary. 1996. *Sacred pathways*. Nashville: Thomas Nelson.

_____. 1998. *The Glorious Pursuit: Embracing the virtues of Christ*. Colorado Springs, CO: NavPress.

Thorndyke, P. W. 1984. Applications of schema theory in cognitive research. In *Tutorials in learning and memory: Essays in honor of Gordon Bower*, ed. J. R. Anderson and S. M. Kosslyn, 167-197. San Francisco: W. H. Freeman.

Tillich, Paul. 1951. *Systematic Theology*. Vol 1. Chicago: University of Chicago Press.

Tomkins, S. S. 1978. Script theory: Differential magnification of affects. In *Nebraska symposium on motivation, 1978: Human emotion*. Current Theory and Research in Motivation. Vol. 26, ed. R. A. Dienstbier, 201-236. Lincoln and London: University of Nebraska Press.

_____. 1991. *Discerning God's will: Ignatius of Loyola's teaching on Christian decision making*. St. Louis: Institute of Jesuit Sources.

Toner, J. J. 1982. *A commentary on Saint Ignatius' rules for the discernment of spirits*. St. Louis, MO: Institute of Jesuit Sources.

_____. 1991. *Discerning God's will: Ignatius of Loyola's teaching on Christian decision making*. St. Louis, MO: Institute of Jesuit Sources.

_____. 1995a. *Spirit of light or darkness: A casebook for studying discernment of spirits*. St. Louis, MO: The Institute of Jesuit Sources.

_____. 1995b. *What is your will, O God?: A casebook for studying discernment of God's will*. St. Louis, MO: The Institute of Jesuit Sources.

Tson-kha-pa. 1978. *Calming the mind and discerning the real: buddhist meditation and the middle view. From the* Lam rim chen mo *of Tson-kha-pa*. Translated by Alex Wayman. Delhi: Motilal Banarsidass.

Tversky, Amos and Daniel Kahneman. 1974. Judgment under uncertainty: Heuristics and biases. *Science* 185:1124-1131. Reprinted in Kahneman, Slovic, and Tversky 1982, 3-20 (page references are to the reprinted publication).

_____. 1981. The framing of decisions and the psychology of choice. *Science* 211 (January 30): 453-58.

Tversky, Barbara and Kathleen Heneway. 1983. Categories of environmental scenes. *Cognitive Psychology* 15:121-149.

Tyrrell, Bernard. 1987. Feelings as apprehensive-intentional responses to values. In *Lonergan Workshop 7*, ed. Fred Lawerence, 331-360. Atlanta: Scholar's Press.

Unger, R. M. 1984. *Passion: An essay on personality*. New York: The Free Press.

Upkong, J. S. 1989. Pluralism and the discernment of spirits. *The Ecumenical Review* 41:416-425.

Varela, F. J., Evan Thompson, and Eleanor Rosch. 1991. *Embodied mind: Cognitive science and human experience.* Cambridge: MIT Press.

Villegas, Diana L. 1997. Discernment in Catherine of Siena. *Theological Studies* 58:19-38.

Walters, Kerry. 1989. The law of apparent reality and aesthetic emotions. *American Psychologist* 44, no. 12 (December): 1545-1546.

Ward, Benedicta. 1989. Discernment: A rare bird. *The Way: Supplement* 64 (spring):10-18.

Wattenmaker, W. D., G. I. Dewey, T. D. Murphy, and D. L. Medin. 1986. Linear separability and concept learning: Relational properties and concept naturalness. *Cognitive Psychology* 18:158-194.

Watts, Fraser and Mark Williams. 1988. *The Psychology of Religious Knowing.* Cambridge: Cambridge University Press. Reprint, London: Geoffrey Chapman.

Weismayer, V. J. 1990. Ein Blick in einen fernen Spiegel: Spätmittelalterliche traktate über die Unterscheidung der Geister. In *Gottes nähe: Religiöse Erfahrung in Mystik und Offenbarung.* Festschrift zum 65. Geburtstag von Josef Sudbrack. ed. Paul Imhof, 110-126. Würzburg: Echter Verlag.

Wesley, John. *The works of John Wesley.* 3d edition. Peabody, MA: Hendrickson

White, John. 1976. *The fight: A practical handbook for Christian living.* Downers Grove: InterVarsity Press.

_____. 1988. *When the Spirit comes in power: Signs and wonders among God's people.* Downers Grove, IL: InterVarsity Press.

Whitehead, A. N. 1929. *Process and reality: An essay in cosmology.* New York: Macmillan.

Whitehead, J. D. and E. E. Whitehead. 1996. *Shadows of the heart: A spirituality of the painful emotions.* New York: Crossroad.

Willard, Dallas. 1993. *In search of guidance: Developing a conversational relationship with God.* Regal Books, 1984. Reprint, San Francisco: Harper/Zondervan (page references are to the reprint edition).

_____. 1998. *The divine conspiracy: Rediscovering our hidden life in God.* San Francisco: HarperSanFrancisco.

Wilson-Kastner, Patricia. 1978. *Coherence in a fragmented world: Jonathan Edwards' theology of the Holy Spirit.* Washington, D.C.: University Press of America.

Wimberly, E. P. 1990. *Prayer in pastoral counseling: Suffering, healing, and discernment.* Louisville, KY: Westminster/John Knox Press.

Wink, Walter. 1984. The power behind the throne. *Sojourners* 13 (September):22-25.

Wittgenstein, Ludwig. 1953. *Philosophical investigations.* 3d ed. Translated by G. E. M. Anscombe. Englewood Cliffs, NJ: Prentice Hall.

Wolff, Pierre. 1993. *Discernment: The art of choosing well.* Liguori, MO: Truimph Books.

Wolters, Clifton. 1980. *A study of wisdom: Three tracts by the author of the* Cloud of Unknowing. Fairacres/Oxford: SLG Press.

Woozley, A. D. 1967. Universals. In *The encyclopedia of philosophy.* Vol. 8. New York: Macmillan Publishing.

Wright, J. H. 1983. Discernment of spirits in the New Testament. In *Spiritual direction: Contemporary readings*, ed. K.G. Culligan, 168-179. New York: Living Flame Press.

Wulf, H. 1965. Unterscheidung der geister. In *Lexicon für Theologie und Kirche*. 2d ed. Vol. 10. Freiburg: Verlag Heider.

Yandell, K. E. 1993. *The epistemology of religious experience* Cambridge: Cambridge University Press.

Yeomans, William. 1989. The refugee experience. *The Way: Supplement* 64 (spring):3-9.

Zaehner, R. C. 1957. *Mysticism sacred and profane*. London: Oxford University Press.

Zajonc, R. B. 1980. Feeling and thinking: Preferences need no inferences. *American Psychologist* 35, no. 2 (February):151-75.

_____. 1984. On the primacy of affect. *American Psychologist* 39, no. 2 (February): 117-123.

Zarate, M. A. and E. R. Smith. 1990. Person categorizing and stereotyping. *Social Cognition* 8, no. 2:161-185.

Index

method, 44-50
multidisciplinary co-
ordination in, 48-49
normative account, 46,
52, 134, 168, 239,
265-266, 303, 342
philosophical, 28-40,
376-377
philosophical theology,
use of, 48, 238-239
psychological, 40-44, 376
review of research, 12-44
specificity, 23-24, 30, 39,
233, 239, 337
in spiritual direction,
333-348
theological, 19-27,
313-316, 376
types/kinds, 305, 313, 377
ascetical strategy
determination, 7
communal decision-
making, 323
evaluation of affective
trends, 2 (*See also*
Affective trends)
evaluation of cultural or
religious trends, 7
evaluation of prophetic
utterances, 14
evaluation of social
issues, 3-4
personal decision making,
3, 7 (*See also* Spiritual
direction)
identification of "spirits",
7 (*See also* "Spirits)
"Discernment of spirits", 7, 17,
64, 69, 124

and "discernment" in early
history, 17
Discernment situation, 322, 324,
335, 352
"Discernment tradition", 19, 176
discretio, 17
Divine-human relationship, 27,
223, 284, 307, 316
Docility, 237, 280, 306, 309,
343
Dubay, Thomas, 15
Edwards, Jonathan, 85, 88-98
appealed to by those evaluating Toronto Blessing, 356
experience of discernment,
94-98
sources, 89-92
Distinguishing Marks and
Religious Affections, 49, 86
context of, 88-98
emphasis on biblical
criteria in, 100, 106,
129
Distinguishing Marks, 49,
98-107, 357, 360
aim, 99
object of discernment in,
99, 130
Parts, First, 99-100
Parts, Second, 100-102,
370
Parts, Third, 103-104
structure, 99
Religious Affections, 49, 107-
129, 358
aim, 109-112
a call to action, 123
object of discernment in,
109-110, 130